I0879844

The Fortress Kingdom

The Fortress Kingdom

The Wars of Æthelflæd and Edward the Elder, 899–927

Paul Hill

Pen & Sword
MILITARY
AN IMPRINT OF PEN & SWORD BOOKS LTD.
YORKSHIRE – PHILADELPHIA

First published in Great Britain in 2022 by
PEN & SWORD MILITARY
An imprint of
Pen & Sword Books Ltd
Yorkshire – Philadelphia

ISBN 978 1 39901 061 0

A CIP catalogue record for this book is available from the British Library

Typeset in 10/12.5 & Ehrhardt MT Std by SJmagic DESIGN SERVICES, India.

Printed and bound in the UK by CPI Group (UK) Ltd.

Pen & Sword Books Ltd incorporates the imprints of Pen & Sword Archaeology, Atlas, Aviation, Battleground, Discovery, Family History, History, Maritime, Military, Naval, Politics, Social History, Transport, True Crime, Claymore Press, Frontline Books, Praetorian Press, Seaforth Publishing and White Owl

For a complete list of Pen & Sword titles please contact

PEN & SWORD BOOKS LTD
47 Church Street, Barnsley, South Yorkshire, S70 2AS, England
E-mail: enquiries@pen-and-sword.co.uk
Website: www.pen-and-sword.co.uk

Or

PEN AND SWORD BOOKS
1950 Lawrence Rd, Havertown, PA 19083, USA
E-mail: Uspen-and-sword@casematepublishers.com
Website: www.penandswordbooks.com

FSC
www.fsc.org
MIX
Paper from responsible sources
FSC® C013604

Contents

PART THREE: THE OFFENSIVE OF 917–918

PART FOUR: SECURING THE NORTH

PART FIVE: ÆTHELSTAN

Photograph Credits

Colour Plates

1. Alfred presents a royal cloak and sword to his grandson Athelstan, c.1909 (tempera on card). Private Collection. © Harry Mileham. All rights reserved 2021/Bridgeman Images.
2. A depiction of Æthelred and Æthelflæd in the stained-glass window in the cloisters of Worcester Cathedral. Designed by James Eadie Reid, Gateshead Stained Glass in 1919. © Paul Hill. Author Collection.
3. Grant of Æthelred and Æthelflæd concerning a land exchange and the gift of a chalice granted to the community of the church of Much Wenlock. British Library, London, UK. © British Library Board. All Rights Reserved/Bridgeman Images.
4. Badbury Rings in Dorset. © Julianelliott | Dreamstime.com.
5. The Cuerdale Hoard. © The Trustees of the British Museum. All rights reserved.
6. Part of the stained glass west window designed by W. T. Carter Shapland at Chester Cathedral. © Paul Hill. Author Collection.
7. The north wall of Chester, looking west. © Paul Hill. Author Collection.
8. Chester, Bonewaldesthorne Tower. © Paul Hill. Author Collection.
9. Chester Cathedral. © Paul Hill. Author Collection.
10. A surviving section of Chester's northern Roman wall. © Paul Hill. Author Collection.
11. Gloucester Cathedral from the site of St Oswald's Priory. © Paul Hill. Author Collection.
12. The remains of St Oswald's Priory in Gloucester. © Paul Hill. Author Collection.
13. St Oswald's Priory, Gloucester. © Paul Hill. Author Collection.
14. Later medieval remains of St Oswald's priory, Gloucester. © Paul Hill. Author Collection.
15. St Michael's Tower at The Cross, central Gloucester. © Paul Hill. Author Collection.
16. Detail from a mural installation depicting Æthelflæd on the Holyhead Road, Wednesbury. © Paul Hill. Author Collection.
17. *Æthelflæd – Warrior Queen of Tamworth* by Luke Perry. Photograph: © Paul Hill. Author Collection.
18. Bedford on the River Great Ouse. © Paul Hill. Author Collection.
19. All Saints Parish Church, Runcorn. © Paul Hill. Author Collection.
20. Detail from *Of Heroes and Industry*. One Red Shoe. Mural at Runcorn High Street. Photograph: © Paul Hill. Author Collection.
21. Llangorse Lake. © Davidmartyn | Dreamstime.com.
22. Replica of the Ethelfloeda drinking fountain statuette, now in the courtyard of Leicester Guildhall. Photograph taken by kind permission of Leicester City Council: Arts and Museums. Photograph: © Paul Hill. Author Collection.

Black and White Photographs

19. Remains of the medieval St Oswald's Priory in Gloucester incorporating earlier wall masonry from the period of Æthelred and Æthelflæd's foundation. © Paul Hill. Author Collection.
20. Remains of the medieval St Oswald's Priory in Gloucester showing earlier wall masonry. © Paul Hill. Author Collection.
21. Remains of medieval St Oswald's Priory in Gloucester showing Anglo-Saxon clerestory window. © Paul Hill. Author Collection.
22. Worcester (south). © Paul Hill. Author Collection.
23. Worcester (north). © Paul Hill. Author Collection.
24. St Helen's on the High Street, Worcester. © Paul Hill. Author Collection.
25. St Helen's on the High Street, Worcester. View in Fish Street. © Paul Hill. Author Collection.
26. St Alban's Worcester. © Paul Hill. Author Collection.
27. St Alban's Worcester, doorway © Paul Hill. Author Collection.
28. Hertford, looking down Fore Street. © Paul Hill. Author Collection.
29. Hertford. Junction of St Andrew Street and Old Cross. © Paul Hill. Author Collection.
30. Hertford. The River Lea from Mill Bridge looking east. © Paul Hill. Author Collection.
31. Tamworth. Looking north from Lady Bridge along Holloway. © Paul Hill. Author Collection.
32. View of Lady Bridge, from the south side of the river at Tamworth. © Paul Hill. Author Collection.
33. Flat Holm and Steep Holm Islands in the Bristol Channel where the Danes who attacked England in 914 fled. © Andy Chisholm | Dreamstime.com.
34. Bedford Market and the Church of St Paul. © Paul Hill. Author Collection.
35. The River Great Ouse at Bedford looking eastwards. © Paul Hill. Author Collection.
36. The entrance to the King's Ditch feature running south of the River Great Ouse at Bedford. © Paul Hill. Author Collection.
37. The King's Ditch at Bedford, looking north. © Paul Hill. Author Collection.
38. View of the probable burh at Runcorn centred on All Saints Church. © Paul Hill. Author Collection.
39. Ethelfleda Bridge showing masonry abutment, on Castle Rock. © Paul Hill. Author Collection.
40. The Queen Ethelfleda Viaduct at Runcorn showing castle-like architectural features (1). © Paul Hill. Author Collection.
41. The Queen Ethelfleda Viaduct at Runcorn showing castle-like architectural features (2). © Paul Hill. Author Collection.
42. The Roman walls at Colchester on the Balkerne Hill (west) side (1). © Paul Hill. Author Collection.
43. The Roman walls at Colchester on the Balkerne Hill (west) side (2). © Paul Hill. Author Collection.
44. St Nicholas Church, Leicester near to the Jewry Wall. © Paul Hill. Author Collection.
45. Diane Gorvin and Philip Bews 'Queen of Mercia', Runcorn. © Paul Hill. Author Collection.

List of Maps and Plans

A Note on the Charters

The charters referred to in this book are noted as 'S' numbers. These relate to P.H. Sawyer's 1968 publication *Anglo-Saxon Charters, an Annotated List and Bibliography*. London. An electronic version is to be found at https://esawyer.lib.cam.ac.uk/about/index.html [accessed 01/12/2020].

Acknowledgements

The making of this book has involved a good deal of travel to many places across England, something which had become much harder than usual during the period in which the book was written. I am very grateful to the staff of several public and private museums and visitor attractions for their kind help, both in person and of course remotely. It has not always been easy to get to places due to recent developments, but wherever I have gone I have been welcomed. Church staff in Bedford and in Tamworth have given me much-appreciated guidance. In particular, to Rachel Pardoe of the Gloucester City Museums Service and her team who organized the photography of the tenth-century grave slab in their collections, I am most grateful. To the staff of Hertford Museum I am grateful too, for their guidance regarding the town's development. At Leicester as well, particularly at the Guildhall, where the delightful replica of the statuette of Ethelfloeda now stands proudly in the courtyard, my thanks for allowing me to spend so long with it. Chester Tourist Information Centre, and everywhere I went in Chester, were all welcoming. I am grateful to the Cathedral and staff for their assistance. Similarly, the staff at Worcester Cathedral have also been most helpful. Thanks also to the staff of the British Library Reading Rooms at St Pancras, where much research has been carried out. They too have had to respond to the pressures of maintaining a public service in the middle of a pandemic. I must also however, thank my wife Lucy, for her forbearance in enduring what has been a very long-lasting passion and in tolerating my sudden disappearances.

Map 1: *Southern Anglo-Saxon England at the beginning of the tenth century.*

Introduction

This book is the second in a series of volumes about the formation of England. The series focusses on the achievements of the family of Alfred the Great (871–99) and their descendants, concentrating on their wars and their lives. Throughout this era, the way in which rulers used their faith as a tool to bring legitimacy to their rulership also played a big part in their lives. In some cases, it was as if the Christian faith itself was defining the ruling classes against the backdrop of pagan practices and Scandinavian settlement. But this was a cosmopolitan world not just in terms of religious practices, but equally importantly of opposing lordships and desperate political and military struggles. The achievements of the children of Alfred is not the only story to be told here. The first book in the series, *The Kingdom of the Anglo-Saxons – the Wars of King Alfred 865 – 899*, recalled the rise of the West Saxon kingdom during an era of great turmoil. The first Danes had caused destruction around the shores of the country, falling upon the Holy Island of Lindisfarne in northern England in 793 and firmly planting themselves off the shores of Ireland. These early incursions had left the English kingdoms' ruling elites only partially affected, until the arrival in 865 of the Great Heathen Army under Ivar, Halfdan and Ubba, the semi-legendary sons of the enigmatic Scandinavian Ragnar Lothbrok.

Although many Danes began to over-winter in England off the coast of Kent from around the 850s (and in Northumbria, probably even earlier), it was the sheer size combined with the resolute intent of the Great Heathen Army which set them apart from so many of their Scandinavian predecessors. The sagas speak of a vengeance mission against the Northumbrian King Ælle (c. 862/67 or c. 867), who had allegedly killed Ragnar by having him put in a pit of snakes, in what was one of the more alarming of his many notable 'deaths'. They may or may not be right. But what is undeniable, is the effect the Great Heathen Army had on England. Northumbria fell to the army in 867 and the Danes installed a local ruler before heading south. The East Anglian King Edmund (855–69) was martyred at their hands in 869 and became not only a saint, but was even commemorated on coinage issued by none other than the later Scandinavian rulers of East Anglia itself.

Mercia, the central Midland English kingdom whose power was unmatched by any other kingdom during the reign of the mighty King Offa (757–96) had experienced a turbulent relationship with its southern neighbour Wessex up until the arrival of the first Danes. A decline in Mercian power and fortune began in the early ninth century amid dynastic strife and the rise of the West Saxon house of Ecgberht, the grandfather of Alfred the Great. At his height Ecgberht was heralded by the writers of the *Anglo-Saxon Chronicle* as the last of the great 'Bretwaldas' of old, a ruler over other kings. He had even at one stage taken London from Mercia and also marched his forces up to the traditional border of Mercia and Northumbria. But Mercia somehow held on, with its warring families vying for the throne in turn. Many of these families seemingly belonged to lineages identifiable by the alliteration of their names. The 'C' dynasty, with its allies from the 'W' dynasty, at times were set against the 'B' dynasty, for example. But these families had pedigrees: some could trace themselves back to ancestors near to the dawn of Mercian kingship, or at least could make a good argument for it. When you could do that, it was all to play for in Anglo-Saxon England. And so from the reign of Coenwulf I (796–821), through the struggles of King Beornwulf (823–6) and his supporters against the East Angles, to the rise of King Wiglaf (827–9 and 830–9) and the reign of Beorhtwulf (840–52), the Mercian story had been one of familiar intrigue played out on a stage overshadowed by the prowling Dane and the gradual rise of the house of Wessex.

But those Danes kept on coming. During the time of the Mercian King Burgred (852–74), who married King Alfred's sister Æthelswith, the dangers were all too real. Two kingdoms had already fallen by 869 and Burgred was vulnerable. The Great Heathen Army came to the Mercian spiritual centre at Repton in Derbyshire in around 873 and the sad result was the ultimate departure of Burgred who ended his days in exile in Rome. In his stead came Ceolwulf II (c. 874–c. 879), propped up by the incoming Danes but still a king in his own right. Described by the *Anglo-Saxon Chronicle* as 'a foolish [*unwisum*] king's thegn', little is really known about Ceolwulf II. The Winchester, or at least pro-West Saxon, version (A) of the chronicle fails even to name him, and the scribe seems to spit out his memory as if it were in some way unpalatable.

There are good reasons for all this. Alfred the Great (871–99) was by 871 the king of Wessex. His story would be a tale told largely from a West Saxon outlook. He was the last of the many sons of King Æthelwulf of Wessex (839–58), the man who had been appointed to Kent by his father Ecgberht, in much the same way as Æthelwulf himself would place his eldest son Æthelstan in charge of Kent and the eastern provinces of an expanded Wessex. Æthelwulf was a pious man and had many sons, four of whom rose to rule Wessex in turn. However, Æthelbald (858–60), the first of these, rose to prominence amid accusations from Alfred's biographer Bishop Asser of lawlessness and scandal. Æthelbald had risen against his father when his father was on pilgrimage to Rome with his young son Alfred. After his father's death Æthelbald had even taken Æthelwulf's new (and rather young) second wife, the Frankish princess Judith, to his own bed. In the last years of Æthelwulf's reign, the kingdom seems to have been geographically shared between father and son during an uncomfortable period. Some stability to a fractured state was restored by Alfred's older brother Æthelberht (860–5). However, at the beginning of his reign Winchester suffered a catastrophic attack by Danes who had come across the Channel from Francia. In 865, the same year as the arrival of the Great Heathen Army, Æthelred I (865–71), Alfred's other brother, the nearest to him in age, became king of Wessex. His reign was dominated by the events which followed his accession and the subsequent collapse of most of the kingdoms north of the Thames.

The Great Heathen Army launched an offensive against Wessex itself in 871, coming to Reading in the winter and successfully repulsing an attack made by Æthelred and his brother Alfred. Just a few days later, Wessex won a much-heralded victory at nearby Ashdown, a place Alfred's biographer Asser had even seen himself, where the battle had raged around a thorn tree. But the West Saxon military system, which relied on the fortitude and reactionary capabilities of its ealdormen, each of whom headed up a shire force (or fyrd) was creaking under the pressure of an attritional war which saw several defeats and a general retreat into the Wessex heartlands in a series of up to nine battles during a tumultuous 871. The campaign was still being fought when Æthelred I succumbed to either illness or injury not long after the Battle of Merton, fought in late March of that year. It had been another hard-fought and costly defeat. The relatively young king left behind him two very important sons, Æthelhelm and Æthelwold, the latter of whom we will meet in our current story.

And so Alfred's Wessex was on its knees in 871. He had become king amid a desperate situation and his brother's children were too young to be realistically considered by the witan (the council of leading lay and church figures in the kingdom, whose agreement was required on the matter of the election of kings, among other things). Although Alfred managed to buy some time for Wessex as the campaigns of 871 petered out and the Danes left for what was then the Mercian town of London, he had a very real problem developing with the sons of his brother and their supporters. By an agreement made between them at a place called Swinbeorg before Æthelred I's death, whichever brother lived the longest was more or less free to inherit all of the wealth in terms of land and treasure and all the other's possessions, except for the limited lands that were due to the other brother's children by way of what seems like compensation. It was an uncomfortable agreement, which Alfred had to revisit later in his reign at a meeting at another place called Langandene. And, as Alfred's will bears testimony, the children of Æthelred I and their supporters were perhaps rightly disgruntled with the arrangement. After all, these young boys were Æthelings (that is, male members of the royal family considered 'throneworthy') descended from a consecrated king. One of them would remember all this for many years to come.

Alfred's reign (871–99) has obviously attracted historians for centuries. There is of course, much we do not know. Moreover, it is certainly the case that the *Anglo-Saxon Chronicle*, in particular, the (A) version, Asser's *Life* and many other later medieval works which drew from these, have an 'Alfredian' bias. But this is not to say the achievement of Alfred was not remarkable. Alfred's Wessex was the last kingdom standing after the collapse and division of Mercia into an 'English' and 'Danish' half generally considered to be roughly to the south and north of Watling Street respectively. Then, during 876, when a branch of the Great Heathen Army under the resilient leader Guthrum launched another dramatic bid from its East Anglian base to deliver the final blow, it seemed Wessex was finished. Guthrum had come first to Wareham in Dorset, then Exeter, then out again to Gloucester after a campaign characterized by broken oaths, murdered hostages and a bizarre loss at sea of 120 vessels of the coast of Swanage. And as the winter of 877 crept icily into 878, the apparent knockout blow was delivered. Into Alfred's royal estate at Chippenham came Guthrum's Danes. Someone had allowed it to happen, but history does not quite say who. Alfred was deserted by some of his men, left to wander the wild fastness of Somerset with some loyal followers. But from an island in a marsh at Athelney, Alfred eventually turned all this misfortune on its head during some of the longest months of his life. He and his Mercian wife Ealhswith had already brought their eldest child, Æthelflæd, into the world and what the young princess must have seen during these dark times hardly bears imagining. An infant boy, her brother Edward, was also brought up during the tumult, although slightly later. To say the experience of their youth greatly affected them both is something of an understatement. Æthelflæd's name probably meant 'noble beauty' or something similar, the Æthel- element being quite common in her father's family. Edward however, whose name meant 'protector of wealth', seems to have been named after his Mercian maternal grandmother Eadburh whom Alfred's biographer Asser says he even met himself, recalling that she was 'a notable woman'.

Alfred famously came crashing back onto the scene by managing to gather an army of the remaining loyal West Saxons and bringing Guthrum to battle at Edington in 878. His victory seems to have been every bit as profound as the 'Alfredian' sources contend. Guthrum, the defeated Dane, was baptised at Aller, moved on to Cirencester and eventually travelled out of Mercia altogether to start, or perhaps re-start, a life in East Anglia as an Anglo-Danish yet Christian king, carrying the baptismal name Æthelstan. A famous treaty between Alfred and Guthrum was drawn up outlining their respective territories and legal responsibilities, although there is no universal agreement as to the date of it. Perhaps around 880 would make sense. Nobody records what happened to the 'foolish' king's thegn, Ceolwulf II of Mercia. But in his stead rose one of the most important men of the whole era, someone we will refer to many times. He was the man who took the English half of Mercia to his heart. This was a place where he most likely had his roots, in the ancient kingdom of the Hwicce based around the central places of Worcester, Gloucester and Winchcombe. He may even have been its ealdorman, although nobody is really certain about his origins. He would go on to marry Alfred's daughter Æthelflæd in the middle of the 880s. His name was Æthelred. And in all the subsequent charters and other literature, he is rarely termed 'king'. Instead, he is given the title variously of 'Ealdorman' or 'Lord' of the Mercians. There is an argument that he may have been 'king' for a very brief period prior to his submission to Alfred sometime before 883. Certainly, he ruled as a monarch in all but name, and his wife Æthelflæd, the 'Lady of the Mercians', would rule in a similar way later.

Alfred had for some time been creating a new entity out of the remains of Anglo-Saxon England in the south, based on the English half of Mercia and the expanded Wessex his family had built before him. It has been called by one eminent historian the 'kingdom of the Anglo-Saxons'.[1] Arguably conceived in the wake of the fall of Ceolwulf II of Mercia and the triumph over Guthrum, this conceptual kingdom comprised the Saxons and Angles of the remaining 'English' parts of the two kingdoms of Mercia and Wessex and it was to be run along family lines. London had been at the heart of the struggles throughout the 870s and 880s. The old trading settlement at Lundenwic centred around Aldwych was abandoned during Alfredian times and the king himself famously 'restored' the burh, or Roman town, of London a little to the east in 886, where after an obscure period of warfare and the possible changing of hands of the old Roman city on more than one occasion, Alfred thoroughly upgraded the place. His biographer Asser says this: '. . . he entrusted it to the care of Æthelred, ealdorman of the Mercians. All the Angles and Saxons – those who had formerly been scattered everywhere and were not in captivity with the pagans – turned willingly to King Alfred and submitted themselves to his lordship.'

Alfred's new kingdom was born. But it would be tested. In the middle of the 880s the Danes came again. A new force, not from the Scandinavian settlements north and east of Watling Street, nor directly from East Anglia, but from the Continent. Alfred had not been idle, however. He had built a series of fortifications across the kingdom, including some in southern Mercia as well as Wessex. They came in a variety of forms. Some were reused Roman defences of ancient towns, whilst others were wooden and stone forts built anew in the landscape, or were re-fortified prehistoric hilltop settlements given a new defensive function after centuries of abandonment. Variously placed at river mouths, strategic crossings and overlooking important road networks, these burhs were listed in a document known as the Burghal Hidage. There were thirty-three of them in total. From the border of Kent to Cornwall, garrisons would meet the threat of incursion. Fortresses would now become one of the many defining features of the kingdom of the Anglo-Saxons. How they exerted their influence over the landscape was of great importance. In 885 the Danes who landed at Rochester were rebuffed and many fled to their vessels after Alfred's land force came to relieve the garrison. Alfred had also reformed the fyrd, or the land army, in this time so that one part of it was always at home tending to the farms of the kingdom whilst the other part served militarily on a rotational basis. Garrison duty, army service, bridge building, watchtower keeping, coastal observance, and even road building were all part of the necessary defence of the kingdom.[2]

Alfred's grand physical and structural restoration of his kingdom had also been accompanied by a spiritual and educational revival across the kingdom. He brought Mercian and Continental scholars to his court. Each of them (including his own biographer Asser and the Bishop of Worcester Wærferth) assisted the king in his programme of translating some great works 'most necessary for all men to know', which provided both lay and clerical leaders with the intellectual apparatus to make Alfred's vision a reality. It was a place where 'praying men, fighting men and working men' were to be considered the tools of society, as Alfred himself said in his translation of Boethius's *Consolation of Philosophy*.

But still the threat from warfare was there. The Danes came again in 893 to Kent. Under a leader named Hæsten, they had come from Francia looking to establish a foothold in England. But Alfred's new system was generally successful, as were the responses of his generals Lord Æthelred of Mercia, Ealdorman Æthelnoth of Somerset and by now one particularly capable Ætheling, Alfred's very own son Edward.

Edward's campaigns in the south were recalled by the chronicler Æthelweard, who wrote in the later tenth century, basing his work on a lost version of the *Anglo-Saxon Chronicle* and probably also drawing on his own family's memories (Æthelweard was descended from Alfred's brother Æthelred I). In these accounts, the young Edward marches across Surrey and brings the Danes to battle at Farnham, where his arrival seems to bolster already existing English troops. In a new era of what would appear to have been great mobility provided by the widespread use of mounted infantry, Edward harried his enemy across the Thames to the north and besieged them on Thorney Island on the Colne. Working closely with his sister's husband Æthelred, who was based at London at the time, in the town Alfred had entrusted to him, the two sub-commanders of the kingdom dealt blow after blow to Hæsten and his forces, until their Essex bases were little more than smouldering ruins. It was a long and detailed campaign lasting from 893 to around 896 and it saw the Danes involved in desperate dashes to the west where they hoped to team up with other Danish groups being sent around the coast from Northumbria and elsewhere. Two great encounters, one at Buttington on the Severn and another later at Bridgnorth, all but did for the Scandinavians who were variously starved or defeated in their hurriedly prepared bases. At Buttington, Alfred had even called-in the Welshmen of Powys who had been provided as part of the mechanics of their earlier submission to the king. It was all a stark contrast to the desperate days of 871. For the Danes and their kin, some found homes in Northumbria and East Anglia and would not forget the campaigns of the 890s. Others, those who lacked money, found vessels and sailed back to the Continent. But despite the peace of Alfred's last few years, he could not hide a fermenting problem, an issue which

1. *Statue of King Alfred in Winchester. By Hamo Thornycroft (1850–1925).*

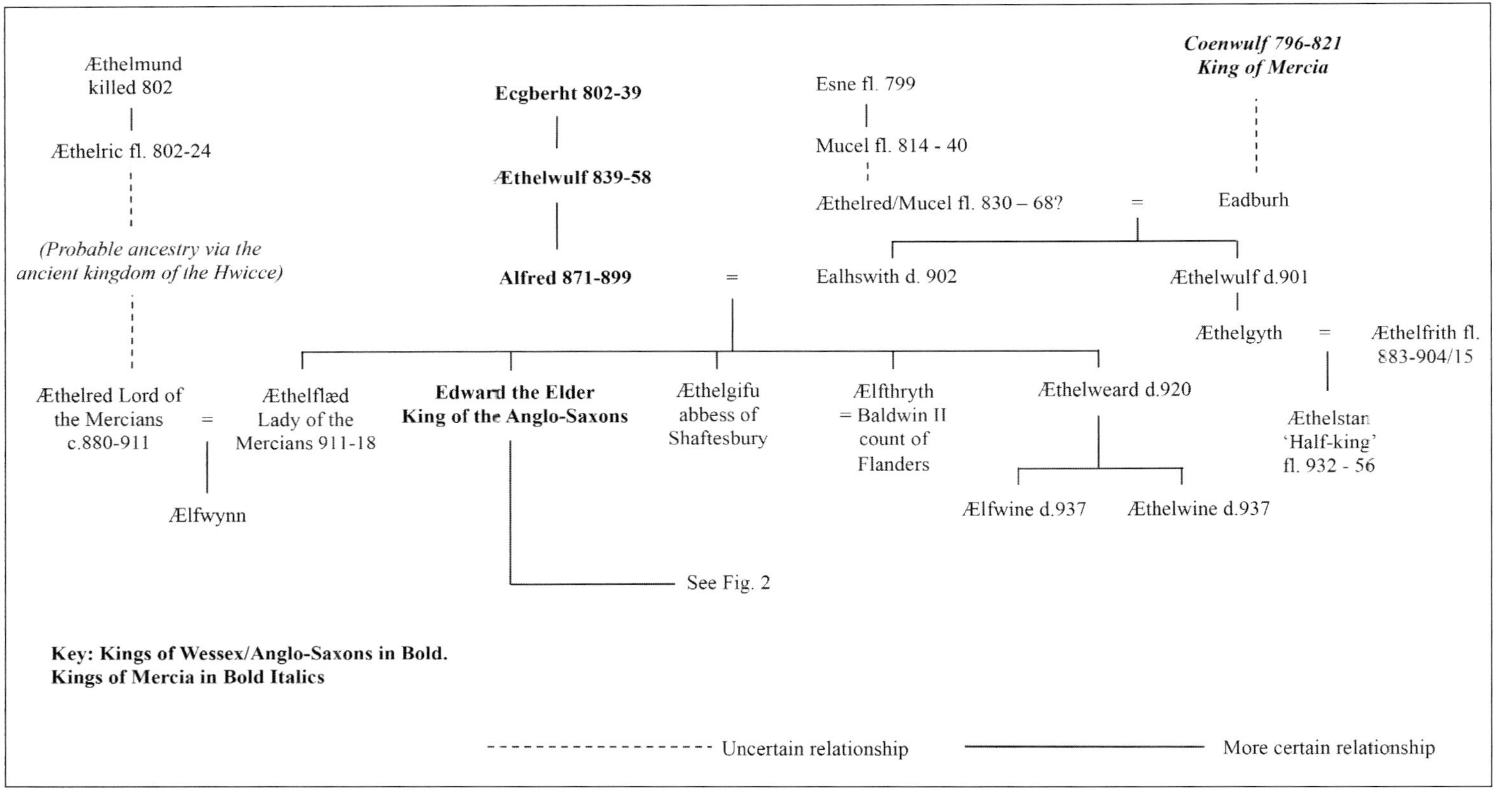

Fig. 1: *The family of Alfred the Great.*

arose in his wider family in the form of the sons of Alfred's brother Æthelred I whose ambitions were fuelled by a perceived injustice.

Certainly, military action was never far away. The Danes of Northumbria and East Anglia were always a potent threat. Guthrum had died in 890 and was replaced by another Dane. And it had been Sigeferth, a Northumbrian leader, who had wreaked havoc around the shores of Wessex in the 890s. Then, in 896 there was another (this time, naval) encounter at an estuary on the south coast in which the English won an attritional battle. Alfred had demanded a new ship design for his kingdom's naval response to the growing threat at sea and the result was a much larger type of vessel than those which the Danes had to hand. There then followed some remarkably bloody naval battles off the coast before the final years of Alfred's reign saw something approaching 'peace' once more.

Throughout this book, Edward will often be referred to as Edward the Elder. This name has well and truly 'stuck' with the king down the ages to modern times. The term, or cognomen, 'the Elder' was first used later in the tenth century to distinguish our King Edward from another King Edward (the Martyr), who reigned in England from 975 to 978. But in 899 there was no such term. King Alfred had done what he could to secure the succession for his son Edward, but there is no doubt that the two sons of Alfred's brother Æthelred I had been sidelined. The fate of the older brother Æthelhelm by the late 890s is not known for sure, but as a succession crisis loomed large, one man was about to do what all Æthelings did if they thought they could manage it. And so, with all that had happened in England over the last few decades, it would be an Englishman, and not a Dane, who would launch the first war of the tenth century.

PART ONE

THE LADY EMERGES

Chapter 1

The Thwarted King

Her Ealhswið forðferde, ⁊ þy ilcan gere wæs þæt gefeoht æt þam Holme Cantwara ⁊ þara Deniscra.

'Here Ealhswith passed away, and the same year was the fight at the Holme of the inhabitants [or men] of Kent and the Danes.'

The *Mercian Register*, or 'Annals of Æthelflæd'. Entry for 902 (C)

As Alfred lay dying in late October 899, we might imagine many of his family gathered around. There was his eldest son Edward, and perhaps Ealhswith, Alfred's wife. Edward had of course been a key beneficiary of Alfred's will, receiving a great swathe of estates from Kent to Cornwall, which included all of the king's booklands in Kent. Stood amongst the attendants and king's thegns rushing back and forth may have been Æthelgifu, the abbess of Shaftesbury whom Alfred had appointed to her position, and whom Asser had described as 'devoted to God through her holy virginity'. Her date of death is unknown though. However, Shaftesbury, an establishment of nuns, had been Alfred's very own foundation and he had looked after it well. There is a Shaftesbury tradition (alluded to in S 357, of disputed authenticity) which indicates that Æthelgifu may have taken the veil on account of bad health, but this cannot be known for sure. She was bequeathed Kingsclere and Candover estates in Hampshire in her father's will and had been described there as her father's 'middle daughter'.[1]

Another daughter, Ælfthryth, was younger than Æthelgifu. She is described by Asser as being fostered 'at all times' at the royal court alongside her brother Edward, 'under the solicitous care of tutors and nurses'. In fact Asser, who knew both brother and sister well, was quite taken with the way they handled themselves in the courtly environment. Both the siblings were friendly and gentle to 'foreigners' and had been obedient to their father. They had 'attentively learned the Psalms, and books in English, and especially English poems . . .' he says. Ælfthryth had been bequeathed estates at Wellow (on the Isle of Wight), Ashton (probably in Wiltshire) and the royal estate at Chippenham. These estates may have passed back to the Crown by one means or another when Ælfthryth went on to marry Baldwin II of Flanders. Baldwin was, incidentally, the son of Judith, who had fled Wessex after her two short marriages into the West Saxon royal family, eventually finding love with Baldwin I, Count of Flanders. This marriage had occurred sometime between 893 and 899, so it is probable that she was abroad at the time of her father's death.

We do not know whether Æthelweard, Alfred's youngest son, was there. He had been sent to the royally established school where alongside other nobility (and no small amount of boys of lesser birth) he learned both Latin and English.

His inheritance in Alfred's will was only marginally less impressive than Edward's, in a similar swathe from Kent to Cornwall, but along a more southerly line. Edward, of course, would also control much of the traditional royal landed wealth and perquisites, provided of course the transition from Ætheling to king ran in his favour. We shall see if it did. Another man may also have been there at Alfred's side, but little is known of him, save for the fact he is described as 'my kinsman' in Alfred's will. He is called Osferth. He may have been a bastard son of the king's, or a relative on Alfred's mother's side, or a son or grandson of one of Alfred's brothers. Alfred's mother Osburh was an enigmatic and puzzling character, and she was also the subject of a sentimental tale in Asser's biography regarding her setting her sons the task of memorizing and reciting a book of poetry (a competition which the young Alfred won). Osferth's connection to Osburh may or may not be indicated by the Os- part of his name, but he may also have been the grandson of Alfred's brother Æthelred I via a mysterious Oswald 'filius regis' who appeared in earlier West Saxon charters. Whatever Osferth's personal heritage, he seems to have stayed around the court for some time. His awarded estates were clustered around Sussex and somewhat hemmed in the small amount awarded to Alfred's nephews there. Whoever he was, Osferth must have played an important part in the leadership of English forces in the struggles of the early tenth century.

Whether Æthelflæd, the eldest daughter of Alfred, was at her father's side in 899 or at her court in Mercia is not known. But she, like her next oldest surviving sibling Edward, had already brought another generation of the family into the world. We will meet the young Æthelstan, Edward's first son, born in around 895, very shortly. But what of Æthelflæd's first, and apparently only, child?

Æthelflæd and Æthelred's daughter was born sometime between their marriage in or around 886 and the outbreak of hostilities with the new Danish host of the early 890s. She was named Ælfwynn. On her birth, which is best placed around 888, the twelfth-century writer William of Malmesbury supplies an account which reveals much of her mother's character, a personality which arguably emulates that of her own grandfather Alfred. Æthelflæd, the mother of Ælfwynn was, he says, '. . . a woman of great soul who, from the difficulty experienced in her first or rather only labour, ever after refused the embraces of her husband, protesting that it was unbecoming for the daughter of a king to give way to a delight which in time produced such painful consequences'.

Whether William of Malmesbury was trying to create an image of Æthelflæd in an ascetic mould is uncertain. Perhaps there is no explanation required for the lack of any further children to the couple, but many are put forward. In some people's view, Æthelflæd's decision to abstain from sexual intercourse is somehow to be seen as a return to 'purity' after a dalliance with carnal pleasure. Alfred too, according to Asser, had once changed his ways from a life of fleshy pleasure to something more godly. Æthelflæd may perhaps have been denying her husband a male heir,[2] a potential figurehead of a Mercian independence movement which might challenge Alfred's vision of Anglo-Saxon unity across the new kingdom. Alternatively, perhaps it is simply the case that Æthelflæd's 'abstinence' was a consequence of the physical difficulties of childbirth, a grim reminder of an unforgiving age, and was given a religious gloss by a much later commentator and admirer. We should remember too that according to Asser, Æthelflæd's mother Ealhswith (who is not specifically named by Asser) had an unspecified number of young children 'who were carried-off in infancy', a sad recurrence surely not lost on her eldest daughter. But whatever the reason behind it, perhaps tellingly, Æthelflæd seems to have made the decision entirely of her own accord.

Ælfwynn's upbringing and education would have been second to none.[3] She will have followed her parents on their journeys through western and southern Mercia. Places such as the burhs at London, Oxford, Worcester, Gloucester and Shrewsbury would have been familiar to her during her childhood. Her education is likely to have been at Worcester, perhaps under the guidance of Bishop Wærferth, a great friend of King Alfred's and a key player in the intellectual reforms which Alfred had instigated across the kingdom. Ælfwynn's mother, however, may have had plans for her to pursue a secular and not a religious life. The charter evidence points to Ælfwynn being around her mother and father's court in her teens, but her early activities are shrouded in mystery until she appears as a fully-grown woman at centre stage in one of Anglo-Saxon England's darkest dramas (see pages 176–8 and 180). In her childhood, it would appear that Ælfwynn was joined at the Mercian court by a certain young boy. This boy, Æthelstan, was King Edward's firstborn son. Æthelstan's extraordinary journey through life is nothing less than the story of the birth of England in its current form. But we don't really know why, as William of Malmesbury contends, he was sent across the hills to Mercia to join with his new foster parents Æthelred and Æthelflæd.

The 'Investiture' of Æthelstan

William of Malmesbury, drawing from an 'ancient volume' he had found about Æthelstan, Edward's first son, tells us that 'at an early age', King Alfred formally lavished great gifts upon him – a scarlet cloak, a gem-encrusted belt and a 'Saxon' sword with a gilded scabbard. The ceremony, he says, was a 'knighting'. The exact date of the ceremony must have been close to the time of Alfred's death in 899. William was using the terminology of his own age when describing the ceremony. Alfred's true intentions are obscure. Some have seen this as an 'investiture' of Æthelstan and have linked it with an acrostic poem probably written by John the Old Saxon (although it could be later and attributable to a different author). Here, the prince is described as 'Sovereign Stone' in a play on his name 'Æthel-stan' and is clearly marked out for some sort of future greatness.[4]

The 'investiture' ceremony recalls Alfred's own experience in Rome as a child where Pope Leo IV (847–55) performed a similar ceremony, investing him as a 'Roman' consul, the meaning of which was probably soon bent to fit in with Alfred's own quest for legitimacy as king. Arguably, Alfred was now providing his grandson with the same continuity of approval for royal rule that he himself had received. Perhaps it was born out of the same 'problem' Æthelstan shared with his grandfather, a question mark over the 'legitimacy' of their parents' union. Whatever the reasons, Æthelstan seems to have come out of it as ultimately 'throneworthy', but much would happen in the years of his youth to make any road to a throne a difficult one to travel.

Shrewsbury

In 901 the Mercian witan convened at a place called in Old English *Scrobbesburh* and in Latin as the *civitate Scrobbensis*. Shrewsbury is a naturally defensible settlement situated high above a bend in the River Severn. During this meeting Æthelflæd and Æthelred granted lands to the monastery at Much Wenlock, an exchange of lands along with a grant from the couple of a beautiful gold chalice in commemoration of St Mildburh (S 221). Mildburh was the eldest daughter of King Merewalh of the Magonsæte. He had founded the monastery at Much Wenlock in 680 and Mildburh become its abbess. The subsequent grant by Æthelflæd and Æthelred is reflective of an often-repeated devotion shown by them to Mercian royal saints and in particular, to those whose reputation was imbued with healing powers. Mildburh was also a virgin and lived a notable saintly life of purity.

The convening of the witan at Shrewsbury in 901 may in part have been to witness the founding of a new burh there. However, its defences remain elusive. Shrewsbury is on top of a high promontory. It is likely the tenth-century burh was an upgrade of a fortified settlement dating to around the time of King Offa. The burh would continue to grow throughout the tenth century and it was here that Æthelflæd is said to have brought the bones of St Alkmund (Ealhmund). St Alkmund's was suppressed in the twelfth century and re-founded as an Augustinian priory at Lilleshall, but the canons evidently thought the foundation was attributable to Æthelflæd.

The boy Æthelstan, who was born around 895, was the first son of Edward by a woman about whom little is known. Her name was Ecgwynn. William of Malmesbury, on whom we rely for an account of her, describes her as an 'illustris femina'.[5] There are hints elsewhere (in the *Life* of St Dunstan) suggesting that she may have been related to the great St Dunstan's family, the figurehead of the later tenth-century ecclesiastical reform movement. The exact nature of her relationship with Edward is debated. Although West Saxon tradition had apparently relegated 'queens' to the position of 'king's wife', there was a later rumour circulating in the 920s that Ecgwynn had been a mere concubine of Edward's. We will see why such rumours were peddled. There is no real evidence of how King Alfred had viewed the union between Ecgwynn and Edward, except to say that it does *seem* that he was fond of the boy Æthelstan.

Why then, did Alfred send his grandson to his daughter's Mercian court? William of Malmesbury is the only one to speak of the event directly in this way, and by using a phrase meaning 'after that . . .' he suggests that it took place not long after the ceremony Alfred had arranged for him (see above, page 12). But there is some further evidence which suggests that the move occurred, and it comes indirectly from Æthelstan himself. In 1304 a dispute between Canterbury and York (Coram Rege Roll, no 178 – Michaelmas 1304 – m 52d), over St Oswald's Priory in Gloucester (see pages 72–3) culminated in a legal hearing at which the prior of St Oswald's, producing one of the first documents at the hearing, cited a now-lost Anglo-Saxon charter concerning privileges granted to St Oswald's in which a 'pact of paternal piety' was referred to as having been pledged by Æthelstan with Æthelred. Interestingly, this same passage also refers to Æthelstan's own father Edward, whose 'paternal wishes' were also being addressed. But whenever that 'pact of paternal piety' was arranged, or indeed what its details were, is not known. The charter referred to by the medieval prior probably dated to around 925 or 926.[6] But, for now though, we must return to the moment when Alfred lay dying a whole generation earlier. Because once again, the family dynamics were changing.

2. *Statue of Ethelfleda. Depicting Æthelflæd and Æthelstan by Edward George Bramwell (1865–1944), outside Tamworth Castle. 1913.*

Around this time Edward took a new wife called Ælfflæd, whom William of Malmesbury refers to as the daughter of *Ethelmi comitis* (Ch. 126), almost certainly implying the late Ealdorman Æthelhelm of Wiltshire, who had been described by the chronicler Æthelweard as 'famous' and who had featured as a principal commander in the wars of the 890s, seemingly always remaining loyal to Alfred. His death is recorded (as ealdorman) in the *Anglo-Saxon Chronicle* for 897. Some people argue, however, for the father of Ælfflæd to have been none other than the *Ætheling* Æthelhelm (the older brother of Æthelwold, who also

3. *Æthelflæd and Æthelstan from the Millenary pageant held at Tamworth in 1913.*

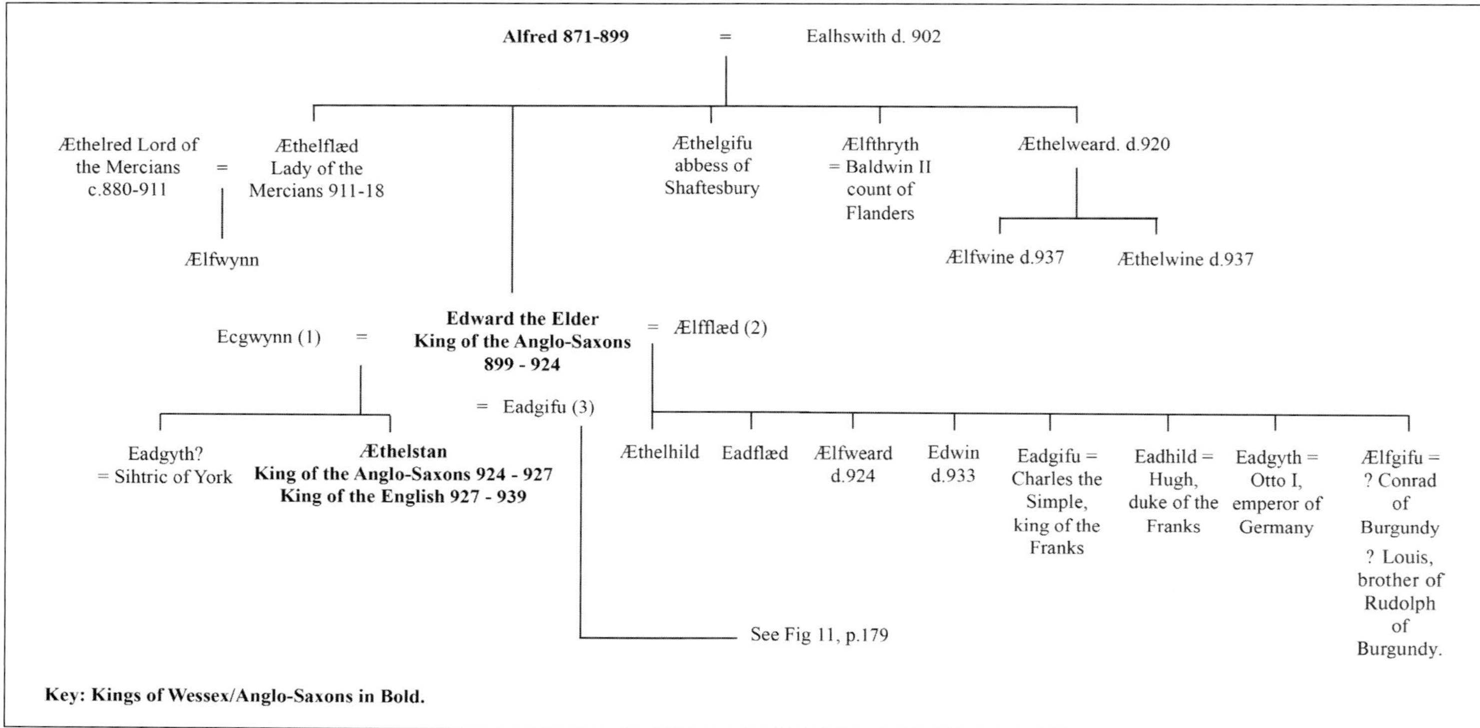

Fig. 2: *The family of Edward the Elder.*

disappears around this time), but it has been considered as unlikely that an Ætheling would serve as an ealdorman.[7] Also, if Edward had indeed married his older cousin's daughter, it may have caused some difficulty with the Church. Would this be too high a price to pay for an olive-branch policy towards the disgruntled family of the late Æthelred I? In some ways though, it would make sense to find Edward reaching out to that branch of the family, as he knew that there was still much consternation in the Æthelwold camp. It would also explain Edward's repudiation of Ecgwynn in a bid to become more politically acceptable to the branch of the family from whom he might expect a challenge. King Alfred's charter of 892 (S 348), however, granting an estate at North Newnton in Wiltshire to Æthelhelm 'my faithful ealdorman', makes no mention of a familial relationship. Moreover, Alfred's will, drawn up probably for a second time in the 880s, when outlining the financial bequests due to his family and close supporters, states 'And to each of my ealdormen 100 mancuses, and to Æthelhelm, Æthelwold and Osferth likewise'. Thus, Alfred seems to be talking of his ealdormen as one 'group' of beneficiaries and then mentions Æthelhelm, Æthelwold and Osferth, his kinsmen, separately in the same sentence as another group. We might expect Ealdorman Æthelhelm to be in the first group, with Ætheling Æthelhelm (who is named) in the second. So if there are two Æthelhelms, *and* if William of Malmesbury is correct, Ælfflæd was the daughter of the ealdorman.

There would be at least two sons and up to six daughters from this second of Edward's marriages. Ecgwynn's fate is unknown and some sympathy for her must surely arise from what little we know of her story. Perhaps she simply passed away or was in some way rejected. And so it seems Alfred sent Æthelstan into Mercia and quite possibly a sister Eadgyth too, born from the same union of Edward and Ecgwynn. The two boys arising from the new marriage of Edward and Ælfflæd were named Ælfweard and Edwin. They were set to become yet another generation of powerful and throneworthy Æthelings. Ælfweard, for example, when no more than an infant, appears on charters of 901 (S 365 and S 366) as a witness listed *above* the six- or seven-year-old Æthelstan.

Perhaps the moving of Æthelstan to his aunt's court in Mercia (whenever this happened) was a shrewd move to secure some dynastic continuity for Alfred's line in Mercia in the wake of his daughter's inability or unwillingness to produce any more heirs. Perhaps it was even a sign of some tension between Alfred and his son Edward, with Edward seeing the issue from his second union as taking precedence over the first and therefore arguing for Æthelstan to be sent away to Mercia. It is likely, however, that Æthelstan's upbringing in Mercia was a product of a good deal of care and attention from his aunt and uncle for what William of Malmesbury calls 'the throne that seemed to await him'. Although some people doubt the authenticity of William of Malmesbury's assertion that Athelstan was brought up in Mercia, there is something to be said for the suggestion that Æthelstan *was* brought up as a Mercian Ætheling with all the connotations that might bring.

Standing outside the Guildhall in bustling Kingston upon Thames is a curious structure. Sitting proudly on a plinth surrounded by Victorian railings styled in the shape of 'Saxon' spears is one very large and very rounded-looking stone. On the sides of the plinth are described the names of seven Anglo-Saxon kings. The stone is a sarsen, or greywether sandstone, block. As early as the time of John Speed in 1627, if not well before, a link had been made between the stone and the coronations of the Saxon kings: here in Kingston 'stood the chair of majesty . . .' says Speed. Long ago, it had been housed in the nearby Saxon chapel of St Mary adjoining the parish church to the south, until that building fell down in 1730. The stone remained beside the church until it was removed in about 1825, where it took up a somewhat unheralded position beside the Elizabethan Guildhall in the Market Place. In 1840 the Town Hall (which became the Market House) was built. The stone was moved again to the yard of the Courts, which is where the present Guildhall stands. But soon would come the stone's great Victorian rebirth.

The *Anglo-Saxon Chronicle* mentions Kingston as a consecration place for just two of the seven kings listed on the plinth of the stone, but Ralph de Diceto, a twelfth-century archdeacon of Middlesex and later Dean of St Paul's, includes in the list the first king of the century, Edward the Elder. Some now dispute the claim that Edward was the first king to be 'crowned' at Kingston and the matter is hardly resolved. There is also the issue to consider of whether or not Edward's 'coronation' saw the first use of the Second Ordo, or whether this was in fact first used later, in 925 (see pages 201–02).[8] The earlier Ordo involved the placement of a helmet on the head of the king and not a crown, hence the potential anachronism of the modern use of the term 'crowning'. For the people of Victorian Kingston, however, the claim for Edward was certainly valid enough, as were the claims for all the others listed on the plinth. So, in 1850, in a ceremony of great civic pride, 'with masonic honours', the stone was promoted to a grand status, provided with its ornate surroundings and placed in front of Clattern House on the roadway and grandly 'inaugurated'. Festivities and events went on well into the late evening of Thursday, 19 September that year including military bands and sporting activities on the Thames. The monument has clearly moved around a bit over the years but has never strayed far from its current location where it came to rest after the building of the Guildhall in 1935. To this day, a visitor to Kingston is reminded of the town's proud Anglo-Saxon royal connections by sculptures on the sides of buildings, friezes on walls and even in the seeming banality of the name for one of its car parks, named 'Seven Kings'. Even the brick walls flanking the A307 and A308 as they carry the town's busy traffic contain decorative brickwork devices depicting arches based on the railings of the Coronation Stone itself.

If Edward was 'crowned' at Kingston, why the place was chosen for the consecration or benediction (contemporary terms) of the king of a 'new' kingdom is an interesting point. By 900 Kingston was already a well-known place in Surrey. In 838, King Ecgberht had made concessions to Canterbury there in return for recognition of his son Æthelwulf as his heir. And it seems the link between Kingston (a royal tun) and the 'legitimacy' of the Anglo-Saxon monarchy was set to continue. There were also good practical reasons why the place should be chosen. It was not far away from here (at Teddington Lock, nowadays) that the Thames became tidal. A bridge was built here in the twelfth century and was said to carry great amounts of traffic. It is likely that the Thames was crossed here in Anglo-Saxon times as well, but by what means, boat, bridge or both, is uncertain. Importantly, Kingston stood right on the boundary between Wessex and Mercia and was thus within a day or two's ride from many important places in the kingdom. It also had a minster church but was not extensively settled. Kingston could accommodate a coronation

4. *The Coronation Stone at Kingston ('inaugurated' in 1850). Seven Anglo-Saxon kings were purportedly 'crowned' at Kingston during the tenth century. Here, Edward the Elder is commemorated in flamboyant writing and in his Old English spelling 'Eadweard'.*

festival with all the food and provisions which that required. There was also plenty of space to set out the tents and house the horses of all the attendants who travelled to the event. And so, on Whitsunday (8 June) 900, Edward the Elder was consecrated as king probably, though not certainly, at Kingston. But before the consecration could take place, there was much to attend to, not least of which was the continuing problem of Æthelwold.

How had Alfred, recently passed, managed to engineer the succession for his son, a rare achievement for the era? Alfred had been packing the witan with supporters ever since his comeback after the Battle of Edington in 878. He secured support for the succession from a number of different groups which he kept close to him. Firstly, there were numerous close relatives such as his wife Ealhswith and her brother Æthelwulf (although both of these two would die within the opening years of Edward's reign). Then there was Æthelweard, Edward's younger brother, who would continue to attest Edward's charters no less than twenty-one times. Osferth was there too, Alfred's possible illegitimate son or kinsman. And then there was Æthelred, Lord of the Mercians, who had joined Alfred's wider family by marriage, whose own supporters would have followed him. Alfred's political appointments also kept up the support. Ealdorman Ordlaf, for example, became Æthelhelm of Wiltshire's replacement in 898. He may have been around the same age as Edward. To these supporters were added the close circle of Mercian, Frankish and Welsh (in the case of Asser) churchmen and administrators who along with the loyal household thegns and servants, all helped to drive the kingdom in the required direction. Bishop Wærferth of Worcester was highly important in this regard. Furthermore, much of the nobility attending the 'coronation' had probably grown up and even campaigned with Edward in the 890s. Many of them may have fought alongside the new king when he was a younger man at Farnham and chased the Danes to Thorney Island. For people like them, it was an obvious development that Alfred's son should be the next king of what was in essence an 'Alfredian' kingdom. But to one man, it was not. And he was biding his time. Soon however, he would demonstrate exactly what he thought about it.

Æthelwold was surprisingly energetic. His actions in the wake of Alfred's death show this to be the case. His obvious fury and sense of betrayal were not entirely unjustified either. If we look at things from Æthelwold's point of view, we might even feel some sympathy. Æthelwold, whom the Winchester, or pro-Wessex (A) version of the *Anglo-Saxon Chronicle* notably does not like describing as an *Ætheling* whereas other versions are less reluctant, now gathered himself for the inevitable challenge to his cousin's throne.

Wimborne

The place where Alfred's brother King Æthelred I of Wessex (865–71) had been buried and where Alfred himself oversaw the obsequies in the troubled year of 871, was Wimborne in Dorset. It was also the place where Æthelred's son Æthelwold firmly planted himself at the beginning Edward the Elder's reign in his stand against his cousin.

A double monastery had been founded by St Cuthburg, sister of King Ine (688–726) of Wessex, before 718. Rudolf of Fulda, in his ninth-century *Life of Leofgyth* (who was educated there), relates that the male and female communities were segregated by 'strong and lofty walls'. Another sister of Ine, Tette, who herself became abbess, had an unusual situation to deal with. After the death of an unpopular and severely disciplinarian nun, it happened that many of the women in the community gathered around her grave cursing her memory and then trampled the freshly-turned earth on the mound. The resultant effect of these combined actions was a new depression in the ground instead of what should have been an intended small rise. Tette united the nuns with her in prayer, after which the grave miraculously reverted to its former state.

On a less humorous note, Wimborne was as symbolic to the West Saxons as Repton had been to a branch of the Mercian royal family before the Great Heathen Army had planted itself right on top of the Mercian mausoleum in 873. It was because of this sort of symbolism that the Danes attacked such places. And this is why the Ætheling Æthelwold came to Wimborne as the son of a consecrated king who was buried there, to symbolically claim his right to the throne himself.

Firstly, let us look at Æthelwold's grievances. His father, Æthelred I (King of Wessex 865–71), had been interred at Wimborne, arguably a West Saxon equivalent of the Mercian Repton. Wimborne was at the centre of a cluster of estates and is believed to have been a royal possession passed from king to king. In other words, the place was synonymous with kingship itself. But it was Winchester and not Wimborne which would feature heavily with Alfred's dynasty. Alfred's plan for the New Minster at Winchester was completed during Edward's reign and seems to have had the support of Grimbald of Saint-Bertin (a scholar invited to England by Alfred) and Plegmund, the Archbishop of Canterbury (890–914/923). This New Minster was supposed to be the royal mausoleum for the kings not just of Wessex, but arguably of the expanded kingdom of the Anglo-Saxons in general. Alfred's grandfather Ecgberht was buried in the Old Minster, and Alfred's father Æthelwulf was brought there too eventually, after initially being buried at Steyning in Sussex. Alfred himself would soon be transferred to the New Minster from the Old Minster. The switch in dynastic emphasis from Wimborne to Winchester, and in particular the idea of the growing influence of the New Minster project, would hardly have been lost on Æthelwold.

There is also the question of legitimacy. Æthelwold may have reminded others that he was not only the son of a consecrated king, but also the son of a rare West Saxon phenomenon, a 'queen', Wulfthryth. She appears in only one charter (S 340), but here she is titled *Regina*. Æthelwold had witnessed one of King Alfred's charters (S 356, thought to date from the 890s, although some say it may be earlier) as 'filius regis' (son of the king) ahead of Edward himself who was styled the same. Drawn up at Malmesbury, this charter, a grant of four hides at Chelworth near Crudwell in Wiltshire to a man named Dudig, is Æthelwold's sole appearance in one of Alfred's charters. If it was drawn up in the 890s, then it begs the question of what Æthelwold had been doing here and why he was seemingly still so important.

If Æthelwold could claim to have been born to a 'queen', the situation with Edward and Æthelflæd was less clear. For much of the recent past, Wulfthryth's case seemingly to be an exception, West Saxon wives of kings were exactly that: merely the 'king's wife' (notwithstanding the Frankish princess Judith, whose marriage to King Æthelwulf in 856 came with a demand for the title of 'queen' from the Frankish king). This curious term had come about according to Asser, who was fed the tale by Alfred, due to the activities of a notorious queen of Wessex named Eadburh who had allegedly poisoned her husband King Beorhtric (786–802) and subsequently fled the country. Asser's tale related that the West Saxons had subsequently kept the wives of kings firmly in the background, not even allowing them to sit beside the king.

And then there is the question of Alfred's will, a clear exclusion of Æthelwold from any realistic basis of landed power in Wessex, at least in terms of an inheritance from Alfred. Æthelwold's brother Æthelhelm, however, had been nominated to receive eight estates to Æthelwold's three, perhaps indicating a slightly more conciliatory feeling towards the older of the Æthelings fathered by Alfred's brother. But significantly, neither of them were bequeathed estates in the more 'important' western part of the kingdom. We find the brothers confined largely to Surrey and Sussex, with estates far away from what they and their supporters might consider their own heartlands. Interestingly, of Æthelwold's three estates in the will (Guildford, Godalming and Steyning), the latter was the first resting place for King Æthelwulf, Æthelwold's (and Edward's) grandfather, who had once returned from pilgrimage to Rome only to find himself confined to the eastern half of the expanded Wessex by his own son Æthelbald. This fact, plus the removal of Æthelwulf's remains to Winchester, probably by Alfred, who will have been wary of the potential symbolism of Steyning, may not have met with the approval of Æthelwold. But by 899, Æthelwold's brother Æthelhelm was no longer in the picture. He had died sometime before the king, at an unknown date. There was now just the fuming Æthelwold, filled with a lifetime's sense of injustice.

So what did Æthelwold do to prosecute his claim? The *Anglo-Saxon Chronicle* says that he rode to the manor of Wimborne and the burh of *Tweoxneam* (or Twynham, a name meaning 'the place between the waters', now Christchurch in Dorset) on the coast. Twynham's existing fortifications may have played a part in his plans. This place had been one of the Alfredian fortifications as listed in the Burghal Hidage. The debate surrounding the date of the document itself continues, with some having it as early as c. 879 and distinctly 'Alfredian' in construct, whilst others have it as late as between 914 and 919 in Edward the Elder's reign, due to the inclusion of Buckingham in the list, a fortification Edward built in 914.[9] But the point about the burhs is that they reflected Alfred's defence-in-depth strategy in his new-look kingdom. And at the dawn of the tenth century, that kingdom was once again under attack, and the mastermind of the assault was a member of the royal family itself.

Æthelwold seized both manors 'without leave of the king and his councillors', although the order in which he did it is not clear. The *Anglo-Saxon Chronicle* implies that Wimborne was first. However, John of Worcester, writing in the twelfth century, implies it was the other way around. Æthelwold's motive for capturing Wimborne is clear. Here, his royal father lay. In fact, to the west seems to have been the heartland of Æthelwold's support. Estates here are a little thin on the ground in Alfred's will, for example. Wimborne is close to the roads leading to Dorchester and Salisbury and it is also at the confluence of the Allen and the Stour (which it is argued may have been navigable between Christchurch and Wimborne). Æthelwold's descent upon this place bears some resemblance to the actions of the Danes at Repton in 873, who came to a place associated with royal memory and laid a symbolic claim to it. But for Æthelwold, there was also a personal angle to it. By sitting here at Wimborne, important to his own branch of the family, in defiance of Edward, Æthelwold was demonstrating a 'new' legitimacy, a symbolic display of an obvious right to rule, and a right to also control the surrounding area. But was the seizing of Wimborne a signal of an intention to divide the kingdom once again along the lines of an east-west split as had been the case in the days of Æthelwold's grandfather, or was the intention even grander than that?

The motive for the capture of Twynham or Christchurch on the coast is less clear, but its position between two rivers and the sea made it a formidable fortification and must indicate that whatever Æthelwold had planned, a naval aspect must surely have played a part. The place was also a port. Moreover, part of the plan must have been to dominate the territory associated with the support of the burh and therefore receive its produce. The fact that he managed to take these places at all indicates that he had enough military muscle to achieve it. This in itself implies a level of support for Æthelwold which is glossed over by the contemporary sources.

Edward had responded to these developments by bringing an army to Badbury Rings. This ancient prehistoric hill fort, with its impressive multiple ramparts, lay near to the junction of the Roman road network four miles to the north-west of Wimborne and Æthelwold was about to discover that Edward had a much bigger force than he did. This ancient site, probably still an assembly point in the local landscape, was large enough and defensible enough to provide some sort of protection for Edward's army. Moreover, by occupying this strategic position, Edward ensured that his cousin could not break out to the west where his family and other supporters probably dwelt. Nor, for that matter, could anyone from the west realistically break through to Wimborne.

It is speculated that Æthelwold was planning a division of Wessex from his new base in the event that he should become the king.[10] This may be the case, but something peculiar happened at Wimborne. Æthelwold had ensconced himself inside and barricaded the gates. He had some supporters with him, but any further support is not documented. The chronicler states that Æthelwold was certainly defiant. In Old English, the phrase is '. . . sæde þæt he wolde oðer oððe þær libban oððe þær licgan', which can be interpreted as 'he said that he would do one of two things: live there or die there'. The use of such an overtly poetic flourish, as was sometimes employed in contemporary heroic poetry, has drawn comment.[11] The use of the verb 'licgan' ('to lie') is thought to mean 'lie slain'. Whoever wrote this into the (A) version of the *Anglo-Saxon Chronicle* certainly knew their heroic poetry. But they knew something else too. Æthelwold's challenge to his royal cousin Edward had been no trifling matter. In fact, the whole episode is reminiscent of another great tale told in the *Anglo-Saxon Chronicle*. In a celebrated entry at the year 755, the rebellion of Cyneheard against King Cynewulf is reported (the main event seeming to take place much later). Here, Cyneheard the brother of Sigeberht (whom Cynewulf had driven into exile) rode to a stronghold known as Merton where he had learned that the king was in company with a woman, and killed the king after a great fight. The next morning, when some of the king's thegns had come to the place, Cyneheard had locked the gates against them, barricading himself and his followers inside, in an act of defiance. There then followed an exchange of offers of money and land and refusals thereof, and a bloodbath of vengeance around the gates of the stronghold, resulting in the death of Cyneheard. But although we might have expected something similar, our Æthelwold's story was not to end in the same way, not yet.

And so we return to Wimborne, where Æthelwold's men have just finishing barricading the gates against Edward. The chronicler tells us Æthelwold had earlier taken a woman who had formerly been consecrated a nun. He had done so without the leave of the king and against the command of the bishops. This has led to much speculation. It was, of course, against the law to abduct a nun. But there is potentially more to it than this. Given that Æthelwold's behaviour during this whole episode seems to smack of symbolic defiance against Edward, the abduction being carried out 'against the king's leave . . .' might well indicate that either Edward or Alfred had been responsible for placing the woman in a nunnery in the first place. But who was the woman? Some people say she may well have been Æthelgifu, the abbess of Shaftesbury, Æthelwold's own cousin. One possibility is that the two were in love and that Æthelgifu's placement at Shaftesbury had been a move to prevent a union between them. It is possible that Æthelwold may have come via Shaftesbury to bring Æthelgifu to the symbolically important place of Wimborne and marry her there. The theory raises more questions than it answers, but something had clearly been burning away at Æthelwold. However, could it really have been a love for his cousin, or at the least the desire to use her for his own dynastic intentions? John of Worcester claims that Æthelwold actually married this nun against her will, although some people see the act as a taking into concubinage of the woman.[12] Whoever she was, she was important politically to Æthelwold, and must have held the key to his legitimacy, otherwise he would not have made the remarkably bold step to take her in the first place.

A combination of the sheer numbers ranged against him and the fact that his passage was blocked to the west must have preyed on Æthelwold's mind. John of Worcester contends that the numerical disadvantage was more than enough. It is not known why Edward did not launch an assault on Wimborne. It may have been a too politically sensitive thing to do. Perhaps he did not want anything to happen to the woman. There seems not to have been a submission, nor even a fight at the gates. Æthelwold took the only option open to him under the circumstances. He stole away from the manor at night and rode off to the north and into the arms of the Northumbrian Danes. The chronicler says that Æthelwold could not be overtaken by the king's riders. It was clear to Æthelwold that he needed more military might if his plans were to be realized. And so he stayed in Northumbria and stirred up support there. As for the nun whom he had taken, she also stole away from Wimborne but seemingly travelled in a different direction. The king's men rode after her too, but the *Anglo-Saxon Chronicle* does not say where she went. John of Worcester, however, says that she was soon taken back to the monastery at Wimborne by Edward's men. If that is right, then her identity might not be consistent with that of Æthelgifu after all.

It is possible Æthelwold's failure to achieve his goal at Wimborne and his subsequent flight to Northumbria are linked. The seizure of Twynham may have anticipated the arrival of a naval contingent which, if it failed to materialize, would have dealt a blow to Æthelwold's bid for power. If this fleet had been a Northumbrian one, then one of Æthelwold's reasons for riding all the way to Northumbria and evading Edward's horsemen may well have been to find out what had happened to it.

It was becoming clear that Æthelwold was far from a spent force. In fact, he was rapidly becoming quite the opposite. It would appear that the Ætheling Æthelwold was soon accepted as 'king' by the Northumbrians. The *Annals of St Neots*, which closely follow a version of the *Anglo-Saxon Chronicle*, describe Æthelwold as both 'king of the Danes' ('rex danorum') and 'king of the Pagans' ('rex paganorum'). These references have attracted much comment. Had the Danes proclaimed Æthelwold as *their* king in Northumbria? The Worcester (D) version of the *Anglo-Saxon Chronicle*, whose chronicler knew a thing or two about northern history, mentions that the Northumbrians 'received him as king and submitted to him'. John of Worcester certainly thought so, too. He says '. . . he fled away by night, and went to Northumbria, where he requested the Danes to allow him to join them, not so much in the capacity of a leader as of a comrade: they, very shortly afterwards, made him their king'. But the actual status of Æthelwold in Northumbria, in terms of who or what he was actually king of, is not fully understood. Tellingly, however, the pro-Wessex (A) version of the *Anglo-Saxon Chronicle* says nothing at all of any submission or acceptance of Edward's cousin as king by the Northumbrians. More telling still, as we have seen (see above, page 20), is the fact that the scribe, throughout the portrayal of his rebellion, is reluctant to accord Æthelwold with the title of 'Ætheling'. Instead, throughout the portrayal of his rebellion, except at the very end, Æthelwold is merely 'Æthelwold' or referred to as Edward's 'father's brother's son'.

To add to the intrigue, coins bearing the name ALWALDUS (and variant spellings) suggestive of AETHELWALDUS were also in circulation from around this time in the north. This coinage is not without its controversies. Such coins have been found in the Cuerdale Hoard and the Silverdale Hoard (see below) and have turned up privately as well. Only in recent decades has the argument for these being linked to Æthelwold gathered pace, based on the similarity they have with the coins of Sigeferth and Cnut, the two Northumbrian Danish leaders dominating York's politics at this time.

Fig. 3: *Coin in the name of ALVALD.DUS, probably* Æthelwold, *cousin of Edward the Elder (obverse). From a coin in the Fitzwilliam Museum (1016.0120).*

The Silverdale Hoard

Dating from the first decade of the tenth century, the Silverdale Hoard was discovered by a metal detectorist in 2011 near Silverdale in Lancashire. The finder reported his discovery to the Portable Antiquities Scheme and the hoard was subsequently analysed by the British Museum.

There are twenty-seven silver coins, ten complete arm rings, two finger rings, thirteen complete ingots (with over a hundred cut at one or both ends), six brooch fragments, a fine wire braid and well over a hundred other fragments of hacksilver. Found inside a lead container deposited face down, it is essentially a hacksilver hoard, with many of the coins bent or pecked and much of the other silver 'tested' in a similar way. Silver was used seemingly in a bullion-style economy at this time, although the move to a fuller 'coin' economy in this region was not far away.[13] The coins are a mixture of Anglo-Saxon, Anglo-Scandinavian and Arabic coins. However, of real interest is one coin bearing the name of AIRDECONVT (probably Harthacnut), a previously unknown Scandinavian ruler in the north. The coin shares similarities with those of two other rulers Sigeferth and Cnut, who ruled in York between c. 895 and 905.

It seems to have been a crowded world in northern England at this time, as the hoard included a type of coin also known from the famous Cuerdale Hoard discovered on the banks of the Ribble in 1840. This type is in the name of ALVVALDVS, believed to be attributable to Æthelwold, the son of Æthelred I, king of Wessex (865–71). Æthelwold unsuccessfully challenged Edward the Elder for the throne between 899 and 902 and fled to the Danes of Northumbria where he himself was received as king.

Fig. 4: *Coin of AIRDECONVT (Harthacnut) from the Silverdale Hoard (obverse).*

We may wonder what sort of promises Æthelwold had made to the Anglo-Danish leadership in York in return for their support. Might it have been the case that in order to secure that support Æthelwold had even renounced his faith to make him more appealing to a seemingly pagan community? It would not be the first time a Christian ruler had done something similar. During his dispute with Charles the Bald in the 860s Pepin II, a great-grandson of Charlemagne, had even 'joined company with the Northmen and lived like one of them' according to the *Annals of St Bertin*. Alternatively, the exact opposite scenario is possible. The reverse of many coins of Sigeferth, Cnut and 'Alwaldus' bear Christian inscriptions. Æthelwold may have persuaded the Danes to *accelerate* their acceptance of Christianity under the watchful eye of the church at York. After all, it is supposed to be around this time (from the late 890s) that the Danes of East Anglia were celebrating on their coinage the martyred English East Anglian King Edmund who had perished at the hands of the Great Heathen Army back in 869.

We cannot really know what sort of accommodation Æthelwold reached with the existing Scandinavian rulers in Northumbria. What we do know from subsequent events is that Æthelwold searched far and wide for that missing ingredient to his success. He needed a fleet and he knew it.

With Æthelwold away somewhere in the north, much was changing in Edward's kingdom in the south. Archbishop Plegmund, Bishop Denewulf of Winchester, Asser (who had been appointed bishop at Sherborne in 895) and Bishop Wærferth of Worcester were all still around, although Grimbald would soon pass away in the very early years of Edward's reign. But it was in the secular ranks where the names and faces of the kingdom's leading figures were changing the most. The witan had a whole new look to it. Many of the names who now appeared regularly on the witness lists of Edward's charters were relatively new. They included Ordlaf, the ealdorman of Wiltshire, only recently appointed in the closing years of Alfred's reign after the death of Æthelhelm. Other faces at Edward's court were Wihtbrord, Deormod (Alfred's *cellerarius* and keeper of the royal stores), Wulfhelm, Ordgar and Heahfrith. But there were some older stalwarts too, who included Osferth, Edward's possible half-brother or kinsman.

New Minster

The building of New Minster at Winchester dominated Edward's early years as king. It was almost certainly the brainchild of his father Alfred the Great. It was built on a site which probably included property given by Alfred to Grimbald, the distinguished churchman and scholar Alfred had brought from the Continent into his service. The purpose of the foundation was to establish a royal dynastic centre for the descendants of Alfred, and arguably for the kings of the Anglo-Saxons in general, but its extreme closeness to Old Minster (among other things) was a cause of some friction throughout the tenth century. So too was its size. The new building, completed in around 903, dwarfed its neighbour for some time until Old Minster gradually caught up with it due to various rebuilds in the tenth century. It was said that the buildings were so close that each community could hear the other's choir singing. Archaeology confirms this uncomfortable intimacy. In one place the buildings were no more than a metre apart.[14]

New Minster became the burial place for Alfred's remains (transferred from Old Minster almost as soon as New Minster had a roof). It also housed the burial of Edward's Mercian mother Ealhswith (who founded nearby Nunnaminster before her death in 902). At least one of Edward's sons (Ælfweard) would be buried here, as would Edward himself (in 924) and his descendant King Edwy in 959. This was after King Edmund I (939–46) had extended the building.

In 1065, a great fire swept through the domestic buildings of New Minster, causing widespread damage, but it was not until 1110 in the reign of Henry I (1100–35), after the vast Norman cathedral had replaced Old Minster, that the community of nearby New Minster was removed to Hyde, a suburb of Winchester. Hyde Abbey was an illustrious building, which housed the transferred bodies of Alfred, Ealhswith and their son Edward. The community survived the damaging civil war of the twelfth century and the building remained intact until the Dissolution of the Monasteries. Hyde Abbey was dissolved in 1538 and after this, a sorry tale of wanton destruction commenced which lasted for centuries. Reckless exploring of the site which incorporated acts of sheer vandalism were carried out, many by those who should have known better.

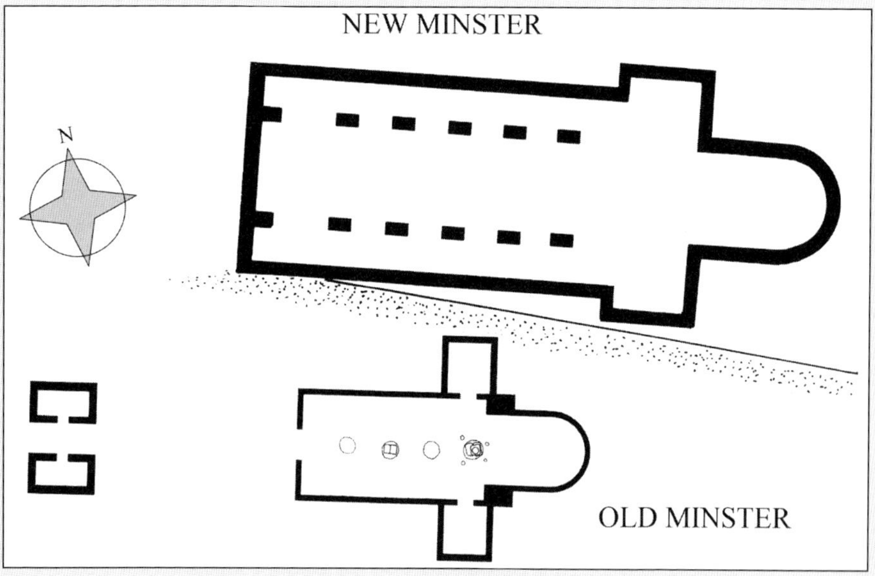

Fig. 5: *Plan view of Winchester New Minster in c. 903 and Old Minster, its neighbour. New Minster, with its aisled basilica and shallow transepts, was similar to a church built by Charlemagne (d. 814) in St Denis in France. Based on a drawing by Simon Hayfield in Biddle, M. (2018).*

Another place where the political climate had changed remarkably was at Winchester itself. The grand project of building the New Minster would set Edward and his immediate supporters on a collision course with Bishop Denewulf. A record of 900 (S 1443) shows Edward acquiring land from Denewulf (and some from the counsellors of the West Saxons) for the building of New Minster in exchange for St Andrew's church. It seems that the work was continued on the project with great energy from the start, reaching completion around the end of 902 or 903. The building was almost certainly meant to be a dynastic foundation as well as arguably a new church for a 'new' burh. On its completion, it was much larger than its historic neighbour, and remained so for some time. But the obvious fact that it had been planted right next door to the 'Old' Minster was not the only source of tension. Edward had also acquired land for New Minster from the cathedral in what looks like a coercive move.[15]

The antagonism continued over the years with land disputes and the occasional dubious document tending to skew the claims of New Minster over its neighbour. The main gripe from the Old Minster community was that it appeared to them that they had not received the full value of the property transfer they felt had been agreed by the king. The implication is that Edward, whose strategy in such things was to favour the exchange of estates and property in such dealings, sometimes did not keep to his side of the agreement. Relations between Denewulf and the king, which at best could be described as 'complicated', were even revealed in writing. When he was pressurised by the king to lease a large and remarkably well documented estate of sixty hides at Beddington in Surrey to Edward, the bishop wrote a letter (S 1444) pleading with the king:

> I, Bishop Denewulf, inform my lord King Edward about the land at Beddington which you were desirous I should lease to you. I have then, my dear lord, now procured from the community in Winchester, both young and old, that they grant it to me with all goodwill, to give it with charter for your lifetime, whether to use yourself or to let on lease to whomsoever you please.
>
> Then there is 70 hides of land, and it is now completely stocked, and when my lord first let it to me, it was quite without stock, and stripped bare by heathen men. And I myself then acquired the stock for it which was afterwards available there. And now we very humbly grant it to you. Moreover, my dear lord, the community are now desirous that it be given back to the foundation after your death.
>
> Now, of the cattle which has survived this severe winter there are 9 full-grown oxen, and 114 full-grown pigs and 50 wethers [castrated rams] besides the sheep and the pigs which the herdsmen have a right to have, 20 of which are full grown; and there are 110 full-grown sheep, and 7 bondsmen and 20 flitches; and there was no more corn there than was prepared for the bishop's farm, and there [are] 90 sown acres.
>
> Then the bishop and the community at Winchester beg that in charity for the love of God and for the holy church you desire no more land of that foundation, for it seems to them an unwelcome demand, so that God need blame neither you nor us for the diminishing in our days; for there was a very great injunction of God about that when men gave those lands to the foundation.

Quite whether Denewulf and the community were as financially upset as he seems to imply is a moot point. Old Minster would in the future compete for glory with its new neighbour with a series of impressive architectural upgrades. But that neighbour, the dynastic foundation for the family of Alfred the Great, would by the end of 903 house the transferred remains of King Alfred himself and his wife Ealhswith. It would also house the learned Grimbald, who may have been destined to base himself there, and the rescued remains of St Judoc, a Breton saint, whose followers in Ponthieu had sailed with their cherished relics across to Wessex. Now, in Winchester, the stage was set for a long-lasting and not altogether harmonious co-existence of the New and the Old Minsters, one which would, however, see a flowering of artistic and cultural works as each viewed the other's achievements no doubt with envy.

The example of King Edward's land acquisition policy as highlighted in the Beddington lease was mirrored elsewhere. Beddington may have suffered badly when the Danes marched through Surrey during Edward's campaigns as an Ætheling in the 890s, or just as likely many years before during the time of his father and grandfather. Although the Beddington lease (the land, incidentally, was still in royal hands in 1066) does not on the face of it have an overt military motivation, many lands acquired by the king did. Between 900 and 904 Edward acquired numerous lands by exchange. These included Plympton in Devon, Chiseldon and Sparcels in Wiltshire, Farmborough, Crowcombe, Compton and Banwell in Somerset, and Portchester in Hampshire. Each of these places had some sort of value to Edward and the example of Portchester (S 372), exchanged for a large tract of land at Bishop's Waltham in Hampshire, may also have had an overt military meaning.

In Mercia, in these early days of Edward's rule, there may have been a slight shift in the relationship between the new king and his English Mercian partners. The charter of 901 (S 221) drawn up at Shrewsbury, concerning a land exchange and a chalice granted to the community of the church of Much Wenlock, includes a description of Æthelred and Æthelflæd as honourably 'holding, governing and defending the monarchy of the Mercians'. A king and queen in all but name, perhaps. It is possible that the Lord of the Mercians, perhaps with the support of an element of the nobility of south-west Mercia, was at this stage tilting Mercia towards greater autonomy from his brother-in-law's overlordship. If so, the combining together of husband and wife in the wording might suggest the Lady of the Mercians felt much the same. But if there *were* some rumblings of Mercian separatism at the beginning of the century, the evidence does not show it bursting into a full-blown movement at this time. It is more likely that the charter is simply flamboyantly stating what had already been the case in Alfred's time: that the Mercian kingdom was ruled by Æthelred and Æthelflæd as part of Alfred's wider vision of a kingdom of the Anglo-Saxons. For example, Æthelred did not produce coinage in his own name. Coinage in Mercia remained in Edward's name, although there are arguments for distinctive Mercian issues (see pages 127–8). There is always going to be a shifting of positions politically amongst all power groups at the transition of one king to another but whether there was such a shift in Mercia between 900 and 902 is difficult to uncover. Any undercurrent of Mercian 'independence' is, however, quite understandable and it is interesting that the concept of its 'monarchy' lingered. The kingdom was all but eliminated from history less than a generation earlier, and yet under the Lord and Lady of the Mercians – albeit as dutiful subordinates to Alfred – it had begun to find its feet once more, if only in the south and west. However, Edward's assertion of himself during these early years certainly secured his position as the most powerful leader in the political set-up south of Watling Street. Besides, in the summer of 902, the greatest threat to his hold on the throne came sailing back into the picture with a long sought-after fleet. Æthelwold, the man who would be king, had landed with a host of Scandinavian shipmen in Essex and, although the (A) version of the *Anglo-Saxon Chronicle* does not admit it, we find in other versions that the people there were submitting to him. Often, the events which followed are described as Æthelwold's 'rebellion'. But in reality, it was a far more serious affair: this was the beginning of a most extraordinary war.

Æthelwold's forces must have been substantial. Not long after its arrival in Essex his army comprised the shipmen of the fleet, East Anglian units under their probable king, Eohric (a leader who seems to have risen to power in the wake of the death of Guthrum in 890), and also the men of the recently submitted population of Essex. Quite where the ships and their crews had come from is not clear at all. The *Anglo-Saxon Chronicle* (D) indicates that the origin of these vessels may even have been far distant. Æthelwold, it says, 'came across the sea here with all the fleet he could get'. Combine this evidence with the apparent time it had taken him to get a fleet at all, and we might well conclude that the Ætheling had either been recruiting shipmen in the north of England, or even abroad. John of Worcester, although writing much later, specifically states that Æthelwold 'returned to England from parts beyond the sea', and that he had purchased some of his fleet, whilst gathering the rest from East Anglia. Speculatively of course, we might suggest a candidate for a Continental recruitment ground on the long-lived Danish enclave of the island of Walcheren at the mouth of the Scheldt, a place where Æthelwold could arguably spend his money well. But despite John of Worcester's tantalizing reference, we cannot be fully sure where the fleet really came from, except that it seems to have been brought together from more than one source.

King Eohric must have taken a leading role in all this. John of Worcester says that Æthelwold had promised the East Anglians a great share in the spoils, a pledge suggestive of both a planned and widespread raiding campaign into Mercia and Wessex. Eohric is a shadowy figure about whom we know very little, but it certainly seems that he was an invaluable ally to Æthelwold. It is not explicitly stated that he was the king of East Anglia, but the references to Æthelwold 'enticing' the East Anglians and having 'enticed' King Eohric might suggest that he was. Sometime later in the year Æthelwold and his army came marching over Watling Street in Mercia and 'thirsting for prey, destroyed everything with fire and sword' says John of Worcester. There is no recorded Mercian intervention as the army progressed across it from east to west. Four miles north-east of Cricklade is a ford across the Thames at a very narrow point of the river. This is at Kempsford. It is possible that the chronicler's description of Æthelwold taking the East Anglians into Mercia and raiding as far as Cricklade before crossing the Thames, refers to this well-known crossing point where the river is shallow enough to ford. But the chronicler's silence on why the Cricklade garrison did not intervene is curious. Their strength, according to the Burghal Hidage (assessed at 1,500 hides), was the equivalent of that of Chichester. Æthelwold's

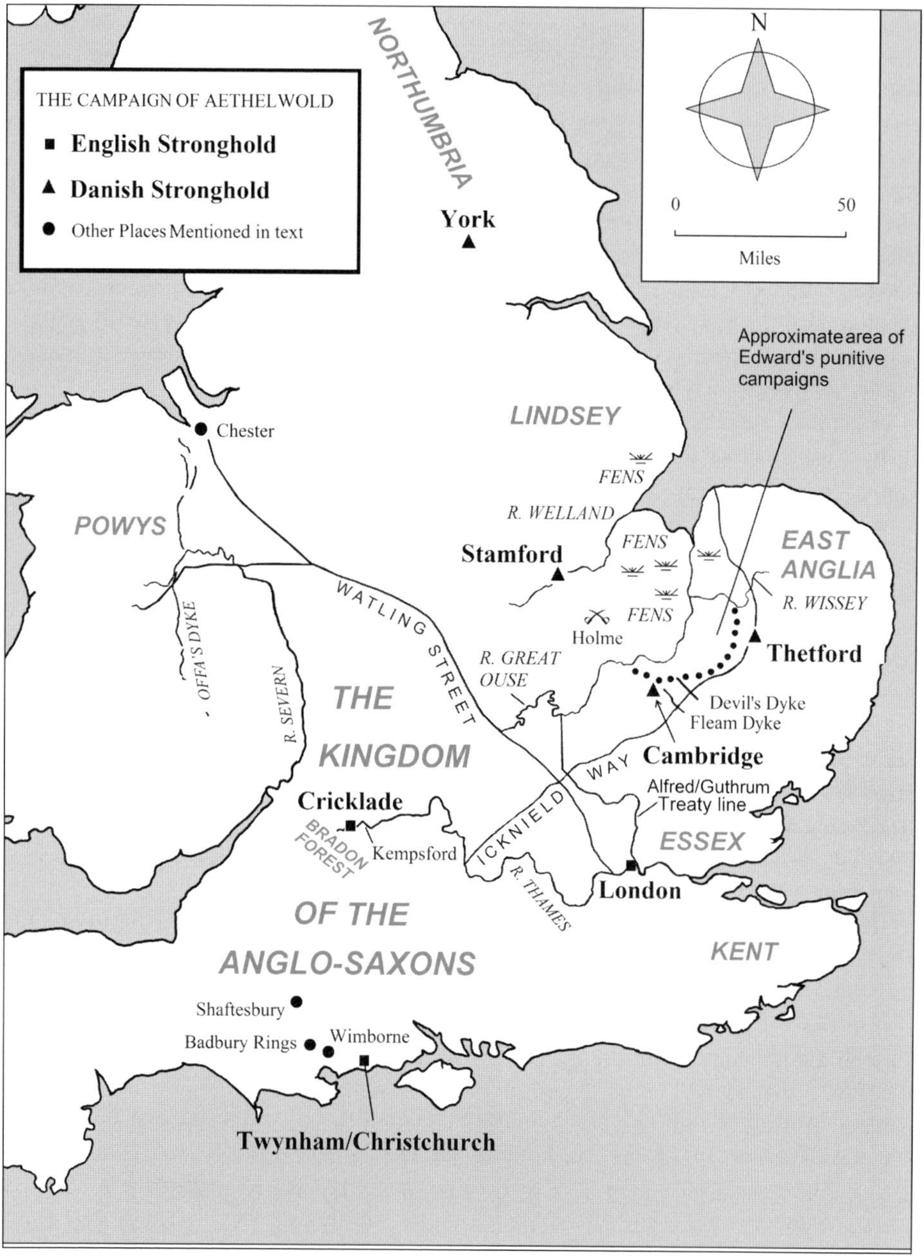

Map 2: *The campaign of Æthelwold.*

forces are recorded as then raiding around the Braydon (Bradon Forest) area and 'taking all that they could grab' before turning home eastwards. But why would the rebel army march all the way across southern Mercia, a militarily sensitive area, simply to seek out a fertile raiding ground and then head home again? Had they had been turned back before reaching their goal?

The chronicler adds that Edward went after his enemy as quickly as he could. This means that the king must have either already been in the area or made good progress from another starting point. Perhaps Ealdorman Ordlaf had come up from Wiltshire, too. But there is another puzzling question. If Æthelwold *had* been turned back, then where was he headed in the first place? Here, the answers are harder to establish and must remain speculative, but the fact that Æthelwold had tried so hard for so long to secure himself a fleet may well be part of it. Æthelwold's heartlands where he could test the strength of his support inside Wessex may well have been directly south of the place where he crossed the Thames. The family of Wulfhere, a man who had turned against King Alfred in 877, were based here, a family arguably linked to the Ætheling's own mother Wulfthryth. In fact, Wulfhere's sedition is revealed in a charter of 901 (S 362). Here, King Edward granted out Wulfhere's forfeited estates, on account of nothing less than treason, referring back to a meeting held in the past at which the leading men of both Wessex and Mercia agreed that he should be deprived of them. This meeting gives a good example of how a resurgent King Alfred viewed rebels. But Wulfhere had earlier witnessed a charter in 868 (S 340) directly after the then queen Wulfthryth (mother of Æthelhelm and Æthelwold). They may perhaps have been related, possibly even brother and sister. The fact that both Wulfhere and his own wife were implicated in the treachery against Edward's father may even indicate that Wulfhere's household had harboured the two Ætheling boys at some stage. So, there appears to be a case for a link between Wulfhere, the lands along the banks of the River Wylie (the lands forfeited), and the group of supporters around Æthelwold. Wulfhere's family did not, as it happens, disappear out of sight or lose all their lands. They were in fact a powerful dynasty in their own right and there is evidence for Wulfhere's own grandson later in the tenth century bequeathing estates known to have once been held by his grandfather. However, what the charter of 901 (S 362) reveals, is a tantalizing glimpse into the tensions at the very top of Anglo-Saxon society and how difficult, long-lasting and sensitive these issues were. It also demonstrates another very important thing: that memories died hard in Anglo-Saxon England.

If Æthelwold had travelled south from Kempsford or Cricklade, he would have come once again to Wimborne and Twynham within a few days' march. Arguably, a supporting fleet could have sailed into Twynham. But it is only guesswork. We may never know if Æthelwold's plan had already been a success, or if he had been stopped in his tracks right in the middle of it. But now, Æthelwold had the full fury of the forces of Edward's kingdom at his heels. The next stage of the war would take place not in the rich green fields of Wessex, but in the misty fenlands of eastern England in a place where the land stubbornly gave way to the sea amid the marshes and watery inlets.

The route Æthelwold took back to the east is not known. Nor is it known whether Edward took the same route in pursuit or headed-off his prey by making an alternative journey. At some point in the campaign the Kent fyrd joined in the hostilities on the king's side. This might show that Edward was either with the men of Kent or detoured to the east of his kingdom to summon that support before heading north. The chronicler's phrase that Edward 'pursued his enemy as quickly as he could gather an army' does not really help. That said, as we shall see, the Kentish contingent would play an extremely important part in the events which followed. Edward's pursuit of his enemy led him into East Anglia, where he raided around the area between the Cambridgeshire Dykes and the River Wissey as far as the fenlands. The river name is *Wusan* as written in the *Anglo-Saxon Chronicle*, which some identify with the Little Ouse situated further south than the Wissey and which flows through Thetford. Both candidates, however, are in roughly the same area. The Dykes in question probably include Devil's Dyke and the Fleam Dyke to the south and east of Cambridge. These linear monuments still rose above the flat landscape, a testimony to Dark Age East Anglian power in centuries gone by. This region is one of the lowest points in England, characterized by big skies and endless waterways dissecting ground which in places is treacherous underfoot. The sequence of events which followed are lost to us. Winter was by now well advanced and when Edward finally decided to call off the campaign in early December, perhaps because his fyrd had reached the end of their term of service, or perhaps because he was satisfied the season's work was over, or maybe even for another reason, he decided to pull back from the fenlands to maintain his cohesion as one force, including the Kent contingent which had joined him on the expedition.

But that contingent from Kent was the source of a problem for Edward. The *Anglo-Saxon Chronicle*, almost in a defensive way, points out that the king had apparently sent seven messengers into their position giving them the order to retreat. But it seems they did not. It has been pointed out that the military forces from Kent at this time may have occupied an interesting position within combined Anglo-Saxon armies, especially when on the offensive in enemy territories.[16] There is a tantalizing potential recollection of their status in John of Salisbury's *Policraticus* written in the latter half of the twelfth century. Referring to the early eleventh century when he says the tradition was in place, and drawing from Wace, another twelfth-century writer, John says the men of Kent formed the first line in the English army, with those of Wiltshire, Devon and Cornwall forming the second. It is not known how far back into Anglo-Saxon history this tradition goes. But one interpretation of this is that the men of Kent were traditionally in the van of the army on the way into enemy territory and covered the rear on the way out. A similar arrangement is known to have existed for the men of Archenfield in the eleventh century when the English army campaigned in Wales. In this latter case, the Welshmen of the border region of Archenfield were allowed to retain certain rights and privileges if they performed these military roles. It is not out of the question that the men of Kent in 902 performed the functions of vanguard and rearguard units in return for a lion's share of the spoils when on offensive campaigns in enemy territory. This would make sense of what was about to happen in the marshy wilderness at Holme. It would also explain why the Kent contingent dallied in defiance of King Edward. They may have been too busy gathering what they believed was theirs by right, in other words, the plunder. And it would also explain why Æthelwold, in the knowledge of the king's absence, and in the depth of winter when supplies were scarce, was tempted to attack.

The leaders of the Kent contingent were Sigewulf and Sigehelm, men whom Edward will have known well. When the king's thegns arrived with their repeated messages to retreat, one can only guess at the response. The decision to remain in the field meant the Kent contingent was vulnerable to attack from Æthelwold. John of Worcester states that the Danes collected their forces into one body to attack when they heard about the Kentish decision not to heed the king's messengers. Nobody really knows what happened to those messengers, whether they were intercepted or merely returned to the king with the bad news. The encounter which then followed is generally referred to as the Battle of the Holme, its precise whereabouts as ill-defined as the boundary between land and water on which it apparently took place. Some have argued that because so many of the nobility of Kent were killed in the battle, we should be looking in Kent itself for the location and not in the fenlands. But this makes no sense of the narrative in the *Anglo-Saxon Chronicle* which says in the context of the raiding between the Dykes and the Wissey, that Edward had wanted to leave the area and that he had wanted his forces to all go out from there together, but that when Edward's seven messengers had failed in their attempts to get the men of Kent to retreat 'they [the Kent fyrd] were surrounded there . . . and they fought there'. The consensus is now that the battle took place around Holme Fen just east of the village of Holme in Cambridgeshire, although a case has been made in the past for an area around Biggleswade.[17] The word Holme may be derived from a word which has a similar form in Scandinavian languages (*Holmr* in Old Norse, for example) and it means (in our context) a 'flat piece of ground surrounded by river or water', perhaps linked to the *Hólmgang* of Old Norse literature, a place of arbitration by combat. The curious thing about this location, if it is correctly identified, is that it is quite a way to the west of the Wissey (and Little Ouse) and the areas of initial raiding undertaken by Edward's forces. But such movement is to be expected. It is conceivable that just prior to the battle, Edward was still pursuing Æthelwold, who may by now have fallen back to the Peterborough area or was headed for the safety of Danish Stamford to the north-west. As for the date, it is often pointed out that the dates given in the various versions of the *Anglo-Saxon Chronicle* are dislocated, providing a date of anywhere between late 902 and 905, but it may be possible to narrow things down a little.

The chronicler Æthelweard was writing about four generations after these events. He generally keeps the reporting of Æthelwold's rebellion to an understandable minimum given that he himself was distantly related to Æthelwold. He tells us that the battle took place five days after the Christian Feast of the Immaculate Conception, which would place it on 13 December 902. This, incidentally, would be just over a week after Edward had lost his royal mother Ealhswith. Whether this loss had any impact on the campaign itself is not possible to determine, as Ealhswith's relationship with her children, which one suspects was very close indeed, is not revealed by any of the surviving literature. She does not appear in Alfredian charters, but does appear as a witness in one of Edward's charters (S 363), a grant, or exchange of land by the king to the familia of the church of Malmesbury. Here, the Mercian lady whose children would go on to lay the foundations of an entire country, is simply styled 'Ealhswið mater regis', the mother of the king. But it is arguable that there was a fondness in people's recollection of Ealhswith, an indication perhaps, that her influence on her family had been great. In the *Metrical Calendar of Hampson*, a tenth-century martyrology named after its nineteenth-century editor, Ealhswith is described in the entry relating to her death for 5 December 902 as 'the true and beloved Lady of the English' (Cotton MS Galba A XVIII). It is high praise indeed for one of the more enigmatic yet clearly important women of Anglo-Saxon England.

Although they seem to have been caught unawares by the Anglo-Danish alliance, the Kent contingent fought very hard under difficult circumstances. We know nothing of the deployment of either side or the tactical development of the battle. We might speculate that as Edward weaved his way through the fens towards Watling Street, the men of Kent had not even set out at all. There is an impression given of a sense of isolation as their force was surrounded. A bitterly contested melee then ensued in which casualties were both attritional and numerous on both sides. The list of the dead as announced in the *Anglo-Saxon Chronicle* is of huge significance. They included the East Anglian King Eohric whom the chronicler Æthelweard thus proclaims 'descended to Orcus', the mythical god of the underworld who famously punished oath-breakers. More importantly for Edward, and catastrophically for the alliance against him, another fatality was Æthelwold himself. He had been perhaps one of the '. . . Two princes of the English, soft of beard . . .' who fell. It is a good example of the risks of committing to open battle in an age where some commanders (such as Edward himself) were often pursuing more strategic goals rather than seeking pitched battles unless they were absolutely necessary. If Edward was receiving any news at all from the misty marshlands, then on hearing of his cousin's death, his emotions would have been mixed. Æthelwold, a man who had almost succeeded in toppling Edward during a long drawn-out and geographically widespread rebellion, had perished. But so too had the flower of the nobility of Kent (according to Æthelweard), the very people with whom Edward's family had struck such a close relationship over the last two or three generations. One King's Thegn is also listed among the dead. The chronicler's account of the battle strikes a defensive tone for Edward. As we have seen, it is as if the chronicler is trying to blame the fyrd of Kent for not heeding the king's call for a retreat. But the possibility remains that the survivors of the Holme had held Edward responsible for some sort of neglect or abandonment of their men. It was a relationship which history would show, needed some considerable reparation. A glance at the casualty list will explain why.

The Battle of the Holme Casualties

Anglo-Danish Alliance
King Eohric
Ætheling Æthelwold (whom the (A) version of the *Anglo-Saxon Chronicle* says had 'enticed' the East Anglian army and 'incited Eohric into hostility)
Beorhtsige/Byrhtsige, son of Ætheling Beorhtnoth/Beornoth
Hold * Ysopa
Hold Oscytel
'. . . and very many others'. (*Anglo-Saxon Chronicle*)

* Hold – a Scandinavian landowner of a rank beneath the status of Jarl but valued in one source as double the wergild of an English thegn

Anglo-Saxon (mainly Kent)
Ealdorman Sigewulf
Ealdorman Sigehelm
Eadwold, king's thegn
Abbot Cenwulf
Sigeberht, son of Sigewulf
Eadwold, son of Acca
'. . . and many others . . .' (*Anglo-Saxon Chronicle*)

With a casualty list like this, it is almost as an afterthought that the chronicler records who actually won the battle. In fact, Henry of Huntington, writing in the twelfth century, even pointed out to his readers that the sources made it impossible for him to tell the outcome, saying that they 'leave that in doubt'. There were more Danes killed than English, but the chronicler admits the alliance held the place of slaughter. If ever there was a pyrrhic victory in early English military history, then this was it. There can hardly have been an inlet or creek in these frozen fenlands which did not run red with blood or was not blocked up by discarded shields and broken bodies. John of Worcester, for the record, has what appears to be two separate entries for the battle. The first, he names as occurring at the Holme and he says the men of Kent 'got the victory', but then he goes on to provide another account based on the *Anglo-Saxon Chronicle* in which he says that the Danes held the place of slaughter.

Æthelweard, our chronicler descended from Æthelwold's father, is perhaps a little cagey about the Battle of the Holme, but he does give it some space in his work and he is dismissive of King Eohric and does not mention Æthelwold. He does mention, however, in suitably watery tones, the two Englishmen who yielded their lives and proceeded to 'explore the foreign regions, under the waves of Acheron'. This may be an oblique reference to the two senior English figures listed in the chronicle, one of which was of course, Æthelwold. But there is another leading Englishman besides Æthelwold listed in the casualties. He is included on the Anglo-Danish alliance side. His name was Beorhtsige or Byrhtsige, and the consensus among most historians is that he was a Mercian.

Beorhtsige's presence in the alliance is intriguing. If he was a Mercian, he and his family may even have been the reason that the alliance had found it so easy to trek across southern Mercia in the early part of the campaign. The son of an Ætheling (Beorhtnoth or Beornoth), Beorhtsige may well have been descended from the Mercian royal line as represented by the 'B' dynasty, which had been involved in the dynastic struggles in Mercia during the latter part of the ninth century. He may also have been the thegn who had witnessed one of King Alfred's later charters at which Edward was present (S 350). Edward, incidentally, signs as 'rex'. If this is the case, then Beorhtsige would have joined the alliance not only in defiance against Edward, the king of the Anglo-Saxons, but also against Edward's 'subordinates' Æthelflæd and Æthelred. His expectations may have been very high indeed, had his side won the war. There is even a hint that his own family may have remained close to the descendants of Wulfhere, as a certain 'Brihtsige' is mentioned in the will of Wulfgar, Wulfhere's grandson (S 1533). But this can only really be speculation. Now, however, in the cold winter of 902, both Ætheling Æthelwold and Beorhtsige lay dead in a watery ditch, their last vision being the giant skies above them, darkened by a murder of carrion crows. Their ambitions had been extinguished and their lives had been cut down by the desperate swordsmen of Kent. Somewhere nearby lay the shattered body of the Danish king Eohric. A new age had dawned in the wake of the Battle of the Holme, perhaps more by accident than design. But it was of spectacular significance to English history. We cannot be sure what England may have looked like or how it would have developed under Æthelwold if he had won the war. Perhaps it would have been more inclusive and Anglo-Danish in outlook, but what Æthelwold's death meant for certain was that for now at least, the line of Alfred was safe.

One mysterious episode mentioned by Æthelweard may be related to the challenge to Edward from Æthelwold in some way. Æthelbald, a man of obscure origin, was consecrated as Archbishop of York in around 900. The event, however, took place in London. This may have been an appointment promoted by Æthelwold and his supporters to establish a firm grip on power in Northumbria, or alternatively it may conceivably have been an Edwardian appointment to thwart the very same. The former is perhaps the more likely in that Edward will have struggled to exercise regal authority in York at this stage. The extent to which the Scandinavian leaders and their followers at York may have lapsed into paganism at this time is also unknown. As for Æthelbald, after the campaign of Æthelwold against Edward came to its watery end at the Holme, nothing more is known of his actions.

We cannot be entirely sure what Æthelflæd thought of her cousin's campaign against the authority of her brother. The *Mercian Register*, the annals which record Æthelflæd's exploits, makes only a reference to 'a battle at the Holme between the people [or forces] of Kent [*Cantwara*] and the Danes'. There is no mention of what must have been a considerable Mercian episode during that campaign. The *Mercian Register*, sometimes referred to as 'The Annals of Æthelflæd', is in fact an extraordinary window into Æthelflæd's remarkable successes not recorded, or at least not surviving, elsewhere.[18] For many, it is an enigmatic text. It is to be found inserted into the *Anglo-Saxon Chronicle* in the versions from Abingdon (B) and (C) as an obvious distinct entity covering the years 902 to 924, whereas in the Worcester (D) version of the chronicle, a scribe has woven in the detail from the annals into the main body of the text, not always successfully, but sometimes providing a little more information, especially at the end, giving the impression that the Worcester scribe may have been working from a more complete original, given that his or her entries extend to 926. The brevity of the entries can be easily overlooked, sometimes they are merely one line only, but they tell the story year by year of the remarkable career of Æthelflæd, only occasionally mentioning her husband. It is perhaps significant that the annals begin with the death of Ealhswith, Æthelflæd's Mercian mother. And crucially the tale is, of course, a distinctly Mercian one. Perhaps owing their origins to a separate Latin poetic *Gesta* or *Life* of Æthelflæd, or alternatively to a now lost and specifically Mercian continuation to the *Anglo-Saxon Chronicle* itself, these annals, written in Old English, provide a blow-by-blow account of the astonishing and otherwise unrecorded tale of one woman's triumphant efforts to fortify Mercia. We will follow her fortunes and those of her brother Edward, tracing the events in what was one of the most emphatic and sustained military campaigns in all of Early Medieval European history. But we must acknowledge that were it not for the information relayed in the *Mercian Register*, or 'The Annals of Æthelflæd', we would be left thinking that our remarkable story was one conceived entirely at or around the court of Edward the Elder.[19]

The challenge to Edward had now receded, along with much of the hope held by the old Mercian line which had fallen at the Holme. Æthelflæd, the 'Lady of the Mercians', must now turn her attentions elsewhere. And there may be a hint as to what seems to have been some inactivity on the part of Mercia at the time of the rebellion against Edward. Æthelflæd's much older husband, Æthelred, 'Lord of the Mercians' was not always in the best of health, if we are to believe a much-debated source called *The Fragmentary Annals of Ireland*, one which we will look at again. It may be that this period was one of those times when his illness had even incapacitated him. And so from around this time, the Lady of the Mercians seems to have involved herself more and more in the government of Mercia as well as in the running of its court. And it would not be long before Æthelflæd was put to the test.

Chapter 2

Ingimund

904 Her mona aþystrode.
905 Her ætywde cometa.
907 Her wæs Ligcester geedniwod.

'904 Here the moon grew dark.
905 Here a comet appeared.
907 Here Chester was restored.'

The *Mercian Register*, or 'Annals of Æthelflæd'.
Entries for 904 to 907 (C)

The death of her cousin Æthelwold and the failure of his challenge against her brother had not been the only news to reach Æthelflæd's Mercian court in 902. The passing of her mother Ealhswith will have brought great sorrow to all. But amid the mourning, ominous news was flooding into Æthelflæd's hall from across the sea. In Ireland, there had been a huge uprising against the Scandinavians.

It was the Norsemen of the Dublin *Longphort* who were on the wrong end of the uprising. The word *Longphort* implies a maritime fortified settlement. And it had been from such settlements that the Scandinavians had dominated the trading networks of the Irish Sea and set themselves up as regional masters. But in its entry for 902, the *Annals of Ulster* had something to say about the tumultuous events which unfolded:

> The heathens were driven from Ireland, i.e. from the fortress [*Longphort*] of Áth Cliath [Dublin], by Mael Finnia son of Flannacán with the men of Brega and by Cerball son of Muiricán, with the Laigin [Leinstermen]; and they abandoned a good number of their ships, and escaped half dead after they had been wounded and broken.

This was no small affair. It was a seismic event, not just for the Irish but for those on the other side of the Irish Sea. Irish records fall silent about Scandinavian activity in Ireland for another 12 years, although it is possible that a remnant of the original Norse settlers stayed behind under some sort of subjection to Irish authority. However, we can pick up the probable Scandinavian refugees in the Welsh annals. The expulsion of the Scandinavians from Dublin seemingly led to new settlements on the Isle of Man, a short-lived settlement on Anglesey and also to many other incursions along the north coast of Wales. But the Welsh also expelled the newcomers. The *Annales Cambriae* says that in 902 a leader called 'Igmunt [Ingimund] came into the island of Môn [Anglesey] and settled Maes Osmeliaun', although another source (which we will analyse in a moment) says that the son of Cadell, son of Rhodri, assembled a force against the Norsemen and drove them out. This reversal led Ingimund to turn further to the east. There then followed a general wider spread of Scandinavian settlers along the western coast of Northumbria from approximately the line of the Mersey right up to Ayrshire, although the written record does not assist in this region. The numbers of Scandinavians involved in the exodus is unclear, but it must have been large. In 1840, the magnificent Cuerdale Hoard of coins, hack-silver, arm rings and other silverware was discovered on the bank of the Ribble at Cuerdale near Preston in Lancashire. There were around 8,600 items of coinage and bullion at the time it was found. The coin evidence, which included coins from Scandinavian York, led to a dating for the hoard to sometime shortly after c. 903. It has not unreasonably been suggested that the hoard may well constitute the war chest of an entire army. But the whole region of modern-day Lancashire and other coastal and inland areas of north-west England are teeming with hoards of silver and small finds from the early tenth century, not to mention the presence of numerous place names indicating a Scandinavian settlement.

Once Ingimund reached the Dee estuary, we are reliant for what happened next on the *Fragmentary Annals of Ireland*. It is the same source which said that the son of Cadell, son of Rhodri, had expelled the Norsemen from Wales. It is a collection of material which survives as a seventeenth-century copy of a fifteenth-century manuscript which itself is based on an eleventh-century compilation. And it is easy to see why some might doubt its authenticity. However, it is an extraordinary work which contains some fantastical and dramatic events and descriptions, and although it is often treated with caution by historians, it does portray Æthelflæd as a 'Queen of the Saxons' in a revealing example of how an independent and non-English (or at least non-West Saxon) source viewed Æthelflæd's status.

Whilst it is possible that the *Fragmentary Annals of Ireland* may have conflated some events, the detail pertaining to Æthelflæd and Æthelred is of real interest, not least because it is highly plausible. For example, we learn of Æthelred's illness here and we are told that he would eventually die of it. And so when Ingimund came to Chester, it was Æthelflæd with whom he sought an audience and not Æthelred. 'Weary of war', Ingimund asked the 'queen' for land in which he could settle and build his dwellings. Æthelflæd (who is named here as *Edelfrida*) gave him lands near Chester where he stayed for a long time. That the area in question comprised the northern and central parts of the Wirral peninsula is given huge support by the vast numbers of Scandinavian and Hiberno-Norse place names across the region. But this is not necessarily to say that Æthelflæd's settlement of Ingimund and his followers was any sort of capitulation. She is most likely to have a struck a deal with Ingimund to protect this corner of Mercia in return for the right to settle the land. The Dee and Mersey estuaries would thus be defended from any unwelcome incursions and the vulnerable flank of north-west Mercia would be secure at a time of great upheaval.

Over time, it appears that Æthelflæd had seemingly employed the threat and not the deterrent. After a period of settlement and consolidation, probably by 906, the temptation of Chester became too great for Ingimund who had long dwelt only on marginal lands in Wirral and desired the fertile (and economically productive) areas dependent upon Chester. As for the Norse-Irish settlement in Wirral, it is something of an understatement to say that there is reasonable evidence for it being widespread. Archaeologists, toponymists, linguists and historians have established overwhelming evidence to show that the people who settled here had created a mini-state of their own in the early tenth century. Speaking predominantly Old Norse, but with a significant Irish element (for example, the name Irby is Old Norse *Irá-býr*, meaning 'settlement of the Irish'), the community established a trading port at Meols. They also created a government centre, or 'Thing', at Thingwall and soon established a boundary with the Mercians defined by Raby to the south and Lower Dibbinsdale and Storeton Hill to the east. There are up to 600 place names in Wirral which have Scandinavian elements of which Tranmere is one. This name is derived from the Old Norse words *trani* (crane) and *melr* (sandbank). The place name evidence suggests that there were also outlier areas of Scandinavian settlement to the south of the boundary, closer to Chester.[1] It is unclear when exactly these settlements were established and the picture is likely to have been complex during the first two decades of the tenth century. But Chester, it seems, was slowly seducing Ingimund and his friends.

The place names also contain a clue to the disaffection of Ingimund and his followers with their surroundings. There are around fifty *kjarr* (carr) names, a word which indicates a marshy area. These are mainly in the north-west of the peninsula, thought to be the earlier settled area. To these, might be added the twenty-four *hólmr* names (a term we have already met in the fenlands). These islands of firm ground in the marshes mainly lie within the original enclave.

The conclusion might seem to be an obvious one. As Ingimund's community grew, it became less able, or less willing, to sustain itself on the marginal lands it had been given. So perhaps there is a ring of authenticity to the story told in the *Fragmentary Annals of Ireland*, which continues with a bold scheme hatched by Ingimund to make a move on

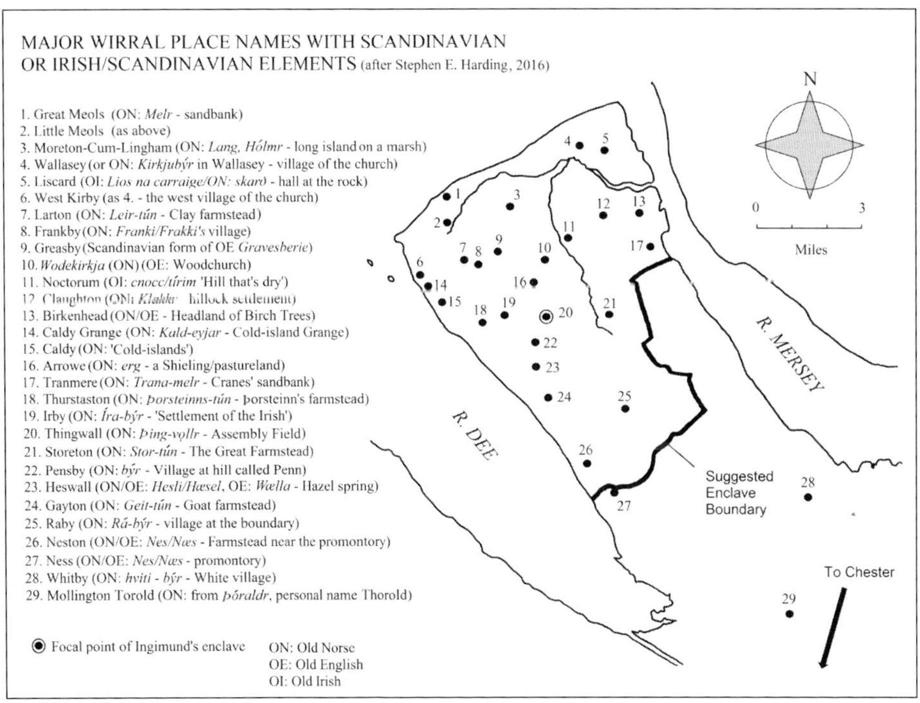

Map 3: *Major Wirral place names with Scandinavian or Irish-Scandinavian elements. After Stephen E. Harding (2016), p. 23.*

Chester. The tale is entertainingly told. It also contains within it two intriguing examples of the stratagem of deceit and one fine example of measure versus counter-measure in an early medieval siege warfare context.

'. . . Hingamund came to the leaders of the Norsemen and the Danes', says the story teller, implying a cultural differentiation amongst the Scandinavians. And then the tale continues:

> . . . he made a great complaint in their presence, and he said that they were not well off without good lands, and that it was right for them all to seize Chester and to possess it with its wealth and its lands. Many great battles and wars arose on account of that. This is what he said: 'Let us beseech and implore them first, and if we do not get them willingly in this way let us contest them by force'.

Perhaps this grand announcement was made at Thingwall where the assembly of the Scandinavians convened. Wherever it was made, Ingimund then brought the assembly to his own house to make his plans with his council, but unknown to him there must have been an agent of the 'queen' present and listening intently. Æthelflæd soon gathered an army 'around her in every direction' and packed it into Chester to augment the garrison. The Scandinavians came to Chester and initially failed to make any impression in their 'beseeching' of the English. Then, on a certain day, we are told that they attacked. On seeing the approaching force, the Mercians of Chester sent messages to Æthelred and Æthelflæd (their exact whereabouts is not specified). But Æthelred, we are told, was so ill he was near to death. Between the two of them however, they gave the messenger some urgent advice to give to the garrison. They were to adopt the stratagem of feigned flight:

> This was the advice they [Æthelflæd and Æthelred] gave: to make battle near the city outside, and the gate of the city should be wide open, and to choose a body of horsemen, concealed on the inside, and those of the people of the city who should be stronger in the battle should flee back into the city as if in defeat, and when the greater number of the forces of the Norsemen came inside the gate of the city the force hidden yonder should close the gate after this band and not admit any more; capture those who came into the city and kill them all. This was all done accordingly, and complete slaughter was thus made of the Danes and Norsemen.

The remaining Scandinavians outside then hatched a plan to attack the wall of the city by making protective hurdles to assist in the undermining or piercing of the walls. But whilst all this was going on there came another ruse from the English. Æthelflæd and her sickly husband sent messengers to the Irishmen in the ranks of the enemy force. The message carried the pointed remark that it was Æthelflæd herself who had 'all authority over the Saxons'. The Irishmen were told that the 'inimical race of pagans' were just as hostile to them as they were to the English and that the Irish contingents should help the English. And so the Irish were told to approach the Danes (but not the Norsemen, who were more like friends to them) and ask them what they demanded for Chester to be betrayed to them. The idea behind the ruse was to bring the Danish element of the army to a place where they could be easily killed when swearing the oaths and laying down their arms, as

Above left and above right: 5 and 6. *Part of the Roman wall of Chester situated between The Northgate and Morgan's Mount. The higher levels are medieval and later in date. This stretch of wall may have been defended in Æthelflæd's time.*

was their custom. It seems to have worked. The place where the Danes were brought must have been carefully chosen because it was here that a trap was sprung and rocks, beams, javelins and spears were hurled down upon them.

The destruction of the Danish element did not deter the Norsemen, according to the story. The assault against the walls of Chester continued in earnest:

> . . . the other forces, the Norsemen, were under the hurdles piercing the walls. What the Saxons did was to throw large rocks so that they destroyed the hurdles over them. What they did in the face of this was to place large posts under the hurdles. What the Saxons and the Irishmen who were among them did was to put all the ale and water of the town in the cauldrons of the town, to boil them and pour them over those who were under the hurdles so that the skins were stripped from them. The answer which the Norsemen gave to this was to spread hides on the hurdles. What the Saxons did was to let loose on the attacking force all the beehives in the town, so that they could not move their legs or hands from the great numbers of bees stinging them. Afterwards they left the city and abandoned it. It was not long after that [before they came] to wage battle again.[2]

Quite when those Norsemen returned is unrecorded, but the earlier statement that Ingimund's desire for Chester had led to 'many great battles and wars . . .' may be reflected in the growing number of military artefacts now being excavated by archaeologists in Wirral which date from around this period. Weapon fragments are being discovered of both English and Scandinavian type and their interpretation

Above and below: 7 and 8. *Built over part of the remains of the Roman headquarters building in central Chester, St Peter's is reputed to be linked to Æthelflæd and Æthelred who transferred the dedication when they re-established as St Werbergh's the minster church formerly dedicated to St Peter and St Paul.*

is only at a very early stage. Some people claim these finds are indicative of one of England's most famous lost battlefields, that of Brunanburh (fought in 937 by an alliance of Northern peoples against the might of the English king and identified by many, but by no means all, as being at or near Bromborough in Wirral). It is an intriguing debate. However, the discoveries might equally be linked to any one of those 'many great battles and wars' fought for the control of Chester and its environs in the early tenth century.

Nothing is known of Ingimund after this curious story of his failure to take Chester, nor indeed of how many times it was attacked thereafter. The archaeological and toponymical evidence would suggest that the Scandinavian presence in the region was a long-term phenomenon. Indeed, the area's Scandinavian character lasted up to 1066 and arguably well beyond it. As for the English record of the events in the area during these years, the *Mercian Register* in its entry for 907 simply reads 'Here Chester was restored'. Whether it was Æthelflæd's response to the attentions of Ingimund which led to the building of a great burh at Chester in 907, or whether that burh had already been built by that year and then had been badly damaged and required restoration (as seems more likely), is not known for sure. Incidentally, John of Worcester attributes the restoration to both Æthelred and Æthelflæd.

Chester soon became a vitally important Mercian fortification on Mercia's north-west frontier. The Lady of the Mercians even established a mint there which struck for her brother Edward. Some of these coins bore Edward's name on one side and a tower on the other. This symbolic celebration of the power of a fortification would continue to be seen in the coinage of Edward's kingdom. As for Chester itself, interestingly, by c. 930 its mint was one of the most important in the country and many of its moneyers bore Scandinavian names.

Chester

The walls of Roman Chester, or Deva, enclosed an area of over 60 acres. In some places Roman masonry can still be seen in the town walls, particularly at the north-eastern sector where the walls tower over the Shropshire Union Canal (see Colour Plate 10). It seems that by the late ninth century some of the space within the walls had become deserted, a far cry from the grand military fortress it had once been, although there was settlement outside the walls to the south and east.

According to Ranulph Higden, a fourteenth-century Chester monk, the remains of St Werburgh (the daughter of the Mercian King Wulfhere who reigned from 658 to 674/5) were removed from Hanbury in 874 and brought to Chester where in the early tenth century they were in the keeping of a college of canons. An ancient church dedicated to St Peter and St Paul may have stood on the site of the present-day cathedral. According to Henry Bradshaw's (d. 1513) verse *Life* of St Werburgh, it was reputed to have been re-dedicated to St Werburgh during Ealdorman Æthelred's time. The dedication of St Peter was thus transferred to a church at the centre of the old Roman fortress. Also associated with Chester and the cult of St Werburgh (with Æthelflæd's involvement) was the cult of St Oswald, an altar for whom was in the nave of the abbey church by the early thirteenth century.[3]

Another Anglo-Saxon church (of St John the Baptist) claims to be Chester's oldest church (with an apparent foundation date in the late seventh century) and was still important in 973 when King Edgar (959–75) ceremoniously paid it a visit. It is situated outside the Roman perimeter and may even have formed the focus for the post-Roman settlement.

The layout of Æthelflæd's burh is not entirely understood, although as at Gloucester, some of the Roman wall on the western and perhaps southern sides are thought to have been dismantled to facilitate an extension to the shoreline of the Dee. This move would then have resulted in an inverted 'L'-shaped fortification with its northern and eastern Roman walls still intact and extended at points A and B on Map 4. Nothing however, is known for sure about Æthelflæd's planning, and there may even be evidence for Saxon re-fortification of the western Roman defences.[4]

Chester would have been prosperous under Æthelflæd, becoming a focal centre for trade, not to mention possessing a thriving mint, producing coins in the name of her brother Edward, but with distinctive reverses (see page 127). The trading connections Chester had with places such as Dublin across the Irish Sea, and its access to the fertile plains beyond it, will have made it a much-prized addition to the Mercian burghal programme.

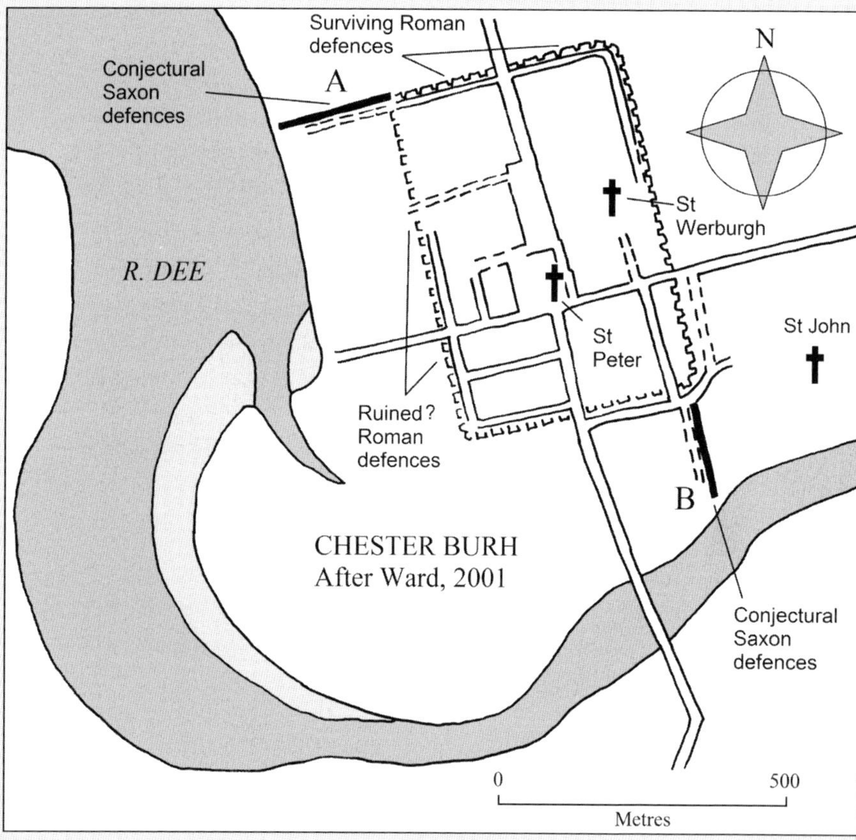

Map 4: *Chester burh. After Ward (2001), p. 163.*

St Werburgh

Saint Werburgh (also spelled Wærburh, Werburh, Werburg or Werburga) was the daughter of King Wulfhere of Mercia (658–74/5) and his wife Eormenhild and thus her royal credentials were impressive indeed, being linked to Kentish and East Anglian royal families through her mother. This element of the Werburgh story probably meant a good deal to Æthelflæd. Always seemingly inclined towards the religious life, Werburgh entered the monastery at Ely where her great aunt Æthelthryth was abbess. Having prospered at Ely, she was later recalled to Mercia by her uncle, King Æthelred (674/5–704). Here, she was put in charge of the nunneries of Mercia. She died in around 700 at her monastery at Threekingham in Lincolnshire after a lifetime of devotion performing miracles and attending to monastic reform.

Perhaps St Werburgh's most famous miracle involved the complete restoration of a cooked and eaten goose which had been seized from the flock of wild geese which Werburgh herself had instructed to be left after the geese had ravaged her land at Weedon (Northamptonshire). Upon restoring the bird to life from just its bones and feathers, the flock never again returned to spoil the land. The saint's healing properties must have been important to Æthelflæd, whose husband Æthelred apparently suffered severe bouts of illness.

Werburgh had wanted to be buried at Hanbury near Repton, although the community at Threekingham locked her body away intending to keep it, before the

Above left and above right: 9 and 10. *Some representations of St Werburgh in Chester. Top – above the east entrance to St Werburgh's, the Roman Catholic Church. Bottom – outside the Cathedral on a First World War memorial. Werburgh also has a shrine within the Cathedral.*

watchmen were overcome by sleep and the locks and bars miraculously fell to the ground. And so Werburgh went to Hanbury. During King Ceolred's reign (709–16) her remains were elevated and found to be uncorrupted. She stayed at Hanbury until the time of the Great Heathen Army's descent on the area in 874, after which her relics were apparently removed (no longer fully intact) to Chester where they remained until her shrine was destroyed in the 1530s.

It is suggested that the move of Werburgh to Chester may in fact be more consistent with Æthelflæd's restoration of Chester in 907 than the period surrounding the descent of the Danes at Repton in the 870s, although there may be room for both arguments. What is certain is that Æthelflæd and her husband made the very most of St Werburgh (and for that matter, St Oswald) at Chester. Subsequently, Werburgh became the patron saint of Chester.

Among Werburgh's many other miracles is a confused tale recorded by Bradshaw and allegedly datable to the reign of Edward the Elder, although seemingly more fitting for the reign of Edward the Confessor (1042–66). At some point the shrine was taken to the walls of the city during a siege by a Welsh king called 'Griffin'. A stone was thrown by one of the besiegers and damaged the shrine. Consequently, the Welsh king and his army were blinded and had to retreat from the walls. Later in 1180, Werburgh's relics assisted in extinguishing a great fire in the city. Always, it seems, Werburgh was a protector of Chester. But she was something else, too. She was a symbol to Æthelflæd and Æthelred of an Anglo-Saxon unity, having links to several ancient dynasties. But perhaps more importantly to Æthelflæd, who chose her saints carefully, she was a royal woman.[5]

Chapter 3

Peace

Her wæs Sancte Oswaldes lic gelæded of Beardanigge on Myrce.
'Here St Oswald's body was brought from Bardney into Mercia.'

The *Mercian Register*, or 'Annals of Æthelflæd'.
Entry for 909 (C)

Whilst Æthelflæd was dealing with the dramatic changes taking place in the north-west of Mercia after 902, there is little to tell us of her brother's dealings with the Danes. These years for Edward seem to have been dominated by his continuing promotion and development of the New Minster project in Winchester and by the inevitable friction this caused with Bishop Denewulf.

Another phenomenon during these early years was a campaign of diocesan reform seemingly spearheaded by the king himself and the Archbishop of Canterbury, Plegmund, which has a complex history.[1] The move to restructure the dioceses across Wessex was one which mainly impacted Winchester and Sherborne. Perhaps having its origins as early as the 890s and again after a council of 905, and against the backdrop of papal dissatisfaction with the English king and a subsequent series of factional dramas in Rome itself, the new division of the West Saxon bishoprics did not occur until after the deaths of Denewulf in 908 (Winchester) and Alfred's biographer Asser in 909 (Sherborne). The dioceses of Winchester and Sherborne were divided up. Winchester was split into Ramsbury for Wiltshire (and Berkshire) and Winchester for Hampshire (and Surrey). Sherborne was further divided into three. Crediton now served Devon (and was further sub-divided to serve the Cornish over the Tamar), Wells served Somerset and Sherborne, Dorset. The policy of reform seems to have benefitted both Edward's New Minster and increased the influence of Canterbury, despite the fact there would be new bishops at the council table. It might be the case that a reduction in the influence of Denewulf's Old Minster at Winchester, and a similar reduction of the influence of Sherborne, a place associated with Æthelwold and Edward's uncles Æthelbald and Æthelberht (who had both been West Saxon kings before Æthelwold's father Æthelred I had taken the throne in 865), was the driving force behind the overall policy. In fact, it is even possible that Edward, apparently like his father Alfred, had always considered King Æthelbald's betrayal of King Æthelwulf (Æthelbald's own father and therefore Edward's grandfather) in the late 850s as a particularly serious crime, one which at the time had the support of the then Bishop of Sherborne himself. But the changes, when they came, would also have some practical benefits as the earlier dioceses of Winchester and Sherborne had been too vast to administer effectively, and the reform brought their organizational framework down to a similar size to the secular shires administered by the ealdormen.

Sometime in the second half of the tenth century a Latin description of all these historic diocesan changes was written in a document known as the 'Plegmund Narrative'. It was written to explain the circumstance for the grant of three estates in Cornwall to the diocese of Crediton, so that Crediton could claim them back from the diocese of St Germans, which had been established later than Crediton. St Dunstan himself also wrote about the events in an attempt to justify the claim of St Germans. The 'narrative' is full of impossible dates and errors and probably represents a compression of events over a number of years from the 890s onwards. For a start, it claims that it had been Pope Formosus in 905 who had 'been moved by great wrath and zeal' and had angrily threatened Edward with a curse unless he proceeded with supplying bishops to vacant dioceses (Formosus had in fact died in 896). Also, the claim in the 'narrative' is that Wessex had been 'completely destitute of any bishop for seven years'. It was not until 909 when Plegmund himself, having had to travel to Rome to obtain a renewed confirmation of his own archbishopric from Pope Sergius III (Plegmund had received his own pallium, a symbolic vestment indicative of the office of bishop, from the now-discredited Pope Formosus), that the reforms could really get underway.

And so the appointments soon followed, but exactly when is not clear. A former deacon at the Old Minster in Winchester named Frithestan became Bishop of Winchester, apparently on the death of Denewulf. Edward's relations with him would be much improved over those of his predecessor. One Athelm (Æthelhelm), a former monk at Glastonbury, became Bishop of Wells and would himself rise to the very highest of positions. Waerstan, who quickly followed the unfortunately short-lived appointee Æthelweard, became Bishop of Sherborne. There certainly does seem to have been a flurry of ecclesiastical appointments in and around the year 909. However, claims repeated by William of Malmesbury in the twelfth century that Plegmund had consecrated seven bishops in one day at Canterbury are difficult to prove. Alongside Frithestan, Athelm and Waerstan (perhaps indicating a date later in 909 to allow for the passing of Æthelweard) had apparently been Eadwulf for Crediton, Beornheah for Sussex and Coenwulf for the Mercians in Dorchester. An Æthelstan was given Ramsbury. All of these men, in varying degrees, would have a part to play in the dramas of their age. And of those, as we shall see, there were many.

The reign of Edward the Elder was, of course, a long and eventful one. However, we are not exactly blessed with a wealth of evidence. Much has been lost, and there are hints in some sources such as in Asser's biography of Edward's father that royal record-keeping was more thorough than surviving material suggests.[2] Asser gives a little glimpse into the king's early years as a child, and the chronicler Æthelweard supplies information not recorded elsewhere about the young Ætheling's military campaigns in the kingdom of his father in the 890s.[3] There are twenty-nine charters (the latest reliable one being from 909, although a disputed Wilton charter may date from 921), most of which are spurious, and two sets of law codes, as well as the various versions of the *Anglo-Saxon Chronicle* of which version (A), usually associated with Winchester, is the most 'Edwardian' in outlook. If William of Malmesbury is to be believed, there is a possibility that Edward may have left a will, but we know nothing of it – a pointer perhaps, to how many other crucial documents we are missing. The second half of Edward's reign in terms of written material is dominated by silence. In around half of his charters, Edward is styled as *Rex Angul Saxonum*, an indication of his position as the inheritor of his father's kingdom of the Anglo-Saxons. In two charters, he is *Rex Anglorum*, and in two others *Rex Saxonum* and in the remainder he is simply King Edward.

As for the early charters, there is some evidence in the early years of the king's reign of another slight shift in the status of the Lord and Lady of the Mercians in some Edwardian charters dating to 903 (S 367, S 367a and S 371). These, it is suggested, shed light on a more cooperative relationship between the rulers within the kingdom of the Anglo-Saxons. One Ealdorman Æthelfrith (who incidentally married Æthelgyth, the cousin of Æthelflæd) had apparently lost some charters in an unspecified fire. He was keen to have new ones drawn up. These were based either on his memories of the old, or when he could not remember, he was given authority to have new ones drawn up in the standard way. The three surviving ones are of this latter type. One (S 367) involves land at Monks Risborough in Buckinghamshire, another (S 367a) land at Islington in Middlesex, and the other (S 371) concerns land at Wrington in Somerset. The appeal to the authorities by Æthelfrith is made to King Edward concerning all three estates, two of which are in Æthelflæd and Æthelred's territory (Risborough and Islington). But the Lord and Lady of the Mercians were clearly present at the gathering which produced these charters, as was their daughter Ælfwynn and numerous bishops from Kent, Sussex and Mercia (but not Wessex). Significantly, the charters refer to Æthelred and Æthelflæd, who were also approached by Æthelfrith by referring to them in a carefully constructed way: '. . . who then held rulership and power over the Mercian people under the aforementioned king' (referring of course, to Edward, who is simply styled as *rex*).[4]

Similarly, the following year, Æthelfrith seems to have been present at a gathering concerning a complex series of sales of land (five hides at Water Eaton), north of Oxford (S 361). Here, it is one Wigferth who makes the appeal jointly to Edward and the Lord and Lady of the Mercians, the old landbook having been lost. The land had passed from the Mercian King Burgred (852–74) and his wife Queen Æthelswith (Edward and Æthelflæd's aunt) to the bishop of Worcester, then to Ceolwulf II (c. 874–c. 879) and then to one Hungyth who had sold it to the claimant Wigferth. Bishop Wærferth of Worcester (c. 872–915) was present at the gathering as well (although he was not the bishop who had briefly held the land). He presumably gave chapter and verse from the Worcester perspective. Again, it is Edward who is acting as overall arbiter and it is he who confirms the sale by Hungyth to Wigferth.

Militarily, however, Edward, the king of the Anglo-Saxons, was still in no position to launch any kind of sustained offensive in the aftermath of his cousin's thwarted challenge. Indeed, this may not have been his plan for some time. Instead, a 'peace' was negotiated. The dating of the treaty made between Edward and the Danes of both Northumbria and East Anglia is generally taken to be 906, although some argue for 905. According to the *Anglo-Saxon Chronicle*, it was Edward himself who was behind it and as the Peterborough (E) version indicates it was an agreement made out of 'necessity' from Edward's perspective. John of Worcester, writing much later and very much impressed by Edward's martial prowess, says that the treaty arose because the East Anglians and the Northumbrians had found Edward to be 'invincible'. The earlier treaty made between Alfred and Guthrum – whatever its exact date – was in dire need of a revisit. There was now a brand new political entity in the north-west of Mercia, and along the shores and hinterland of what became Lancashire. The border in the south Midlands was more fluid than ever. It is probable that the salient of English land as defined in the earlier treaty, with its northernmost border running along the twisting River Great Ouse, had entirely collapsed back onto the River Ouzel, thus representing a significant Danish encroachment on English territory. Moreover, a number of Scandinavian place names on the English side of Watling Street may suggest further encroachment to the north of the salient just inside Æthelred and Æthelflæd's territory, although it is equally possible Watling Street did not mark the exact line of the boundary in this area at this time.

The details of the treaty reached at a place called *Yttingaforda* (Tiddingford) are unknown. We might expect it to have included territorial agreements. The location of the meeting may even have been the exact same place where the treaty of Alfred and Guthrum had been drawn up all those years before. There are two candidates for the site of Tiddingford where it was said that 'they confirmed the peace'. Both sites are situated on the western side of modern-day Leighton Buzzard. One of these is at Tiddenfoot Waterside Park and the other is merely half a mile west at a gentle hill known as Tiddingford Hill. Both sites share one thing in common. They are very close to the River Ouzel and dominate the ford across it. Edward was clearly meeting the Danish lords at the frontier between his patrimony and theirs. And just three miles or so to the east of here, Watling Street ran in a south-east to north-west line across the heart of Mercia.[5]

Edward and Æthelred were clearly concerned about the loss of English territory in this south-east Mercian area. There is evidence to suggest that the re-establishment of Englishmen with a landed interest in these areas was a matter of deliberate Edwardian policy around this time and that the king of the Anglo-Saxons and the Lord of the Mercians were both prepared to encourage the purchasing of estates from the Danes. A confirmation charter of five hides to the thegn Ealdred, dating to two years after the end of Edward's reign, records that both Edward and Æthelred had required the land to be purchased from the Danes at Chalgrave and Tebworth for ten pounds of gold and silver (S 396). This land was near to where the Icknield Way passes over Watling Street and carries on towards East Anglia. To what extent this policy was repeated up and down the line of Watling Street on the Scandinavian side of the divide is unknown, but this accrual of land for what would appear to be strategic military purposes may also be matched by Edward's other policy of acquiring ecclesiastical lands usually by exchange agreements, coerced or otherwise. The impression given is that the 'peace' was an uneasy one, and that Edward was doing what all good commanders-in-chief do in times of peace. He was preparing for war.

The peace of Tiddingford lasted, as far as can be seen, for around two to three years. Unless of course, there were several unrecorded peace agreements in the meantime. But then someone broke it. No-one really knows who. Were it not for an extraordinary statement made by the chronicler Æthelweard, we might think that very little had happened until 'peace' was broken. Here is what he says in his entry for the year 909:

> After one year, the barbarians broke the peace with King Eadweard, and with Æthelred, who then ruled the Northumbrian and Mercian areas. The fields of the Mercians were ravaged on all sides by the throng we spoke about, and deeply, as far as the streams of the Avon, where the boundary of the West Saxons and Mercians begins.

So, just one year had passed when the barbarians broke the peace. If Æthelweard is accurate, then the 'peace' cannot have been that concluded at Tiddingford for which the consensus suggests a date of 906. More spectacular, however, is the assertion that the peace which was broken was one agreed between the northerners and both Edward and Æthelred 'who then ruled the Northumbrian and Mercian areas'. The structure of the sentence in its Latin form may mean that Æthelweard was trying to say that Æthelred at this time was ruling not only over the Mercian, but over the Northumbrian 'areas' too. It is, to say the least, a remarkable statement. No other compelling evidence exists of such a Mercian hegemony at this stage. One phenomenon which *may* support the notion, however, is the larger than usual amount of silver hoards deposited in the north-west of England attributable to the opening decades of the tenth century. Many arguments exist for the motivations behind the deposition of hoards. Some have argued that the intention of the depositor was to return to the hoard one day, thus the items represent a form a safe-keeping. Others have pointed to the interesting idea (mentioned by the thirteenth-century Icelandic historian Snorri Sturluson) that the wealth buried in this life would be available in the afterlife. The hoards of this period in the north-west of England, such as the colossal Cuerdale Hoard (see Colour Plate 5) and the recently discovered Silverdale hoard (page 26) consist of a mixture of hacksilver, ingots and coinage. The region thus presents as the most silver-rich in the country. Distributed as far north as Penrith in Cumbria and around the coast of Lancashire, and in the hinterland around Morcambe Bay, and also around the eastern side of Chester, these deposits of silver may generally indicate a period of political instability. It is arguable that the king of the Anglo-Saxons and his Mercian allies had for some time viewed the expulsion of the Norse from Dublin as a threat to their own increasing power and ambition in central and northern England. These hoards of silver seem to be deposited at nodal points of routeways around halfway between Dublin and York, this being the very sector of the country which it would seem was hugely important for the kings of the Anglo-Saxons to drive a wedge through, to prevent political and geographical union between these two great centres.[6]

Some evidence may exist to suggest an economic and political vulnerability in York around this time, which might just have been exploited by Æthelred. From around c. 905 the coinage of York was replaced by an anonymous issue which lasted for around 15 to 20 years. It was of a poorer quality than its predecessors, at around half the weight standard. On one side of the coins was the name of York (EBORAICE/EBORAICE CIVITAS) and on the other was SCI PETRI MO (Saint Peter's Money). Perhaps there was indeed an absence of clear secular leadership in York during these years after the rule of Sigeferth, Cnut and (briefly) Æthelwold. Perhaps the glue which held York together at this time was the archbishop and the Church.

Because of the difficult structure of the sentence in Æthelweard, it is possible it might have had Edward and not Æthelred as its subject, although we know Æthelred to have been a pugnacious and expansion-minded Mercian leader. Æthelweard had a unique gift for giving us these special nuggets of information. His knowledge of Mercian history seems to have been remarkably comprehensive. But Æthelweard neglects to tell us something that the *Anglo-Saxon Chronicle* does not. Prior to the invasion of the northerners, Edward had himself sent an army from both Wessex *and* Mercia into the north: '. . . and it raided the north raiding-army [Norðhere] very greatly, both men and every kind of property, and killed many men of those Danish and were inside there for five weeks.'

This little excerpt comes from a modern translation of the (A) version of the chronicle. Recently, one historian has looked again at the wording.[7] It is observed that the use of the term 'Norðhere' to describe the northerners in this case is in fact the only use of the compound term in the entire chronicle. Elsewhere, the chronicler uses terms for East Anglians and Northumbrians when there is a need to make the distinction. But here, we have a different term. It is possible that the 'Norðhere' were not in fact the 'Danes' of York, or those of the Five Boroughs in the eastern Midlands, nor indeed those of a much-weakened East Anglia. They may have been the newly-arrived Hiberno-Norse who had flooded into the west coast of Lancashire and settled on the north-west border of Mercia. Their settlement seems to have been particularly strong in the lands between the Ribble and the Mersey and in Cumbria to the north. It may have been these men who had displaced Englishmen (some are known in this period to have sought new lords further east), and some of them may have combined with Ingimund to apply pressure on Chester, which we will recall, was most likely attacked more than once.

The campaign launched against the Scandinavians in 909 bears the hallmarks of a punitive measure, one of reduction and devastation, a cowering into submission of rebellious forces, caught in their very homelands by a massive combined Anglo-Saxon army from the south. The medieval chronicler Roger of Wendover in his *Flowers of History* entry for 909 says that the campaign was conducted in response to a rebellion. Although he was several centuries distant from events, it is possible that Edward and Æthelred were conducting a campaign to enforce the submission of the Hiberno-Norse to an expanded Mercian patrimony under Æthelred, whose rule was in some way being resented by the newcomers. We do not know enough about Æthelred's illness to rule out the idea that he could not have taken such an energetic approach. The *Anglo-Saxon Chronicle*'s reference to 'those Danish' need not contradict such an assessment, as the scribes of Winchester and the south in general are likely to refer to most Scandinavians as 'Danes', since this was a collective term often used. The campaign may well have ended with an agreement or treaty. It is possible this agreement was the one which was broken by the men of the north as they attempted to throw off the yoke of the kingdom of the Anglo-Saxons under its Mercian sub-king Æthelred. This might explain their subsequent choice to raid deep into the heartland of Æthelred's patrimony, as reported by Æthelweard. And it might explain why they came down to the borders of Mercia and Wessex, as if to suggest the anger was mainly ranged against Æthelred's domain. If this is the case, the men who broke the peace could well have been from either of the Scandinavian groups (that is, those of York or those of the north-west), or perhaps a much-feared alliance of both. Another possibility is that Edward the Elder's five-week campaign was a response to the terms of the treaty at Tiddingford, in that the Danes of York may have asked for assistance against the newcomers as part of this agreement and therefore, by conducting a campaign against them, Edward was fulfilling both his political obligation to York and providing the assistance of an overlord to Æthelred of Mercia by quelling an uprising. Once again, we are reminded how little we know and how much we would like to know.

Many historians take the punitive five-week campaign to have been conducted against the Danes of the eastern side of the 'Danelaw' and not those Scandinavians of the north-west. One reason put forward for the joint campaign of Edward and Æthelred in 909 being conducted in the region of Lindsey (Lincolnshire) and not in the north-west at all, is the chronicler's statement that in this year the bones of St Oswald, the great early Northumbrian king, were retrieved from Bardney. The saint's relics, or at least some of them (Bardney was not the only home to parts of Oswald's body), were brought to Æthelred's new minster in Gloucester, which was either then and there, or likely later, re-dedicated to the royal saint.[8] Some see this as a consequence of a campaign conducted in the area by the joint Anglo-Saxon forces, whilst others see it as an independent action amounting to a 'daring' raid into enemy territory conducted by a small group of Mercians. Others still, argue for the retrieval of these relics (not known to have been challenged by the Danes) as a part of some other agreement, maybe even a clause of the Tiddingford treaty. It is possible that the relics of St Guthlac may also have been translated from the fenland monastery at Crowland to Hereford during the same episode and perhaps under an equivalent agreement. But if Æthelweard's assertion of Mercian hegemony over the north is correct, then it may be no surprise that Oswald, so important to Æthelflæd and Æthelred, was retrieved at this particular time.

Perhaps by coincidence, the Worcester Manuscript (D) of the *Anglo-Saxon Chronicle* places the retrieval of St Oswald's 'body' at the year 906, the same year as the conclusion of that 'peace', but this version of the chronicle has a jumbled chronology in the early tenth century, and weaves in material from the *Mercian Register* with some discomfort in terms of dating. It is conceivable that none of these theories are correct. The twelfth-century historian William of Malmesbury intriguingly states that the relics of St Oswald were translated because at that time both Æthelred and Æthelflæd 'had all Mercia under their power'. This could indicate that the move was one which the Lord and Lady of Mercia felt they were simply entitled to. Oswald and his story (see below) was of huge symbolism to the children of Alfred the Great.

Relics were more than merely 'useful' in many ways. The income generated from early medieval 'tourism' is something which is often cited, but there is probably a more straightforward explanation for Æthelred and Æthelflæd's concern with saintly relics, and it is almost certainly an enthusiasm they passed on to their nephew, the young Æthelstan. Canon VII of The Second Council of Nicaea in 787 had elevated the importance of relics in that no church should be consecrated without them. Moreover, since the advent of the Danes and the persistent attacks on monasteries from the late eighth century onwards, the promotion of saints had notably fallen into the hands of the secular leaders of Anglo-Saxon England and here Æthelred and Æthelflæd were an example to every Christian Mercian. To collect and donate relics was a way of increasing the prestige of the ruler, and in these cases, the founder of new churches. They were also essential for some of the important mechanics of government such as oath-swearing and slave-freeing (manumissions) and other legal matters, thus providing for a binding mechanism in the eyes of God. Æthelred and Æthelflæd chose their relics very carefully and were keen to acquire them and venerate them when and wherever they could within their own patrimony. And with Oswald, the saint who pretty much had everything a contemporary English ruler could want, the urge to have him brought into the heartland of Æthelred and Æthelflæd's domain must have been overwhelming. We might add to this the notion that King Alfred's children seem to have been convinced they were descended from none other than Oswald himself. It has even been suggested that the saint's powers of healing were probably of special interest to Æthelred, whose illness seems to have been prolonged.[9] The same could also be said of the couple's interest in St Werburgh and St Mildburh too. This experience of her husband's illness was similar in some ways to Æthelflæd's experience of her own father Alfred's famous long-term suffering and protracted search for a cure. So, whatever the reason was, whether it was part of a grand strategy, an opportunist grab, or an obvious entitlement at a time of increased power, a desire for a cure for her husband's illness, or a bid for the ultimate statement of political legitimacy, or even all of these things, Oswald came to Gloucester.

Saint Oswald

The cult of St Oswald, whose feast day is on 5 August, was one of the more famous royal saintly cults in early medieval England. His fame even spread throughout Europe. It is certainly no accident that Oswald's relics were brought to the new burh at Gloucester where they would attract pilgrims. Æthelflæd and her husband clearly wished to be associated with Oswald. They often brought the bones of royal saints (usually with a distinct Mercian connection) into their newly-established burhs as part of an overt display of public legitimization of their right to rule, as well as providing a spiritual and economic foundation for those places. For the Lady of the Mercians, however, there was a personal, spiritual and even imperial affiliation with Oswald.

Oswald was king of Northumbria from 634 to 641/2. The son of Æthelfrith of Bernicia, he defeated the king of Gwynedd Cadwallon ap Cadfan at the Battle of Heavenfield in 633/4 and united both Bernicia and Deira into one Christian realm. The Venerable Bede (*Ecclesiastical History* III.2), writing in the subsequent century, relates a tale of Oswald erecting a wooden cross before the battle, holding it firm in the ground until his men could fill the earth around it. Splinters from the cross were said later to have great healing powers.

Oswald was himself killed in battle at Maserfield (apparently at Oswestry, or maybe elsewhere in Powys) in 641/2, defeated by the last great pagan king of Mercia, Penda. After a dying prayer for his warriors, Oswald's body was dismembered and placed on stakes. Soon, the place where he died was associated with miracles and people even took earth from the site, leaving a large hole in the ground.

Oswald's brother King Oswiu (642–70) retrieved Oswald's bones the year after his death. But it was his daughter, Oswald's niece Osthryth (d. 697), who brought the main part of the remains to Bardney, whose monks were only persuaded by a miracle to accept them. Oswald's head and one of his arms had separate journeys to Lindisfarne and Bamburgh and subsequent medieval histories surrounding his remains were played out at Durham and Peterborough respectively. Osthryth's sister the saintly Ælfflæd (abbess of Whitby, who died in 714) has even been suggested as an inspiration for King Alfred naming his daughter Æthelflæd. Osthryth married Æthelred I of Mercia (675–704) and it is here that we might see a parallel between the actions of Osthyrth and those of Æthelflæd two centuries later. Both women were responsible for the movement or translation of Oswald's relics. The shrine at Bardney seems to have attracted much attention. It was even keenly adorned by none other than King Offa (757–96). But by 909, much had changed at the site, and it is generally thought the place was attacked by Danes at least once in the 870s.

Oswald's relics were layered with meaning, particularly for Æthelflæd. Firstly, Oswald had been a Christian 'unifier' of English peoples. Æthelflæd may have considered herself to be much the same, just as her father had been. Moreover, she may have seen herself as distantly related to Oswald, who had married the daughter of Cynegils, the King of Wessex, although it is not known how long this line ran. However, the manipulation of royal lineages was fairly common. The continental Saxon Hrotsvitha, writing later in the tenth century, believed Alfred's granddaughter Eadgyth (who married the Holy Roman Emperor Otto I) to be descended from King Oswald, describing this as a 'blessed lineage'.

One final association may go a long way to explaining how Æthelflæd viewed Oswald, regardless of any spurious or actual dynastic ties. Bede's *Historia ecclesiastica* models Oswald partly on the Roman Emperor Constantine. Both were great Christian rulers, both were linked to the north of England (Constantine being acclaimed emperor in York in 306) and both won military battles apparently supported by their faith. To this can be added the well-known story of Helena's (Constantine's mother) discovery of the True Cross in Palestine and its associated miracles. It is no surprise then, that Oswald's remains found a new home in a newly-built and richly-adorned church in a restored old Roman city at Gloucester. Here, as in other places rebuilt by Alfred and his daughter, the memory of Rome was re-branded and given a very Anglo-Saxon character. And few who visited Gloucester in those days can have doubted who was in charge.

We should not underestimate the extent to which Mercia was beginning to reassert itself after years of adversity. Certainly, the resurgence of western Mercia under Æthelred and Æthelflæd was a startling phenomenon. And if we are to believe Æthelweard and William of Malmesbury, by 909 their power extended right across the ancient kingdom and perhaps even to the north of it. But of course, Æthelweard reminds us that something was about to happen to put the kingdom of the Anglo-Saxons to the test. A raid from the north, deep into the heart of Mercia, would result in one of the most crucial battles of Anglo-Saxon history. And yet, very little is known of it. It was a battle which in many ways defined the next generation of Englishmen and women and made possible the extraordinarily well coordinated events of the years between 910 and 924. The story of the birth of England was about to enter another gripping chapter. In true Anglo-Saxon style, it would be an episode heralded by the ringing sounds of the sword's edge crashing against shield walls on a field named after an ancient pagan God – none other than God of War, Woden himself.

Chapter 4

The Battle of Tettenhall, 5 August 910

On þysum gere Engle ⁊ Dene gefuhton æt Teotanheale, ⁊ Engle sige namon. ⁊ þy ilcan geare Æðelflæd getimbrede þa burh æt Bremesbyrig.

'In this year English and Danes fought at Tettenhall and the English took the victory. And the same year Æthelflæd built the stronghold at *Bremesbyrig*.'

The *Mercian Register*, or 'Annals of Æthelflæd'. Entry for 910 (C)

So, the 'barbarians' broke the peace with Edward and Æthelred and ravaged the fields of Mercia as far as the borders of Wessex, according to Æthelweard (who leaves out the joint reduction by the Anglo-Saxons of the army in the north). However, there is confusion with the dating of events in many of the sources and much of it is irreconcilable. For example, the Worcester (D) version of the *Anglo-Saxon Chronicle* has a battle near Tettenhall on 6 August 909 and then goes on to mention it again by name in 910 and then gives the background to it and the list of casualties in an encounter described in the subsequent year. The Worcester manuscript is not the only one to give us more than one battle. It is, however, generally accepted that there was but one 'Battle of Tettenhall', although, as we shall see, the important parts of the campaign seem to have occurred over a broad landscape and the encounter probably had several stages. There are numerous accounts, not all of them contemporary and some of them contradictory, but we can get a broad picture of what happened, when it happened, and who fell on the field.

First, the *Anglo-Saxon Chronicle* – in its various forms – provides important background, and includes a detailed knowledge of the fallen. It was the army in Northumbria (this time mentioned as 'on Norðhymbrum') who 'broke the peace' and 'scorned every peace which King Edward and his councillors offered them'. They then raided across Mercia, says the chronicler. The king, we are told, had gathered 100 ships and was at the time in Kent. His ships came east along the south coast towards him. It then seems that the raiders believed that Edward had the bulk of his forces aboard these ships so that the raiders believed 'they might go unfought wherever they wanted'. But when Edward had learned that the enemy had come south on a raid, he 'sent his army both from Wessex and from Mercia, and they got in front of the raiding army from behind when it was on its way home, and then fought with them and put the raiding-army to flight, and killed many thousands of it; and king Ecwils was killed there'.

This is what the pro-Edward (A) version tells us. It gives us no real idea of the geographic location of the battle and it only mentions one important casualty whom it refers to as King Ecwils. But the Abingdon version (B) supplies a fuller casualty list at the year 911 (for 910), having already summed up the battle in its entry for the previous year by simply saying 'In this year, English and Danes fought at Tettenhall and the English took the victory': 'And King Eowils was killed there, and King Healfden and Earl Ohter and

Earl Scurfa, and Othulf the Hold, and Benesing the Hold, and Anlaf the Black ['swarthy' or 'infamous'], and Thurferth the Hold, and Osferth Hlytta [soothsayer] and Guthferth the Hold and Agmund the Hold and Guthferth.' The *Annals of St Neots* adds one more casualty to the list, a mysterious man named Eagellus, whom it combines with Agmund as '*primates paganorum*', or 'chief of the Heathens'.

Æthelweard gives us a little more. After telling us the Danes had raided around the streams of the Avon', he says (according to the modern translation) 'they were transported across the River Severn into the West Country and there they ravaged great ravagings'. 'But', says Æthelweard,

> . . . when rejoicing in rich spoil they returned towards home, they were still engaged in crossing to the east side of the river Severn over a pons, to give the Latin spelling, which is called [C]antbricge by the common people. Suddenly squadrons of both Mercians and West Saxons, having formed battle-order, moved against the opposing force. They joined battle without protracted delay on the field of Wednesfield; the English enjoyed the blessing of victory; the army of the Danes fled, overcome by armed force. These events are recounted as done on the fifth day of the month of August. There fell three of their kings in that same 'storm' [or 'battle' would be the right thing to say], that is to say Healfdene and Eywysl, and Inwaer also hastened to the hall of the infernal one, and so did senior chiefs of theirs, both jarls and other noblemen.

And so the name Inwaer (Ivar) is added to the casualty list and thus Æthelweard provides us with a familiar-sounding list of Scandinavian kings, some reminiscent of the men of the Great Heathen Army who were active in the 860s across England and Ireland. This has prompted some to suggest that some of these men may be descendants of that very family operating out of Dublin, who had recently been displaced in 902 and were now based in the north-west of England. Some other hints that many of the northern army which fell at Tettenhall may have emanated from this same stock of displaced Scandinavians, is the assertion by some that the Hold Agmund (a listed casualty) has his memory preserved in the form of 'Amounderness', a large swathe of land north of the Ribble. Some have even sought to link the name Agmund with the intrepid Ingimund whose celebrated activities around Chester preoccupied Mercian defence policy in the opening years of the century. However, no link between the names, except for their rough similarity, can yet be proved.[1]

We cannot be entirely certain exactly who these fallen men were or whether they came from York, the English north-west or even from the Danish garrisons of the eastern Mercian areas. But there are some observations to be made from all the accounts. Firstly, everyone seems to agree that the Scandinavians raided into Mercia. Edward, who was in Kent preparing a naval force for action elsewhere, perhaps in the north-east or possibly even overseas, seems to have initially been surprised by the move and then to have organized a joint Mercian and West Saxon force (as one might expect of the king of the Anglo-Saxons) to march against the enemy. Whether Æthelred and Æthelflæd commanded the Mercian contingent is not said. But Tettenhall, as we shall see, is in English Mercian territory and the events were said to have taken place on 5 August, St Oswald's Day. With symbolism this powerful, it is difficult to imagine that they were not involved. By telling us that the English 'got in front of the raiding army from behind when it was on its way home' the chronicler implies a degree of shadowing. This strategy was widely adopted by early medieval armies. It was a way of ensuring that you kept up knowledge of your enemy whilst maintaining just the right distance. The English must have known for some time of the enemy's movements through Mercia and were able to anticipate its homeward journey. This all implies the use of scouts and, importantly, the use of speed made possible by mounted forces.

It is Æthelweard who provides us with the notion that there was an element of surprise about the English onslaught. This would certainly explain the calamitous casualty list. The names of the dead may well have come to the English chroniclers via confirmation of the names of the fallen coerced from captured men at the battlefield itself. It is likely that this encounter, or series of encounters, was one where the odds were consistently stacked against the Scandinavians.

So, where exactly did the battle take place? Æthelweard says the Danes were in the process of crossing the Severn over a bridge at *[C]antbricge*, almost certainly Quatford just south of Bridgnorth. However, Quatford and Bridgnorth are approximately 12 miles from Tettenhall (which is on the north-west outskirts of modern Wolverhampton). The Worcester (D) version of the *Anglo-Saxon Chronicle* (in one of its numerous mentions of the encounter) says a battle took place *near* Tettenhall (see Map 5, page 67). Moreover, Æthelweard adds a unique reference into the mix. His 'Field of Wednesfield' is written in Latin as *Vuodnesfelda campo*. In Anglian areas (such as here, in the region of Tettenhall) it is suggested that 'camp' had a meaning of 'battle, fight, contest or dispute' as opposed to its alternative meaning elsewhere in the south of England of 'open land or field'. And it is at Wednesfield (Woden's Field), a further three miles east of Tettenhall, where in 1513, a field name of Camp Feld (in the area of Wadden's Brook) once existed, that the final encounter of the Tettenhall campaign is thought to have taken place.[2]

The evidence is patchy to say the least, but it may represent an initial ambush conducted by a Mercian shadowing force on their Scandinavian enemies as they headed over the bridge at Quatford, followed by a second encounter where the enemy was stopped in its tracks in the region of Tettenhall by another combined English force on the field at Wednesfield. It is even possible that in this main battle, there were two separate actions, one at Tettenhall and one at Wednesfield. The two or more separate actions in the same campaign might explain the confusion in the chronicles and the conflating of events. We are missing a huge amount of information, but what little we have suggests that the superior knowledge of the landscape lay emphatically with the Anglo-Saxons. They attacked their enemy at its most vulnerable moment, then stopped it from reaching the lands beyond Watling Street in an encounter from which few of the Scandinavian leaders and the men of their retinues survived. Whoever these fallen men were, their absence from the stage of northern English politics after their annihilation in 910 probably contributed to the remarkable shift in the approach taken by Edward and his sister's armies over the next few years. The rulers of the kingdom of the Anglo-Saxons would combine to assert their authority in places previously lost for generations. But one of these rulers was nearing the end. He may even have been injured at Tettenhall and was certainly not able to direct the building of a new burh at *Bremesbyrig* (see below, pages 66–70) a project which was instead, overseen by his redoubtable wife.

Above and below: 11 and 12. *Plaque in Ethelfleda Memorial Gardens (top) and Ethelfleda Terrace (bottom), Wednesbury.*

In the entry in the *Mercian Register* for 911 'Æþered Myrcna hlaford', Æthelred, Lord of the Mercians, is recorded as having died. The announcement is kept very simple:

> Ða ðæs oþres geares gefor Æþered Myrcna hlaford.
> 'Then in this, the next year, Æthelred, lord of the Mercians, departed.'

He was buried 'in the fortress called Gloucester' says Æthelweard, amid what one imagines were scenes of deep mourning. This man had been a close ally of both King Alfred (who had left him a sword worth 100 mancuses in his will) and Edward the Elder. He had fought shoulder-to-shoulder with both Anglo-Saxon kings, father and son, and had seemingly devoted himself to the great family project. John of Worcester adds the following wording in his entry for the year 912 (for 911): 'After a well spent life Aethered [*sic*], a most honourable man, ealdorman and patrician, lord and subregulus of the Mercians, died: after whose death, his wife Aegelfled [*sic*], daughter of King Alfred, kept possession for some time, and with a strong hand, of the kingdom of the Mercians . . .'

He left behind him a much rejuvenated and confident Mercia. He also left behind his daughter Ælfwynn, his foster-son Æthelstan and most importantly for the future of England, his 'Myrcna hlæfdige', Æthelflæd. For Æthelflæd, the Lady of the Mercians, the time had come. She assumed the leadership in Mercia and became its queen in all but name. Alongside her brother Edward, she would now write a whole new chapter in the history of Anglo-Saxon England.

Wednesbury

Local tradition suggests that Æthelflæd built an otherwise unrecorded burh at Wednesbury, roughly equidistant between modern Walsall and Dudley, four miles to the south-east of Wednesfield and thus not far from the field of the Battle of Tettenhall. The name may mean 'the burh associated with Woden'. Evidence for the burh is inconclusive but this has not prevented the tradition developing into a notable civic pride movement expressed in the form of a street name 'Ethelfleda Terrace' and an extraordinary ornamental gateway by the bus station known as The Caryatid Gateway, designed by the sculptor Steve Field. Here, Æthelflæd forms a caryatid on the left side. Also, there is a plaque in the Ethelfleda Memorial Gardens proclaiming the site to be on the '. . . fighting platform of the stronghold built by Ethelfleda . . .'. There is also a large mural on the Holyhead Road sporting a combative-looking Æthelflæd wielding a spear. All these suggestions are not as extraordinary as they may seem. It is possible the summit of Church Hill, linked once to the old god Woden, may have been the focus of the settlement, burh or some other sort of military presence in Æthelflæd's time, providing commanding views of the routeways in the local landscape.

Although it is not recorded in the *Mercian Register* as one of the burhs founded by the Lady of the Mercians, the circumstantial case for the connection is strong. The tradition was certainly known to Robert Plot, who in 1686 wrote in his *The Natural History of Staffordshire* that 'The renowned Ethelfleda, who governed the kingdom of

Above and right: 13 and 14. *Æthelflæd sculpture (left side): The Caryatid Gateway, Wednesbury Bus Station. By Steve Field and John Vaughan. Stainless steel and limestone. 2004.*

Mercia with so good conduct, fortify'd this Town against the Danes who infested her Nation'. There were apparently traces of an ancient fortification visible on the hilltop in 1813 too. In 2008 archaeological enquiries revealed a substantial ditch running around part of the contour of Church Hill yielding early medieval pottery. The site was long thought to have been an earlier Iron Age hilltop settlement or fortification and it is likely that it does stretch back into the prehistoric period.[3]

Above and below: 15 and 16. *Saint Bartholomew's Church at Wednesbury.*

St Bartholomew's Church sits on top of the hill, its early history shrouded in mystery. It is possible that an earlier dedication (such as that at Stafford) was to St Beorhthelm (Bertelin). As an aside, at Runcorn (see page 123) the present All Saints Church, the focal point of the Mercian burh, was formerly dedicated to St Bertelin and then to St Bartholomew. But the case for Wednesbury's church connections to St Bertelin is unclear. The idea that the Lady of the Mercians placed a fortification here in a region which saw one of the greatest battles of the age, cannot be discounted.

17. *Mural installation on Holyhead Road, Wednesbury depicting* Æthelflæd. *Part of the Wednesbury reliefs. Designed by Steve Field. Steel. 2007. (See also Colour Plate 16.)*

Chapter 5
Bremesbyrig

Whilst her husband was struggling with the illness or injury which would probably be the one that claimed his life, Æthelflæd had gathered her witan around her and began urgently to assess the vulnerabilities of Mercia in the wake of the Tettenhall campaign. Despite the crushing success of the final encounter, it must have been of grave concern that the enemy had come into Mercia so deeply and raided so widely without being stopped earlier. The defensive network of major fortifications in her heartland area included Worcester, Hereford, Gloucester, Shrewsbury and probably Winchcombe. To the north of course was the restored fortification at Chester, but in the context of Tettenhall, this might be considered to lie in a different sector. The *Mercian Register* in chronicles (B) and (C) records that Æthelflæd built the stronghold at *Bremesbyrig* after the battle at Tettenhall. The word *getimbrede* (for which the translation usually given is merely 'built') probably means more specifically 'provided with a wooden stockade or enclosure'. The term (and its grammatical variants) is frequently used when describing the provision of a burh in this period. So, if Æthelflæd *getimbrede þa burh æt Bremesbyrig*, it has been pointed out that she may have provided a pre-existing 'burh' or enclosure with new timber defences.[1] It is also notable (elsewhere in the chronicles) that when describing the provision of stone walls to a pre-existing fortification, the (A) chronicler uses the term *worhte*, implying 'worked' in preference to *timbrede* (see page 147 for a description of Edward's revision of the Towcester defences in 917).

It is significant that Æthelflæd constructed *Bremesbyrig* during the lifetime of her husband. Æthelflæd was clearly now taking the lead in Mercian affairs. Whether this is due to her husband's suspected ill-health, however, is not certain. The Worcester (D) version of the *Anglo-Saxon Chronicle* names the stronghold as *Bremesburh* and also attributes its construction to Æthelflæd, although it continues to report the Battle of Tettenhall two more times.

The location of *Bremesbyrig* is not known for sure. There have been a number of candidates put forward over the years. One of these, Bromborough in Wirral, whilst it might make sense in respect of being a forward defence for Chester on the English side of the territory carved out by Ingimund, is often proposed as a candidate for the events of the next generation surrounding the Battle of Brunanburh in 937. It is not beyond imagination that it could be the answer to both quests. However, to equate Bromborough with Æthelflæd's fortification of *Bremesbyrig* does not explain the presence of an intermediate 's' in the name of Æthelflæd's burh which is not apparent in early spellings of Bromborough. What is apparent, is that the *Bremes-* element may well come from a personal name, but the man who gave it to the place is entirely unknown. Another potential site, this time on the southern side of Chester, is Beeston Castle, which is a medieval castle built on a promontory amid much earlier prehistoric fortifications.

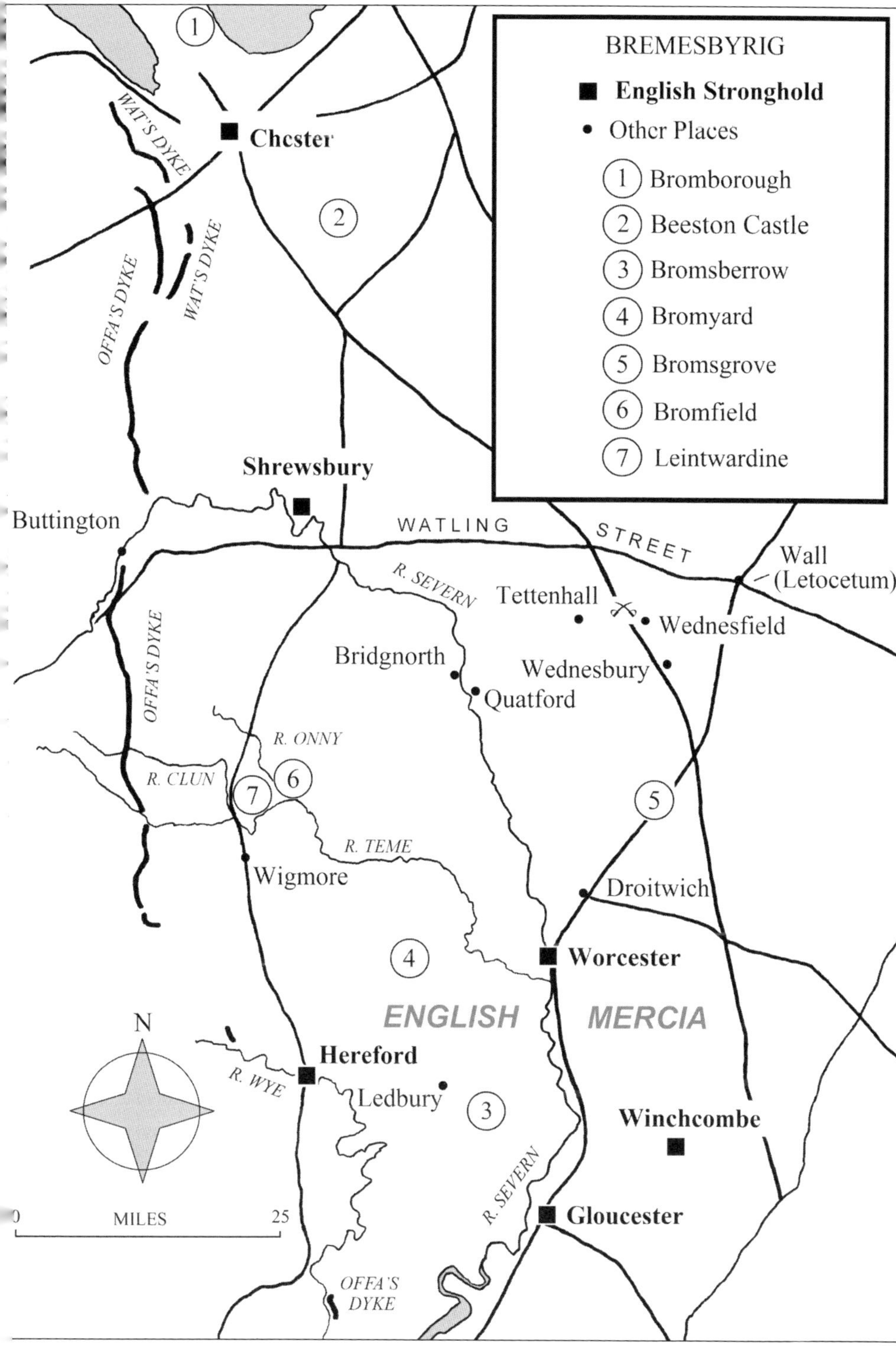

Map 5: *Possible locations for* Bremesbyrig.

Whether any link can be made to Æthelflæd here remains to be seen, and the site has been extensively excavated with no evidential link, but it is clearly a location with wide-ranging views across Cheshire to the Mersey and would fit with how Æthelflæd viewed the concept of inter-visibility in the Mercian landscape. However, the prospect of a full-sized burh of the type which Æthelflæd was known to go on to build elsewhere seems remote, although a late Saxon presence of some sort on this hilltop site cannot and should not be discounted.[2]

Another candidate, Bromsberrow in Gloucestershire is roughly 10 miles north-west of Gloucester and thus sits inside the triangle of fortifications provided by Hereford, Worcester and Gloucester. It is at the convergence of the later Hereford, Worcester and Gloucester shires. The rules surrounding the building of a 'new' burh are not known, but situating such defences at boundary locations might make sense. Some, however, argue that the placement of a fortification here would not have been necessary given the garrisons of the aforesaid three forts would have had this land covered. But we do not know enough about where exactly the Scandinavians penetrated on their raid. If they had come directly between the three major fortifications it would make sense to subsequently plug the gap, although the same could be said for Bromyard situated in the valley of the Frome in Herefordshire and conceivably controlling access in and out of the area of the 'triangle' of fortifications. Bromyard is known from at least c. 840 to have been an important settlement which later grew to become a key market town in the region, but etymologically it is hard to make it fit with *Bremesbyrig*, despite it being an attractive proposition. The early spelling 'Brommgeard' is thought to mean 'enclosure where broom or gorse grew', although alternative local folklore tradition has it that the 'Brom' element was synonymous with Frome. It is difficult to imagine the men of tenth-century Bromyard having no say at all in the defence of their area, but whether they are the men of *Bremesbyrig* remains uncertain.

Bromsgrove in Worcestershire, situated around 19 miles to the south-east of Bridgnorth and about 18 miles to the south of the region of Tettenhall, is another very good candidate.[3] Being just 13 miles north-east of Worcester, it was situated on the main Roman road between Droitwich and Wall (Letocetum). A burh here would extend the protected area towards the north-east and it was within a day's march of Wednesbury (although the exact date of Wednesbury's construction is shrouded in mystery) and thence to Watling Street. The placement of *Bremesbyrig* at Bromsgrove would make perfect sense in the wake of the previous invasion which sparked the Tettenhall campaign, and it does seem that the *Mercian Register*'s mention of the building of the fortification is a reaction to that very campaign, being designed to prevent such destructive penetration into western Mercia from the north, particularly providing a forward 'shield' for important economic centres such as Worcester and Droitwich. The economic aspect of the placement of a burh here might be important: the royal retention of the wagon-shilling and load-penny at Droitwich, as mentioned in Æthelred and Æthelflæd's charter of a grant of privileges to Worcester (S 223, see page 79) shows concern for the economic influence of this salt-producing area on the royal coffers from at least the 890s, with more than a hint in that charter that it always had been a concern.

The layout of Bromsgrove is familiar to students of Anglo-Saxon burhs. It displays a linear 'High Street' model shared by many other known burhs, although there are no hints of the burghal perimeter. But here again, with Bromsgrove, the evidence can be said to be confusing and even contradictory: it has been suggested that there are etymological problems.[4] Bromsgrove's earliest mentions are consistent with the name in its current form. A document of c. 804 names it as *Bremesgraf* (S 1187) and in 1086 at the time of the Domesday survey it is *Bremesgrave*, neither of which contain the byrig/burh element pointing to a fortification. The place name is thought to mean 'the wood belonging to Breme', indicative of a personal name. But, is it possible that in 910 the settlement was upgraded and then referred to as *Bremesbyrig* (at least in the eyes of the author of *Mercian Register*)?

The Domesday reference is possibly revealing. It would seem that Bromsgrove was fairly prosperous at that time. The estate was a royal manor and possessed a significant rural territory, a characteristic of a number of burhs of the ninth and tenth centuries. In fact, eighteen subsidiary berewicks or settlements are referred to, radiating up to 12 miles from the settlement. Because the Domesday entry also includes a reference to a priest, it is generally believed that the place may have had a minster church. This is also based on the sheer size of the estate and the clearly obvious siting of St John's church.[5] The medieval parish of St John's is considered to be unusually large. The church itself cannot be dated on surviving fabric to anything earlier than the late twelfth century. However, its position on a rise overlooking a communication network is reminiscent of St Bartholomew's at Wednesbury (see page 65) and also to the hilltop minster church at Hanbury, both of which are not without their proposed Æthelflædan connections. The archaeological evidence still eludes, but Bromsgrove has remained a popular – and on the face of it – strategically convincing candidate for *Bremesbyrig*.

Yet another candidate is potentially at Bromfield, a village near Ludlow in Shropshire, which is situated at the confluence of the rivers Teme and Onny. Although the manor of Bromfield is certainly pre-Conquest, and the Bromfield Priory was founded some time before 1061, there is no structural archaeological evidence to suggest that the Bromfield site is that of *Bremesbyrig*. Its antiquity is not in dispute, however, as this was the area in which an early Anglo-Saxon inhumation cemetery was discovered, dating from the sixth to seventh centuries. This cemetery is associated with a much earlier site, a Roman marching camp, situated just to the north of the present-day village and much mutilated by quarrying works. Bromfield's position in the landscape is, however, of note in terms of the burh-building programme of Æthelflæd. It is 20 miles from where a burh at Chirbury would be built five years hence, 19 miles from the Bridgnorth/Quatford area, and 20 miles from Hereford. Intriguingly, it is also 20 miles from Shrewsbury. If the general rule for Alfredian West Saxon burhs (that they were built no more than around 20 miles apart) is applicable to the burh programme in West Mercia, then we might expect to find *Bremesbyrig* right here, controlling the confluence of these two rivers and dominating the nearby south-to-north Roman road. To add to the mystery is another potential candidate just five miles to the west of Bromfield. This is Leintwardine, situated at the confluence of the Clun and the Teme. A Roman settlement named Bravinium once stood here and there are still some visible ramparts dating to the late second century. The settlement appears in Domesday Book as *Lenteurde*, though there is nothing to plug the gap between Roman and the late Saxon, save some distinctive early tenth-century pottery (see page 100), which is not enough at this stage to indicate the presence of an entire burh, but the position of the site, like that of Bromfield, is of note. An English presence here would be consistent with a defensive stand against incursion from Wales, which arguably was not the priority in the aftermath of Tettenhall. The earliest stonework in the church of St Mary Magdalene is a blocked-up western doorway, which does not assist in pushing the foundation any further back. However, it is thought to be linked to at least two 'tot' sites (lookout or signalling sites) of the tenth century and thus would be linked into the defensive network of Æthelflæd's era. These sites are at Totteridge Hill and Hopton Castle Titterhill. The pottery was apparently found near the church which sits in the middle of the Roman perimeter. If Leintwardine is not *Bremesbyrig* or any of the other 'missing' forts of Æthelflæd's era, then it is clearly something. Its tantalizing evidence reminds us that not everywhere which received the attention of Æthelflæd or her husband in this era went on to become a fully urban place, and there is still much to learn from investigating places like it.[6]

Wherever *Bremesbyrig* was, we can safely assume Æthelflæd was behind its construction. Her rise to power in the wake of her husband's death, however, is another matter. Not since Queen Seaxburh of Wessex (died c. 674) had briefly assumed control of the kingdom in the seventh century had a woman come to power like this. But Æthelflæd was different. In Seaxburh's case there was the involvement of sub-kings and questions over the queen's legitimacy and an uncomfortable power struggle. Not so with Æthelflæd. Her rise to sole power was merely an extension of what had gone before. She was to rule as the Lady of the Mercians, a female version of the Lord of the Mercians. And there is no good surviving evidence of any objection to her rise to power.[7] But there was something unusual which happened at around this time. The *Anglo-Saxon Chronicle* explicitly records that 'King Edward succeeded to London Town and to Oxford, and all the lands which pertained thereto'. This 'seizure' of London and Oxford by Edward at the time of the death of Æthelred has been taken by some to be a mark of aggression against his sister, but it may in fact be something more straightforward. When Æthelflæd and her husband had married in around 886, London was awarded to Æthelred perhaps as part of a dowry arrangement by King Alfred. In 911, at the death of Æthelred, Edward might be seen to simply be reclaiming what was his right as king of the Anglo-Saxons, with Oxford having been the other town in the gift, now reverting to Edward. Whatever the reason for the reversion to Edward of the two vitally important fortifications (and regional centres of trade) in the south-east of Mercia, the new arrangement must have led to a new approach to the ongoing war between the children of Alfred and the Danish lordships. It is probably at this time that brother and sister met for a revision of territorial responsibilities. Edward, with his newly-acquired forts of London and Oxford, would go on to conduct most of his campaigns east of the line of the Fosse Way, whereas Æthelflæd and her loyal followers campaigned to the west of this line and north of Watling Street on the western side. This area to the west of Wychwood Forest (especially at its southern end) was the heartland of the patrimony of the late Æthelred. But this division of responsibilities, if indeed it did occur in this way, was not likely to have been decided arbitrarily. It may even be that Edward's armies were pitted against the Danish armies south of the Welland who were arguably affiliated in some way to the Scandinavian leadership in East Anglia, whereas the armies faced by Æthelflæd may have been affiliated to York.

Above and below: 18 and 19. *Remains of the medieval St Oswald's Priory in Gloucester incorporating earlier wall masonry from the period of Æthelred and Æthelflæd's foundation.*

Both brother and sister must surely have communicated often on the subject of strategy. This cannot be in dispute. History would show that their approach to the domination and subsequent expansion of English-held territory would be reliant on one thing above all others: the Anglo-Saxon burh or fortification. Neither of them wasted any time in organizing their resources in order to conduct the first recognizable phase of this policy.

The New Minster and Later Medieval Priory of St Oswald, Gloucester

The new minster at Gloucester was said by William of Malmesbury (*Gesta Pontificum, 293*) to have been founded by Æthelflæd and her husband Æthelred during the time of King Alfred. This would place it somewhere between c. 886 and c. 900 with a date in the 890s seeming most likely to coincide with the building of the new burh in Gloucester. The church, like its neighbour, was also originally dedicated to St Peter. It is described as having been handsomely endowed. Its eventual destruction in the seventeenth century came after a long history as the priory of St Oswald. According to the *Life of St Mildburg* the church was commonly called 'Golden' on account of its abundant ornamentation. It attracted pilgrims to Gloucester from far and wide.

The church saw its cultural heyday during and after the reign of King Æthelstan (925–39) in the decades after the translation of the bones of St Oswald in 909. A prior of St Oswald's who was involved in a plea hearing heard before Edward I in 1304 ascribed the foundation of the church to Æthelred '*primicerius* of the Mercians', citing a charter of Æthelstan in favour of the house which stated that Æthelstan was acting in accordance with a 'pact of paternal piety' with Æthelred and also acting in accordance with the wishes of his own father Edward the Elder.

Although sumptuously adorned, the building in its first and second phases was of modest proportions compared to New Minster at Winchester and very small compared to Carolingian churches, some of which also featured a similar western apse. It was built to a traditional insular plan with an unaisled nave and north, south and east porticus. The outer walls appear to have been limewashed and a bell was made for the church.

Excavations have uncovered evidence for rich wall paintings on a division at the east end of the nave and blank areas of wall plaster probably reserved for wall hangings. There was also a small gold book fitting and a possible fragment of gilding from a metal object perhaps from a reliquary casket. Also discovered were richly-decorated grave slabs (see Colour Plate 27), probably originally brightly painted and perhaps even those belonging to one or both of the tombs of the founders Æthelred and Æthelflæd. William of Malmesbury contended that the tombs were discovered in the south porticus during a twelfth-century enlargement of the church, although the *Mercian Register* records Æthelflæd as interred in the east porticus of 'St Peter's church' (now thought to imply her own foundation of the new minster, and not the older one nearby). It is not clear if the church acquired the dedication to St Oswald

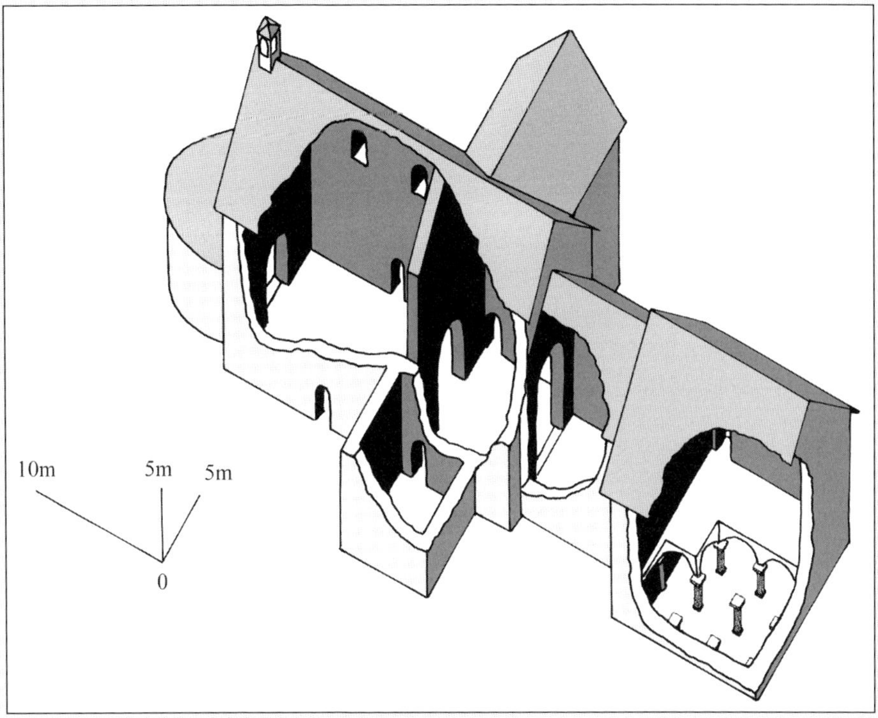

Fig. 6: *Reconstruction of Period II of the new minster, Gloucester (later the medieval St Oswald's Priory) c. 920, showing separate crypt construction at east end, and unusual western apse. After Jean Williamson, in Heighway, C. and Bryant, R. (1999).*

immediately after the translation of his bones in 909 or later in the century. By the early eleventh century the name of Oswald was certainly being used. An eastern porticus would usually imply a burial in the chancel, but here an additional sunken crypt was built at the east end of the church. It is thought that in this crypt (similar in construction to that at Repton) once lay the bodies of Æthelflæd and Æthelred and just possibly, the relics of St Oswald himself.

One final tantalizing suggestion has been made regarding the siting of the church. It was built over a Roman cemetery near to where an arm of the Severn and some of its tributaries once flowed to form something of a low-lying island. In effect, it was partially 'defensible'. Moreover, incorporated into the fabric of the earliest church were several eighth and ninth-century broken cross shaft fragments perhaps indicting that here was also a Middle Saxon sacred site which had somehow become desecrated. The temptation is to find an explanation for that desecration and reach the conclusion that it was here where the Danes set their tents in 877 before they parcelled out Mercia and launched an offensive against Alfred. But for this, there is no direct evidence. However, the building of a church on a sacred site which became dedicated to St Oswald and which probably housed the tombs of its founders who effectively rebuilt Mercia, may be imbued with more symbolism than we can possibly imagine.[8]

Left and below: 20 and 21. *Remains of the medieval St Oswald's Priory in Gloucester showing earlier wall masonry (centre, top picture) from the period of Æthelred and Æthelflæd's foundation. The bottom of an Anglo-Saxon clerestory window can be seen just beneath where the bird is flying (bottom picture).*

PART TWO

THE FORTRESSES OF THE CONQUEST

Chapter 6

How Did a Fortress Work?

During the 880s, when King Alfred's defensive burh-building programme was arguably at its height, across the whole of Wessex and in parts of Mercia, many central places were either having their existing defences restored or upgraded, or were simply being built anew amid a strategic military landscape. However, archaeological evidence is emerging for an earlier date for the construction of a great number of 'burghal' defences in places which eventually became towns across both Wessex and Mercia, leading to speculation that the Alfredian period of reform was but an episode in a much longer story. Mercian centres, in particular those at Tamworth, Hereford and Winchcombe, have been shown to have much earlier Anglo-Saxon defences than those attributed to Æthelflæd's time. In Winchester in Wessex, for example, the work of Alfred's brothers who preceded him as king is thought to be just as significant as Alfred's own efforts in the town. However, there is no doubt that the existing systems and structures of civil defence across both Wessex and Mercia received royal attention during the late ninth and early tenth centuries.[1]

Many burhs emerged as important market towns later in the tenth century, continuing with a royally backed and deliberate economic purpose, but some did not. Some burhs may even have held this economic function, at least in embryonic form, from the outset. Those other 'burhs' would therefore be better off being termed as 'strongholds', it is suggested. Some people now say the term 'burh' should only really be applied to the more permanent fortifications such as those which continued to develop and be settled during the late ninth, tenth and eleventh centuries. But the word has a very long usage in Old English and its meaning has been revisited in recent years.[2] In essence, the word may merely refer to a high-status ditched enclosure. It has been used throughout the period in reference to defended earlier Iron Age hill forts (Badbury Rings being an example), monastic enclosures (Peterborough), aristocratic and royal residences (Bamburgh), and proto-urban and urban settlements (any number of 'burys or 'boroughs').[3] The origin of the word 'burh' is from the old English verb *beorgan* 'to protect or shelter'.[4] It has subsequently become synonymous with the proto-urban spaces characterized by the fortifications of the Alfredian and post-Alfredian era, which in turn have become interlinked with the story of early English urbanization, none of which helps in establishing how the fortresses of Edward and Æthelflæd actually worked. As a rule of thumb, it is safe to say that when the 'burhs' built by Alfred's children were established, the driving force was not to create a 'town' in the modern sense, despite the fact that this did indeed occur in many places. The establishment of such central places affected the control of military movement and of economic commodities, and the subjection of the surrounding districts. In some cases an overt legitimization programme is arguably discerned through the establishment of churches. In other words, there was a great symbolism to these places, too.

As we shall see, although the burhs Edward and his sister built were clearly part of a wider strategy and shared important characteristics, there is some merit in taking each foundation as it comes. Some places like Winchester, for example, were having their Roman defences restored and street layouts put down in the ninth century. But it was not just restored Roman defences which appeared in the landscape. As part of the wider network of defences, some Iron Age hill forts were once again reused where their position had a contemporary strategic need. Planned regular new burhs had already been built, such as that at Cricklade, as had smaller irregular strongholds. In Alfred's time and in Æthelflæd and Edward's time, the overriding factor in the placement of their fortifications was exactly that: placement. River crossings, estuaries and promontories overlooking routeways were all important. The idea behind the establishment of Anglo-Saxon fortresses of this period, whether we call them burhs or strongholds, was to obviously provide immediate protection for those inside it, but to also control movement in the landscape. The economic, social, political and ecclesiastical aspects of many of these places were also important, with royal backing, but those strongholds, particularly small ones, which had served their function militarily were left undeveloped when their strategic placement waned in importance.

Although Alfred's biographer Asser spoke of the king's regret that some of his demanded fortifications were begun too late in a time of necessity, the sheer scale of the programme was nonetheless impressive. This is not to say that King Alfred was the sole architect of the idea of the Anglo-Saxon defensive settlement as a whole, however. Far from it, in fact. As far back as the reign of the great Mercian King Offa (757–96), fortifications were being erected to counter the threat from the Danes. Furthermore, the 'three common burdens', the so-called *trinoda necessitas* of bridge-work (brycggeweorc), fortress-work (burh-bot) and expeditionary service (fyrd-færeld), duties incumbent on the holders of bookland, are traditionally said to date from the reign of King Æthelbald of Mercia (d. 757). But we can be sure that Alfred demanded much from the men of his kingdom. An entry in the *Anglo-Saxon Chronicle* shows how he reorganized military provision throughout his kingdom, a notice which probably refers to reforms stretching back into the 880s: 'The king had separated his army into two, so that there was always half at home and half out, except for those men who had to hold the fortresses.'

Asser, writing probably in around 893 (although there is an argument for a date in the later 880s) went on to mention that the enemy often 'burst in by land and sea (or, as frequently happens, by both!)'. It would seem to be a reasonable suggestion that the Alfredian burghal programme was designed to prevent both such occurrences by placing fortifications no more than around 20 miles apart, thus providing a place of refuge for the people of the kingdom. Whilst this provided a defensive depth in the hinterland, the burhs placed at river estuaries prevented enemy ingress up those rivers and therefore denied access to the road systems, Roman or otherwise, inland. Others, it is argued, were placed near to royal estates to afford them the protection they required.

In short, a burh or stronghold of the type we are considering in the context of the wars of the early tenth century dominated the territory which was dependent upon it. Its manpower was drawn from that district. The Burghal Hidage, the document which lists the mainly West Saxon burhs, shows how many hides (a unit of assessment roughly equivalent to a measure of land supporting a peasant family) 'belonged' to each burh. None of the different versions of the Burghal Hidage lists all thirty-three forts. One of the versions, known as the Nowell transcript (thanks to the sixteenth-century historian who transcribed it before its demise in a fire of 1731) has an appendix which states: 'If every hide is represented by one man, then every pole of wall can be manned by four men. Then for the maintenance of twenty poles of wall, eighty hides are required, and for a furlong one hundred and sixty hides are required by the same reckoning.'

A pole is 5½ yards, so it has been possible in some cases to assess the accuracy of the mathematics against the surviving circuits of some burhs, with Winchester's 2,400 hides theoretically providing for 9,900ft of walls. The Roman walls are in fact a very close 9,954ft in total. The later medieval versions have an appendix which is thought to have originally read, 'That is all 27,000 hides (and seventy which belong to it) and thirty burhs belong to the West Saxons'.

The hidages listed in the two groups of manuscripts which constitute the Burghal Hidage are as follows:

Eorpeburnan	324
Hastings	500
Lewes	1,300
Burpham	720
Chichester	1,500
Portchester	500
Southampton	150
Winchester	2,400
Wilton	1,400
Chisbury	700
Shaftesbury	700
Twynam (Christchurch, Dorset)	470
Wareham	1,600
Bridport	760
Exeter	734
Halwell	300
Lydford	140
Pilton	360
Watchet	513
Axbridge	400
Lyng	100
Langport	600
Bath	1,000
Malmesbury	1,200
Cricklade	1,500
Oxford	1,400
Wallingford	2,400
Buckingham	1,600
Sashes	1,000
Eashing	600
Southwark	1,800
(Worcester)	1,200
(Warwick)	2,400

Fig. 7: *The Burghal Hidage*

It is certainly a sizeable garrison capability. There is every reason to believe that a significant portion of the kingdom's population were required to perform fortress duty. Whether the paper assessment was quite the same as the reality on the ground is impossible to say for certain. But when we combine all this with some other factors in the defence of the kingdom, which had clearly been there for some time, we can see that Anglo-Saxon governments of this period can hardly be accused of being idle in providing for the defence of the people. Across the kingdom there were various trackways described as 'herepaths' (herepæð), 'herestreets' (herestræt) and ' hereways' (hereweg). A 'here' is generally taken to indicate 'army'. These roadways, streets or pathways connected burhs and other nodal points to one another. Not necessarily reused Roman roads, they aided communication and movement across the kingdom. Many of those identified across Wessex for example, would seem to act as something of a 'B Road' system in conjunction with the principal Roman arteries.

But there is other evidence for defensive provision. A system of beacons would seem to have been in use for some time. Carefully positioned on hillsides, these beacons were lit to give warning of coastal invasion, sending their visible message way back into the hinterland. With one watch or guard point visible to another, the speed with which a signal could travel was probably quite quick. Charters from the period contain the compound word *weard-setl*. This means 'a place where guard is kept, or 'the place of those who keep watch or guard'. As early as the reign of Cuthred of Wessex (740–56), a 'weard setle' is mentioned in the bounds of a charter (S 258) for 749 referring to Highclere in Hampshire. It is also known that there were numerous mustering places for Anglo-Saxon armies at this time and we might assume that the burhs themselves formed an important part of this activity. Ecgbryhtes Stane, the place where Alfred gathered his forces before his victory at Edington in 878, is perhaps one of the more celebrated examples. Recognized regional assembly points across Wessex and Mercia would also have performed a similar function.

One of the earliest burhs established by Æthelred and Æthelflæd involved the renovation of the ancient Roman town of Worcester. This is not to say that its defences had not been attended to by previous Mercian rulers, but Æthelred and Æthelflæd's approach is recorded in writing. The document (S 223) describing this huge undertaking dates probably to the 890s and was drawn up with the consent of King Alfred. It gives a good idea of the sort of detailed planning which must have gone into the building of many of the burhs of the period. The document is a grant of rights to the church of St Peter at Worcester and near the beginning of the text is the phrase '. . . at the request of Bishop Wærferth, their friend Ealdorman Æthelred and Æthelflæd have ordered the building of the burh at Worcester for the protection of all the people and also that the worship of God may be celebrated therein'. The town was expanded beyond its Roman perimeter, enclosed by an earthen rampart, with the River Severn protecting it on the west. We are told about the things that went on within the burh and how they were to be organized. It was an example of church and secular leadership working together. Tolls, for example, were levied on salt from Droitwich and were to remain in the king's hands: '. . . the wagon-shilling and the load-penny at Droitwich are to go to the king as they always have done'. Land taxes

Above and below: 22 and 23. *Worcester from south to north. The cathedral is situated in the older, southern part of the town. All Saints Church (far left, bottom picture) marks the probable northern extent of the tenth-century burh.*

were levied and fines were to be imposed on rogue traders and for those caught fighting. There were fines for theft too. There was a tax for the upkeep of the walls and numerous other crimes which were punishable by compensation payments. Half of all such revenues were to go to the Church. There was clearly market trading in the burh (and outside), as the charter also indicated that Æthelred and Æthelflæd 'desire to give half to God and St Peter and to the lord of the church that the foundation may be more honourably maintained' of their rights 'both in market and in street', both inside and outside the burh. In return, the bishop had arranged for a number of divine offices to be appointed in honour of Æthelred and Æthelflæd both for the duration of their lifetime and after death. During lifetime, the psalm *De profundis* was to be sung and after death *Laudate Dominum*. Every Saturday thirty psalms and a Mass were to be performed both during life and after death. And so, the 'new' burh at Worcester would provide both a physical and spiritual protection for the people and for the founding couple.

It is easy to imagine a bustling mercantile settlement in the expanded Worcester of the early tenth century and it is equally possible to see other places such as Shrewsbury, Chester, Hereford and Gloucester in a similar light. But as we rejoin Edward and his sister in 912, a year after the departure of Lord Æthelred, we can be sure that the idea of the central stronghold was a key to their strategies in their respective areas. What had not happened yet was a switch to an overt offensive into areas held by Danish lords, but the foundations for this were being laid. And we can be sure that wherever Edward and Æthelflæd built their burhs, they were not alone in the landscape.

Chapter 7

Scergeate 912 (Æthelflæd)

Her com Æþelflæd Myrcna hlæfdige on þone halgan æfen Inuentione Sancte Crucis to Scergeate ⁊ þær ða burh getimbrede, ⁊ þæs ilcan geares þa æt Bricge.

Here, on the holy eve of the Invention of the Holy Cross [2 May] Æthelflæd, Lady of the Mercians, came to *Scergeate* and built a stronghold there, and the same year that at Bridgnorth.

The *Mercian Register*, or 'Annals of Æthelflæd'.
Entry for 912 (C)

This is the entry for the *Mercian Register* for the year 912, accompanied by its modern translation. In a terse sentence, the record reveals that Æthelflæd had come in person to oversee the engineering works at both *Scergeate* and *Bricge*. She knew her landscape well: she was schooled in the contemporary art of military geography and had sat at her father's side in many a military and 'urban' planning meeting, one in particular in 898 when the ongoing project of restoring London was the topic of discussion (S 1628). She was perfectly confident in overseeing surveying operations in preparation for fortification building. We might imagine that Æthelflæd scoured the landscape with an expert eye much like her father had done when he was looking for a suitable site around Hertford in the 890s.

So, Æthelflæd's next recorded fortification (after *Bremesbyrig*) was at a place called *Scergeate*, a word which means 'boundary gap, or gate/opening'. She had come here 'on the holy eve of the Invention of the Holy Cross'. The author of the *Mercian Register* may be dropping a hint as to the 'Mercian' significance of the event. It had been St Helena, the mother of the fourth-century Roman Emperor Constantine, who had discovered the True Cross on a trip to Palestine in 326. It had been the same saint who was the subject of Cynewulf's Old English poem *Elene* which retold the story. Helena's coinage was arguably an inspiration for the only known coinage of a Mercian queen, Queen Cynethryth (the wife of King Offa), who died in 798. The link between St Helena (who is also the patron saint of Abingdon and Colchester) through Cynethryth to Æthelflæd, seems also to have been based on the mutual experience of motherhood and a significant share in 'royal' power. Her importance to Æthelflæd is probably also reflected at Worcester. The church of St Helen was one of the earliest churches in Worcester, occupying a central place on what is now the High Street of the city at the junction with Fish Street, and regarded as the 'mother church'. Dating from the pre-Saxon or Romano-British period, the church is still there today (though with much later stonework) and represents a striking continuity of Christian worship in the city. It would have been an important place in the newly-refurbished burh which

Æthelflæd and her husband had renovated 'for the protection of all the people' in the 890s. Its early history is not fully known, but its origins in the Roman period are perhaps further emphasized by its position, almost abutting the defences of the Roman part of the town on the inside at the junction with the subsequent northern expansion. In fact, just at the western end of Fish Street, on what is now Deansway, sits another church building, St Alban's, inside the old Roman perimeter which probably also originated in the Romano-British period and no doubt had a significance in Æthelflæd and Æthelred's time.

Perhaps the *Mercian Register*'s author was signalling the beginning of a distinctly Mercian enterprise, as Æthelflæd now set out on her own in 912 to fortify the region. Sadly, we are again left with a puzzle as to the location of *Scergeate*. The name gives us no clue as to which 'boundary' or which 'gate' we are to be considering. However, the boundaries of regional tribes, still a potent cultural force in early tenth-century Mercia, may have had something to do with the placement of those burhs which were built 'anew', so to speak. The sixteenth-century antiquary John Leland believed *Scergeate* (which he called 'Scorgate') to be somewhere in Gloucestershire on the Severn 'repaired by Ethelfleda', and it does seem that Æthelflæd's concerns at this stage were to secure the Severn Valley and her western flank. By placing fortifications at strategic locations up and down the River Severn, she would be effectively preventing any northern army breaking through to the west, whilst also protecting western Mercia from incursion from the west itself. There has been much speculation as to where *Scergeate* may have lain, if indeed it was on the Severn at all. One historian

Above left, above right and overleaf: 24, 25, 26 and 27. *Two very early church foundations in Worcester may have held some significance for* Æthelflæd. *St Helen's on the High Street (24 and 25 – view in Fish Street) and St Alban's (26 and 27 – doorway).* *See page 189.*

has postulated that it may lie on the Severn in the Wyre Forest in the Bewdley area, being situated as part of Æthelflæd's advance up the Severn valley.[1] If so, it would place it neatly equidistant between Worcester and the fortification which would soon be built at or very near to Bridgnorth. But we lack any further evidence to place *Scergeate* here. That said, if the identification for *Bremesbyrig* is correct for Bromsgrove, the strategy could conceivably be to throw a protective arc around the northern access routes into Worcester.

Whitchurch in Shropshire has also been put forward. It was known by the time of the Domesday survey as 'Westune' and its present name comes from its Norman-period 'white' church. It is at a place where the Welsh border today thrusts into England, almost as if it were stubbornly clinging to long-cherished lands. Whitchurch also lies along a branch of the Roman road from Wroxeter to Chester. It remained an important settlement long after the Norman Conquest and its strategic importance can hardly be denied. The parish church of St Alkmund's (a favoured saint of Æthelflæd), situated on a hill in the centre of the town, is thought to have been founded by Æthelflæd in 912, although this is not certain. Today, it is a fine example of Georgian ecclesiastical architecture. But what is certain is that Æthelflæd was heavily involved in the promotion of Mercian royal saints, although the mere presence of the church may not necessarily assist in placing *Scergeate* here. The place has a Roman heritage too, being the site of a fort and accompanying settlement called Mediolanum. Despite the lack of archaeological evidence of a tenth-century burh, the siting of Whitchurch, lying more or less equidistant between Shrewsbury and Chester, has something to recommend it. In the Domesday survey it is recorded as having an impressive forty-one households, and having been in the possession of Harold Godwinson in 1066 and then of William de Warrenne in 1086. It was in the largest 20 per cent of all settlements recorded in the survey, surely pointing to a earlier and long-standing importance. But in our period not only would Whitchurch defend a notable 'gap' in the landscape and secure the corridor between Shrewsbury and Chester, it would also be the area where King Edward would be campaigning in the last days of his reign, spent at Farndon, half way between Whitchurch and Chester (see page 189). Whitchurch, it seems, whether it is *Scergeate* or any of our other 'lost' burhs, may yet have an Æthelflædan story to tell.

Recently, a case has been put forward for either Little Shrawardine or its near neighbour Shrawardine in central Shropshire, situated at a major ford on the Severn, only seven miles west of Shrewsbury.[2] Both of these neighbours have post-Conquest castles, as if to reinforce an earlier importance. The proposed site lies on a right-angled bend in the Severn. It is thought to have been the meeting point of the dioceses of Hereford, Lichfield and St Asaph. The area is on a boundary between the folk groups of the Wreocensætan and Magonsætan and a deviation in the boundary here to include the opposite bank of the river is thought to be significant and is something which historians have also observed at Quatford. The possibility therefore, that this may have once been a double burh straddling the Severn has been postulated. Archaeological proof of any of this is yet to be established, and for now, Little Shrawardine and its neighbour remain an intriguing mystery.

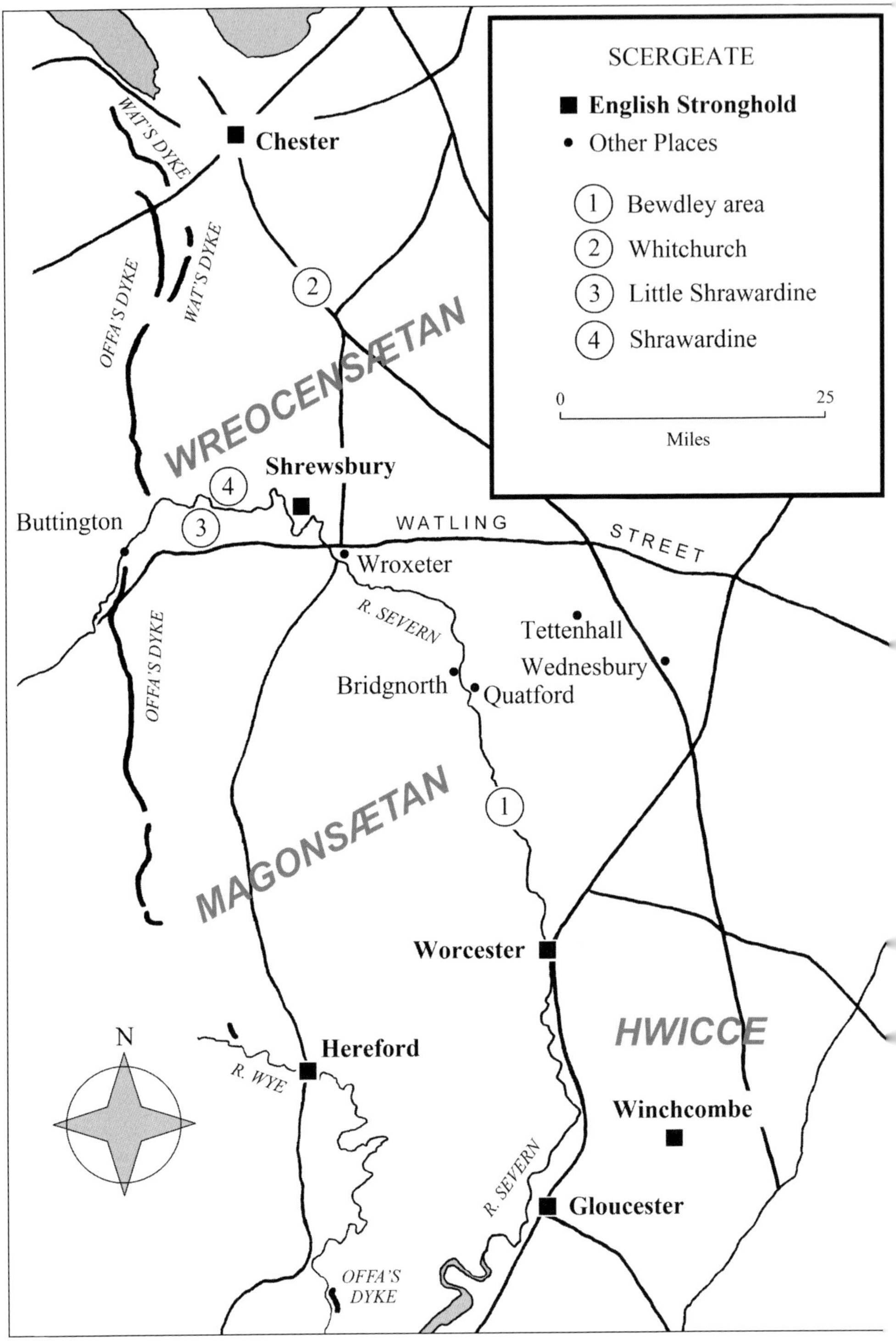

Map 6: *Possible locations for the burh of* Scergeate.

Chapter 8

Bricge 912 (Æthelflæd)

On the face of it, Æthelflæd's building of the burh at Bridgnorth might seem to be less of a mystery. But a closer examination of the contention that her burh was at modern Bridgnorth raises some interesting issues. We cannot be sure that the construction of *Bricge* was contemporary with *Scergeate* or if it followed on from it. The wording of the *Mercian Register* suggests the latter scenario, and we know from later accounts of Edward's reign that it could take on average around two or more months to build a burh (see page 135 regarding Towcester, although Buckingham seems to have taken just four weeks). If this is the case, and if *Bricge* and *Scergeate* were consecutively constructed, Æthelflæd's engineers and fyrdsmen will have had *Bricge* operational around late August or early September in 912.

This locality was of great strategic significance, being roughly the place where the Danes encamped between 894 and 895 and the place where a different group of Danes, returning northwards in 910, crossed the Severn and were tailed by a Mercian army in the lead-up to the fight at Tettenhall. It has been argued that this place, known as *Bricge*, *Brycge* or *Cwatbrycge*, was at Quatford.[1] The problem is compounded however, by the name *Brig* also being an early name for Bridgnorth (whose second element 'north' was added in the thirteenth century), just two miles to the north-west of Quatford. After the Norman Conquest, Robert de Bellême, Earl of Shrewsbury, transferred the 'oppidim de Quatfort' to Bridgnorth. This would have been when an earlier post-Conquest motte was abandoned at Quatford. It was at this point, in 1101, that John of Worcester tells us that Robert 'began to repair and surround with a broad and lofty wall . . . the castle which Ethelfleda, lady of the Mercians, had formerly built . . . at a place called in the Saxon tongue *Brycge*, on the west bank of the River Severn'. This reference to the *west* side of the river has led people to place Æthelflæd's burh at Bridgnorth, where the later castle was built.

There is, of course, a powerful strategic argument for there being some continuity at Bridgnorth from Æthelflæd's time to that of the rebellious Norman earl's time. Bridgnorth Castle is built on a promontory overlooking the Severn. It is also on the western side. Some people therefore, argue that because of John of Worcester's statement, Bridgnorth is indeed the *Mercian Register*'s *Bricge* and therefore Æthelflæd's burh. It is an argument augmented by the fact that St Leonard's Church (barely half a mile to the north of the Norman castle) contains earlier Anglo-Saxon stonework and that the twelfth-century bailey of the castle most likely follows Æthelflæd's burghal perimeter (calculated as enclosing a plausible 5.7 hectares) and the argument may seem to be sealed by twelfth and thirteenth-century exchequer accounts of the castle, which describe a dungeon at 'Ethelfleda's Tower'. But this romantic acknowledgement of Æthelflæd's legacy is hardly evidence for her fortification. Nor is the curious oval ringwork structure sometimes put

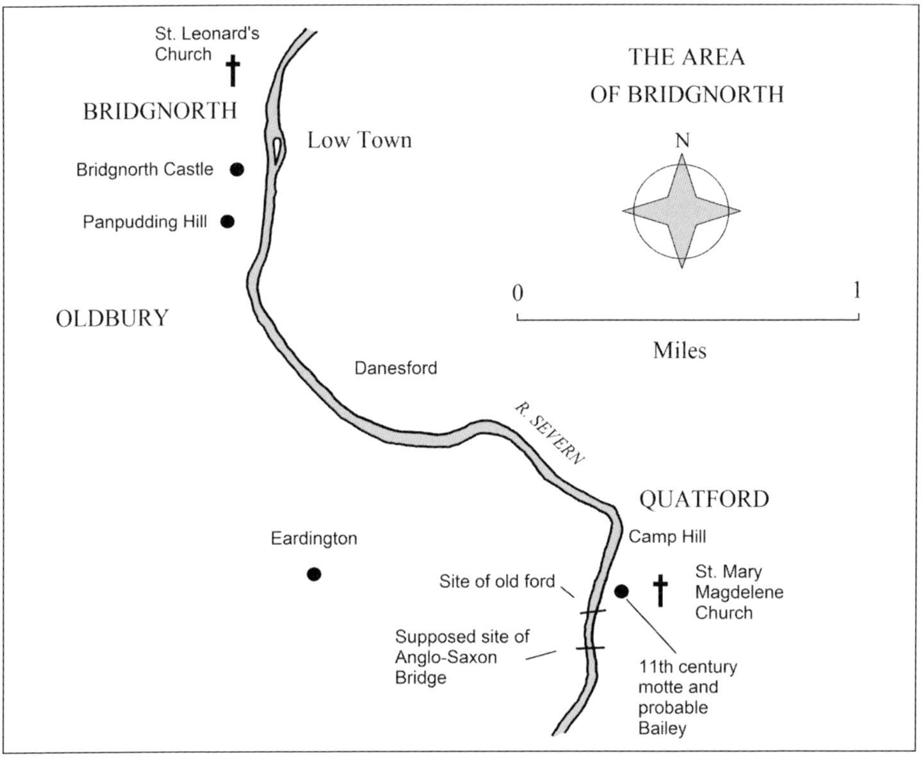

Map 7: *The area of Bridgnorth.*

forward as a burghal candidate, 84m wide at its widest point, situated to the south of the Bridgnorth promontory (but still on the western side of the Severn) at Panpudding Hill. This structure's form is consistent with what in Norman times would have been a siege- or counter-castle constructed by Henry I (1100–35) in his war against the rebellious Earl of Shrewsbury.

There is a school of thought (perhaps, a too dismissive one) that John of Worcester was mistaken in his assertion about the transfer by Robert de Bellême of Æthelflæd's fortification being on the *west* side of the Severn, and the suggestion is that much of the other evidence – such that it is – points to Quatford, where the earlier Norman motte is on the *eastern* side. By knocking out John of Worcester's claim as an error (a controversial step), the field might seem to be open. So, is there any strength in the argument that Æthelflæd's burh was in fact at Quatford? Firstly, we should take a look at Oldbury. This is not at Quatford, but is merely half a mile to the south-west of Bridgnorth Castle and less than two miles to the north-west of Quatford. Its name 'Oldbury' is evocative, if not demonstrative, of a disused burh and it is also recorded in Domesday Book. It may even be that the materials incorporated into the nearby ringwork of Henry I came from here. But as we have seen 'burh' can simply mean 'enclosure'. Placing Æthelflæd's burh at Oldbury, attractive though it is, would mean removing it from close proximity to the Severn (admittedly by only half a mile) and this would make the association of a bridge an improbability. And yet both Bridgnorth and Quatford sit right on top of the river.

We know that *Brycge* was an alternative name for *Cwatbrycge*, which was at or very near Quatford. Its name appears to have travelled with it to modern Bridgnorth during Robert de Bellême's regional upheaval. But prior to this, it is almost certain that a pre-Conquest bridge existed at *Cwatbrycge* (i.e. Quatford) and it makes perfect sense for Æthelflæd to plant her burh here. It is no surprise therefore, that an early Norman motte was built here too, as is so often the case in other Anglo-Saxon burhs (where the motte is usually erected in a corner). So, if Æthelflæd's burh was in fact at Quatford, and not as many people contend at Bridgnorth, what physical evidence is there? Map 7 shows the area of Bridgnorth and possible candidates for the location of the burh. The area around Camp Hill has the early Norman motte virtually on top of the River Severn. Just to the south of here – a matter of yards – was thought to be the bridge. Adjacent and slightly to the north-east of the motte is an open area of land roughly square in shape, with its south-east corner truncated by a natural valley feature. It lies on the eastern side of the modern A442

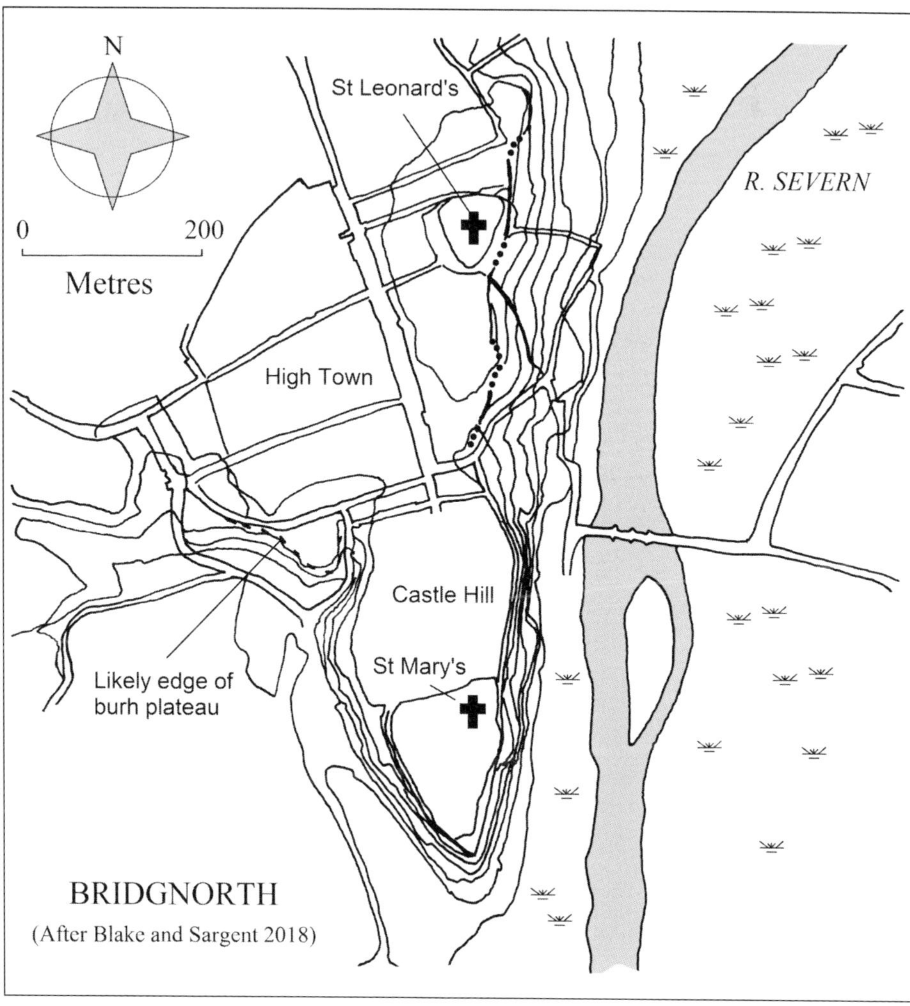

Map 8: *Bridgnorth.*

road, just to the north of St Mary Magdalene Church. There are plenty of candidates for Æthelflæd's burh in this area, but if *Bricge* is not at Bridgnorth after all, then there is a chance it may have lain here at Camp Hill, right on top of a ford (and by Æthelflæd's time, a bridge) where even a modest garrison could have challenged a Danish or Welsh army heading east.

But the argument for Bridgnorth itself will not go away, and is probably quite rightly the consensus. Many of Æthelflæd's burhs were built on plateaux.[2] Such a plateau exists to the north of the castle in the High Town area on the east side of the High Street. It would thus incorporate St Leonard's church, after all. This general planning phenomenon of a plateau, encompassing a church, with natural slopes and drops forming the edges, is often repeated in Æthelflæd's burhs, with particular emphasis being laid on the church foundation. Recently brought to light, it is a useful template in the hunt for those burhs yet to be identified. The debate over the identity of the Æthelflædan burh continues today. Without solid archaeological evidence, it is unlikely to be resolved in the near future. As far as *Bricge* is concerned, the clamour from the Bridgnorth camp is the loudest, although Quatford was clearly important in the later ninth and tenth centuries. We are left, however, only with the teasing clues in the Shropshire landscape, not all of which can lead to the answers.

Chapter 9

Hertford 912/13 and Witham 913 (Edward)

As the autumn of 912 gave way to winter, Edward the Elder looked to start his phase of the grand plan in his own sector in the south-east Midlands. News will have reached him of the successful completion of his sister's fortifications of *Scergeate* and *Bricge* and he will have felt confident that English Mercia had at least begun to secure its western flank and consolidate its centre. It was around Martinmas, on 11 November 912, that Edward brought his army and engineers to Hertford. He ordered his men to build the 'more northerly stronghold' there, between the Maran (the modern-day River Mimram), the Beane and the Lea. The work began on the northern side of the Lea and the south side of the Beane, in an area centred on modern-day Old Cross. The work will have taken a few months and may well have been fully completed by the spring or early summer of 913.

By the summer of 913, Edward's strategic intent would be clear to anyone living in Essex. 'Between Rogation Days and midsummer,' says the (A) version of the *Anglo-Saxon Chronicle*, Edward took a part of his army to Maldon in Essex 'and camped there while they made and built the stronghold at Witham'. Rogation Days were a period of processions for several days preceding Ascension Day. But the *Annals of St Neots* say this all took place about the Feast of St John the Baptist, which is on 24 June. So, Edward's march across Essex seems to have taken place much nearer to midsummer. While the work at Witham continued, says the chronicler, 'a good part of the people who were earlier under control of Danish men submitted to him'. This is no great surprise. Edward's military presence at Hertford may already have persuaded some of the people dwelling in the western part of Essex to submit to him. Also, Witham lies on the Roman road to Colchester, then a Danish stronghold. It is more or less level on a west-to-east line with Hertford's position 31 miles further west. Edward's intention is barely concealed. He was cutting off Essex from the Danes and forcing the submission of the people by imposing a burh at an important location. The memories of Æthelwold's challenge to the throne and of his cousin's success in Essex cannot have been far from his mind as Edward watched the crowds of people flock towards him in the summer of 913. Meanwhile, the garrison that he had left at Hertford had begun their work on the south side of the Lea. Another fortification was being built there, too. This time, it seems to have been a grander affair, with evidence in the street pattern of careful planning. This newer southern burh was centred on the present marketplace and Salisbury Square further to the north, its purpose in conjunction with the northern burh being to control movement up and down the Lea as well as across the ford. It had its main east-west axis along Maidenhead Street and Railway Street and its southern limit south of another parallel thoroughfare, Fore Street. On its western side, but still within the

28. *Hertford. Looking east past the War Memorial down Fore Street, one of the two main thoroughfares of Edward's southern burh.*

bounds of the southern burh, ran a road down to the Lea, to this day still called The Wash. Edward, the king of the Anglo-Saxons, was finally flexing all the muscles of the English military machine.[1]

An event is recorded in the *Anglo-Saxon Chronicle* (A), under the entry for 913.[2] It occurred 'after Easter', when the Danes launched their own strike against the kingdom of the Anglo-Saxons. The Danes of Leicester and Northampton were surely aware of the fortification programme being undertaken by the commanders of the kingdom to their south. And so, it was a combined force from these two Danish-controlled strongholds who 'broke the peace' (an often-repeated phrase used by the chronicler indicating the existence of one of many a lost treaty). The Danes poured over Watling Street probably as a mounted force and struck deep into the heart of English territory,

29. *Hertford. Junction of St Andrew Street and Old Cross, the historic heart of the northernmost of Edward's burhs.*

reaching Hook Norton on the periphery of Wychwood, east of the Fosse Way. Here, at Hook Norton and its surrounding areas, they slaughtered many men before turning home, says the chronicler. The first of those who turned home soon joined with another independent mounted unit and attacked Luton – an indicator, perhaps, of an unrecorded Anglo-Saxon burh there. But they were soundly defeated by what the chronicler refers to as 'the people of the land'. The victory was so emphatic that after their enemy had fled the field, the Anglo-Saxons could pick over the spoils of war, which included the booty initially taken by the Danes in their earlier raid and the best part of their horses and weapons. Nothing is recorded of the battle, but due to its close proximity, it is tempting to suggest the garrison of the newly-constructed burh at Hertford had played some part in the campaign. In fact, William of Malmesbury, although writing much later, emphasizes the spirit of the people in Edward's time, speaking of such forces rushing out of their fortifications to take on the enemy and surpassing them 'both in number and warlike skill'. 'Thus the enemy . . .,' he says, 'became an object of contempt to the soldiery, and of derision to the king.' This era of new-found high morale and confidence amongst the English people may not be so far-fetched as it seems. And someone else was once again at work in the Mercian landscape during 913. While her brother was making progress in Essex, around 115 miles to the north-west his sister was planning something emotional, remarkable and long-lasting. The Lady of the Mercians was about to embark upon the next phase in her grand strategy. With the west for now as secure as it could be, the time had come to reclaim the very beating heart of Mercia.

30. *Hertford. The River Lea from Mill Bridge looking east. To the left was the earlier northern burh and to the right was the subsequent planned southern burh.*

Chapter 10

Tamworth and Stafford 913 (Æthelflæd)

Her Gode forgyfendum for Æþelflæd Myrcna hlæfdige mid eallum Myrcum to Tamaweorðige ⁊ þa burh þær getimbrede on foreweardne sumor, ⁊ þæs foran to Hlafmæssan þa æt Stæfforda.

'Here, God helping, Æthelflæd, Lady of the Mercians, went with all the Mercians to Tamworth, and then built the stronghold there early in the summer, and afterwards before Lammas that at Stafford.'

The *Mercian Register*, or 'Annals of Æthelflæd'. Entry for 913 (C)

So, it happened with God's help. And it is significant that the Lady of the Mercians had gone there 'with all the Mercians'. This ancient 'capital' of Mercia, the much-heralded seat of earlier kings including King Offa (757–96), had for nearly two generations lain on the frontier of Danish-held territory. It had receded in importance over this period, after being attacked by the Danes in 874.[1] For Æthelflæd, the next phase of her project was to push north and west from her late husband's heartlands. The securing of the Severn valley and her western flank had made this next phase possible. Now, it would be the rivers Tame and Sow, tributaries of the Trent, and even the Trent itself at its western end, which would set the boundaries for the next operation. This phase would push English Mercian influence towards the kingdom's historic heartlands. It is also possible that the appointment during Æthelflæd's period of rule of Bishop Ælfwine (or Ælle) at Lichfield, situated between Stafford and Tamworth just north of Watling Street, was linked to the military expansion undertaken at this time by the Lady of the Mercians. These fortifications would provide a protective shield for Lichfield. Ælfwine remained a key figure not only during Æthelflæd's time, but also over the next two decades, and he may well have been responsible for some of the key documents of the early tenth century. And so, with God's help, amid scenes of imaginable joy, Æthelflæd brought the Mercian people into Tamworth. There was no recorded resistance. Warriors, churchmen, carpenters, merchants, smiths, bakers, butchers, tanners and millers will have all come to Tamworth with the army. Almost certainly at Æthelflæd's side, as she had no doubt been when the Mercian army were working on *Scergeate* and *Bricge*, was her daughter Ælfwynn and quite possibly her nephew, Æthelstan.

Tamworth guarded the crossing of the Tame. Any garrison there could easily cover the junction of the two Roman roads of Watling Street and the northern bound Ryknild Street which led towards Derby. Notwithstanding the overt symbolism of Tamworth to the English people of Mercia, the shift of emphasis by Æthelflæd in moving to little more than a day's march from one of the principal Danish boroughs at Derby would have impacted on the minds of the commanders there, let alone to any Danes nearby at Repton. And as if to reinforce the confidence of the English, the Lady of the Mercians built, or rather,

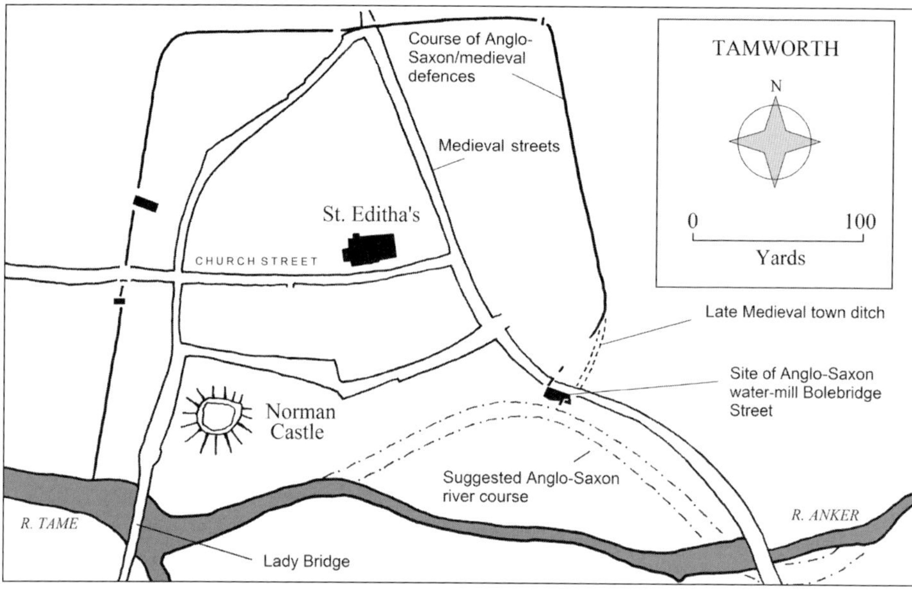

Map 9: *The burh at Tamworth.*

31. *Tamworth. A later Norman castle was erected in the south-west corner of Æthelflæd's burh. Looking north from Lady Bridge along Holloway, the modern road follows the probable line of the internal road on the west side of the burh.*

32. *View of Lady Bridge, from the south side of the river looking towards the burh at Tamworth.*

rebuilt the burh at Tamworth on the northern side of the junction of the Tame and the Anker. Æthelflæd's burh at Tamworth is estimated to have enclosed an area of 23 hectares (about 57 acres). A bank of turf, clay and gravel was topped with a timber palisade in front of which was a great ditch, the whole perimeter structure measuring 8m across. With gate towers and wooden walkways, Tamworth was being given some special treatment by the Mercian engineers, revisiting the efforts of earlier great kings. Within the burh Æthelflæd had her palace, although traces of it have proved elusive. Also, within the perimeter was the church located at the site now occupied by St Editha's parish church in the centre.

Tamworth soon developed an urban identity, later acquiring a mint, whereas it would seem that *Scergeate* did not. The newly-installed garrison here would be capable of countering raids from Repton, Derby and even Leicester to the east. And so this phase of Æthelflæd's programme was more overtly symbolic and at the same time more offensive than the first, as would be demonstrated by the end of the year with the building of another crucially important burh at Stafford. This place also went on to become an urban centre. And between these centres in 913 and for years to come, a chain of signalling sites were woven into the landscape, bringing quick warnings of enemy movement. The Lady of the Mercians was throwing down the gauntlet to the enemy up to and beyond Watling Street, and it seems, that for the time being, her enemy had very few answers.

The feast of Lammas is celebrated to mark the first fruits of harvest. The Old English word for it was 'hlaf-mas', or put simply in modern English, 'Loaf-Mass'. It was celebrated on 1 August. For Æthelflæd to have built her burh at Stafford before

Lammas means that for much of July the Mercians would have been furiously busy at both Tamworth and Stafford, finishing the first burh and beginning the next. For this second burh of the year, Æthelflæd had chosen a place where just a small community existed. It was also a place where the River Sow was fordable. The first part of the name 'stæðe-ford' means 'landing area for vessels'. It may further indicate the strategic importance of the place. The Stafford site was carefully chosen for a number of other reasons. It was a peninsula of sand and gravel surrounded on three sides by a bend in the river and to the north-east of the settlement was marshy land. It was virtually hemmed in by these natural features and this meant that its northern man-made defences were quite short.[2]

According to Mercian tradition, a saint called Beorhthelm had established a hermitage on the site in the eighth century at a place then called Betheney. His story is very obscure and may even be conflated with that of another man of the same name and with later legends. Tradition has it that he had once been a Mercian prince who fell in love with an Irish princess and brought her to England where he left her in a forest in dire need of a midwife. When he returned to her she had been devoured by wolves and this awful event is what had triggered his life as a hermit. The story is probably borrowed from that of St Bertelme of Fécamp. Another of his names, along with Bettelin and Bertram, is St Bertelin. Although legend says that St Bertelin subsequently moved to Ilam in Dovedale where he is supposed to have ended his life (and where the tale of the wolves features), the link to Stafford was not lost on Æthelflæd, who established a minster church in the saint's name, close to where the parish church of St Mary now stands. He became the patron saint of Stafford. The remains of the medieval chapel of St Bertelin's can still be seen, beneath which may well lie the evidence for Æthelflæd's church. The saint's feast day is on 10 August, which may perhaps have coincided with the completion of the burh at Stafford. However, what marks Æthelflæd's Stafford out from the other burhs she had built to this point is the extraordinary amount of building activity at the site, as well as the evidence for it being a focus of agricultural and of course, military activity.

At Stafford, we are fortunate in having over 50 years of archaeological investigations to inform us. These excavations have been going on intermittently since 1954, and one particular discovery in the 1970s demonstrated the holistic approach Æthelflæd was adopting in her burh-building programme. A proliferation of a type of pottery, wheel-thrown and tempered with a rounded quartz sand, which archaeologists call Stafford Ware, was being found in some quantity.[3] Then, in 1977 just south of Tipping Street, came the discovery of Stafford Ware kilns, followed by another excavation in 1994 of a kiln in Salter Street. Although there is evidence of earlier pottery production at Stafford and much agricultural activity predating Æthelflæd by a good few decades, there is clearly a case for an explosion of activity in Æthelflæd's era. The idea that Æthelflæd merely walked into a deserted site is beginning to slip away. Instead, a more remarkable picture is forming. Æthelflæd did almost everything in her life very carefully indeed and with great purpose. It seems the establishment of Stafford in 913 was based on securing and protecting what was already a centre for Mercian taxation and agricultural surpluses established earlier.[4] This would explain why Æthelflæd put an army in it.

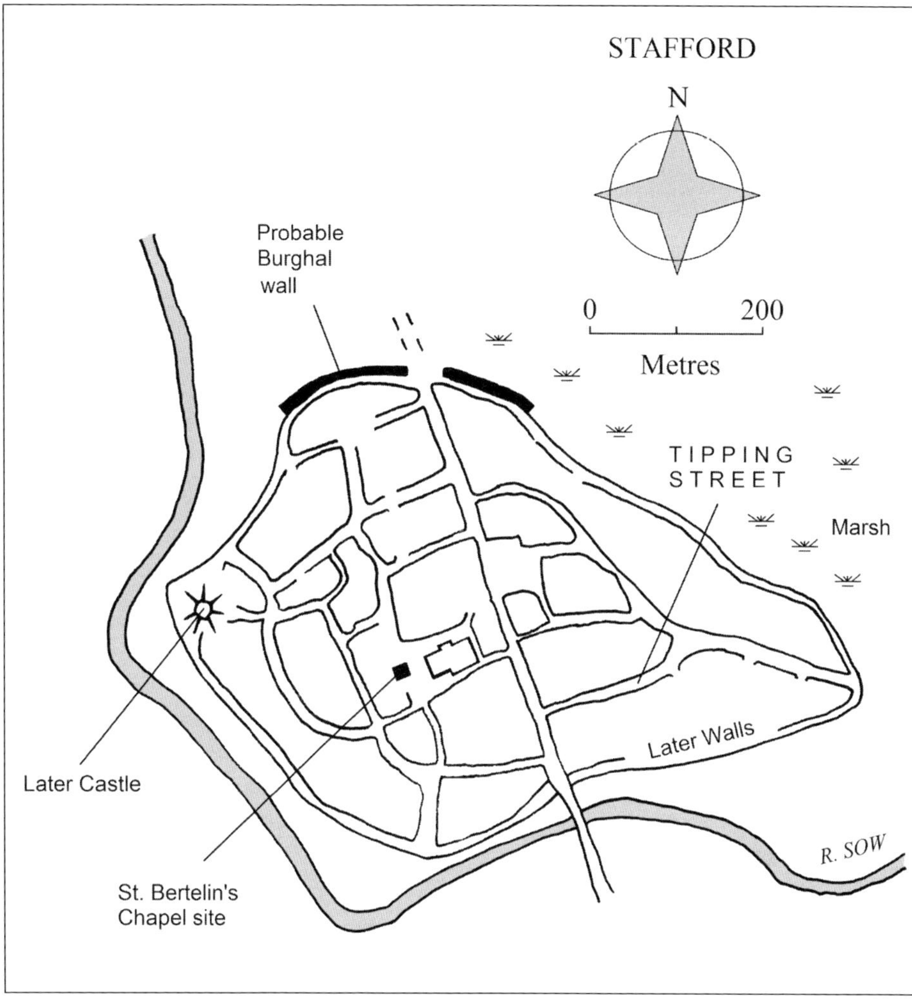

Map 10: *Stafford, with later medieval street layout.*

The area to the north of St Bertelin's was given over to grain processing and associated baking activities. A smithy and stable blocks laid to the east. On the east side of the main axial roads were pottery workshops producing bowls, lamps, pots and jars. These workshops were accompanied by areas showing evidence of animal butchery. The archaeologist who directed the excavations concluded that the main purpose of the place in the early tenth century was as a production site for pottery and animal foodstuffs in support of what must surely have been an Anglo-Saxon army.[5] The burh which encompassed all this activity is thought to have been roughly rectangular in outline, although the extent and form of the outer defences is not fully known. Perhaps the inspiration for Æthelflæd's burh comes from none other than Rome itself. Its shape is thought to have been akin to that of a Roman fort with what would appear to have been an Anglo-Saxon equivalent of a Roman vicus (a supporting settlement) to the east.

Moreover, the pottery of the burh's kilns is observed to model its forms on the Roman Trent Vale ware of a bygone era. It is possible that Æthelflæd was deliberately invoking Rome as a way of symbolically emphasizing her right to rule. All of this, together with evidence for a mint (of a slightly later date) at Stafford, provides a picture of a thriving military settlement with attendant artisanal support, confident and aggressive in its outlook. One can imagine the transient population of herdsmen, merchants, craftsmen and shield makers, smiths and others swelling the population as they delivered the goods to support the army at Stafford.

The way in which Stafford Ware was distributed across the landscape is of significance, as it demonstrates the close relationships between the burghal garrisons of Æthelflæd's territory. Excavated examples of the pottery have been discovered in large quantities at Hereford, Chester and Shrewsbury, and other places include Lichfield, Dublin, Rocester, Barton Blount, Gloucester, Tamworth, Cold Norton, Grange Cow Worth in Ellesmere Port, Tatton Park, Leintwardine and Wroxeter. With the obvious exception of the Dublin example (which shows either a trade in the pottery itself or an example of other goods such as salt being transported in Stafford-type vessels, presumably out of Chester), the distribution as shown in Map 11 could well indicate the sites which had a military connection to the main production centre at Stafford, all within the domain of the Lady of the Mercians. Wroxeter, the ancient Roman settlement of Viroconium Cornoviorum, whose history continued into the post-Roman period as an important regional centre, is of note. St Andrew's church certainly contains Anglo-Saxon fabric, but it is not known to what extent the ancient settlement was reoccupied in Æthelflæd's time, let alone whether it could be considered as a candidate for any of the lost burhs. Some of these places however, we can assume would have had modest garrisons. One exception, that of Barton Blount, would appear to be more civilian in character and its position just 10 miles west of Danish Derby may or may not reflect a later settlement than the time we are considering here.

A clearer picture is now emerging of Æthelflæd's Mercia being well organized and militarily potent, capable of providing a significant military presence in the landscape. The adoption by Æthelflæd of Roman influences in both burghal design and the material culture that was associated with these sites was arguably a reflection of the approach

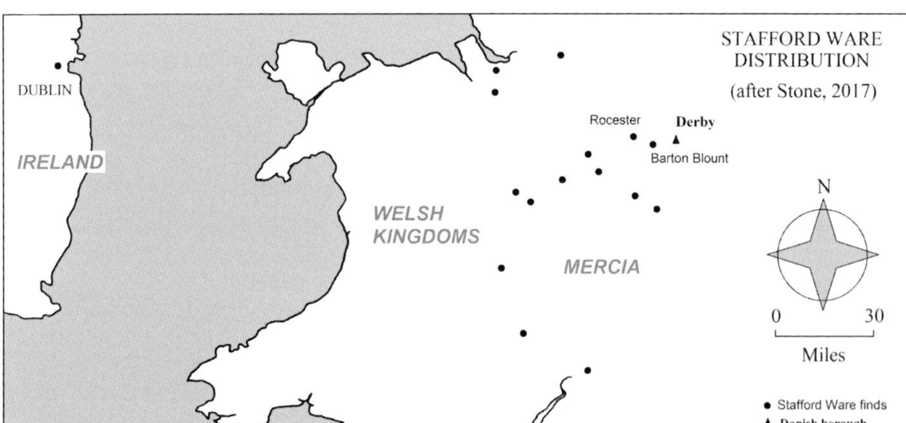

Map 11: *Distribution of Stafford Ware pottery. After Stone (2017).*

Map 12: *The war at the end of 913.*

her father took in Wessex in the previous generation. Her establishment of churches in these burhs, each conspicuously dedicated to royal and/or Mercian saints, was part of a legitimization of her right to rule. And it was this long-lived relationship between her family and Rome which she may well have felt was an overwhelmingly important aspect of her life, a factor which marked her out from the leaders of the forces ranged against her. The building, worshiping, farming and industrial activity would continue across western Mercia into 914, as Æthelflæd sought to consolidate her domains. And, as she spent the mild winter of 913 with her thegns and churchmen, probably in the burh she had refurbished with her late husband at Worcester, she may rightly have felt that Mercia was slowly being born again under her rule, and in some ways, even in her own image.

Chapter 11

Eddisbury and Warwick 914 (Æthelflæd)

Þa ðæs oþre geare þa æt Eadesbyrig on foreweardne sumor, ⁊ þæs ilcan geres eft on ufeweardne hærfest þa æt Wæringwicum.

'Then in this, the next year, [was made] that [stronghold] at Eddisbury in early summer; and later in the same year, late in harvest-time, that at Warwick.'

The *Mercian Register*, or 'Annals of Æthelflæd'. Entry for 914 (C)

The *Mercian Register* does not differentiate between different types of burh. Like the other versions of the *Anglo-Saxon Chronicle*, it makes no distinction between fortifications restored from their Roman heyday, or built afresh at strategic locations to echo the form of Roman camps, or indeed those which were built at much more ancient locations such as Iron Age hill forts. The burh at Eddisbury would appear to fall into the latter category. It did not go on to become an urban centre, but there may be good reason to believe that this was not its purpose. There are two chief candidates for the first of Æthelflæd's fortifications of 914 and they both contain the name Eddisbury, and they are both in Cheshire.

One candidate is at Rainow, Macclesfield. However, despite the presence of an undated bank and ditch here on the edge of the Pennines (and therefore on the borders of Danish and English-held territory in 914), there is little else to recommend this Eddisbury as the tenth-century fortification. There are no major routeways through the area, for example. That said, little investigative work has been carried out here. Much more favourable however, due to its geographical location and some useful archaeological evidence, is the Castle Ditch hill fort near Eddisbury Hill situated in the Delamere forest, which is close to the Roman road leading from Chester to the long-abandoned Roman fortification at Manchester and thence to York. The conclusions might seem to be obvious. With commanding views over the landscape, this hilltop site was re-fortified by Æthelflæd to protect Chester's north-east flank from incursions along the Roman road, and to protect the area from seaborne invasion from the Mersey Estuary. Also, less than a day's march to the east were the renowned salt producing centres, heavily exploited by the Romans, such as Northwich, Middlewich and Nantwich (the latter is listed as having eight salt houses in 1086). So it is not out of the question that another motive for the building of Eddisbury was for the protection of the regional economy.

Archaeology has moved the debate forwards but not without a setback or two.[1] In the 1930s seven phases of activity were identified at the site of which the last but one phase was seen as Anglo-Saxon. 'Dark Age' huts were found and sherds of pottery attributed then to the same era, would seem to have clinched the matter, except for the fact that the sherds no longer exist and were said by the excavator to have been very similar to some sherds from the Iron Age hill fort at Old Oswestry in Shropshire, which subsequent ceramic analysis has placed firmly in the Late Iron Age. Better results came in 2010 and 2011 when fifteen trenches were dug on the main enclosure and on both ramparts, and at Merrick's Hill (the site of a medieval hunting lodge) a further five trenches were dug. The consequences of these investigations are twelve identified phases of occupation and activity. In the north-east corner of the main hill fort set into the inside face of the inner rampart was a clay oven, a sample from which was subjected to archaeomagnetic dating and which returned a rather impressive last firing date of between c. 745 and 980 AD.[2] The discovery is not universally accepted as final proof of Æthelflæd's burh, but given the paucity of evidence for burhs such as *Bremesbyrig* and *Scergeate*, the discovery of a probable tenth-century oven might seem to some to be manna from heaven. But not everyone is convinced about a location for Eddisbury in Cheshire at all. It has been suggested that Eddisbury is to be seen as a temporary fort positioned elsewhere, and in the context of the constructions at Tamworth, Stafford and Warwick. The argument here would be that the fort would have been constructed in the wake of the 913 raid into the Hook Norton area in order to counter a repetition of such an event. The area around High Cross, where the Fosse Way intersects with Watling Street is suggested, but no particular location is promoted.[3] But if Æthelflæd's burhs at Tamworth and Stafford (913) triggered the Danish raids into the Hook Norton area (apparently at Easter 913), then there would be an argument for that raid having taken place at Easter 914 instead, given that Stafford, the latter of the two English burhs was erected around 1 August 913. And to say that version (A) of the *Anglo-Saxon Chronicle* with its difficult chronology leaves a little room for that argument is an understatement. If that is the case, then we might ask to what extent the raid into the Hook Norton area was designed to link in with the tumultuous events of 914 in the Severn Estuary, which we will look at shortly. But of course, we cannot know what precisely prompted the raid, nor can we be certain of the exact chronology.

The year 914 was packed with incident across the British Isles. There were a number of Scandinavian groups active in the Irish Sea that year. One of these groups had also been active in Brittany. The Bretons, under Alan the Great, had achieved notable successes against the raiders in 891 and 892, but after Alan's death in 907 the Scandinavians returned in numbers and devastated the region for many years, with Alan's successor Gourmaëlon being slain around 913 to 914, and the monastery of Saint Winwaloe at Landévennec being destroyed. These raids began a whole generation of Scandinavian ascendancy in Brittany. And it was from one or more of these Scandinavian enclaves on the coast of Brittany that many ships set sail in the summer of 914 for England.

There were two jarls with the fleet. The chronicler calls its leaders Othor (*Óttar* in Old Norse, *Oitir* in the Irish account) and Hroald. The first of these is perhaps identifiable. He is thought to have been a member of the Dublin-based Norse group who both before and after the expulsion of 902 were ranged against the sons and grandsons of Ivar for control over the Irish Sea, and by association the re-establishment of the corridor of power between Dublin and York. The *Anglo-Saxon Chronicle* (A) says the fleet 'went around west until they got into the mouth of the Severn, and raided in Wales everywhere by sea, where it suited them . . .'. But this was no ordinary raid, and some of these Scandinavians may have been no strangers to the shores of the Severn. John of Worcester, although writing two centuries later, says that 'nearly nineteen years before [they] had quitted Britain and gone into Gaul . . .'. Some of these crews may well have been the men who had fled England after the *Quatbricg* episode a generation earlier, preferring to seek their fortune on the Seine instead. On their return to England, they sailed up the Severn and brought widespread misery around the Severn Estuary, but significantly, they chose to attack the south coast of Gwent and then moved into the ancient Welsh kingdom of Ergyng (or Archenfield), centred on the lands between the rivers Monnow and Wye south of Hereford, presumably preferring not to sail right into the hornet's nest of Gloucester and its surrounding burhs.

The Scandinavians conducted raids in this border area and captured a man named Cameleac (Cyfeiliog), 'bishop in Archenfield', and then they 'led him with them to the ships'. The capture of this little-known churchman caused some concern. But that concern is recorded not in the *Mercian Register*, but instead is recorded in the (A) version of the *Anglo-Saxon Chronicle*. It was the king of the Anglo-Saxons, and not his sister, who ransomed the bishop back from the raiders for forty pounds. Why this would be the case, particularly when this all seems to have happened on Æthelflæd's doorstep, is a puzzle which may have a solution. Edward's intervention could be interpreted as that expected of an overlord. The Mercians under Æthelred, despite a defeat at the Battle of Conwy in 881, had bounced back in terms of their hegemony over many of the Welsh kingdoms and had even campaigned alongside Anarawd of Gwynedd as he looked to impose himself in the south, perhaps in return for recognition of Mercian overlordship. But back in King Alfred's time, the southern kingdoms of Wales had been driven to seek out Alfred for protection due to the 'tyranny' of Æthelred. But now, such allegiance to Winchester existed only in the south-east of Wales. The kingdom of Brycheiniog had almost certainly submitted to Æthelflæd by this time. Therefore, Ergyng, along with Gwent (including Glywysing), was possibly one of the few kingdoms still subject to Edward.

Nothing is explicitly recorded of Æthelflæd's response to the developments on her borders, but we are entitled to conclude that she was never idle. If the chronology is correct, then she may have been preoccupied with the building of the burh at Eddisbury. Alternatively, she may have left a sub-commander in charge of that project and marched south. After Edward's payment of the ransom for the bishop, the Scandinavians 'wanted to go on a raid against Archenfield'. But they were met by the men from Hereford, Gloucester 'and the nearest strongholds', a phrase which perhaps indicates the deployment of men from one or more of the lost Æthelflædan burhs, the most likely candidate being *Bremesbyrig*. There is nothing to tell us that Æthelflæd had gone with the armies of Hereford and Gloucester into Ergyng. Then again, there is also nothing in the chronicle's text to say that Æthelflæd, the natural commander of these garrisons, did *not* do so. However, the episode's absence from the *Mercian Register* is troubling. If the (A) version of the *Anglo-Saxon Chronicle* at this stage represents an 'Edwardian' chronicle, it may be that because this episode was directly linked to matters of Edwardian lordship, that it was recorded there and not in the *Mercian Register*. Perhaps Edward exercised his role as supreme overlord, as king of the Anglo-Saxons, to call in aid from his sister's heartlands or simply asked for the help which she willingly supplied. Either way, the result was somewhat emphatic.

We do not know where the battle took place, although it is sometimes suggested that the site was at or near Killdane field in Weston-under-Penyard close to the site of the old Roman settlement of Ariconium. The combined garrisons took the victory and killed Hroald and the brother of Jarl Othor 'and a great part' of the invaders. The survivors were driven into an enclosure of some sort, mentioned as a 'pearruc' (loosely interpreted as an 'enclosed area' in Modern English, but noticeably not described as a 'burh'). Here, they were besieged until they gave hostages and promised to leave Edward's domain, says the *Anglo-Saxon Chronicle*. It is of note that the 'domain' in question is not cited as that of Æthelflæd. There was, of course, an immediate concern for the king. The Scandinavians had left the area on their ships and Edward therefore knew that it was necessary to protect the north-west coast of Wessex on the southern side of the Severn Estuary from a seaborne threat. The king had put the coastal watches and fortifications on alert everywhere from Cornwall eastwards to the mouth of the Avon 'so that they dared seek land nowhere on that side'. But they still did. They 'stole up by night' twice on the shore of Edward's kingdom, just east of the burh at Watchet and then again at Porlock. The chronicler is unambiguous about the consequences:

> Then on each occasion they were hit, so that few came away, except only those who swam out to the ships. And then they settled out into the island at Flat Holm [or Steep Holm, according to other versions] until the time came that they were very short of food, and many men perished with hunger, because they could not get any food. Then they went from there to Dyfed, and then out to Ireland, and this was in harvest time.

There were no victories to be had in England for the Scandinavians from Brittany. The choice of either Flat Holm or Steep Holm as a place of refuge is interesting, given that these islands are just a short sail away from the beginning of the Roman road at the mouth of the River Axe which could take its traveller right into central Wessex and to Old Sarum and thence to Winchester. But no such temptation was taken by the Danes. For those who had remembered the campaign of 895 to 896, the outcome must have felt painfully familiar. Defeat, followed by near starvation and much loss of life amongst the crews. But the force was not so depleted that it could not raid Dyfed before sailing to Ireland, where the *Annals of Ulster* record its arrival in Waterford harbour. In a later entry in these annals (see pages 159–63 for the battle at Corbridge), we learn the name of one of the other leaders within Othor's force. He was a man named Gragabai (from *Krakabeinn*, a curious name, which could mean 'crowfoot', 'bone breaker' or even 'leg breaker'). This warrior presumably replaced the slain Hroald at the head of his warband. Ominously for the Irish, the period during which the native dynasties had experienced some respite from the Scandinavian menace after the great fightback and expulsion of 902 was coming to an abrupt end. This fleet was the first major Scandinavian fleet to be seen in Ireland since those times, and very soon, there would be more.

33. *Flat Holm and Steep Holm Islands in the Bristol Channel near the mouth of the Severn Estuary where the Danes who attacked England in 914 fled.*

Othor's was not the only Scandinavian fleet to be active in the Irish Sea that year. A notice in the *Annals of Ulster* tells of a man who would have a startling impact on northern politics across the British Isles over the next few years. In Old Norse, his name was Røgnvaldr. In the Irish text, he is described as Ragnall *ua Ímar* (a grandson of Ivar), and in the *Anglo-Saxon Chronicle* he is given the name Rægnald. After the expulsion of the Scandinavians from Ireland in 902 Rægnald seems to have established himself in Man and parts of Galloway. It is quite possible that he and Sihtric, a kinsman (possibly even a brother) who was also another grandson of Ivar, were the very Scandinavians who had set up bases in the north-west of England, these being the communities to which Ingimund had appealed during his push for Chester in the years after 902.

The entry concerning Ragnall or Rægnald in the *Annals of Ulster* records a naval victory off the coast of Man against a fellow Scandinavian named Bardr Ottarson whom it is tempting to see as a son of Othor, but who some argue was his brother, the two of them being sons of another Óttar, 'son of larnkné'. Rægnald however, was the emphatic victor of this Irish Sea bloodbath and it set him on the road to wider power. However, over the next year or two, Othor's force at Waterford was joined by others, although this force seems to have been defeated by and submitted to Rægnald when the latter 'came against' Waterford in 917. Also, in 917, Sihtric took Dublin in the wake of a victory at a battle at Confey, which ended Leinster's stiff resistance to the returning Scandinavians.

The re-establishment of a descendant of Ivar in Dublin and the rise of another grandson (Rægnald) who was soon to turn his attention firmly towards Northumbria after his recent victories, would bring concern not only to the Irish, but to Edward and his sister. The spectre of a huge corridor of power spanning the trade routes of the Irish

Sea and stretching from Dublin to York, dominated by one Scandinavian dynasty, might become once again a reality in due course. But for now, late into the harvest of 914, not long after the fleet from Brittany had sailed off to Ireland, Æthelflæd turned her attention to her burh-building programme once more, and to the ongoing campaign against the Danes of central England. She marched to Warwick, a settlement on her eastern flank. Just a few miles from the Fosse Way, the Roman road which may have defined Edward's and Æthelflæd's individual campaigning sectors, the Lady of the Mercians began work at yet another Mercian centre, a town which to this day fondly remembers her.

Warwick obviously went on to become an important medieval defensive site, with Warwick Castle being the seat of the Earls of Warwick after the Norman Conquest. Æthelflæd's burh is thought to have been traced in later centuries by the oval-shaped medieval wall circuit of the town which encompasses the summit of the hill overlooking the River Avon. Here, at the southern end, the later castle was built. There are commanding views from this location and they are mainly to the south and east, overlooking the river valley. It would seem to be an ideal site for a burh, although little archaeological evidence has come to light except that some excavations have revealed the possible centre of Æthelflæd's burghal earthworks under Market Street to the north-west of the castle and north of the High Street.[4] Although Æthelflæd will forever be associated with Warwick, the name 'Ethelfleda's Mound' is affectionately given to what was in fact a Norman structure. There is much archaeology to discover regarding Æthelflæd's burh at Warwick,

Fig. 8: *Æthelflæd as depicted on a plaque in Warwick at the end of Jury Street marking the 1,100th anniversary of the foundation of the burh in 2014.*

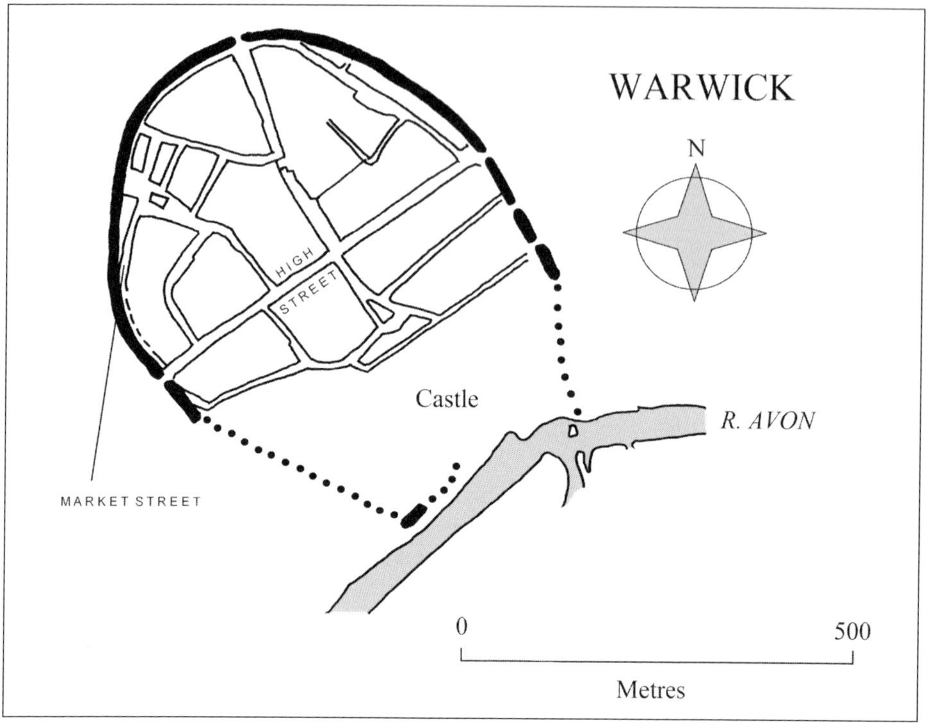

Map 13: *Warwick.*

and when the evidence comes, it is hardly likely to undermine the importance of the place during this phase of the Mercian fortification programme.

As the work continued in the late harvest of 914 at Warwick, just 30 miles to the south-east in Edward's sector, the engineers and craftsmen of the kingdom accompanied their king to Buckingham. The two commanders of the Anglo-Saxons, brother and sister, were now geographically very close to one another. There must have been much communication between the two of them at this time, and meetings between officials from the two allied courts. Even direct communication between Æthelflæd and her brother are not out of the question. Perhaps at this stage, there was a royal revision of the Burghal Hidage (see pages 77–8). Less speculatively, we can be sure that as the work continued at Warwick late in the year, the king's engineers were also busy.

Chapter 12

Buckingham 914 (Edward)

> . . . King Edward went to Buckingham with his army, and stayed there four weeks, and before he went from there made both of the strongholds each side of the river.
>
> *Anglo-Saxon Chronicle* (A)

The move to Buckingham is recorded as taking place 'before Martinmas' (11 November). By the time of its completion, the gap which was exploited by the Danish raid down to Hook Norton in 913, if that is indeed when it had occurred, would be significantly smaller. Buckingham was truly a frontier fortress. Situated on the River Great Ouse less than seven miles from Passenham on Watling Street, it sat precariously close to the border which had once been described further north by the salient of land agreed in the Alfred-Guthrum treaty, but which now had probably collapsed back at least to the old Roman road. In fact, it is suggested that Scandinavian encroachment had taken place since that treaty, which brought the frontier right to the doorstep of Buckingham. Some argue for the existence of an Alfredian burh at Buckingham from at least c. 880. It is an argument linked to the ongoing debate about the date of the Burghal Hidage document in general, this being centred on whether King Alfred's burghal programme as represented in the document (including its Mercian fortresses, of which Buckingham is one) dates from this earlier period, or whether it is an Edwardian revision of the same, dating soon after his own efforts at Buckingham in late 914. The debate is likely to continue, but it does seem highly unlikely that there was no military presence in such an obvious frontier settlement during Alfred's period of resurgence in the 880s. The fact that Edward spent just four weeks at Buckingham building both strongholds either side of the river may indicate that there were previous defences in existence that needed upgrading. Four weeks is around half the time it seems to have taken to construct other burhs. Again, the term used is 'geworhte . . .' (see pages 66 and 147) possibly indicating a stone upgrade. The four-week stay may also indicate that the king had some regional administrative business to deal with in terms of the organization and assessment of the burghal territories as they now stood.

The chronicle's reference to 'both of the strongholds' combined with the paucity of archaeological evidence for a twin burh at Buckingham has led to some suggestions that the southern burh was not finished and instead a new stronghold may have been built several miles to the north-east of Buckingham at Newport Pagnell.[1] Although there is no definitive evidence for this, Buckingham does seem to have been designed to work in coordination with other burhs in the region, these being Oxford, Sashes and Wallingford, with a probable military presence at Aylesbury (as its name may suggest) south of Buckingham. Together, and in conjunction with the burh at London and the twin burhs at Hertford, these places will have covered the south-east Mercian sector up to Watling Street which had been under the control of Edward himself since 911.

With the establishment (or re-establishment) of the burh at Buckingham, came the requisite obligation imposed on the wider territory for the landowners of that area to submit to the king at the fortress. And at this time the king's presence at the burh at Buckingham, along with the furious activity of his army at work there, placed pressure on the Danes of Bedford. The *Anglo-Saxon Chronicle* (A) demonstrates the effects of Edward's fortification programme in this frontier zone: 'And Jarl Thurcytel sought him out as lord, and all of the holds, and almost all the principal men who belonged to Bedford, and also many of those who belonged to Northampton.' We now have a name of one of the Danish war leaders in this sector. For Thurcytel to 'seek out' Edward as lord was a significant step to make. It implies an overwhelming military presence on his doorstep. Also, the possible movement of an English garrison to Newport in late 914, into the salient of land lost between 900 and 914, may not be as far-fetched as it sounds. With deep supply lines and reinforcements available to Edward from Buckingham, Oxford, Aylesbury, London and Hertford, Jarl Thurcytel may well have felt hemmed in by the king and must have therefore persuaded most of his men at Bedford that resistance was futile. To a slightly lesser extent, the Danes at Northampton may have felt a similar pressure if a military presence at Newport had taken (as seems likely) a significant chunk out of their southern territories. As with the other burhs built by Edward and his sister, the mechanics of submission, that is, the reorganization of land-holding and calling-in of allegiance in the newly-acquired burghal territories, played a significant part in establishing royal rule. And so, with Edward's burh at Witham having been built in Essex the previous year and the drive into the collapsed salient of the old Alfred-Guthrum treaty, the king was taking the war deeper into territory previously dominated by Danish lordship. And it would not be too long before his sister would do the same.

Chapter 13

Chirbury and *Weardbyrig* 915 (Æthelflæd)

Þa ðæs oþre geare on ufan midne winter þa æt Cyricbyrig, ⁊ þa æt Weardbyrig . . .

'Then in this, the next year after mid-winter [was built] that stronghold at Chirbury, and then that at *Weardbyrig* . . .'

The *Mercian Register*, or 'Annals of Æthelflæd'.
First part of the entry for 915 (C)

As the winter of 914 inexorably marched into the cold opening weeks of 915, the Lady of the Mercians turned her attention to another border operation, the building of a fortress at Chirbury. The position of Chirbury, situated in a bend of the River Camlad on the Welsh border just two miles east of Offa's Dyke and only around eleven miles from the then capital of Powys at Mathrafal, has led to speculation that Æthelflæd was concerned to secure herself from attack from the Welsh. This is quite conceivable. However, Chirbury (a name which implies a 'fortress or enclosure with a church') is also a little over six miles from Buttington. It is not out of the question that Æthelflæd's main concern in the winter of 914 to 915 was to provide protection from any returning Danes who had used this routeway into Mercia before. Moreover, the fortification at Chirbury (which is now just a small village in the Vale of Montgomery) may well have been an extension or rebuilding of the one which the English used in the run-up to the siege of Buttington a generation earlier, a siege at which the Welsh participated on the English side.

Chirbury is unwilling to yield its tenth-century archaeology to investigators.[1] That said, not a great deal of work has taken place there. It may also be that a red herring has got in the way, too. Just beyond the western edge of the village is a square earthwork situated in what is known as King's Orchard or Castle Field. It encloses only 0.3 hectares and yet it has been excavated in the past (in 1953 and 1958) in the hope it might represent some part – or all – of the Anglo-Saxon fortification. But no evidence of such was found. Its position overlooking the east-west trackway may still be significant, and may be linked in some way to the burh, but equally may date from another age. No evidence of any settlement was found in the excavations, however. A far more likely position for the burh at Chirbury would be a few hundred metres to the east of this feature in Chirbury itself, where the church of St Michael forms the focus of what is now a settlement of a few hundred people. The church is largely of twelfth and thirteenth-century construction, and was once part of the Chirbury Priory founded in 1190, which was thought to be constructed over an Anglo-Saxon minster. Excavations in 2003 around the church found a heavily robbed-out potential Anglo-Saxon foundation wall, but nothing datable or definitive. In Welsh, the village at Chirbury is known as Llanffynhonwen ('church of the white well'), perhaps indicating the importance of a pre-Christian centre for worship.

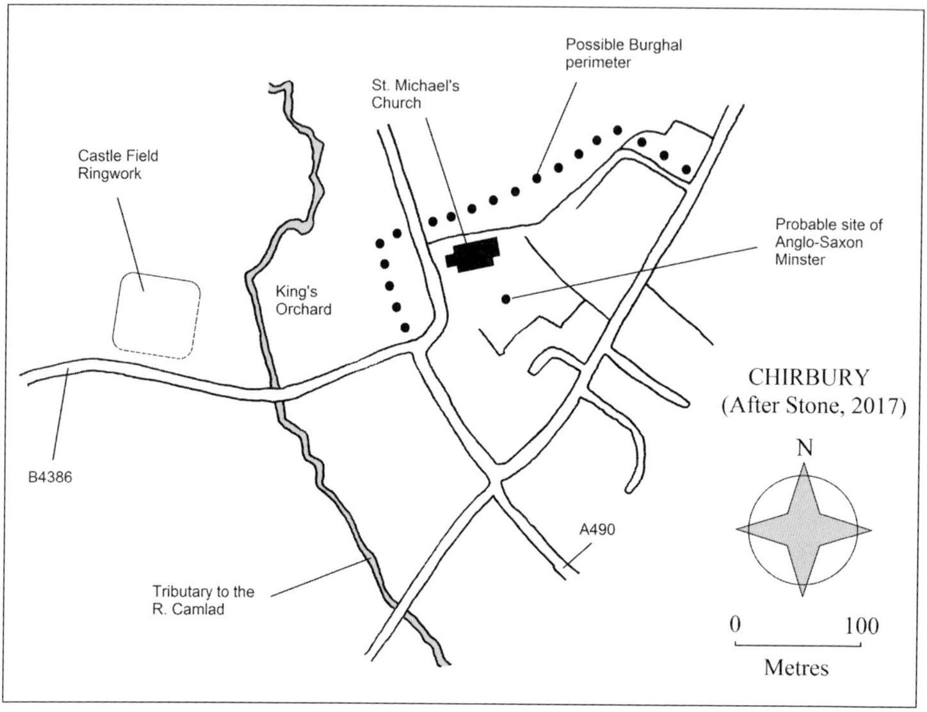

Map 14: *Chirbury. After Stone (2017).*

Quite what archaeological secrets are held beneath the church or in the bumps of the half-forgotten surrounding fields, are yet to be revealed. Map 14 shows the tentative shape of the burh at Chirbury.

If Chirbury is elusive to us, then the fortress Æthelflæd built almost immediately afterwards in 915 at *Weardbyrig* (a name meaning 'watch fortification') has become invisible. And yet, *Weardbyrig* seems to have possessed a mint[2] and was even the focus for brief governmental activity. On 9 September 915, Æthelflæd granted a charter (S 225) to her thegn Eadric, of ten hides of land at *Fernbeorgen* (probably Farnborough in Warwickshire, although some argue for Berkshire). This grant was made whilst the Lady of the Mercians was at *Weardbyrig,* presumably overseeing the final stages of the work on the burh. The charter's surviving text is both thirteenth-century and corrupt, and its date (in the text, as 878), is too early. But if this document preserves any accuracies, then it contains some interesting information. Firstly, Æthelflæd's title is of note. Through the mercy of Christ, she is described as 'gubernacula regens Merciorum', or 'directing the government of the Mercians'. Eadric is given the right to purchase ten hides of land from one Wulflaf, whose great-great grandfather held the original land book from King Offa, which was subsequently destroyed in a fire. If the Farnborough (*Fernbeorgen*) in the grant relates to that in Warwickshire, then this land would be around eight miles east of the Fosse Way and 10 miles to the north-east of the area around Hook Norton which had so recently been ravaged. Alternatively, the Berkshire candidate would be consistent with land granted later in the tenth and again in the eleventh century to another thegn and to

Abingdon Abbey respectively. Wherever the Farnborough in question was (and it is not thought to be the Farnborough in Hampshire), it was clearly a Mercian concern. But it is the witness list in the charter which supplies the most interest.

Sometimes, the issuing of royal or governmental documents from burhs in this period is thought to coincide with the foundation of the burh itself, even though the estates being dealt with in the document may be somewhere else. So the witness list to this particular charter is thought to also represent the Mercian dignitaries present at the foundation of the burh at *Weardbyrig*. Amongst these were three abbots, four bishops, an ealdorman and other senior figures. One of the names of the senior churchmen, some considerable way down the list, is that of 'Egberht *abbas*', an obscure man who may be the same man who appears in our story in the summer after this charter was originally drawn up (see page 132). Another name, although mistakenly copied as indicative of a bishop, is spelled the way we might expect Æthelflæd's daughter to have spelled her name. 'Ælfwyn *ep*. (for *episcopus*)' is thought to represent none other than Ælfwynn, who for some time, seems to have closely followed her mother's itinerant entourage throughout Mercia. Ælfwine (Ælle), the Bishop of Lichfield, is listed separately as the third witness and his name is spelled the male way, so 'Ælfwyn *ep*.' is not a mistake for him. If the identification of Ælfwynn is correct, then she is fittingly listed second behind her mother, an indication of both her rise in importance within the Mercian court and of a shocking drama to come (see pages 177–8).[3]

But where exactly had all these dignitaries gathered? Is there any evidence at all for the location of Æthelflæd's *Weardbyrig*? One suggestion, which places *Weardbyrig* right on the frontier of the war zone in 915, is that the burh was situated at Tutbury on the confluence of the rivers Trent and Dove, where the Roman road from Watling Street (heading north out of Worcester through Roman Letocetum to Derby, passes nearby), and where, just a few miles away, sits the old Mercian royal centre at Repton, recently beset in the 870s by the Great Heathen Army. The claim is made partly on the basis that the word 'tot' (a 'lookout') is interchangeable with 'weard' (a place where a guard or watch is kept).[4] Stafford Ware has also been discovered here, and the implication is certainly that of an Anglo-Saxon military presence, but whether that qualifies the place for a full-scale burghal garrison, is another question. However, this is more evidence than we normally get, although, if Tutbury is in fact *Weardbyrig*, it has yet to physically manifest itself in the form of structures. The proximity of nearby Hanbury, where the church of St Werburgh incorporates two Anglo-Saxon crosses built into the west wall, may also be significant. Should the Tutbury case be the correct one, it would represent the most advanced position of all of Æthelflæd's burhs we have so far considered, being just less that 10 miles from Derby and virtually on top of Repton.

But Tutbury is not the only candidate for *Weardbyrig*. Suggestions for the site being in Nottinghamshire have been put forward in the past, but this is surely far too easterly a location for an English fortress at this stage of the war. In another direction, Warborough in Oxfordshire has been promoted as the location, but again, this seems to be far away from the theatre of the war in 915, and if Warborough *was* a burh, it would likely have been built at the behest of King Edward, in whose military sector it was, and not by the Lady of the Mercians.[5] William Camden, the great antiquarian, had thought *Weardbyrig* to be identical to Wednesbury, and although attractive, this cannot be philologically proven. Another candidate, Whitchurch in Shropshire, already in the running for the unidentified

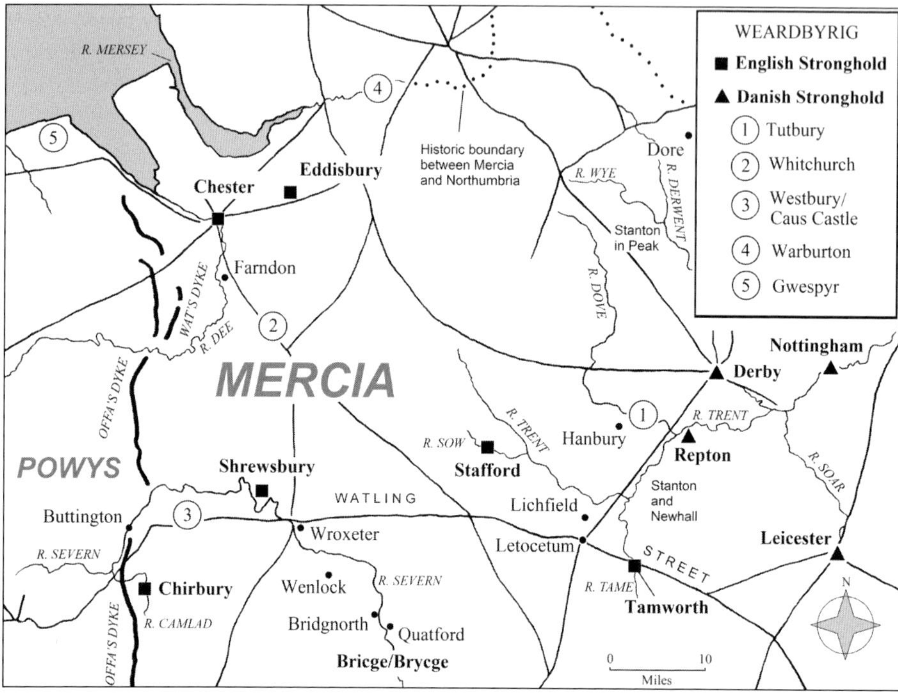

Map 15: *Possible locations for* Weardbyrig.

fort of *Scergeate* (see above, page 85), has also been put forward for *Weardbyrig*. It is not surprising to find the arguments for *Scergeate* coinciding with those for *Weardbyrig*. In fact, another *Weardbyrig* candidate, Westbury in Shropshire midway between Shrewsbury and Buttington, may represent one of a series of forts in this sector of which the *Scergeate* candidates at Shrawardine were numbered (see Map 6, page 86). A case has been made for Caus Castle near Westbury.[6] This Iron Age hill fort was apparently refortified in medieval times, with a high narrow-topped motte and large outer bailey. The inner bailey contained a medieval borough probably created by Roger Corbet in 1198, which by the fourteenth century had fifty-eight burgesses living there. But it is possible that all this later development overlies what is essentially an Anglo-Saxon burh. Over halfway towards Buttington (the site of a great battle in the 890s at which King Alfred's commanders defeated the Danes), the case for Caus Castle is strong. An *Anglo-Saxon Chronicle* entry for 1053 mentions that the 'Welsh men killed a great part of the English people of the guard near Westbury', perhaps indicating an ambush on an English patrol. But the identification of that particular Westbury remains obscure. If *Weardbyrig* was indeed here, it will have worked in conjunction with its neighbour Chirbury as a 'watch-fort' defending ingress from the west, dominating Watling Street (see Map 15).

Two other candidates are to be found, both frequently promoted. The first of these is at Warburton in Greater Manchester. Historically part of Cheshire, it stands on the south side of the River Mersey and its oldest church is dedicated to St Werburgh. However, rather than the name Warburton meaning something like '*Weardbyrig*-ton' as we might hope, it is more likely to indicate that the 'tun' itself is named after a Werburgh (who,

Above: 1. *Alfred presents a royal cloak and sword to his grandson Athelstan, c. 1909 (tempera on card). Mileham, Harry (1873–1957). Private Collection. The ceremony was described as a 'knighting' by William of Malmesbury, who drawing from an 'ancient volume' he had found, says Æthelstan was thereafter brought up at the court of his uncle and aunt Æthelred and Æthelflæd.* (© Harry Mileham. All rights reserved 2021/ Bridgeman Images)

Right: 2. *A depiction of Æthelred and Æthelflæd in the stained glass window in the cloisters at Worcester Cathedral. Designed by James Eadie Reid, Gateshead Stained Glass in 1919.*

3. *A charter of 901 (S 221) drawn up at Shrewsbury, concerning a land exchange and the gift of a gold chalice granted to the community of the church of Much Wenlock. It includes a description of Æthelred and Æthelflæd as honourably 'holding, governing and defending the monarchy of the Mercians'.*

4. *Badbury Rings in Dorset, a prehistoric hill fort, where Edward the Elder camped with his army during the rebellion of his cousin Æthelwold at the beginning of his reign.*

5. *The Cuerdale Hoard. Found in 1840 beside the River Ribble in Lancashire at Cuerdale near Preston. Containing around 8,600 items of silver coins and bullion when found, it weighed some 40kg. Bone pins found with the treasure suggest it may have been bagged up in separate portions. It is thought to date to the opening years of the tenth century and is probably to be seen in the context of the expulsion of the Scandinavians from Ireland in 902.*

Right: 6. *Part of the stained glass west window designed by W.T. Carter Shapland at Chester Cathedral, section showing Æthelflæd, or 'Ethelfleda'. The window, made in 1961, contains seven other notables of the 'Holy Family' including St Werburgh and St Oswald.*

Below: 7. *The north wall of Chester, looking west. Over to the right, beyond the houses and hills, was the Scandinavian enclave founded by Ingimund. Chester would feature heavily in the wars of the first decade of the tenth century.*

8. *Bonewaldesthorne Tower, Chester, with spur wall leading down to the Water Tower. Although this beautiful construction is later medieval in date (first recorded in 1249 and probably rebuilt in the fourteenth century), it carries an unusual name. Tradition suggests that it was named after one of Æthelflæd's warriors.*

9. *Chester Cathedral. Although it became a Benedictine abbey in 1092 and later the cathedral in 1541, an earlier church here was reputed to have been re-dedicated to St Werburgh during Æthelflæd and Ealdorman Æthelred's time.*

10. *A surviving section of Chester's northern Roman wall, showing a line of moulded cornice. The extent of Æthelflæd's refurbishment of Chester's walls is unknown, but is likely to have been along this northern line and along the eastern walls too. The tenth-century upgrade is thought to have extended the defences to the river front.*

11. *Gloucester Cathedral from the site of St Oswald's priory. The* Mercian Register *or 'Annals of Æthelflæd' entry for 909 says 'Here St Oswald's body was brought from Bardney into Mercia'.*

12. *The remains of St Oswald's Priory in Gloucester. Æthelflæd and her husband built a church here initially dedicated to St Peter, then later to Oswald. The founders were almost certainly buried here, in the crypt of the earlier church.*

13. *St Oswald's Priory, Gloucester. Some parts of the wall above the arches incorporate original Anglo-Saxon stonework.*

Above: 14. *Later medieval remains of St Oswald's Priory, Gloucester.*

Left: 15. *St Michael's Tower at The Cross, central Gloucester. This had marked the highest point in the old Roman fort. Æthelflæd and Æthelred greatly restored Gloucester in the late ninth and early tenth centuries, including a planned street layout.*

Left: 16. *Detail from a mural installation depicting Æthelflæd on the Holyhead Road, Wednesbury. Part of the Wednesbury reliefs. Designed by Steve Field. Steel. 2007. Words by local poet Brendan Hawthorne.*

Below: 17. Æthelflæd - Warrior Queen of Tamworth *by Luke Perry. 2018. At an impressive 6m high, 'Æthelflæd' stands on a roundabout outside the railway station. She shows visitors their way into central Tamworth.*

18. *Bedford on the River Great Ouse. A settlement existed on the north side of the river (the rough centre of which is marked by the Church of St Paul) from at least the time of King Offa. In 915 Edward the Elder built a southern burh across the river after receiving the submission of the Bedford Danes.*

19. *All Saints Parish Church, Runcorn. The earliest church on this site may have been dedicated to St Bertelin. Æthelflæd founded the burh and probably the church, in 915.*

Left: 20. *Detail from* Of Heroes and Industry. *One Red Shoe. 2011. Mural at Runcorn High Street. Æthelflæd forms the 'R' of Runcorn.* *See also page 169.*

Below: 21. *Llangorse Lake. The* Mercian Register, *or 'Annals of Æthelflæd' entry for 916 says '. . . Æthelflæd sent an army into Wales and broke down Brecon Mere, and there took the wife of the king as one of thirty-four'.*

Above left: 22. *Replica of the Ethelfloeda drinking fountain statuette, now in the courtyard of Leicester Guildhall. Bequeathed by Edith Gittins (1845–1910) to the County Borough of Leicester, the original fountain with Benjamin Fletcher's statuette was unveiled in Victoria Park in 1922.*

Above right: 23. *Detail of replica of Benjamin Fletcher's Ethelfloeda drinking fountain statuette, now in the courtyard of Leicester Guildhall.*

24. *St Nicholas Church and the Roman remains at Jewry Wall, Leicester. Æthelflæd took Leicester 'peaceably' into her control in 918.*

Above: 25. *Colchester. The Balkerne Gate. The largest surviving Roman gateway in Britain. It is not known how this was utilized during Edward's 917 refurbishment of the burh. The* Anglo-Saxon Chronicle *records that Edward returned to Colchester later the same year and '. . . improved the stronghold and restored it where it was broken down earlier'.*

Left: 26. *Æthelflæd is represented here in a thirteenth-century cartulary (collection of charters) of Abingdon Abbey, draped in a blue mantle and holding a sceptre in her right hand and offering her left hand with palm upwards. The other ruler (top left) is her aunt Æthelswith, who like Æthelflæd herself, once ran the Mercian court.* (© The British Library Board. BL. MS Cotton Claudius B. VI, f. 14)

Above: 27. *Probably originally brightly painted, this grave cover, excavated at St Oswald's Priory in Gloucester, displays artistic parallels with other tenth-century works of art. It is not beyond imagination that it may have once provided the cover to one of either Æthelred or Æthelflæd's tombs.* (© Gloucester Museums Service)

Right: 28. *The Coronation Stone at Kingston in Surrey with the name of Æthelstan on the plinth along with other English kings of the tenth century.*

29. *Kingston Market Place, Surrey. All Saints Church is in the background. The coronation of King Æthelstan, Edward the Elder's first son, took place close to here in 925.*

30. *The Vale of York Hoard, containing over 600 coins and over 60 silver fragments. The cup is decorated with running animals and has close Carolingian parallels. The hoard may have been deposited during a period of unrest around the time of King Æthelstan's descent on York in 927.*

confusingly, is not thought to be the famous saint, but a different Werburgh).[7] This would explain the later eleventh-century spelling of the place name as *Warburgtune*. But if Warburton is to be dismissed as a candidate for *Weardbyrig*, it should be done so with caution. It is in an ideal location for either a burh or, at the very least, a structure consistent with a signalling or lookout provision in the area. Warburton may yet yield its Anglo-Saxon secrets.

It is hardly in doubt that Æthelflæd's north-west frontier was of serious concern to her, particularly after the events in and around Chester in the opening years of the century. If the defence of the mouth of the River Dee was part of this concern, then the argument put forward in recent years for *Weardbyrig* being at Gwespyr (a Welsh form of the word 'Westburh') near Llanasa in Clwyd, not far from Prestatyn, would make some sense.[8] This narrow coastal plain of Flintshire is argued to have been in English hands at the time, and a fort here would certainly do the job of alerting Chester and other burhs of any incursions from Ireland, not to mention any from the Welsh themselves. The argument is partly based on the notion that 'weard' sites are actually linked into the coastal defence system of Anglo-Saxon England, and that the views offered by Gwespyr would fit the bill perfectly. The *Anglo-Saxon Chronicle* entry for the year 1053 (mentioned above) might equally apply to this particular 'Westburh'.

Wherever *Weardbyrig* lay, it was important enough to be minting coins for several decades in the tenth century. The finds of coins from this mint are few and far between, but examples from Ireland, Skye and Chester might just help swing the argument towards Caus Castle near Westbury or to Gwespyr, although such an important identification should hardly rest on such a small sample of evidence. The *Weardbyrig* coins, for example, bear similarities in design to those produced at Gloucester, Hereford and Stafford. One moneyer is also known from the Shrewsbury mint.

What is clear is that Æthelflæd was busier than ever in 915. She had probably finished, or was just finishing, the project at *Weardbyrig* in early September, just days before the celebrations of the Holy Cross commenced. Her next endeavour would be a fortification at Runcorn in Cheshire, which she would turn her attention to before mid-winter. If *Weardbyrig* was at either Gwespyr or Warburton, the move to Runcorn could easily be seen as part of a concerted programme to protect the north-west frontier. If instead it was at Caus Castle, then the move to Runcorn was a new, but still vitally important, strategic departure. But just before she moved her army through Chester and onwards to the pinch point at Runcorn where the Mersey significantly narrows, her brother – if we can rely on the chronology of the *Anglo-Saxon Chronicle* – was gathering his own forces in the south. One year after the submission of Jarl Thurcytel, Edward moved on Bedford.

Chapter 14

Bedford (Edward) and Runcorn 915 (Æthelflæd)

> Here in this year, before Martinmas, King Edward went with his army to Bedford and took possession of the stronghold, and almost all the garrison who had earlier dwelt there turned to him. And he stayed there four weeks, and before he went from there he ordered the stronghold on the south bank of the river to be built.
>
> *Anglo-Saxon Chronicle* (A)

Why had it taken a whole year, from one Martinmas (11 November) to another, for Edward to move on Bedford? We recall that Jarl Thurcytel had 'sought out' Edward as lord at the end of 914 when the king was at Buckingham. But it had not been a total submission. Although Thurcytel and 'all the holds' had sought out Edward's lordship, along with 'almost all the principal men who belonged to Bedford' and also 'many of those who belonged to Northampton', not everyone had done so. The administration of all this must have taken some time, along with protracted negotiations with the remaining forces.

An alternative explanation for the seeming delay in Edward's moving on Bedford might be that he was waiting for his sister to finish her work at *Weardbyrig*, but the taking of Bedford seems not to have been related strategically to Æthelflæd's fort. Whatever the reason, Edward built a second fortress at Bedford, this time on the south side of the River Great Ouse. The twin fort would have the combined advantage of blocking river traffic and of establishing an imposing garrison in a frontier region.

Bedford was not without its significance to the English Mercians. When Edward came here that winter, he may have visited the tomb of King Offa, who had died at nearby Offley and had been brought to a chapel by the river at Bedford in 796. After all, Edward, like his sister, had Mercian blood in his veins. But if he did pay his respects to the famous old king, he would have done so with some plans and diagrams under his arm. Soon, he would be consumed by the immense project facing him, a project which he ordered to be commenced before he left the place. The northern fortress was probably built even earlier than Alfred's time, and was centred roughly on the present-day St Paul's Square. Its perimeter has been debated for years, and was once thought to have been bounded on the north side by St Peter's Church near St Peter's Street, with the church itself acting as a sort of gatehouse. However, this notion has been subsequently revised, leaving St Peter's as an extra-mural church and the perimeter of the northern burh has been reduced a little in size, although its scale is still somewhat impressive (see Map 16).

On the south side, the newer burh was situated either side of modern-day St Mary's Street running south-north. A notable feature which is traditionally attributed to the

Right: 34. *Bedford Market and the Church of St Paul represent the probable centre of the northernmost Anglo-Saxon burh, which may trace its origins all the way back to the time of King Offa, long before Alfred and his son Edward upgraded the settlement's defences.*

Below: 35. *The River Great Ouse at Bedford looking eastwards down river towards Tempsford. This river formed part of the famous boundary between Alfred and Guthrum and was in a frontier zone during the wars of Edward the Elder in 915.*

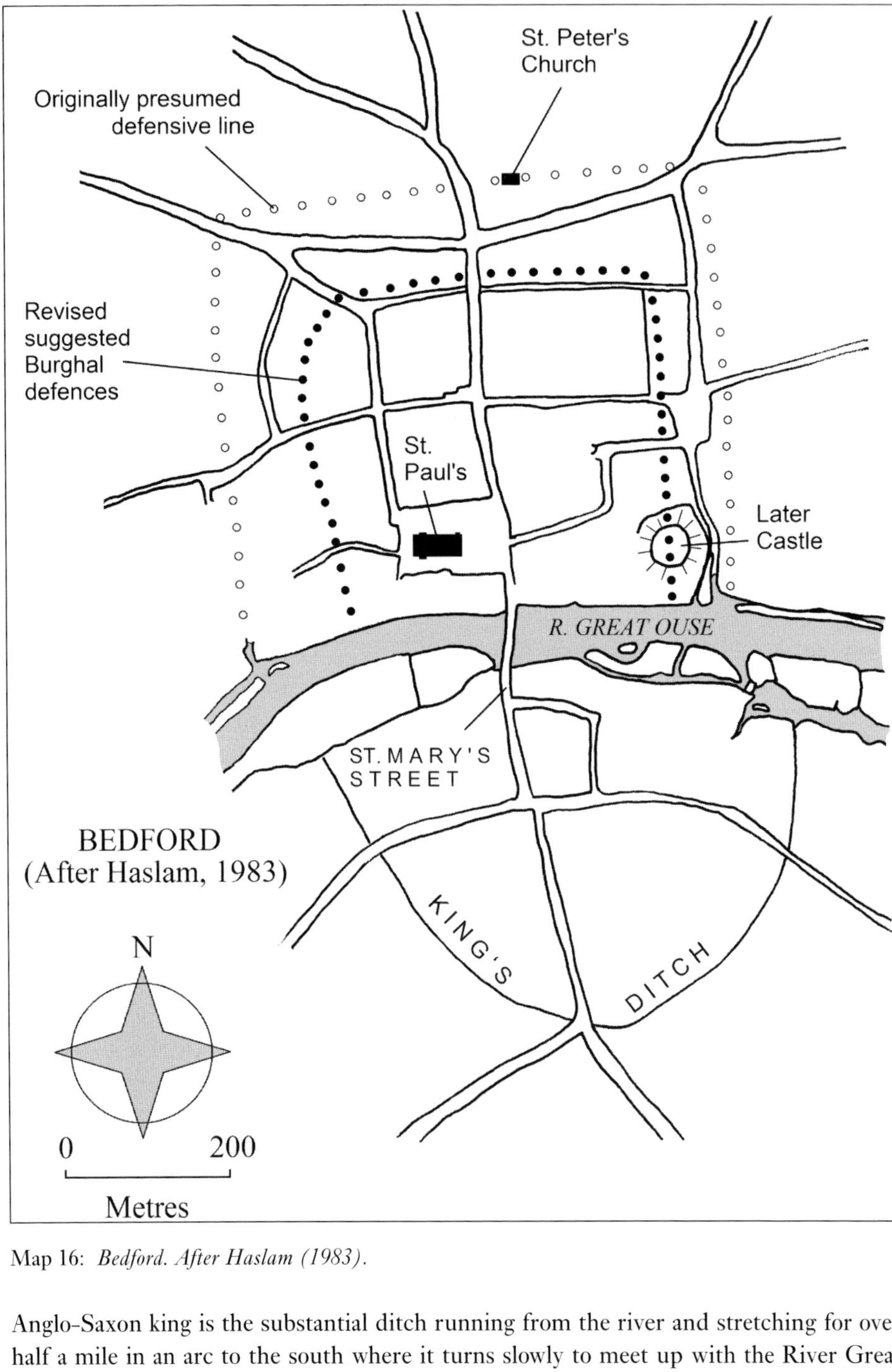

Map 16: *Bedford. After Haslam (1983).*

Anglo-Saxon king is the substantial ditch running from the river and stretching for over half a mile in an arc to the south where it turns slowly to meet up with the River Great Ouse once more. This, called 'The King's Ditch', is still to be seen in some places, and even today, it has a water flow in places. The actual antiquity of the ditch is not certain, although by later medieval times, the building of fish ponds belonging to St John's Hospital, which tapped into the flow of the ditch in the south-east corner of the southern burh, may provide evidence that the ditch predates the medieval era.[1]

The sequence of events at Bedford cannot be known for sure, but the way it is worded in the *Anglo-Saxon Chronicle* suggests that Edward went 'with his army' (*mid fierde*) and 'took possession' (*beget þa burg*) of Bedford. This would presumably have been the earlier Mercian settlement north of the river. Then, almost all, but not quite all, of the garrison (*burgware*) who had earlier dwelt there, 'turned to him' (*cirdon*, from the verb *cirran*, to turn). The king then stayed there for four weeks (like he had done at Buckingham). These four weeks must have been occupied by administrating the submissions, the oath-taking and the geographical reorganization of the burghal district. It would also have involved the planning for the building of the southern burh, which Edward did not order to be commenced until 'before he went out from there'.

Whether Thurcytel was an impediment or an enabler to all this is difficult to say. He is not heard of again until the next summer. The work on the southern burh would have continued in earnest and the presence of a garrison here, will have threatened the few remaining Danes of Northampton and as events would show, those Danes stationed further down the River Great Ouse at Huntingdon. Edward's takeover of Bedford had created something which would be seen again in the years which followed. Culturally, politically and militarily, Bedford was now an Anglo-Danish centre.

Above left: 36. *The entrance to the King's Ditch feature running south of the River Great Ouse at Bedford. This ditch, once ran in a great loop around the southern side of Bedford, and is argued by some to have been constructed at the time Edward the Elder built the southernmost burh at the settlement in 915.*

Above right: 37. *The King's Ditch at Bedford, looking north as it disappears under Bedford Girls' School towards the River Great Ouse.*

38. *View of the probable burh at Runcorn centred on All Saints Church to the right. View taken from the Silver Jubilee Bridge looking east. The Manchester Ship Canal is centre left.*

As Edward was preparing to leave Bedford, his sister was moving her entourage to the Runcorn Gap on the Mersey. The second part of the entry in the *Mercian Register* for the year 915, which mentions the founding of Chirbury and *Weardbyrig* goes on to say:

> . . . ⁊ ðy ilcan gere foran to middan wintra þa æt Rumcofan
> '. . .and in the same year before midwinter [was built] that at Runcorn.'

Here at Runcorn, the river narrows significantly. This stretch of the Mersey is known as the Runcorn Gap. There was once a natural feature on the south side, now partly removed, at a place called Castle Rock. It stood opposite another promontory on the north side of the river at Widnes. Æthelflæd's strategic intentions might seem to be clear enough. The maritime and military traffic between York and Dublin could be easily checked from here. The activities of Rægnald and Sihtric so recently in the Irish Sea will have played a great part in Æthelflæd's planning. It is not inconceivable that after the establishment of the burh at Runcorn, Æthelflæd even brought a small fleet here. Runcorn would also have proved useful in this vital area of north-west Mercia in that it will have worked with Chester and Eddisbury in providing mutually supportive garrisons, each of whom were within a day's march from one another.

39. *The affectionately named Ethelfleda Bridge (opened in 1868), also known as the Runcorn Railway Bridge or Britannia Bridge, showing masonry abutment on the much-truncated Castle Rock. The Silver Jubilee Bridge is in the foreground.*

In Old English, Runcorn was spelled *Rumcofan*. It means 'at the broad [or "roomy"] cover or cove', an allusion to the extraordinary widening of the Mersey creating a lagoon-like opening in this area. Æthelflæd's burh was for a long time widely believed to have been at Castle Rock, but the evidence may be misleading. In the 1860s, engineering works all but obliterated the promontory to improve navigation. Any further evidence here will have been removed once more by the building of the Manchester Ship Canal

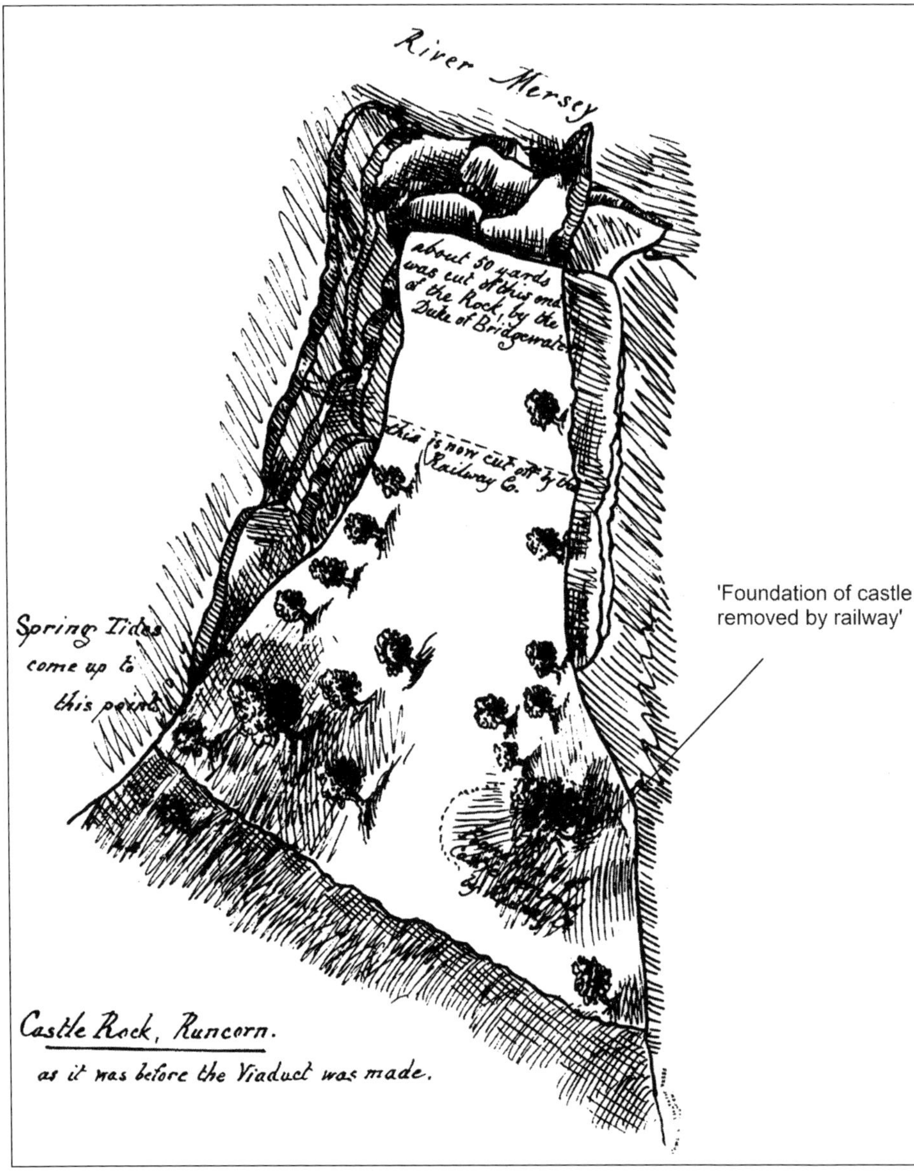

Fig. 9: *The promontory at Castle Rock from Beaumont, W. (1873),* A History of the Castle of Halton and the Priory or Abbey of Norton. *Showing features from J.H. Hanshall's work in his 1823* History of the County Palatine of Chester.

between 1887 and 1894, which passes right through the site. However, a drawing was made before all this work (see Fig. 9), showing that the promontory had been roughly triangular in shape and enclosed a modest area of 1.5 hectares.[2] Cut off from the mainland to the south by a narrow water-filled ditch, this 'fortification' appears to have been bounded by a rampart on all of its sides. But this confined area at Castle Rock may not have been Æthelflæd's burh of Runcorn. For a start, it would be unlike any other of her fortifications, and furthermore, it is too small. It may represent (as some antiquarians suggested) a small and later medieval construction, or it may be only a part of Æthelflæd's building work.

Visitors to the area today are overwhelmed by the sight of the two giant bridges over the Mersey. The modern Silver Jubilee Bridge carries the A533 over the river, but right next to it is a remarkable piece of Victorian engineering. The charmingly-named Queen Ethelfleda Viaduct leads up to the bridge variously also known as Runcorn Railway Bridge, Ethelfleda Bridge or Britannia Bridge. It was opened in 1868 and carried the West Coast main line across the Mersey. One of its massive masonry abutments on the southern shore is thought to stand on the site of the 'burh' at Castle Rock. Perhaps, in an affectionate memorial to the ancient fortification, the stonework of the Victorian structure is castellated. But the now mainly destroyed promontory at Runcorn may only have been a small part of the Æthelflædan burh, if any part at all. As at Stafford, the Lady of the Mercians is thought to have established a church dedicated to the Mercian St Beorhthelm (Bertelin) often identified with the parish church of All Saints Church at Runcorn.[3] This church is several hundred yards to the east of the promontory at Castle Rock. If this church represents the focal point of Æthelflæd's burh, as so many of her churches did, then Castle Rock might be a post-Conquest red-herring, or at best, an extension of the

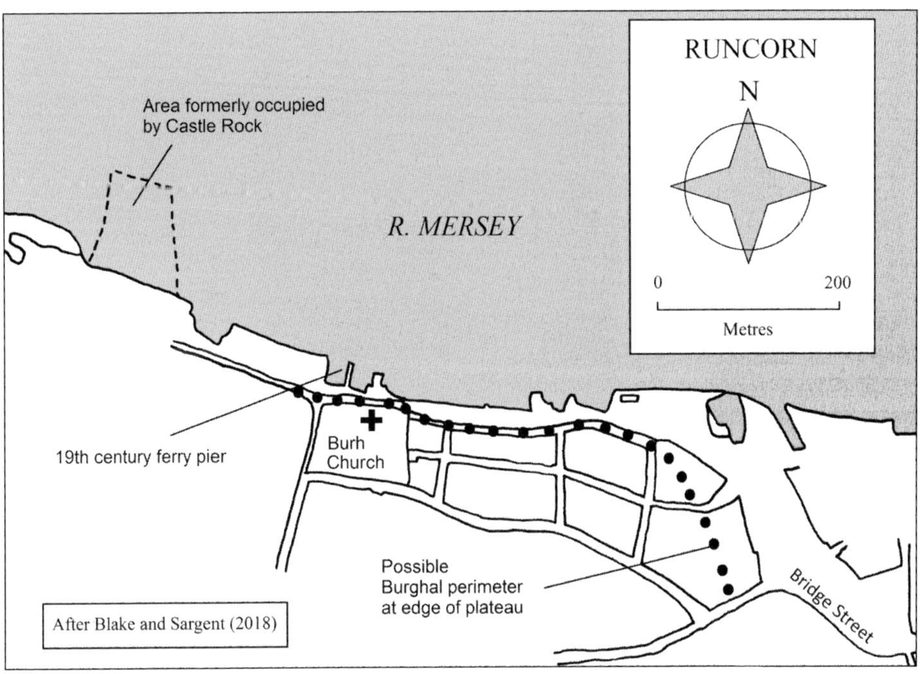

Map 17: *Runcorn. After Blake and Sargent (2018).*

Above and opposite: 40 and 41. *The Queen Ethelfleda Viaduct at Runcorn showing castle-like architectural features.*

Anglo-Saxon burh in its north-west corner, perhaps built as a coastal watchtower. It is now thought that Runcorn, like many of Æthelflæd's other burhs, was built on a plateau, which would make perfect sense if it were located to the east of Castle Rock.[4] The bounds suggested are Bridge Street at the eastern end of the town, the steep inclines to the south providing the southern border of the burh and the land which falls away to the Mersey on the west providing the western edge of the plateau. Runcorn's location and function as a burh may have seemed to be straight forward enough, but here, as in so many other places, the evidence is still somewhat hidden.

What Æthelflæd did during the opening months of 916 is not recorded. The burh building of the previous year may have occupied her administratively. However, for both Æthelflæd and her brother, the year would be another busy one. Edward would continue his drive to the east, and this time, he had some unfinished business in Essex.

Chapter 15

Maldon 916 (Edward)

> Here in this year, before midsummer [24 June], King Edward went to Maldon and built the stronghold and established it before he went from there. And the same year, with the peace and help of King Edward, Jarl Thurcytel went across the sea to the land of the Franks with those men who wanted to follow him.
>
> *Anglo-Saxon Chronicle* (A)

Edward had already been to Maldon in the late spring or early summer of 913 when he had brought an army there to camp whilst he built the burh at Witham. During the first part of 916, it became necessary for the king to come once more to Maldon and this time build a burh right here where the River Chelmer empties into the wide Blackwater Estuary. It is not known for sure what prompted the venture. Maldon's unusual proximity to Witham is a puzzling aspect, but it may have been decided by the king when he was here in 913 that Maldon itself could function very well as a combined burghal garrison and naval base in the next stage of the war. The king would certainly need coastal support if the reduction into submission of East Anglia was any part of his plan.

The burh-building activity at Maldon was certainly as industrious as any of Edward's other burghal projects, and it would soon acquire a mint as well. Some have speculated that the Chelmer itself may have been provided with a barrier near its mouth at this time, although there is admittedly no evidence for it.[1] Although based on limited excavation evidence, it is generally thought that Edward's burh was set back from the waterfront and that its bounds ran on higher ground clockwise from Beeleigh Road, across London Road, south towards St Peter's Hospital and then west and north over London Road and along Dykes Chase. John of Worcester's later recording of 'the unconquered King Eadweard' and his rebuilding of Maldon (attributed by John to 917) states that the king did not leave there 'until he had strengthened it with a garrison'. But this may be John of Worcester's take on the *Anglo-Saxon Chronicle*'s assertion that Edward 'established it before he went from there'.

At some stage in the year of 916, Jarl Thurcytel seems to have gone abroad. The circumstances are not known for sure, but the jarl gathered those of his men who wished to follow him and went to the land of the Franks. The presumably small band of men sailed with the king's help to Francia and may well have participated in the Danish settlement of this area of northern France in ancient Neustria, which had become the patrimony of the first Scandinavian counts of Rouen. In England, however, the departure of Thurcytel can only have left Edward stronger in Bedford and its dependant areas. Whether Thurcytel had been coerced into leaving due to some impropriety towards the king or simply chose to lead his men into a new adventure in a land where there was more to be won for an ambitious warlord is a matter of pure speculation.

Other Danish commanders in places such as Huntingdon, Cambridge, Colchester, Northampton and Leicester must have felt it coming, a feeling of inexorable pressure against their communities. To the north of them, their allied warlords at Derby, Stamford, Nottingham and Lincoln must have been anxious too. A line of English fortresses had now sprung up over the last five years, from Maldon in the east to the concentration of strongholds around the base of the Wirral peninsula and on the Mersey Estuary. The flanks of the kingdom of the Anglo-Saxons were to some extent secured. Moreover, Æthelflæd's fortresses on the north-west frontier – on the face of it a defensive programme – may even have begun to look ominously to the Danes like a springboard for an offensive against which they would struggle to defend themselves without support from one another. This period of fortress building by the brother and sister partnership is sometimes referred to as the 're-conquest' of the 'Danelaw'. It is a paradigm with stubborn characteristics. However, it was neither a 're-conquest', nor was it exclusively in the 'Danelaw' (which appears to have been a slightly later concept). What Edward and Æthelflæd were undertaking was a *conquest* of territory in its own right. Land was falling into their hands which had never been part of their immediate family's domains, although they could both lay philosophical claims to it by distant lineage. Their methods were very similar: build a burh, organize or reorganize the territories dependent upon it, and call in submission from those around. For her part, Æthelflæd's process of legitimizing her power was to build churches dedicated to saints with strong Mercian or familial connections at the heart of her burhs, almost as spiritual landmarks displaying divine approval. The two commanders do not necessarily have to have seen eye-to-eye over every detail of policy in a complex political world in which Mercian and West Saxon empathies still jarred with one another, but we should be clear about one thing. This was always going to be a family affair. That is how Anglo-Saxon politics worked.

For Edward and Æthelflæd, any switch to a more overt offensive, after so many years of consolidation, would depend upon timing. And in the middle of 916, as Edward was heading out towards Maldon, he might have expected his sister to be making her plans for the strategic switch to the offensive in her sector of the kingdom. No doubt Æthelflæd's plans were well advanced in this respect. However, an event occurred in Wales which may have paused the grand plan for a short while. It was an event recorded by the *Mercian Register* in an unusually detailed entry in which the author clearly expresses some revulsion, and it reveals just how capable and resolute a leader the Lady of the Mercians could be.

The Coinage of Edward the Elder

Rarely are the minting places of Edward's coins shown, although some early pennies from Bath (whose reeve is mentioned in the *Anglo-Saxon Chronicle* as passing away in 905) are known bearing the name of the town. However, the majority of Edward's coins are of the 'Two Line' type brought in by Alfred in the later years of his reign. From about 910 a rare type appears from London and Canterbury with a rose design on the obverse.

During the central years of Edward's reign a series of coins appear with ornamental designs on the reverse (see Fig. 10). Some of the moneyers whose names appear on these issues are known from later mint-signed coins struck after Edward's reign. They appear from around 910 and last until around 920 when they are replaced once more by the 'Two Line' reverse which now incorporated a linear circle between the inscription and the beaded edge. It can be deduced that these ornamental reverse types emanated from western Mercia, in the patrimony of Æthelflæd. Chester, Shrewsbury, Hereford and Gloucester feature. Although neither the Lady of the Mercians nor her late husband appear to have struck coins in their own name, the occurrence of these ornamental types, although struck in Edward's name, may represent his sister's

Fig. 10 (a): *Obverse and (b) reverse of silver penny of Edward the Elder, 'Two Line' type. Moneyer EADMVND.*

10 (c): *Silver penny (reverse) of Edward the Elder, Church Tower type. North-west mint, probably Chester, c. 910–15.*

10 (d): *Silver penny (reverse) of Edward the Elder, 'Hand of Providence' type. Moneyer AÐULF. Middle period, West Mercian mint.*

desire to express her own (and specifically Mercian) influence over coinage under her control. Designs include a tower or reliquary (associated with Chester); a church; a 'Hand of Providence' (Shrewsbury); flowers and floral motifs (with fronds curved in the shape of an 'M'), a bird; and two large rosettes.

By the end of Edward's reign, the king appears to have had moneyers striking for him at Bath, Canterbury, Chester, Chichester, Derby, Exeter, Hereford, London, Oxford, Shaftesbury, Shrewsbury, Southampton, Stafford, Wallingford, Wareham and Winchester. Although there are likely to have been other burhs minting for Edward, this list of burhs with active moneyers (including their dependant territories) is arguably roughly geographically consistent with bounds of Edward's 'kingdom of the Anglo-Saxons' as it stood towards the end of his reign. East Anglia (at least in Norfolk), although with a good degree of imitative coins, is not thought to have been directly under Edward's monetary control, although this does not preclude any military or political alliances the East Anglian Danes may have made with the king.[2]

PART THREE

THE OFFENSIVE OF 917–918

Chapter 16

Æthelflæd and the Welsh

Her wæs Ecgbriht abbud unscyldig ofslegen foran to middan sumera on .xvi. Kł. Iuł. – þy ilcan dæge wæs Sancte Ciricius tid þæs ðroweres – mid his geferum. ⁊ ðæs embe þreo niht sende Æþelflæd fyrde on Wealas ⁊ abræc Brecenanmere ⁊ þær genam ðæs cinges wif feower ⁊ ðritiga sume.

'Here before midsummer, on 16 June, Abbot Ecgberht, guiltless, was killed with his companions. The same day it was the festival of St Cyricus the martyr. And three days later Æthelflæd sent an army into Wales and broke down Brecon Mere, and there took the wife of the king as one of thirty-four.'

The *Mercian Register*, or 'Annals of Æthelflæd'. Entry for 916 (C)

The Lady of the Mercians can hardly be accused of hesitation. The fact that it took just a matter of days and not weeks to organize a punitive expedition against Brycheiniog hints strongly at the force being drawn from a battle-ready garrison already established at a Mercian burh or burhs. Hereford of course lends itself as an obvious, though not necessarily exclusive, candidate.

The journey from Hereford to Llangorse Lake, where the king of Brycheiniog had his crannog, is a little under 30 miles as the crow flies. Today, it is one of the more pleasant trips anyone could take across the countryside bordering England and Wales, featuring a verdant carpet of fertile fields and forests surrounding the undulating hills. Æthelflæd's men may have taken the route out of Hereford to the north and followed the Roman road which hugs the banks of the Wye, or alternatively they may have taken an early southerly turn off this road, crossed the Wye and headed through Ergyng, picking up additional warriors to lead them into Wales along the Usk valley and round the southern side of Llangorse Lake. It is also possible the River Lynfi, a tributary of the Wye may have been used amphibiously. The English army commanded by Æthelflæd made this journey just three days after the shocking news of the murder of Abbot Ecgberht and his men. The mood would have been a sombre one amongst the warriors in the Mercian army.

Nobody today quite knows the identity of this Ecgberht, although he was clearly important to Æthelflæd. He may have been the same churchman who witnessed the charter granted at *Weardbyrig* (S 225, for which see above, page 112) and could therefore have been associated with an institution greatly favoured by Æthelflæd. If so, he may have been part of Æthelflæd's wider household and this would explain the nature of her reaction. Bonds of friendship and loyalty within any ruler's household were of great importance, but seem to have been particularly so for Æthelflæd. Ecgberht, or *Ecgbriht* as he is spelled in the *Mercian Register*, may have been travelling through South Wales when he was set upon and killed, unless his assailants had penetrated into England. He may even have been acting as a Mercian envoy on a mission whose purpose is now long lost. If so, he would have been travelling under the protection of the Lady of the Mercians. The king of Brycheiniog, a man who would probably have been duty-bound to protect members of Æthelflæd's household as they came through his kingdom, may well have made a fateful error either by act or omission regarding the slaying of Ecgberht. At this time it is probable that Brycheiniog, unlike Gwent, was subject to Æthelflæd.[1] The perpetrators of the crime against Ecgberht are not identified, nor indeed is the motive. The implication might be that they were pagans, since the 'guiltless' abbot is arguably being portrayed as a martyr. This may be why the chronicle reminds us that it was a feast day when he was slain. The reaction from Æthelflæd, however, was telling.

By 916, the situation in Wales was almost unrecognizable from the arrangement Asser reports in the time of Alfred, around 893. All the Welsh bar the combined south-east kingdoms of Glywysing and Gwent had at some stage turned to Mercia in return for military assistance in what had by now become a campaign of internal conquest in Wales represented by the ambitions of the sons of Rhodri, referred to collectively as the *Merfynion* (named after Merfyn Frych, the dynasty's ninth-century founder). The identity of the unfortunate king of Brycheiniog is uncertain, but he is not thought to have been of the *Merfynion*. A later account (that of Caradoc of Llancarvan) even has him as a Dane marrying into Welsh royalty. In fact, the kings of Brycheiniog are thought to have had at least a partially Irish ancestry. A certain Tewdwr is recorded in the 930s and this may be the king in question, or possibly his father, a man known in tradition to have the name Griffi ap Elise

The *Mercian Register* records 16 June as the festival day of St Cyricus the Martyr. This saint is relatively obscure, but his story must have been of significance to the compiler of the annal, and to Æthelflæd herself. Cyricus was a child saint who was reputedly prayed to for the welfare of the family and for children's recovery from illnesses. For this reason alone, there may be a significance for Æthelflæd. Her experiences in that regard had arguably been traumatic. Cyricus's mother was called Julitta. Their story emanates from Tarsus in the year 304. During a period of Christian persecution, Julitta had fled to Tarsus with her three-year-old son, only to fall into the hands of the governor there. During the torturing of his mother who refused to worship idols, the boy scratched the governor's face and proclaimed his Christianity. He was then killed when he was hurled to the floor. His mother rejoiced at the death of her son, since he had earned his martyrdom before her. Then, she was duly martyred too. Saint Cyricus was popular in France in the early medieval period, partly because some relics were brought back from Antioch by a fourth-century bishop of Auxerre. Also, the Emperor Charlemagne had apparently dreamed he was saved by the child saint from being killed by a wild boar during a hunt. The child vowed to save the emperor if he would clothe his naked body. The saint was less popular in England, though his feast day did feature in tenth-century Welsh law. The mention of St Cyricus in the *Mercian Register* certainly serves to highlight the indignation of the author of the annals.

The implication of the account in the *Mercian Register* is that Æthelflæd took her army on the campaign in person. Although it says that she 'sent' the force, the wording which follows this section shows that it was Æthelflæd herself who 'broke down' Brecon Mere. When the army arrived at Llangorse Lake, they would have been met with an extraordinary sight. A wooden dwelling much like those from many centuries before, rising in the swirling Celtic mist from a glass-like watery setting. An artificial crannog had been built on the northern part of the lake, with a causeway leading from the shore to the island. On this island in the lake stood just a few halls and ancillary buildings. The remains of the island can still be seen today. Archaeological work has established that the oak timbers for the palisade were felled between 889 and 893 and it is generally thought that this structure (a type of feature more common in Ireland) was built by the king of Brycheiniog in response to the Scandinavian presence at Quatford, when the Danes were known to have ravaged the Welsh countryside from their base there. However, it is equally likely that the defensive island was built in response to aggression from the rising power of the *Merfynion* or even from Mercia.

This small fortification, constructed on an island of brushwood and sandstone boulders, is the only crannog in Wales. Measuring just 40m by 30m, it was a D-shaped structure with its straight side parallel to the shore and a causeway just 3m wide which linked the island to the shore some 50m away. The archaeological work has uncovered evidence for burning at one stage in the site's history and it is tempting to link this with Æthelflæd's attack. Also discovered amid the charred remains was a burnt lump of textile which experts have managed to show was once a fine linen and silk item displaying birds surrounded by vines. It may even have been owned by the Welsh queen herself.[2]

Whether Æthelflæd brought her own boats, or got her warriors to shoot fire-arrows from the shore, or simply stormed the causeway by surprise, is not known. Nor is the reason for the Welsh king's absence. However, the taking of his wife as one of a curiously specific 'thirty-four' people, sent out a strong message. The Lady of the Mercians took the role of lordship no less seriously than her husband, brother or her late father. Any attack on her household would be met with retaliation on the household of the perpetrator. This punitive strike had been devised to destroy the very essence of Æthelflæd's enemy: his household. By doing it so effectively, she had also showed her own household what their loyalty meant to her.[3]

One can only imagine the humiliation felt by the Welsh king when he gazed upon the burning remains of the crannog. We do not know what happened to the prisoners. We might assume that a subsequent re-submission of Brycheiniog soon took place. If so, it would have been a very public event. And this episode had shown something else, too. Amid all the distraction and strife caused by the wars with the Danes, the ruler of Mercia had shown that she could successfully reinforce Mercian hegemony over a client kingdom in Wales. But there were others in Britain who might equally have been nervous. To any Dane living in England who learnt of the events on a distant Celtic lake, Æthelflæd had, at the very least, shown she could take an army beyond the borders of her country and terrify her enemies.

Chapter 17

Spring and Summer 917

The events of the opening months of the war of 917 are not recorded. That year, Easter fell on 13 April. Sometime before this, says the (A) version of the *Anglo-Saxon Chronicle*, King Edward ordered a stronghold to be built at Towcester. This was an old Roman fortress on the Tove, which centuries earlier had gone by the name of Lactodurum. Recalling its Roman function, the English simply called it *Tofeceastre*, the 'castle, or fortification, on the Tove'. The place lay on top of Watling Street and the refortification of the ancient fort will have directly threatened the Danes at Northampton just eight miles to the north-east. The road junction here had Watling Street going off to the south-east, while another Roman road stretched south towards Oxford and Dorchester. Arguably, Towcester was the last piece of the jigsaw in this area for the brother-and-sister partnership. The ability of the Danish lords to penetrate south of Watling Street was being severely challenged, and it seems their own leadership knew it. This region would now become the very epicentre of the war and the pace of events dramatically quickened.

Edward's men must have worked furiously on Towcester's refurbishment, because the chronicler records that at Rogationtide another burh was built at a place called *Wigingamere.* Rogationtide was a series of prayers, fasting and processions which included the observation of the Litany of Saints. It occurred over a four-day period leading up to Ascension, 40 days after Easter. This means that Towcester was probably operational in around two months. The location of *Wigingamere* however, has been much discussed. Candidates range from an unlikely (though interestingly sited) Wigmore in Herefordshire (see Map 5, p. 67), situated deep in Æthelflæd's territory on the Roman road out of Hereford to Wroxeter, to Wigmore Pond north of Olmstead Green in Cambridgeshire, perhaps too far into enemy territory at this stage of the war to be realistically considered.

The likelihood is that Edward's burh of *Wigingamere* was situated well within his own sector (see Map 18) and not too far from the freshly-installed garrison at Towcester, who were hastily exchanging their adzes and shovels for swords and spears as their comrades from another command headed out to *Wigingamere*.

There are two principal candidates.[1] The first of these is perhaps the favourite. It is at Old Linslade, a little to the north of Leighton Buzzard very close to Tiddingford, where the treaty of 906 was agreed. This location, just two miles to the north-east of Wing, would have placed the fortification in a bend of the River Ouzel on its western bank. Here, it would be equidistant from Hertford and Towcester. The site, it is argued, would have been near a region of marsh from which the name *Wigingamere* could derive. But there is difficulty here, as in many of the unidentified forts of this period. Nearby Wing itself and Wingrave may also be good candidates. But here at Old Linslade, the name of *Wigingamere* is thought to have come from the old tribal boundary between the Yttingas and Wigingas, with the *(ge)mære* element meaning a boundary.

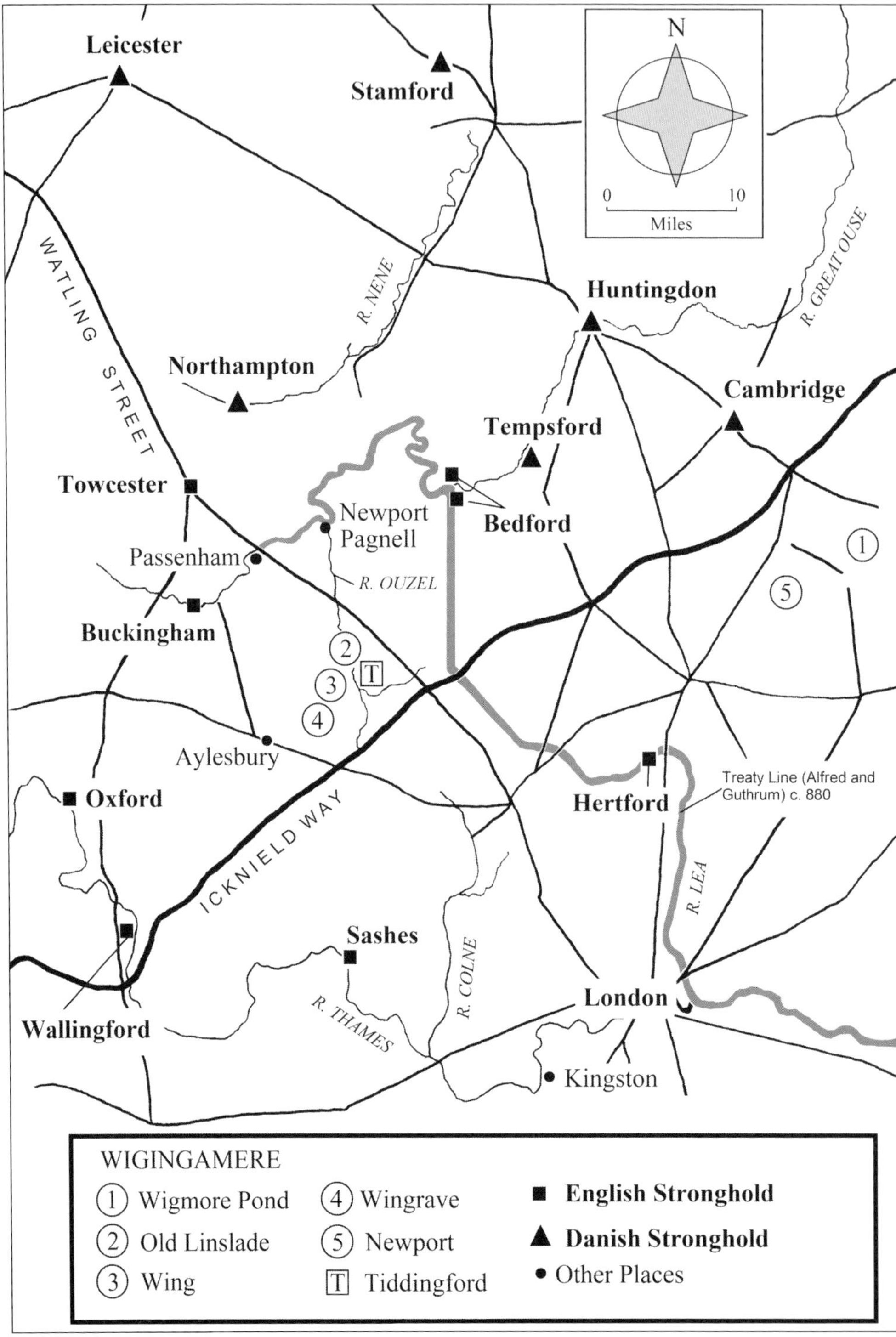

Map 18: *Possible candidates for Edward's burh at* Wigingamere.

Newport in northern Essex has also been given as a potential candidate. This location is only a few miles south of Saffron Walden and is on the River Cam. The Wicken Water is just half a mile to the west and this may also have given *Wigingamere* its name. But for the war to be thrust this deep into Danish territory at this stage is again problematic, although it is certainly the case that by now, events were moving fast.

Somewhere between midsummer (24 June) and Lammas (1 August), although the chronicler places Lammas before midsummer in his sentence the Danes 'broke the peace' (an indication that there may have been yet another treaty after the recent spate of burh building). This seems to have been a direct consequence of the recent pressure. The armies of Northampton, Leicester and 'north of there' marched to Towcester, says the chronicler. They 'thought that they would be able to break it down', says the chronicler. This was an important moment. There are only rare glimpses of coordination between the various Scandinavian-dominated power groups north of Watling Street, but here we have a clear example of what must have been exactly that. It may be that the Danes were taking advantage of Edward's field force having left the area after installing a garrison at Towcester. But it is the phrase 'north of there' which potentially holds the key. A combined army from Northampton and Leicester would have been large, despite some of the men of Northampton having already gone over to Edward when the king was at Buckingham. But for the Danes to have to drawn men from the lands dependent upon any part or all of Derby, Nottingham or Stamford might be implied by the phrase. If so, we can imagine the force which came to Towcester and set up camp outside the new fortress was of a reasonable size. Quite what arrangements its leaders had made for the defence of their respective home fortifications that summer is not known.

But the Danes were ill-equipped for a protracted siege, and they were impatient, too. They tried in vain all day to break Towcester, but Edward's refurbished walls held firm and the garrison successfully withstood the attackers until it received reinforcements. The Danes could see that their actions had drawn English reinforcements to the burh. What then followed was a switch in strategy from the Danish commanders. They took to night raids in small bands, pouncing on unsuspecting men and seizing livestock and other property. They penetrated the region between Bern Wood and the probable English fortification at Aylesbury. The reason for the change in approach may have been both political and strategic. Bern Wood was a forest stretching across Buckinghamshire into Oxfordshire almost as far as Aylesbury. The land here apparently belonged to the king. It was roughly 35 miles south of Watling Street and the raids may have been designed to demonstrate that the Danes could still reach well into Edward's kingdom if they wished. But there is something else. Nothing is mentioned as to why the garrisons at Oxford, Buckingham and Wigingamere did not venture out to hunt down the raiders. Perhaps they did. Despite all the suffering caused, the combined army of Leicester and Northampton and those brought from further north failed in their primary goal of neutralizing Towcester, but the raid into the south may have been a screen for the next stage of Danish movement.

The Leicester-Northampton army was not the only one operating in the south Midlands that summer, by any means. Whilst parts of this group were raiding after their failed attempt on Towcester, another army 'at the same time' drawn from Huntingdon and East Anglia came to Tempsford at the confluence of the Ivel and the Ouse (see Map 19a).

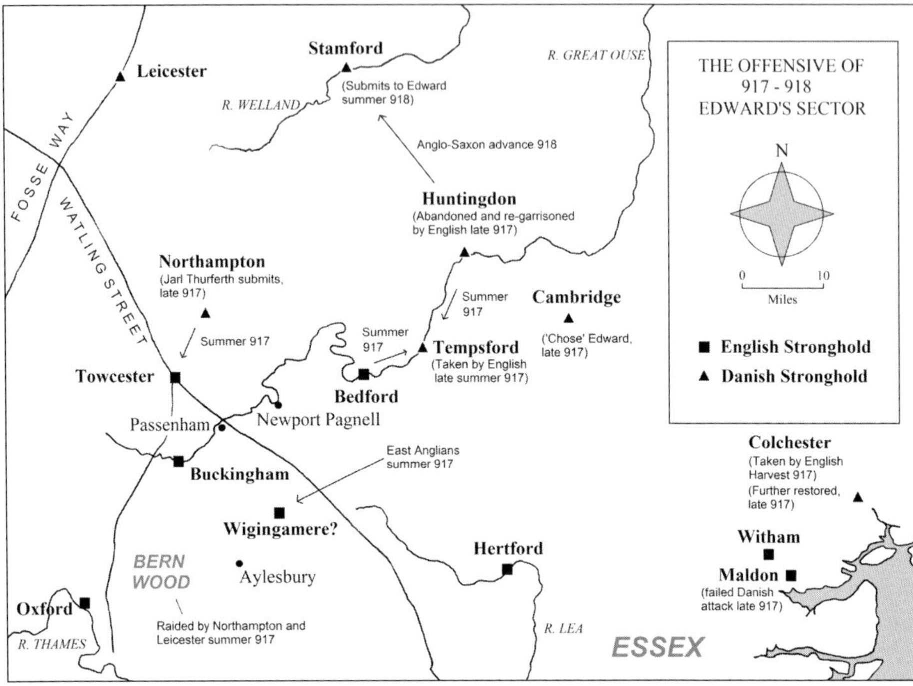

Above and below: Map 19: *The offensive of 917–18.*
a) *Edward's sector.*
b) *Æthelflæd's sector.*

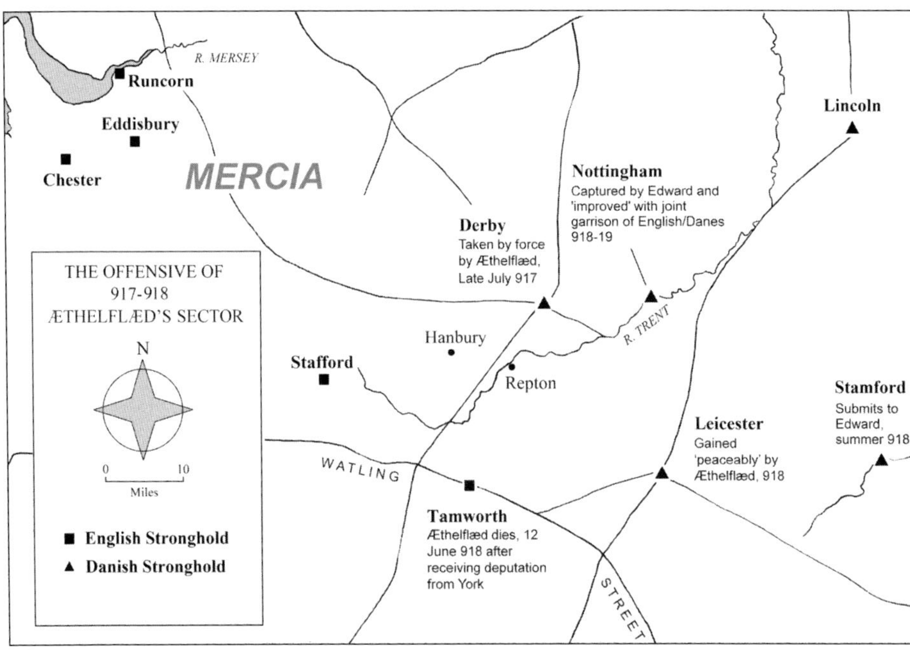

The Huntingdon contingent had even abandoned their fortification at home and brought their entire community forward, nearer to the front line. The Danish concern here must have been the obvious threat created by Edward's combined Anglo-Danish army at Bedford, just 10 miles upstream along the River Great Ouse, and also a desire to 'recover' (a term used by John of Worcester) local lands lost to the Anglo-Saxon king.

Nothing is known of the location of the Danish fort at Tempsford, although just four miles upstream at Willington are mysterious earthworks taken by one early twentieth-century antiquarian to be indicative of a riverine camp, complete with inner and outer harbours built in the Scandinavian fashion. Later that same century, limited excavations came to no firm conclusion, except to give rise to speculation that the site may in fact have been a later medieval construct. For some time, however people believed the Tempsford site to be at Gannock's Castle, a site which may be later medieval in date and small in size. However, it is felt that this site is in the right area, being close to the confluence of the two rivers.[2] The Huntingdon-East Anglian army now at Tempsford set its sights on attacking Bedford. The chronicler says they 'got at' Bedford but a sortie by the garrison from Bedford soundly defeated the Danes, killing 'a good part of them'. It is not known who these Bedford men were, but it is likely that they were a combined force of Englishmen and those Danes who stayed behind when Jarl Thurcytel had departed (see page 110). The survivors from this battle seem to have made it back to Tempsford, which for the time being would continue to play a part in the war.

'Then yet again after that', says the chronicler, another army was raised against the English. This time, it was drawn from East Anglia and parts of Mercia (although John of Worcester curiously has Essex, perhaps implying that part of the force was drawn from Danish occupied Colchester). This army – the third raised in the summer – went to the new fortification at *Wigingamere*. They, like their comrades at Towcester, were not successful in breaking it down. The garrison withstood a short siege and the Danes contented themselves with seizing cattle in the vicinity before they went away. Had this third 'army group' united with those at Tempsford earlier, then the outcome of this stage of the war may have been different, unless of course some of its East Anglians were the same men who had participated in the failed attack on the men of Bedford. And so it would appear that despite there being good evidence for cooperation amongst the different Danish-led groups in the early part of the campaign, there was little coordination between the three groups themselves subsequently. This meant that their separate attacks on parts of Edward's defensive infrastructure were each too weak to be individually successful. Moreover, the system of fyrd rotation and regional garrisons employed by Edward and his sister across the wider kingdom meant that any attempt to besiege English forces would soon be met by a relief force, as happened at Towcester and most likely at *Wigingamere*, too.

It was time for Edward to launch a counter-offensive. As the summer wore on, his target was the second of the three Danish groups, that at Tempsford. Defeated recently by the men of Bedford, this force may well have been numerically weak. It was, however, ensconced behind the walls of the Tempsford fortification. The force which took on the job of attacking Tempsford was drawn from 'the nearest strongholds' and was described as 'a great tribe' gathering in Edward's domain. Presumably, these garrisons were in south-east Mercia under Edward's direct command such as Bedford, Buckingham, Towcester and *Wigingamere*. They may also have included Aylesbury and Newport Pagnell, if the arguments for burhs here are accepted. The wording of the chronicle does not imply that Edward led the force in person, however, and it may be that the drive against Tempsford was led by one of Edward's sub-commanders.

Tempsford was attacked by the large English force. They were able to persevere against it, probably because no relieving force came to its aid. The English are described as fighting against the fortification 'until they broke it down'. Once they had broken into it, they killed those who put up resistance and seized the others. The reported casualty list is interesting. We learn of some more Danish names. Among the dead behind the walls of Tempsford were a 'king' (perhaps the king of East Anglia), and 'Jarl Toglos, and his son, and Jarl Manna and his brother'. It is possible that Toglos and Manna had initially been at Huntingdon before the move to Tempsford. As for the identity of the dead king, some have sought to link him to the mysterious Guthrum II,[3] a supposed successor to King Eohric of East Anglia. However, the existence, let alone the role of this character is doubted by some. The impact of the victory at Tempsford may have been very significant. The Anglo-Saxon king could look now at pushing forward towards the abandoned Huntingdon encampment and to the edge of the Fens. By doing this, the king would secure a strategic victory. He would drive a wedge between the two other 'army groups'. On the west side of the wedge were still the Leicester-Northampton group and on the east side were the third army group of the year, based in East Anglia and quite probably partly operating out of Colchester. John of Worcester indicates that this Tempsford episode had been a turning point. He too, follows the chronicle in listing the casualties, and like the chronicler, emphasizes the seizure of prisoners too. But he also says that from now on 'the English power increased from day to day'. The Danish move from Huntington to Tempsford had failed.

Around the time that the assault on Tempsford was being carried out in Edward's sector, some 70 miles to the north-west, Æthelflæd was preparing to exploit the distraction of the lords of northern and central Mercia who may have sent men to assist with the Leicester-Northampton group who had attacked Towcester earlier in the summer. At long last, the Lady of the Mercians was moving her armies into the territories which had been held by Danes for nearly two generations. As her brother drove up the Tempsford-Huntingdon axis in south-east and central Mercia, Æthelflæd brought an army to Derby, one of the five (and most westerly) of the great Danish boroughs to the north of Watling Street. But she would soon discover that some things come with a price.

Chapter 18

Derby, Late July 917

Her Æþelflæd Myrcna hlæfdige, Gode fultumgendum foran to Hlæfmæssan begeat þa burh mid eallum þam ðe þærto hyrde þe ys haten Deoraby. þær wæron eac ofslegene hyre þegna feower ðe hire besorge wæron binnan þam gatum.

'Here before Lammas, God Helping, Æthelflæd, Lady of the Mercians, took possession of the stronghold which is called Derby, together with all that belonged to it; also four of her thegns, who were dear to her, were killed there inside the gates.'

The *Mercian Register*, or 'Annals of Æthelflæd'. Entry for 917 (C)

Derby is in fact, a Danish word. '*Djura-by*' may have meant something like 'deer village', or perhaps more prosaically 'village on the Derwent'. In Old English, it seems to have taken the form 'Deoraby'. But the place once had the different name of Northworthy. This had been the place where King Alfred's loyal Berkshire Ealdorman Æthelwulf, who had fought so bravely for Alfred before losing his own life, was taken for burial in 871 after the disastrous battle at Reading in a year of battles against the Great Heathen Army which had nearly extinguished England's last remaining Anglo-Saxon kingdom.

In 917, Derby was a very different place than it had been in 871. The abandoned Roman settlement of *Derventio* stood at the junction of five major Roman roads here in the very centre of old northern Mercia. Today, this place is called Little Chester and is just to the north of the modern city of Derby. Many people argue that the Danes must have come here, to the east bank of the Derwent, and restored the place. Opposite it, an earlier fort had stood on the other bank, but had long been abandoned. The Romans returned to the area on a number of occasions and occupied it several times. In the third century, *Derventio* acquired stone walls and gates, and also its status as a small urban settlement but was abandoned before the end of the century. It may have been that these structures still stood when the Danes arrived in the late ninth century.[1] The Anglo-Saxons had obviously settled in the area as well, as Ealdorman Æthelwulf's posthumous journey suggests. Northworthy is thought to have had a minster church long associated with Mercian royalty and which housed the tomb-shrine of Saint Alkmund. The Lady of the Mercians herself is almost certainly the driving force behind the early tenth century translation of Saint Alkmund's relics to Shrewsbury.

It is difficult not to see Æthelflæd's assault on Derby as arising from shared intelligence and forward planning with her brother and his commanders. The timing of it could not have been better. She was strong enough to have done this earlier, but chose to do it in late July when some proportion of the garrison had almost certainly joined in with the war further south. But if the move was timed to coincide with Edward's great thrust towards Tempsford, then it could also be interpreted as a means of preventing any reinforcements being sent from Derby and its dependant territories down to the theatre of war in

Edward's sector. Quite *how* Æthelflæd did it, is another matter. Most people believe that the approach was from the west and therefore the force of the attack would have fallen on the west gate of the Danish fort. Despite no evidence, this seems a reasonable-enough suggestion, although the Roman road direct from Tamworth in the south is another line of approach. The army Æthelflæd took to Derby may have been drawn from any number of the recently-built Mercian burhs, along with senior noblemen and their retainers. But the assault was a brutal affair. Siege equipment was not unknown in tenth-century England. There is even a near-contemporary riddle whose subject is thought to be a battering ram cut from a tree. Æthelflæd's engineers may have fashioned just such an item or items. The other weaponry and equipment at her disposal would have been scaling ladders, fire-arrows and torches, and a host of men armed with swords, sidearms and spears, each carrying shields. One way or another, the army got through the gates. They were fiercely resisted by a garrison who had clearly not all gone south. But the casualties were hard for the Lady to bear. A loyal thegn and his retinue were highly valuable. Æthelflæd clearly felt a bond not just of lordship, but of friendship too. And now she had lost four of those friends in one single action. Their identities may never be known, although there is a charter (S 224) believed to date from around 914 in which Æthelflæd granted two hides of land at *Stantun* to one Ealhhelm. This place is thought to either be Stanton in Peak in Derbyshire, or Stanton and Newhall, also in Derbyshire (see Map 15, page 114).

It is very unusual for the contemporary sources to describe a ruler in terms of the affection they held for their thegns. But here in the *Mercian Register*, we have exactly that. The use of the word *besorge*, meaning 'dear or beloved', is not all that common and implies a deeply-held care on the part of Æthelflæd. We have already seen just how close she was to members of her household if the evidence of the expedition to *Brecenanmere* is anything to go by. It has been argued that the use of the more emotive *besorge* may even enshrine a tradition of 'sorrow' being part of a woman's work.[2] But perhaps with this intriguing window into Æthelflæd's feelings, we are glimpsing a rare thing indeed: a real person leaping from the pages of history.

In the aftermath of the victory at Derby, Æthelflæd may have reflected a little. As she buried her friends and probably made arrangements for the relics of St Alkmund to be brought to Shrewsbury, she could at least look upon the horrors of battle with some sense of achievement. She had brought her men to war and taken a key fortress. With the victory came a big prize. The lands which had been dependent upon Derby were now hers to organize, and an enlarged domain and income was surely the result. A great swathe of land once subjected to Scandinavian overlords was now back in traditional Mercian hands, stretching from the Derwent westwards to Chester and the Welsh borders. Her fame was spreading across the north of England and over the sea in Ireland, too. There, Æthelflæd was no mere Lady of the Mercians. That was a term applied in the English sources. To the Irish, this woman was nothing less than a queen. Exactly what the Mercian thegnhood thought of her title cannot be known. But there was something which was now becoming obvious. Whilst the Alfredian idea of a 'kingdom of the Anglo-Saxons' was certainly being upheld by Edward the Elder, who often styled himself as its figurehead, the family's lordship was spreading directly into new areas, thanks to the efforts of both Edward and his sister. This made that 'kingdom' more of a reality and less of an ideal. Now, an older concept was returning to the Midlands after years of consolidation and defence. We have noted before that memories die hard in Anglo-Saxon England. Æthelflæd's offensive to the east and her capture of Derby may well have meant something highly significant to the ealdorman and thegns who followed her, particularly as it was bought at such a cost. Mercia, their ancient and much loved kingdom, was being slowly restored. The *Mercian Register* or 'Annals of Æthelflæd' are not to be seen as a celebration of the notion of Mercian separatism, however. They are, however, likely to be the Æthelflædan equivalent of the Edwardian chronicles, both of which follow the deeds of Alfred's leading children in their different endeavours. In that respect, the absence of the recording of the taking of Derby in the (A) version of the *Anglo-Saxon Chronicle* is probably understandable. But clearly something profound was happening in Mercia.

Huganus, Derby and the Danes

There is an entertaining and fanciful tale about Æthelflæd's capture of Derby preserved in David Powel's *Historie of Cambria* (1584). The story attempts to link the attack on the Welsh kingdom of Brycheiniog in 916 with the assault on Derby in 917. Citing as its origin a tale from the medieval chronicler and monk John Castoreus (John le Bever, John of London, fl. 1310), it goes as follows.

A 'Welsh' king named Huganus, who is in fact a Dane who married into Welsh royalty according to Caradoc of Llancarvan, feeling that King Edward was preoccupied elsewhere, brought an army into the king's land. In response, Æthelflæd took her own force to 'Brecknocke, and putting Huganus to flight, took his wife and 34 [*sic*] men captiues, and lead them with hir to Mercia'. This prompted Huganus to flee to Derby with 15 household men and 200 warriors where he then allied himself with the Danes. But Æthelflæd, of course, followed him. She entered the gates but Huganus resisted 'and slue foure of hir chiefe officers'. Her saviour was her steward Gwyane, the lord of the Isle of Ely, who set fire to the gates and furiously set about the Britons. Huganus was overwhelmed and chose to die by the sword rather than to surrender himself to a woman.

The story provides an imaginative and completely different motive for Æthelflæd's assault on Derby. With no real basis in checkable facts, and with a legendary central character, the tale may simply be a conflation of several events mixed with creative writing, but no account of Æthelflæd's capture of Derby seems quite complete without it.

Chapter 19

The Autumn Onslaught

The campaigning would get even more intense before 917 was over. The English now began to mobilize from Kent, Surrey and those parts of Essex loyal to Edward, which by now was much of it. The king's sub-commanders called their retainers and fyrdsmen together. It was still harvest time, perhaps the most challenging time of year to be launching a military land campaign. And yet, the Alfredian reforms of the army and the rotation system he imposed had ensured there was always a contingent tending the fields. This arrangement made Edward's armies less 'seasonal' and consequently, there was greater military capacity all year round. Also, to supplement the forces being raised in the countryside, the king had drawn armies from 'the nearest strongholds everywhere' too. The logistics alone must have been considerable. Deciding who to leave at the garrisons, how to provision the field armies and keep the mounts fed and watered, how to arrange forward supply dumps and which roads and tracks to send the scouts down, were all decisions made by the royal horse-thegns and other officers working with the king's sub-commanders. The sheer numbers in this army would also have been impressive. Three combined shire fyrds and numerous detachments from the burhs of south-east Mercia came together to form a force probably just as large as the one which had attacked Tempsford. No doubt, the Kent fyrdsmen led the way when the army crossed into Essex and headed towards one of the most famous of the old Roman colonia at Colchester. That place was now, in late 917, a place which had been a Danish stronghold for some time.

The siege at Colchester does not seem to have lasted long. The chronicler indicates that it was over before the end of the same harvest period. But the walls of Roman Colchester were high and some of them can even be seen today, particularly along Balkerne Hill. By some unknown means, the English forces prevailed in the siege and the result was bloody carnage within the walls. They killed who they could find and seized everything inside, 'except for the men who fled away over the wall'. The chronicler perhaps implies here that the final push may have caused some desperation amongst the defenders.

The capture of Colchester was an important moment in Edward's wars. It put increasing pressure on the East Anglian leadership to respond, or else risk catastrophic defeat themselves. They had lost many men this year already and their recourse to warriors of their own kindred or even of those who owed service was being stretched. And yet their answer was to organize a counter-offensive. The (A) version of the *Anglo-Saxon Chronicle*, which we have been following through this phase of the war, says that the East Anglians had 'enticed' some 'Vikings' (*wicinga*) into service. The geographical origin of these Vikings is unknown, but their role as booty-hunting independent units is certain, otherwise the chronicler would not have bothered to distinguish them from the East

Above and below: 42 and 43. *The Roman walls at Colchester on the Balkerne Hill (west) side. Colchester played a key role in Edward's war in the autumn of 917.*

Anglian force. As to the identity of the chronicler himself, an interesting theory has been put forward that the man who may have played a strong part in writing this section of the chronicle from 912 to about 920 may have been Alfred's youngest son, Æthelweard,[1] not to be confused with the later tenth-century chronicler Æthelweard from whom we have extracted so much material already. The latter Æthelweard was descended from Alfred's royal brother King Æthelred I of Wessex (865–71), whereas Alfred's son Æthelweard, who lived until 920, would father two sons Ælfwine and Æthelwine, who would go on to participate in the greatest battle of all of early English history in 937. If the theory about the attribution of the penmanship of Alfred's youngest son is correct, then it would explain a lot. The theory is based largely on linguistic arguments, such as often-repeated phrases throughout the work, but it is possible to see something more: a secular, perhaps even military, mind at work in the text. This Æthelweard would have been the well-educated brother of the king, a man of Wessex likely to exalt Edward's achievements and less likely to wax lyrical about his older sister's work in distant Mercia. He would not necessarily have held any animosity towards Æthelflæd and may have worked for Edward in the knowledge that someone in Mercia was covering his sister's tale, which, as we have seen, they certainly were. Moreover, Æthelweard would have held military office within his brother's kingdom and it is not out of the question that he even commanded one of the armies mentioned in the wars of 917 and earlier. There may be clues in the (A) version of the chronicle that its author may just have known a thing or two about military matters. Is there not an intriguing attention to detail when discussing the disposition of named Danish leaders? Is there not a curious account of Danes launching themselves over a Colchester wall in the face of the Anglo-Saxon onslaught, an event perhaps recorded by an eyewitness?

We cannot know what promises were made to the 'Vikings' by the East Anglians, but they chose to join them in a campaign which saw them both head out not to Colchester, but to Maldon in Essex, thinking 'that they would avenge their injuries'. The other reason for the chronicler's distinction between the East Anglians and the 'Vikings' is revealed by the way he talks of them together '. . . þæs landheres ge þara wicinga': he implies that he is talking on the one hand about an East Anglian land force, and on the other, about a 'Viking' and no doubt, naval one.

The recruitment of the Vikings, whom the chronicler soon informs us were *æscmanna* (or 'askr-men'), indicates that the plan was to attack Maldon by both land and sea in the two-pronged approach which the Danes had so often employed before. The 'askr', incidentally, was a typical Scandinavian vessel of the era. The plan to attack Maldon must have had, as its desired consequence, the isolation of newly won Anglo-Saxon Colchester. If Witham could be overcome as well, there was every chance the English could be surrounded at their new stronghold due to the fact that the Roman road from London to Colchester would thus be interdicted.

It started well enough. The Danes may have been in the ascendancy and close to taking Maldon before English reinforcements apparently came to relieve the place. The arrival of those reinforcements persuaded the East Anglians to break off their attack and to march away. But the English combined their field army with their garrison and 'went after' the Danes, bringing them to battle, 'killing many hundreds of them, both of askr-men and of others.' The East Anglian attempt at driving a wedge through northern

Essex and isolating Colchester had failed. The Anglo-Saxon machine was seemingly unstoppable. Whoever was writing about it, however biased he may have been, certainly knew it.

The English armies mentioned so far in the (A) version of the chronicle, when portraying the war in the south-east Midlands, did not all necessarily have Edward as their immediate commander. The king of course was what we might call their commander-in-chief. They are described variously as either being drawn from garrisons or from the regional fyrds. But as soon as the harvest of 917 was over, it was indeed Edward himself who the chronicler describes as personally leading a West Saxon fyrd (*Westsexna fierde*) to Passenham on Watling Street. Passenham is situated within easy reach of the burhs at Buckingham, Towcester, Newport Pagnell (if the argument for its existence is correct) and Bedford. When Edward brought the West Saxon fyrd here, he brought them to the southernmost apex of the territory which had been dominated by the Northampton Danes. From Passenham, a contingent of the army was sent nine miles to the north-west, up the Roman road, with cartloads of masonry, to refortify the burghal walls at Towcester in stone: '. . . sæt þær [at Passenham] þa hwile þe mon worhte þa burg æt Tofeceastre mid stanwealle . . .'.What is interesting about this passage in the *Anglo-Saxon Chronicle* is that when Edward's West Saxon forces appear, they seem to be doing much more than just fighting. A certain disposition towards military engineering is notable. This was after all, the king's army. But the capability may even have extended to his sub-commanders. And perhaps it is the appearance of these wagonloads of masonry, supplies and supporting soldiery which explains what happened next.

It was too much for one Danish leader to bear. Faced with a similar predicament to that of Jarl Thurcytel of Bedford previously, another Dane, the leader of the Northampton army whose dependencies stretched as far as the River Welland many miles to the north, turned to Edward. With this Dane came all his holds and senior warriors, and if John of Worcester is to be believed, some subject Englishmen too. His name was Jarl Thurferth. They 'sought him [Edward] as their lord and protector' says the chronicler, who not unsurprisingly, uses the language of lordship. The army of Northampton was capitulating.

There is no sign that Jarl Thurferth ever slipped away to the Continent or in any way turned his back on his new lord and protector. Unlike Thurcytel who three years earlier had felt he could not make it work, Thurferth may have retained his position and his lands in service of the king. Passenham's proximity to the other burhs of the region would now show its merits. It was time for the rotation of the fyrd. Those who had campaigned so hard up until now were sent home to see to the management of the end of the harvest on their estates, while the newly-arrived fyrdsmen marched out to Huntingdon where Edward had commanded that they restore the fortification recently abandoned by the Danes. Edward, who had suffered an embarrassing hiatus in the fyrd rotation system in the 890s during the wars of his father, had now clearly learned how to efficiently organize it, so that the incoming forces arrived as the outgoing forces left. Here at Huntingdon, a familiar pattern repeated itself. The local people submitted to the king and sought his protection. Edward stayed at Huntingdon while his messengers rode around the countryside bringing news to churches and villages of Edward's recent conquests. By installing a garrison at Huntingdon, he had effectively cut the Danes of Leicester and Stamford off from those in East Anglia and Essex. It is no surprise therefore that at this stage of the war, Edward chose to take his army down to Colchester sometime before 11 November (Martinmas), where once again, his men were put to the task of repairing the very walls the Anglo-Saxons had overcome in their recent successful siege of the place. Incidentally, John of Worcester adds that the garrison Edward then placed here consisted of 'stipendary' men, a reference to a possible recollection not recorded elsewhere of King Edward's usage of mercenaries at this stage of his campaign when clearly his manpower resources were stretched. But it is only a passing comment, as if it were taken for granted (mercenaries in John of Worcester's twelfth century were common enough). We are not given any more information as to the garrison's origins. But if it is true, it may have been a temporary or expedient measure designed to ensure Colchester's loyalty in an area (namely Essex) which had wavered one way and another for a generation or so. The administrative organization of the dependant lands of Colchester would have presumably followed on after regional submission was secured.

Here at Colchester, where Edward may have rebuilt the royal vill, that regional submission was indeed secured. Some remarkably public events were played out. A great number of people (*folc*) from East Anglia and from Essex who were earlier under the control of the Danes, 'turned to' Edward. It was an indication that the grip of the East Anglian Scandinavian lords was dramatically weakening. But then, the chronicler reports in terms as triumphant as possible, an arrangement which may show that Edward was not as entirely all-conquering as his chronicler might have liked. The 'army' of East Anglia, by which he means those very Scandinavian lords, 'swore union with him: that they wanted all that he wanted, and would keep peace with all with whom the king wanted to keep peace, both on sea and on land.' It is the language of political cooperation. Something very similar is found in Edward's second (Exeter) law code in which the king beseeches his own councillors to do exactly this (see page 181). In fact, the whole deal sounds more like a description of an alliance which bound the East Anglians to the Edwardian will, the binding mechanism being a regional or even national oath to the king of the Anglo-Saxons, something Edward's own father had been keen to promote in the wake of events at London in 886.

There was another group however, a group whose discourse with Edward was quite different and much more like that of the groups who had submitted earlier. At long last, the Danes of Cambridge, who for generations had caused so much trouble to Edward's father, 'separately (*synderlice* is the word used, which implies something which is done apart from something else) chose Edward for their lord and protector, and confirmed that with oaths just as he determined'. In other words, Edward secured a separate submission from Cambridge on his own terms. We cannot be sure how long Edward stayed at Cambridge. However, due to an incident recorded in the *Liber Eliensis*, a twelfth-century Latin compilation (II.25), which occurred much later in the tenth century around 975, we know Edward may have dealt with land apportionment and regional submission here, like he had done elsewhere. The later tenth-century incident in question revolved around a lawsuit concerning the estate at Bluntisham in Huntingdonshire. The sons of a Dane known as Boga of Hemingford wanted to reclaim this estate because they believed it was theirs by hereditary right. Their maternal uncle, a man named Tope, should have inherited the estate from his grandmother who 'in the flower of her virginity' had:

> Gone across from Bluntisham and petitioned King Edward at Cambridge at the time when Earl Toli [probably Jarl Toglos, who was killed at Tempsford in 917] had taken possession of Huntingdonshire against the king by force and, for this reason, she should by right have held the land as her own.

The sons of Boga contended (in 975) that the submission to Edward made by their female relative had been a voluntary one and therefore one presumes the basis of their claim was that they did not believe the estate should have been forfeit. But the court did not see it that way. 'The wise old men of the district' had even remembered when Earl Toli had been killed (a full 58 years earlier) and more importantly, they remembered the sequence of events. They rejected the claim on the grounds that the woman had not made her submission to Edward in time, and that the brothers' claim that the visit of the woman to Edward had come at a time when Earl Toli had possession of Huntingdonshire was chronologically wrong. The king had overrun Huntingdon before he had come to Cambridge, they said. 'There was no land so free in the whole of Huntingdonshire that it could not be lost through forfeiture,' they said.

In 975 Bluntisham was in the hands of an Englishman named Wulfnoth who was trying to sell it to Bishop Æthelwold. The wise men had decided in favour of Wulfnoth being allowed to sell the land. A huge meeting was then held (with men from six hundreds) to which Wulfnoth and the sons of Boga were summoned. The charter for the land was produced by a monk of Ely. But it was decided that the sons of Boga had lied about Tope and his grandmother. Besides, the actual possession of the charter was important. Wulfnoth was able to produce more than a thousand men to vouch for him 'through their sworn testimony'. But the sons of Boga 'would not accept the oath'. Everyone decided that Wulfnoth should have Bluntisham and they would support him in future. After this, Bishop Æthelwold gave Wulfnoth the outstanding money for the land and a warhorse worth three marks.

This story has a number of facets of Anglo-Saxon law running through it, not least of which is the impressive communal gathering in support of Wulfnoth occurring at the later meeting. But it might be possible to conclude that at Huntingdon in 917 Edward and his legal team had combined to confiscate Bluntisham which then passed into royal hands, after which the king presumably quickly awarded it as bookland to Wulfnoth's unnamed ancestor. One cannot help but wonder if this episode demonstrates the general mechanics of Anglo-Saxon conquest beyond Watling Street during Edward's years. First, the military campaign needed to be won. And in this, the taking and/or building of fortresses was clearly the *modus operandi* of the king of the Anglo-Saxons (and for that matter, his sister). A Dane could quite easily be confirmed in his or her possession of an estate, provided a 'voluntary' submission had been made. After all, this was never a war of annihilation. But if submission came late, or not at all, the land was confiscated.[2] And in respect of the Bluntisham estate, that submission had not come at the right time and the claimants had lied about the original circumstances.

It had been an action-packed year for both Edward and his sister. Their campaigns, and those of their subordinates, had begun to reshape the political map of lowland Britain. But there was much still to do. Whether the siblings met over the winter cannot be proved: there is simply no evidence for it. But what happened next in the war indicates that the spirit of coordination and cooperation was still very much in the ascendancy. Christmas came and went. There is no sign of a counter-offensive against either of the children of Alfred in their respective domains. Then, as the New Year opened, the Lady of the Mercians asked her thegns to slip on their mailcoats and grab their bags of provisions once more. Her choice of destination, a troublesome stronghold in the very centre of England, would come as no surprise to anyone in her army, and even less so to the Danes who dwelt there.

Chapter 20

Leicester and Stamford 918

Her heo begeat on hire geweald mid Godes fultume on foreweardne gear gesybsumlice þa burh æt Ligraceastre, ⁊ se mæsta dæl þæs herges þe ðærto hirde wearð underþeoded.

'Here in the early part of this year, with God's help, she peaceably got in her control the stronghold at Leicester, and the most part of the raiding-armies that belonged to it were subjected.'

The *Mercian Register*, or 'Annals of Æthelflæd'.
First part of the entry for 918 (C)

The *Mercian Register* once again provides detail where the (A) version of the chronicle remains silent. It would seem that Æthelflæd was just as much of a 'peace-weaver' and shrewd negotiator as she was a hardened war leader. The diplomatic art in Anglo-Saxon England was often a role taken up by royal women. Æthelflæd would have learned these valuable political skills in the court of her father, under her mother's tutelage, before she was transferred to the Mercian court, where she took firm control of the running of it. Her own aunt had done exactly the same when she had married the Mercian King Burgred many years before. We do not know the full nature of Æthelflæd's relationship with her aunt Æthelswith, particularly in the early years of her life, but one suspects there was a great influence here, too.

Quite how Leicester was peaceably won, whereas the taking of Derby had been a bloodbath, remains a mystery. The most likely scenario is that Æthelflæd arrived at Leicester with an impressive army and during the subsequent parley between the Lady of the Mercians and the Leicester leaders, one or two obvious points were made. The fact that the Leicester leaders were in an impossible situation was one. To their south, the Dane Thurcytel had long departed Bedford and Jarl Thurferth of Northampton had gone over to the king. Jarl Toglos was dead and so too were many of his men. An allied king had also fallen at Tempsford. Cambridge had submitted to Edward. To their north-west, Derby had been overrun by Mercian forces, and presumably Æthelflæd had been busy administrating the local landscape and dealing with submissions and confiscations. They would have been reminded too, that there was no real hope of alliances to the east. Edward's forces at Huntingdon and his agreement with East Anglia had made this impossible. Arguably, Leicester still had a 'friendly' Nottingham, Stamford and Lincoln at their disposal, but it must have been obvious the walls were closing in. And so, in early 918, there was no apparent fighting as Leicester held the gates of its stronghold open for Æthelflæd. Except to say that the 'most part' of its warbands capitulated, implying that a few of them did not. What Æthelflæd did next in Leicester is not clear, though tradition says she may have founded or restored a church on the site of the later medieval church of St Mary de Castro, associated with the post-Conquest castle. Similarly, it is not entirely certain what Æthelflæd's relationship was with the church which is now St Nicholas Church, overlooking the Roman remains at Jewry Wall. This church had a long history, probably as an earlier minster church and inside the building are two well-preserved windows.[1]

44. *St Nicholas Church, Leicester near to the Jewry Wall. The pillar in the foreground is apparently Roman.*

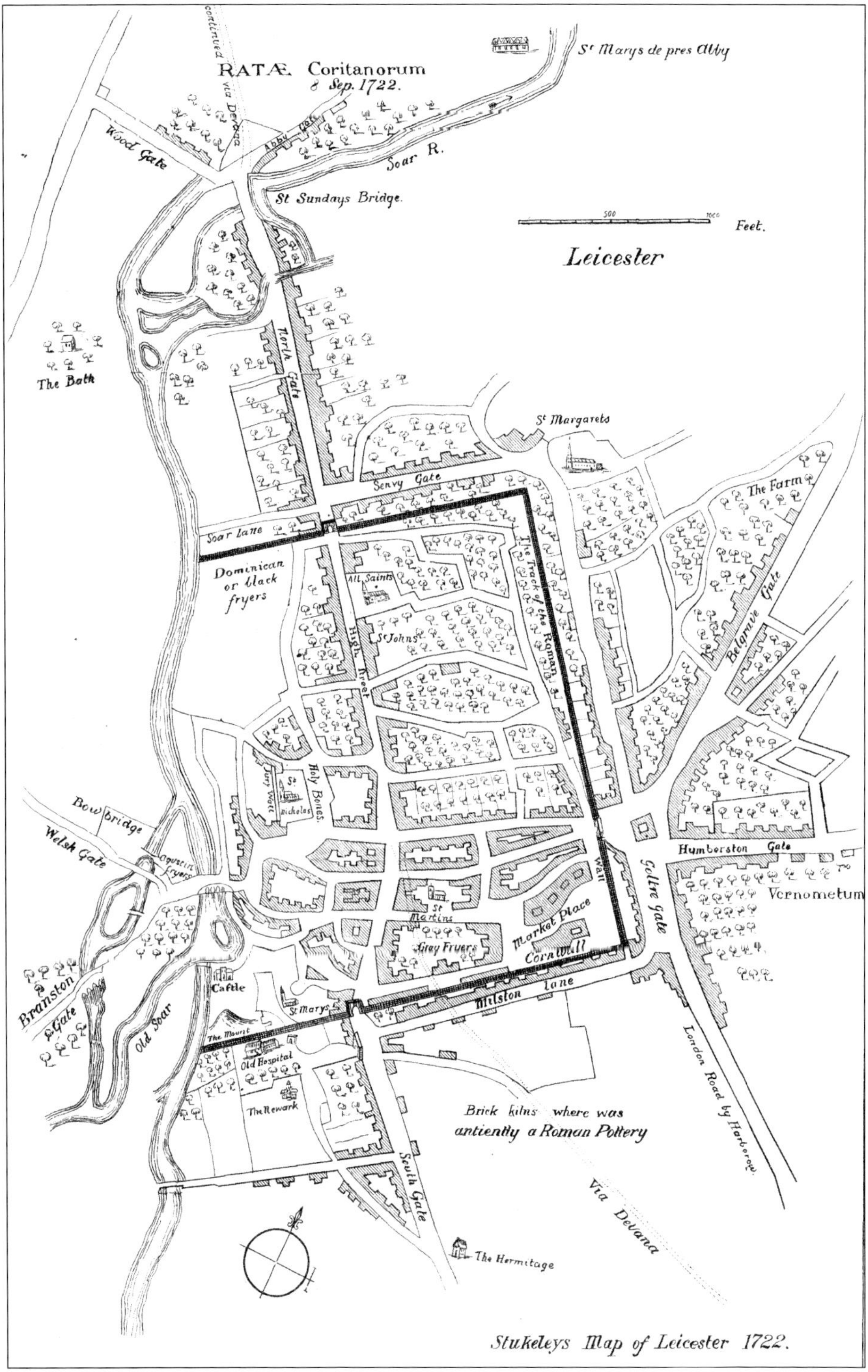

Map 20: *Stukeley's map of Leicester 1722.*

Both a resurgent English Mercia and the Danes of Leicester may well have benefitted from the bringing of Leicester into Mercian overlordship. Events in the north were beginning to make everyone – Englishman and Dane – look over their shoulders. The threat presented by Rægnald to the political status quo was growing. It may be for this reason that the *Mercian Register* goes on to say:

> ⁊ hæfdon eac Eforwicingas hire gehaten, ⁊ sume on wedde geseald, sume mid aþum gefæstnod, þæt hi on hyre rædenne beon woldon.

> 'And also the York-folk had promised her – and some of them granted so by pledge, some confirmed with oaths – that they would be at her disposition.'

The mixture of pledge and oath may represent the cultural diversity in York around this time, with Anglian, Danish and even other Scandinavian practices being in play. We are not told where this remarkable offer was made, but that it was made at all, is a testimony to the reputation of the Lady of the Mercians. We will return to Æthelflæd's role as power broker in the colourful north. But first, whilst she was completing her negotiations, her brother was making his plans to move on Stamford and bring his armies up to the line of the Welland. And sometime after 11 May, he did precisely that. What his sister achieved at Leicester through skilful statecraft backed with the threat of force, Edward would have to achieve at Stamford with rather less subtlety. Once again, the burh builders in the king's army sharpened their tools.

Edward's first action on arrival at Stamford was to order the building of the southern burh opposite the Danes' own fortified settlement on the other side of the river. Stamford had been a prosperous borough under the Danes. It is likely that around the time of the fall of Burgred of Mercia in the middle of the 870s, the Danes had come here to an already existing estate centre and then went on to occupy it and enhance it. The settlement was on rising ground on the north bank of the Welland. There was an important Roman road however, just a half a mile west, which crossed the river at a place called Stanford (literally, 'Stone Ford'). This was Ermine Street. It had once carried much Roman traffic from London to Lincoln and York, and it was still a vital artery in the tenth century.

Here at Stamford, the Danes had direct access to the North Sea, as the Welland was navigable to Stamford. Not only this, but Stamford in the late ninth and early tenth century boasted a remarkable pottery industry producing white buff or grey fabric pots and jars which developed into early forms of glazed ware, which archaeologists have noted bear a striking similarity in terms of influence and parallels with centres in northern France, particularly around the Beauvais area. The link between the Danes of the region north of Watling Street and northern France must have been stronger than the texts let on. Perhaps it is no surprise after all, that Jarl Thurcytel of Bedford chose a new life there when he turned his back on service with the English king. The archaeologists who discovered the Stamford Ware kilns, have also discovered part of a double-ditched enclosure, believed to have been topped with a palisade. This was just to the south-east of what was the later Norman castle. This is thought to be the northern burh which Edward took over and then commenced the building of the southern burh linked by a bridge. Each of these burhs would then have been assigned a burghal territory by the king and his planners.[2]

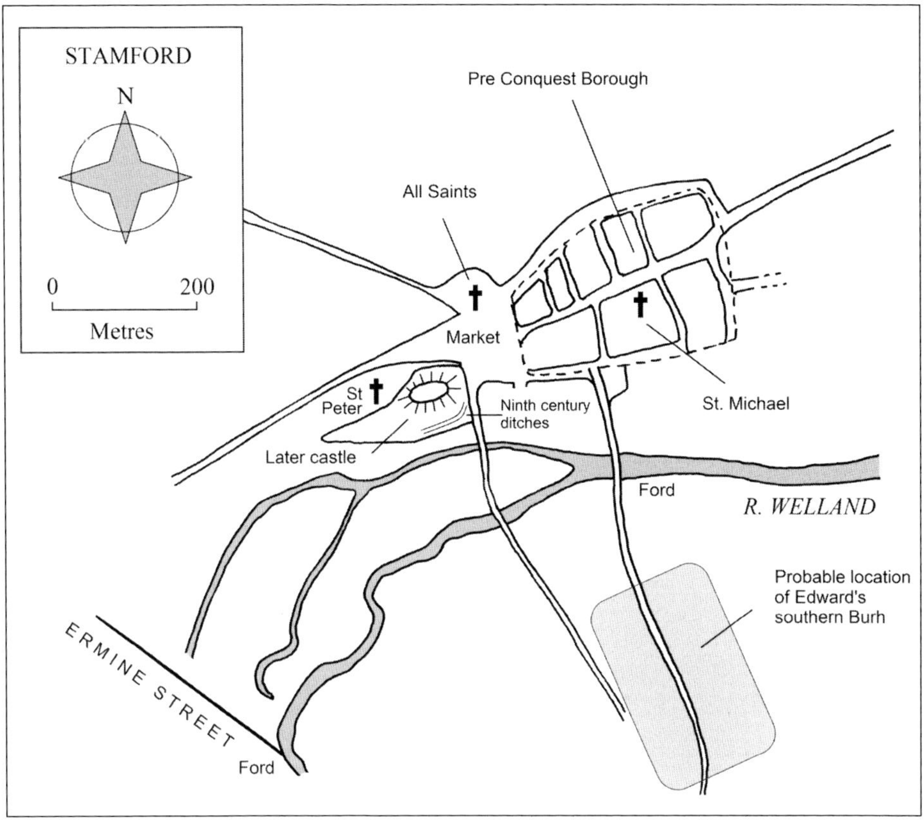

Map 21: *Stamford. After Mahany and Roffe (1983).*

It is not known precisely how quickly the Danes of Stamford submitted to the king of the Anglo-Saxons. Like others before them, however, they are recorded as seeking Edward as their lord. It was another in a string of submissions which raise the question of how seemingly easily they came. There is no question that Edward and his sister were anything other than consummate commanders. Their campaigns had simply given their enemies no choice but to turn to them, time after time, whether coerced by military might or persuaded by unassailable logic. But there was something troubling everyone on the political stage in Britain at this time. If there had been an apparent void left in the north by the defeat of the Scandinavians at Tettenhall in 910, then it was about to be filled. York, under new leadership, would rise again.

PART FOUR

SECURING THE NORTH

Chapter 21

The Battle of Corbridge

In the far north-east of England, there had risen to power an Anglo-Saxon dynasty of lords based at Bamburgh. Eadwulf, the ruler of this autonomous realm, was purported to have been a friend of King Alfred's, so says the *Historia de Sancto Cuthberto*, an eleventh-century compilation. He ruled until 913 when he was murdered by a rival named Eadred, whose origins are obscure. There is some speculation that Eadwulf may have held some sway in York for a few years up to the time of his death. The speculation is of course invited by the lack of clear chronological evidence for events in the north in this period and the general assumption that there was a power vacuum at York after the Battle of Tettenhall. Some even speculate that the vacuum may stretch as far back as the Treaty of Tiddingford in 906. However, the murdered Eadwulf was succeeded by his son Ealdred and moreover the friendship Eadwulf had shared with Alfred was also matched by that of Ealdred and King Edward, says the same northern source. Speculation is also rife that Ealdred may have at least intermittently continued his father's hegemony over York between c. 914 and c. 917. But it is the arrival of Rægnald into the already-colourful picture, which signals a sea change at York, a city where since 916 the Anglo-Saxon Archbishop Hrotheweard had become a pivotal figure and who must have been at least partly responsible for decision making at a high level on both secular and religious matters.

The *Fragmentary Annals of Ireland* contain a story of alliances which involve many of the power-groups of the north. The authenticity of the account is often called into question, as are the annals themselves, but they are worthy of exploration. As for Æthelflæd's role in all of this, much vaunted by this particular source, we need to remember that according to the *Mercian Register*, the Lady of the Mercians was taking Derby before 1 August 917 and was in Leicester in the early part of 918 and was by the early summer of that year back in Tamworth, where in all probability, she received the deputation from the people of York around late May or early June, unless of course, they had made the trip down from York to Leicester slightly earlier in the year. With that time frame in mind, what are we to make of the following entry, which most people take to be pertinent to the situation in 917 to 918, in the *Fragmentary Annals of Ireland*?

> Æthelflæd, by her own cleverness, made peace with the men of Alba and with the Britons, so that whenever the same race should come to attack her, they would rise to help her. If it were against them that they came, she would take arms with them. While this continued, the men of Alba and the Britons overcame the settlements of the Norsemen and destroyed and sacked them. The king of the Norsemen [potentially either Sihtric or Rægnald] came after that and sacked Strathclyde, and plundered the land. But the enemy was ineffectual against Strathclyde.

The entry in the *Fragmentary Annals of Ireland* is actually part of the entry for the year 914. Alba was effectively the kingdom of Scotland in its earlier form. From 900 it had been ruled by Constantín mac Áeda (900–43), a man who reigned long into the tenth century and experienced many twists of fortune. The other polity mentioned here is Strathclyde. Although it is in modern Scotland, it was not 'Scottish' in a cultural sense, but was 'British' or Welsh instead. Its people spoke a language similar to Old Welsh known as Cumbric. Strathclyde was situated in what the Welsh called *Hen Ogledd*, or the 'Old North'. The centre of this ancient kingdom seems to have moved to Govan in the wake of the Scandinavian sack of Dumbarton Rock in c. 870. Records are scarce for the chronology of Strathclyde after c. 870, but the *Chronicle of the Kings of Alba* does mention one Dyfnwal 'king of the Britons' dying during the reign of Constantín, where he is listed first in a list of four kings, each of whom died in quick succession of one another and all of whom were Irish (apart from Dyfnwal). Because the three Irish kings are known from other sources to have died in 915, 916 and 919, the date for Dyfnwal's death is placed at around 915 at the latest and could even have been 914. This means that the man who did business with Æthelflæd was either the outgoing Dyfnwal or one of his successors, perhaps Owain, his son.

The passage in the *Fragmentary Annals of Ireland* which mentions the 'clever' Æthelflæd and her alliances against the Norse, comes directly after an extraordinary tale of the Lady of the Mercians' martial prowess. This passage has been taken by many to indicate that Æthelflæd was involved in a famous battle in the north of England which occurred at Corbridge, which we will examine shortly. The date for this battle is problematic, with most sources placing it in 918 and one important one suggesting two battles, one in 914 and one in 918. So, here is what the *Fragmentary Annals of Ireland* say about Æthelflæd:

> In that year great armies of Dark Foreigners and Fair Foreigners, Danish and Norwegian Vikings came again to attack the Saxons, after the installation of Sitric grandson of Imar as king. They challenged the Saxons to battle, and the Saxons did not delay, but came at once to attack the pagans. A hard and ferocious battle was fought between them, and there was great energy and heat and contention on both sides. Much noble blood was spilled in this battle; nevertheless, it was the Saxons who won victory and spoils after massacring the pagans. For the king of the pagans was taken ill, and he was carried out of the battle to a forest nearby, and he died there.
>
> Now Oittir [*sic*], the most greatly esteemed earl in this battle, when he saw the Saxons slaughtering his people, fled into a dense wood near him, along with those of his people who survived. A huge throng of Saxons came after him, and they surrounded the wood. The Queen commanded them to hack down all of the forest with their swords and battleaxes, and they did so. First they felled the trees, and then all the pagans who were in the wood were killed. The pagans were slaughtered by the Queen like that, so that her fame spread in all directions.

Does this extraordinary account refer to the first of the two battles of Corbridge in the north-east of England in 914, or is it really telling us about something else? The whole story bears a remarkable similarity to the events described in the *Anglo-Saxon Chronicle* (from the West Saxon perspective) for 914 when Jarls Othor and Hroald came up the

Severn and kidnapped a Welsh bishop, causing a response from Edward and the raising of armies from Hereford and Gloucester (see page 104). It is possible that the *Fragmentary Annals of Ireland* are simply helping us with the Mercian side of this same tale. And it would certainly make sense that the Lady of the Mercians would seek northern alliances in the wake of the departure of the Scandinavians to Ireland.

Jarl Othor's force which sailed up the Severn and wreaked havoc in 914 finally fetched up in Waterford in Ireland. Also, we have noted that Sihtric and Rægnald re-established themselves in Ireland in 917 with the former taking Dublin (see page 106). The passage quoted above says the action in the wood took place after the installation of Sihtric as king, which confusingly would bring events forward to sometime after 917 and not 914 after all. So, we cannot be entirely sure whether to place Æthelflæd's 'clever' northern alliance in 914 or somewhere between 917 and 918.

The evidence is notoriously difficult to interpret regarding what Rægnald did next in his bid to spread his power across northern England and ultimately capture the prize of York. Indeed, his involvement in affairs east of the Pennines is poorly understood from about 913 up to 918. If Æthelflæd was not involved in the battle at Corbridge, whether it was in 914 or 918 or even both, she certainly would have been interested in its outcome. She does not *seem* to have been there in person (unless we assign the *Fragmentary Annals* account to that particular battle), but we cannot rule out the possibility of a Mercian contingent fighting in support of Ealdred and Constantín. However, we are still left with the problem of where to place the battle of Corbridge, if indeed there was only one of them.

In an entry for 918, the *Annals of Ulster* say that it all went like this: Rægnald (Ragnall), Jarl Othor and Gragabai left Ireland and 'proceeded afterwards against the men of Scotland'. The latter, however, 'moved against them, and they all met on the bank of the Tyne in northern Saxonland'. The pagan army divided into four batallions (a plausible development we have seen many times before). One of these was led by Guthfrith, another grandson of Ivar. Another was led by the two jarls, another by the 'young lords' and the final one by Rægnald himself which was deployed in ambush. The Scots then routed the three batallions they could see. Othor and Gragabai were killed. But then Rægnald launched into the rear of the Scottish army, causing many casualties until nightfall when the battle was broken off. No Scottish leaders were 'cut off' by this ambush, say the *Annals*. The implication is that there was an English contingent fighting on the Scottish side, as the term 'northern Saxonland' might suggest. The overall result of the battle could be interpreted either as a pyrrhic victory for the Scots or a last-minute victory for Rægnald, bought at heavy cost.

The *Chronicle of the Kings of Alba* has a more terse account. A battle at 'Tinemore' took place in the eighteenth year of Constantín's reign (918), between Constantín and Rægnald, and the Scots had the victory. An English source adds more colour to the picture, but is also the source of the confusion over the two separate dates for the battle or battles (914 and 918 respectively). The *Historia de Sancto Cuthberto* (HSC 22) describes a battle which it then links with the confiscation of lands of Cuthbert's community by a Scandinavian leader named Onlafbald in defiance of Bishop Cuthheard. Cuthheard was thought to have died by 915 at the latest, hence the attribution of an early date for the battle described at HSC 22 in the *Historia*. However, the sources which mention his death are both late and unreliable. The story in HSC 22 tells the tale of an Englishman named Alfred who fled across the Pennines to get away from the Norse settlers. This Alfred came to Chester-le-Street where he served Bishop Cuthheard, who gave him land. Then, 'King Rægnald came with a great multitude of ships and occupied the territory of Ealdred . . .', whom, we recall, was King Edward's friend at Bamburgh. Ealdred was then 'driven off' (indicating an early battle) and went to Scotland, seeking help from Constantín. Ealdred then brought Constantín to a battle against Rægnald at Corbridge. But this battle was a resounding victory for Rægnald, not Constantín. Alfred, the man who had come east, was fighting on Ealdred's side and was put to flight. As for Ealdred, only he and his brother Uhtred survived amongst the senior English leadership. Two sections later (HSC 24), comes the description of what seems to be another battle, which includes the same participants, but which better fits the 918 scenario. To put it simply, if that is at all possible, it is now thought the author of the *Historia* has taken the same battle account from two sources and got confused about Cuthheard's dates and Onlafbald's land dealings and therefore has given us two battles of Corbridge and not one.[1]

The position of Corbridge is interesting. It is four miles east of Hexham on the Roman Dere Street, which goes from York into Lothian. Here, on the banks of the Tyne at the river crossing, the battle was fought. If the *Annals of Ulster* are correct, then it looks like Rægnald was on his way north and the allies intercepted him. But had he marched up from further south on foot, or had he brought his ships into the mouth of the Tyne as is suggested? If so, the sea journey from his bases west of the Pennines must have been very long indeed unless he dragged his vessels across land, a phenomenon not entirely out of the question but inherently unlikely. Rægnald's intention would therefore seem to have been to confront the northern alliance and gamble on a victory by knocking out one or both of them in battle, thus leaving himself free to take control of York and its dependant territories to the south. If so, it was certainly a risky, but perhaps necessary strategy. York, incidentally, is a full 80 miles to the south of Corbridge.

If there was just the one battle of Corbridge, then subsequent events in the north would show it to have been a strategic victory for Rægnald in that he is recorded as taking York in its aftermath. Unfortunately, the *Anglo-Saxon Chronicle*'s dating of this event to 923, as reported in the Worcester (D) and Peterborough (E) versions, is dislocated. The *Annals of Ulster* for example, generally regarded here as reliable, report Rægnald's (Ragnall's) death in 921. This leaves us with having to place a date for the battle earlier than that. The deputation of the men of York to Æthelflæd seems to have taken place after her acquisition of Leicester early in 918. The date for Corbridge hinges on whether these promises from York to the Mercian ruler came through fear of Rægnald taking York, or immediately in the wake of it, and consequently it also hinges on when exactly Rægnald walked into York and changed the complexion of the northern world. The problem is, that we have no exact date for that.

What we do have a date for, however, is a seismic event occurring just 12 days before midsummer in 918. It was an event which would have left the alliance-seeking men of York vulnerable to a political take-over from Rægnald, or through their weakness, acquiescent in it. It would also have left King Edward with an unexpected problem of the very first magnitude, if his dream of expanding the kingdom of the Anglo-Saxons was to be continued. Constantín, the Scottish king, Ealdred of Bamburgh, Owain the king of

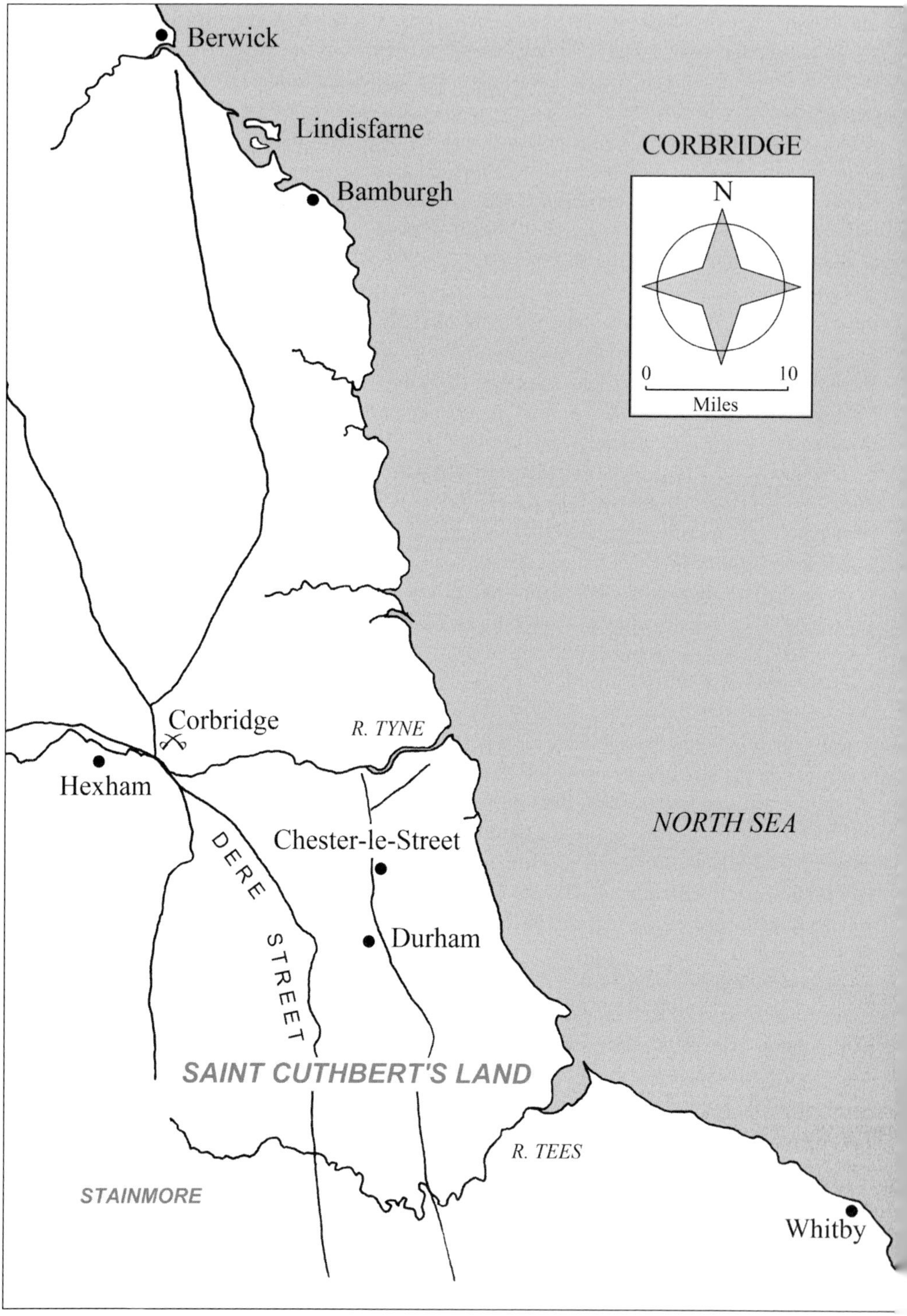

Map 22: *The location of the Battle of Corbridge.*

Strathclyde, and each and every one of the Welsh kings would all have paused in their halls when messengers ran to them, bringing the shocking news. The *Annales Cambriae* has an entry for the death of the English 'queen'. Also, across the sea in Ireland, where by now the reputation of one of English history's most extraordinary women had spread, the news also filtered through. It was recorded in many sources either side of the Irish Sea, of course. But the Irish, so seemingly enamoured by the deeds of an English 'queen', report in the *Annals of Ulster* (918.5) in the entry after the battle on the banks of the Tyne, that 'Ethelfled [*sic*], a very famous queen of the Saxons, dies'. If she had had anything to do with Corbridge at all, it would have been one of her last major acts.

In Mercia, the world must have come to a crashing halt. The headline is even recorded by the (A) chronicler, not usually given to mentioning the Lady of Mercians. He duly noted Æthelflæd's death, calling her by her name and mentioning her as Edward's sister, an event which occurred whilst the king was still at Stamford. But the author of the *Mercian Register* also had something to say. Æthelflæd's death seems to have occurred soon after the men of York had come to her with their promises:

> Ac swiðe hrædlice þæs ðe hi þæs geworden hæfde, heo gefor .xii. nihtun ær middan sumera binnan Tamaweorþige ðy eahtoþan geare þæs ðe heo Myrcna anweald mid riht hlaforddome healdende wæs, ⁊ hyre lic lið binnan Gleawcestre on þam east portice Sancte Petres cyrcean.
>
> 'But very quickly after they had done that, she departed, 12 nights before midsummer, inside Tamworth, the eighth year that she held control of Mercia with rightful lordship; and her body lies inside Gloucester in the east side-chapel of St Peter's Church.'

Across Mercia, the feeling must have been one of immense loss. The woman who had rebuilt vast tracts of the ancient kingdom had departed. Henceforth, the community at Worcester would say Mass every Saturday for Æthelflæd's soul and thrice daily recite *Laudate Dominum*, as they had done for her husband. It is difficult not to see the death of Æthelflæd as a catastrophe for the Mercians. She had departed at the height of her fame, just when an extraordinary grand family project was nearing its most crucial stages. Her burh-building programme had been exceptionally energetic. The recorded fortifications attributed to her included those mentioned in the *Mercian Register* and elsewhere specifically as burhs, such as *Bremesbyrig*, *Scergeate*, *Bricge*, Tamworth, Stafford, Eddisbury, Warwick, Chirbury, *Weardbyrig* and Runcorn. We might add to these fortifications those at Chester, Hereford, Shrewsbury, Wednesbury, Winchcombe, Gloucester and Worcester, all of which exhibit varying degrees of tenth-century archaeological evidence, circumstantial or otherwise, not to mention the strongholds taken by Æthelflæd at Derby and Leicester. As for those burhs such as *Scergeate* and *Weardbyrig* which seem elusive to this day, it is worth considering that these difficulties might arise from their contemporary success as forts in a changing landscape, and not from their failures as central places. Perhaps one day, work carried out by the trowels and shovels of the archaeologists and the cotton-gloved hands of the archivists will reveal more secrets at Bromsgrove, Leintwardine, Shrawardine, Tutbury, Caus Castle and Whitchurch, front-runners for some of these missing places, each of which surely had a part to play in Æthelflæd's grand designs.

In generations to come, there would be many a noble woman and indeed, even queens and mothers of kings who bore her name, such was the esteem in which she was held amongst Mercians and across England as a whole. At least five important women shared her name in the tenth century and there is even a suggestion that it was a popular name beyond these five. Edward must surely have been devastated by the news of his sister's death when the messengers rode to Stamford. From both a personal and political point of view, it came as a body blow. Their relationship had clearly been close. But they will not have seen everything in the exact same way, since they both had control of different and very ancient kingdoms within the overarching project of Edward's wider kingdom of the Anglo-Saxons. However, William of Malmesbury, writing in the twelfth century, said of Æthelflæd

> . . . she was a powerful accession to his [Edward's] party, the delight of his subjects, the dread of his enemies . . . This spirited heroine assisted her brother greatly with her advice; she was of equal service in building cities, nor could you easily discern whether it were more owing to fortune or her own exertions, that a woman should be able to protect men at home, and to intimidate them abroad.

William of Malmesbury couches his praise of Æthelflæd in terms of what she brought to Edward's plans and campaigns, perhaps underplaying the truly independent nature of this most powerful Anglo-Saxon woman. But he does acknowledge that Edward's subjects were infatuated by her and that those who stood against her were in fear of her. But William's praise is valuable nonetheless. It has even been argued that William of Malmesbury modelled his account of his formidable contemporary Matilda (d. 1167) on Æthelflæd in his later *Historia Novella*.[2] Matilda's familial connections stretched back to the line of the house of Wessex and in William's time she was struggling for the throne of England against her cousin King Stephen (1135–54). But William was hardly the only medieval writer impressed by the deeds of the Lady of the Mercians. To Caradoc of Llancarvan she was a woman 'of singular virtues' who 'greatly strengthened the Mercian kingdom'. John of Worcester called her 'a very virtuous woman, and renowned for her prudence and justice'. He also pointedly remarks that she had held a 'firm but moderate undivided sway over the Mercians' and importantly, that she had left her daughter as heir to the kingdom. The idea that Æthelflæd had been a 'Lady' by title and not a 'queen', was completely lost on, or ignored by, another twelfth-century historian, Henry of Huntingdon, who burst into verse in his praise of her. He even tampered with her gender by way of some sort of 'compliment'. Translations vary, but the sentiment is clear:

> Heroic Elflede [*sic*]! Great in martial fame,
> A man in valour, woman though in name;
> Thee warlike hosts, thee, nature too obey'd,
> Conqu'ror o'er both, though born by sex a maid.
> Chang'd be thy name, such honour triumphs bring,

A queen by title, but in deeds a king.
Heroes before the Mercian heroine quail'd:
Cæsar himself to win such glory fail'd.

Henry of Huntingdon was not trying to be 'sexist' here in the way we might understand the term today. For him, although he misunderstood her familial relations, Æthelflæd had clearly achieved (and even surpassed) the deeds more commonly achieved by great men of the past and his poem should be seen as high praise indeed, perhaps even deriving itself from an earlier source. The praise has kept coming down the centuries on and off. As those centuries wore on, some depictions of Æthelflæd emerge, albeit in a stylized form. A collection of charters (a cartulary) dating from the thirteenth century from Abingdon Abbey shows her seated, draped in a blue mantle and holding a sceptre in her right hand and offering her left hand with palm upwards as if issuing a proclamation (BL. MS Cotton Claudius B VI, folio 14r; see Colour Plate 26). In contrast, another thirteenth-century depiction in a genealogy has her almost as a nun in a possible confusion with her younger sister Æthelgifu whom King Alfred had made abbess at Shaftesbury (BL. MS Royal 14 B V). She is mentioned here in French as 'La Sage' – 'the wise'. And wisdom once again appears in the following century when Æthelflæd is depicted again as 'La Sage' where she wears a headdress of contemporary style in another genealogical chronicle (BL. MS Royal 14 B VI). And in the sumptuous fourteenth-century Chaworth Roll, a genealogy of English kings dating initially to the 1320s with exquisite green-tinted roundels, the reference is once again to wisdom. Æthelflæd is again described in Anglo-Norman French, the language of the English aristocracy of the time. Although it borrows its detail from William of Malmesbury and possibly elsewhere, the recollection of Æthelflæd (translated below) some 400 years after her death, is still powerful:

> This Alfled [*sic*] was the most wise of all lay women. With her intelligence and her knowledge she greatly helped her brother Edward to govern the kingdom. When she was married to earl Edrid [Æthelred] to whom her father had given her, she bore him a son [*sic*]; thereafter she never allowed her lord to sleep with her carnally, for she said that the lineage of queens should not practice or love sensuality where there was such suffering in giving birth.[3]

Æthelflæd makes intermittent appearances over the centuries, with long gaps, and cameos in a play or two here and there. But her 'appearance' in Henry Bradshaw's (d. 1513) verse *Life* of St Werburgh, whilst deriving material again from William of Malmesbury, contains detail that perhaps only a monk of Chester could feel entitled to proclaim:

Also we may note, holdyng none opinion,
This lady Elflede of her charite
Of the sayd mother-churche translate the patron,
Caused the sayd oratorie reconciled to be
In the honour of the most blessed trinite
And of saynt Oswalde, martyr and kynge,
For the Loue she had to hym continuynge.

The yere of our lorde .ix. hundreth and .viii.
This noble duchesse with mycel royalte
Reedified Chestre and fortified it full right,
Churche house and wall, decayed piteousle.
Thus brought vnto ruyne was Chestre cite
First, by Ethelfride, kyng of Northumberlande,
And by danes norwaies, vexyng all Englande.

Also she enlarged this sayd old cite
With newe myghty walles stronge all-about,
Almost by proporcion double in quantite
To the forther byldynge brought without dout;
She compassed in the castell enemies to hold out
Within the sayd Walles, to defende the towne
Agaynst danes and walshemen, to dryue them all downe.

After the deth of her husband Ethelrede
She ruled the realme of mercelande manfully,
Buylded churches and townes repared in dede,
As Staforde Warwike Thomwort and Shirisbury;
Of newe she edified Runcorn and Edisbury.
The body of saynt Oswalde also she translate
From Bardeney to Gloucetur, there to be tumulate:

Where she edified a noble monastery,
With licence of her brother afore nominate,
In honour of saint Peter ouer the blessed body
Of the sayd saynt Oswalde kyng and martyr coronate.
In wiche monastery this lady was tumulate,
The yere of our lorde .ix. hundreth and nyntene;
Whom myn auctor prayseth in this wordes serene . . .

For the Victorians, the memory of her father was the more overpowering force, though as we have seen, her importance was not lost on the engineers of the Queen Ethelfleda Viaduct at Runcorn (see pages 123–4). The twentieth century, however, possibly because of the frequent millennial celebrations of the founding of the various named Mercian Æthelflædan burhs, saw a flowering of appreciation for Æthelflæd, who thus remained entrenched in the imaginations of many people in the heart of England. Perhaps the most touching statue of this era is that by Edward George Bramwell (1913), still standing today outside Tamworth Castle (see page 14).

One of the foremost Anglo-Saxon scholars of the twentieth century, Sir Frank Stenton, said of Æthelflæd 'The record of the fortresses which she built for the protection of Mercia shows that she had an eye for country, and the ability to forecast the movements of her enemies'. And yet for so long, Æthelflæd has had to play second fiddle in the national imagination not only to countless men, but also to other prominent

Above and right: 45 and 46. *'Queen of Mercia', Runcorn. Diane Gorvin and Philip Bews. 1994. Commissioned by Halton Borough Council and the Manchester Ship Canal Company.*

women of different eras. Both Boudicca (the famous British leader of the Iceni tribe who led an insurrection against the Romans in AD 60 to 61) and Elizabeth I (1558–1603) have rightly earned their places in history. However, neither of them can place their story at the very moment of the birth of England. In fact, the first of them predated that whole concept by hundreds of years and was not 'English' at all. But anachronistic comparisons are perhaps unfair to all. Suffice it to say that the burgeoning recognition in towns

47. *Originally on Wigg Island overlooking the Mersey, Angela Sidwell's 2009 statue of Æthelflæd and two other companions ('Watch on the Mersey') now stand proudly outside the Brindley Theatre, Runcorn.*

48. *Iron fence on Runcorn waterfront commemorating 'Aethelfreada'. At the site of the former Transporter Bridge.*

49. Of Heroes and Industry. *Fiona and Neil Osborne. One Red Shoe. 2011. Mural at Runcorn.* Æthelflæd *forms the 'R' of Runcorn.*

and churches across England of the life and work of Æthelflæd in the form of statues, stained-glass windows and public events such as were seen in Gloucester and Tamworth in 2018 at the millennial commemorations of Æthelflæd's passing, are to be warmly welcomed. At last, the Lady of the Mercians is stepping out of the mist, capturing us in her warm embrace. The woman whose strong hands and wise mind nurtured the infant England will never be forgotten.

We have seen how Æthelflæd's memory crops up in more places than merely at the list of burhs recorded in the *Mercian Register*. Wednesbury, for example (see above, pages 62–5), proudly promotes its connections with the Lady of the Mercians. Sometimes, the memory may be based on the suspected early link of still extant (though rededicated) churches to Æthelflæd. At Churchdown in Gloucestershire, the church of St Bartholomew sits picturesquely amid an Iron Age hill fort, echoing the situation at another St Bartholomew's at Wednesbury. Although the existing church building dates from the Norman and later medieval periods, the belief that it had an earlier connection with Æthelflæd was promoted by a Gloucestershire antiquarian, Reverend William Bazeley. It is perhaps not so wild an idea. Above the north porch is a medieval room in which it is believed the canons of St Oswald's Priory (see pages 72–4) stayed when they served as parish priests, having travelled out from Gloucester. In the early twentieth century St Bartholomew's was superseded by the new parish church dedicated to St Andrew, situated in the village slightly to the north-east. And even here in the village, at St Andrews (to the south side of the church) archaeology has shown connections with the late Saxon period, with excavations revealing ditches, a few sherds of limestone tempered ware, a strap end and postholes prompting speculation that the village in Late Saxon times was an agricultural settlement.[4] Small wonder then, that we find a stained-glass window of Æthelflæd, complete with crown and sceptre, at St Andrew's in Churchdown, designed by George Cooper-Abbs in 1934. Another church, where Æthelflæd is commemorated in the form of a stained-glass window is at St Barnabas's Church in Bromborough in Wirral, near to where she is believed to have founded a monastery in the area around the year 912. 'Countess Ethelfleda' is the title awarded to her in the window. Little is known of the tenth-century history of this place, but outside the church stands a reconstructed and rather fragmentary Anglo-Saxon cross purportedly dating to the ninth or tenth century, the fragments having been found apparently during the demolition of the church in 1863. The position of the church and monastery would be right near the edge (on the English side) of the Scandinavian enclave established by Ingimund's portion of the exiles from Ireland in the early tenth century.

At Leicester, a drinking fountain surmounted by a statuette of Æthelflæd was bequeathed by Edith Gittins (1845–1910) to the County Borough of Leicester. Gittins was an artist, feminist and staunch admirer of Æthelflæd with whom she identified. She actively promoted women's rights and social reform. She also believed that her choice of Æthelflæd not only would raise the profile of the value of women in society but also fitted in with notions of Anglo-Saxon civic identity. Originally intended for the High Street, it was instead unveiled on 3 August 1922 in Victoria Park. The structure was to be called 'Ethelfloeda's Fountain' and it was to be made by Benjamin Fletcher and Crossland McClure. The statuette was unfortunately stolen in 1978, but a replica originally created by Benjamin Fletcher now stands in the courtyard of Leicester Guildhall.[5]

So there are plenty of memorials to Æthelflæd in later times, some alluding to the acts which made her famous in her own time. But are there any roughly contemporary texts other than the *Mercian Register* which might shed some light on Æthelflæd? Recent scholarship has brought to light one such text, the little known Paris Bibliothèque nationale, Latin 5574, fols 1-39, which may well provide us with a glimpse as to the spiritual inspiration for Æthelflæd.[6] If we combine her knowledge of this text with her sure

50. *Replica of the 1922 Ethelfloeda drinking fountain statuette, now in the courtyard of Leicester Guildhall.*

knowledge of Aldhelm's (c. 639–709) famous treatise on chastity and the tenth-century translation of the life of the Mercian St Guthlac, all of which were circulating in her time, we start to perhaps understand the spiritual drive behind Æthelflæd. Dating to around 900, the Latin 5574 mentioned above is believed to be of Mercian (probably Worcester) origin and must surely have had the approval of the Lady of the Mercians.

The overwhelming theme within the five hagiographies it contains is that of the heroic yet martyred woman. Female martyrs, who gained their immortality through courage and suffering in a world of great violence, are at the heart of the work. Saint Juliana of Nicomedia is represented here by an almost complete *Life*. She was martyred in c. 304 and became a patron saint of sickness. Saint Margaret of Antioch, the only female saint famous for subduing a dragon, is also here. Her suffering at the hands of her pagan Roman persecutor and her miraculous escape from the dragon's symbolic 'womb' may be why this particular virgin martyr became the patron saint of childbirth and she was surely of great importance to Æthelflæd. Margaret had even said that pregnant women who invoke her would escape the dangers of childbirth as would their infants. And then there is St Helena, whose influence over Mercian ruling women has already been seen (see above, page 82).

According to the *Mercian Register* Æthelflæd had ruled Mercia since the death of her husband 'with rightful lordship'. It is a curious phrase with some hint of a Mercian recollection that there may have been those who thought that lordship *not* to be rightful. Whether those who thought this were Mercian or West Saxon in outlook is unknown. Æthelflæd had ruled as a Mercian ruler, and to some a 'queen' and also as a loyal – although occasionally independent – allied commander to her brother. She had done so by displaying the overt piety of her father and she seems to have shared his moral, if not political, outlook in life. And in Mercia, people had a very different understanding of their 'royal' women. They were not held in the background like they apparently were in Wessex. People will have known the importance of Æthelflæd's maternal lineage through her Mercian mother Ealhswith, her grandmother Eadburh and thence back to Coenwulf (796–821). Æthelflæd's own aunt Æthelswith had experienced rule in Mercia alongside her husband Burgred. Both women would have quickly learned the art of the *frythwebba* or 'peace-weaver', a traditional role for royal women, but for Æthelflæd the experience of rule was more direct and involved an overt and symbolic justification programme as she and her forces established or re-established a Mercian presence in place after place, bringing the bones of carefully chosen saints into the churches. Perhaps the symbolism behind those royal saints, many Mercian, was to reassure as well as justify. There need not be any cynicism implied on Æthelflæd's part. She is likely to have been truly devoted to the saints. Memories of the great female figures of the Mercian past must still have been current at the time of Æthelflæd's death, and her brother Edward, half Mercian himself, knew it. It may be significant that John of Worcester refers to Æthelflæd as leaving her 'kingdom' to her daughter. The Mercians had their own idea as to who was going to succeed the first 'Lady of the Mercians'. And, as it turned out, it would be the second.

Chapter 22

A New Lady

Æthelflæd's body was probably taken to St Editha's church in Tamworth immediately after her death. She was washed, clothed and shrouded in linen and then possibly taken to Lichfield just seven miles to the north-west. Here, she may have lain on a bier and been blessed by her friend, Bishop Ælfwine. Then the journey to Gloucester was organized. This procession would have been accompanied by a guard of honour of at least thirty of Æthelflæd's warriors and a host of household staff, not to mention clerical officials. It is tempting to assume that her daughter Ælfwynn and nephew Æthelstan were there too, as seems most likely.[1]

It is to that daughter we now turn. She was the first and only woman in Anglo-Saxon history to succeed another woman as a ruler of any region, let alone one with such a grand heritage as Mercia. But her tale contains a very dark moment. So, who was Ælfwynn, the second Lady of the Mercians?[2] It is likely that she was earmarked for the Mercian succession by her parents and the Mercian witan many years before her mother died. The scant record of her life up to 918 would suggest (mainly from her signatures on charter witness lists) that she had been present in the Princes Risborough area in 903/4, at Worcester in 904 and at the burh of *Weardbyrig* in 915.

When she was no more than 16 years old, Ælfwynn was included as the third life in a lease by Bishop Wærferth of a large enclosure in Worcester and an estate at Barbourne. This charter of 904 (S 1280) contains the phrase '. . . And if Ælfwyn [*sic*] survives them [her parents], it shall similarly remain uncontested as long as she lives; and after the death of the three of them, it shall be given back without dispute to the lord of the church for the souls of the three of them . . .'. The assumption would appear to be that Ælfwynn was the heir to her parents' possessions. So, when Æthelflæd died in June 918, it is likely that she inherited this Worcester property.

Ælfwynn's appearance on a joint grant to Æthelfrith *Dux* (S 367 and S 367a, a renewal of a grant replacing an earlier document lost in a fire) is also of note. It was for thirty hides at Monk's Risborough, Buckinghamshire. Æthelfrith, a senior figure in the Mercian set-up and a man of probable West Saxon background exercising power in south-east Mercia since Alfred's days, had clearly thought it necessary to appeal to King Edward as well as both Æthelred and Æthelflæd in this document (see above, page 51). Ælfwynn appears sixteenth in the witness list after the bishops and magnates, but before the abbots and ministers. But it seems that Ælfwynn grew in importance after the death of her father in 911. The charter issued at *Weardbyrig* in September 915 catapults her up the rankings – if the identification of Ælfwyn *ep.* (for *episcopus*) – is correctly recognized as a copyists' mistake.

That Ælfwynn did succeed her mother as Lady of the Mercians cannot be in doubt. John of Worcester's statement that '. . . she left an only daughter, named Aelfwinna [*sic*], by the subregulus Athered [*sic*], heir to her kingdom' speaks volumes. The *Mercian Register* explicitly states the succession to be the case in its entry for 919 (although the content is generally thought to be more accurately dated to December 918, due to the wording of the entry). Here, we are reminded of the brutal pragmatism of Anglo-Saxon politics:

> Her eac wearð Æþeredes dohtor Myrcna hlafordes ælces anwealdes on Myrcum benumen, ⁊ on Westsexe aleded þrim wucum ær middan wintra; seo wæs haten Ælfwyn.
>
> 'Here also [a phrase suggestive of a continuation of the preceding 918 entry] the daughter of Æthelred, Lord of the Mercians, was deprived of all control in Mercia, and was led into Wessex three weeks before Midwinter; she was called Ælfwynn.'

For someone to be 'deprived of all control' must surely mean that they had obtained that control in the first place. So, between her mother's death in June and Ælfwynn's curious deposition in December 918, what had happened to lead King Edward to take such a dramatic and ruthless step? And why does it seem on the face of it to have been a move unopposed by the Mercian witan? And most intriguingly of all, what ever happened to Ælfwynn?

Firstly, we turn to the sequence of events as reported in the *Anglo-Saxon Chronicle* and its Mercian insertion, the *Mercian Register*. It is not easy to reconcile the two. The pro-Wessex (A) version of the *Anglo-Saxon Chronicle* has it as follows.

1. Æthelflæd dies at Tamworth 12 days before midsummer 918.
2. Edward 'rides' to the stronghold [*þa burg*] of Tamworth and takes it, then 'all the nation of the land of Mercia which was earlier subject to Æthelflæd turned to him, and the kings of Wales: Hywel and Clydog and Idwal and all the race of the Welsh, sought him as their lord'.
3. From Tamworth Edward goes to Nottingham, captures it, and orders it to be improved and occupied both with Englishmen and Danes. All the people who were settled in the land of Mercia, both Danish and English, turned to him.

There is, of course, no mention of Ælfwynn. The *Mercian Register*, however, simply has this:

1. Æthelflæd dies at Tamworth 12 days before midsummer 918, in the eighth year of her 'rightful lordship' and is taken to Gloucester.
2. Ælfwynn, daughter of Æthelred, is deprived of all control in Mercia and led into Wessex three weeks before Midwinter [December 918].

So, we have Æthelflæd dying in the summer of 918 and Ælfwynn succeeding her, and not being 'deposed' until three weeks before Midwinter, which would have placed the deposition in the opening week of December.

The general feeling amongst historians is that the author of the (A) version has compressed the timeline for the understandable political purpose of glossing over the brief rule of Edward's niece in Mercia, and that the events described go well into 919. If so, this would put the submission of the Mercians to Edward and the visit and submission of the Welsh *after* the deposition of his niece. But this is by no means conclusive. The evidence is capable of a great variety of interpretations.

Firstly, Edward must have acted swiftly on hearing of his sister's death. But the chronicler's claim that he 'rode' to Tamworth in the aftermath of Æthelflæd's death is of interest. The word used is *gerad*, which whilst having 'mounted' connotations, can also be used in the context of 'overrode', or may even mean 'took into his possession'. John of Worcester goes as far as saying that Edward 'reduced Tamworth to submit to him' on hearing of Æthelflæd's death. If Edward had come to Tamworth to secure his niece's allegiance and perhaps even promote her accession, the language of the chronicle shows the approach to be somewhat overbearing. Perhaps he came to impose his own rule instead. The king does not seem to have removed Ælfwynn immediately, however, and so her departure from political life cannot have been his priority from the start. It is understandable that the (A) version of the chronicle makes no mention of Ælfwynn at all. It simply left her out of the story. It is quite possible Edward came to Tamworth as king of the Anglo-Saxons and immediately secured his niece's allegiance. But is it conceivable that at this stage, the nation of Mercia that had been subject to Æthelflæd (that is, all of Mercia except those parts still under control of the remaining Danish armies, and those parts ceded to Edward on Æthelred's death in 911) 'turned to him'? The word used by the chronicler is *cierde*, arising from the verb *cirran*, 'to turn'. We encountered the same word when the men of Bedford had turned to Edward in 915. It is thought to be a fairly neutral term and does not imply bonds of lordship.[3] So, the situation in mid-June 918 might either be that Edward came to Tamworth with a sizable force and secured his niece's submission, or took full control from the outset. If the former scenario is correct, what promises or arrangements were made with the Mercians regarding Ælfwynn's status as a *subregulus* to Edward are unknown. If the latter scenario is correct, Edward's delay in dealing with the obvious issue of Ælfwynn's political potency would require explanation.

The next thing to have happened is the submission of the Welsh kings. Here, we may have the compressed version of events. These kings were Hywel (Hywel Dda, the long-reigning king of Dyfed), Clydog (Powys) and Idwal (Gwynedd), all collectively of the *Merfynion*. Both Hywel and Clydog were the sons of Cadell ap Rhodri, who had earlier replaced the sons of Hyfaidd in Dyfed. Idwal was the son of Anarawd ap Rhodri, the highly active king of Gwynedd, whom he succeeded in 916. These rulers represented the second generation (that is, 'grandsons') of Rhodri. The account of their submission to Edward is an emphatic statement whereby the impetus comes from the Welsh side, like we have seen before amongst the Danes of the Midlands, in that they 'sought him as their Lord', or so it was said. This is different to the Mercians 'turning' to Edward. These three kings, it is thought, were effectively transferring their bonds of lordship from their earlier overlord (Æthelflæd) to their new one, Edward. For this to be the case, the Welsh submission may have come after early December 918 when Ælfwynn was deposed and Edward assumed full control of Mercia, unless of course, he had done so already.

All of this leaves us wondering if the Nottingham campaign came before or after the deposition of Ælfwynn. It must not be forgotten that Edward was still in the process of completing his drive to the north and his conquest of areas still under Danish lordship.

Æthelflæd, his chief partner in all this campaigning, was no longer at the head of the Mercian army. It seems likely that Edward assumed overall command of a combined Anglo-Saxon army as he headed out to Nottingham, a stronghold which may well have been his late sister's next target. It does not seem likely that Ælfwynn commanded any part of the army. In fact, it is more likely that Æthelstan, a tested warrior of 23 years of age, although curiously absent from the records, lead the Mercian army. The English army successfully captured Nottingham. We are not told how it was done, but it was a far different outcome than that which Edward's father Alfred and his uncle Æthelred I had faced in 868. Once achieved, Edward ordered the Nottingham fort to be 'improved' and occupied by a joint garrison of Englishmen and Danes, a phenomenon now becoming increasingly familiar. Also, Edward's capture of Nottingham and the subsequent engineering works which seem to have included a large-scale ditch and rampart, resulted in 'all the people that was settled in the land of Mercia, both Danish and English . . .' turning to him.

Developments at Nottingham seem to have led to the turning of almost all of historic Mercia to Edward, bar Lincoln and its dependencies. This may be because Lincoln was still in some way beholden to York and, particularly, the new political set-up under Rægnald. Some, however, contend that Lincoln itself was included in this submission as the wording of the chronicle might suggest, but there is no explicit mention of the city. Edward's concerns about Rægnald and York were certainly real enough, but the situation in Mercia, although murky in the accounts, was by late November 918, clearly beginning to occupy Edward's mind. Something had changed since the summer.

Ælfwynn had seemingly remained a spinster during her mother's lifetime. Nobody seems to know why. Ælfwynn's mother Æthelflæd had chosen not to remarry after her husband's death in 911 and we have noted her attitude towards childbirth and carnal pleasures as reported by William of Malmesbury (see page 176). But whether this position transferred to her daughter is debatable. Ælfwynn was around 30 years old by now, and apparently childless. Constitutional crises of this magnitude can often be brought about by lack of suitable heirs. If it is the case that Æthelflæd wished for the Mercian succession to pass down the female royal line (which is hardly out of the question), Ælfwynn would still have needed to produce children. There is some speculation that when the men of York had come to Ælfwynn's mother in the early summer of 918, they may have brought a marriage proposal with them. This cannot be proved. There is also an argument that there is some room for the proposition that it had been Æthelstan himself who was destined to marry his own cousin, despite the obvious consternation this would cause with the Church in a new atmosphere of religious reform which followed on from the death of Bishop Wærferth of Worcester, around 915 or 916.[4] But this too cannot be proved. Rumours that Ælfwynn had been destined to marry into the York regime are given spurious support by a possibly fictitious tale preserved in Powel's edition of the *The History of Wales* of Caradoc of Llancarvan (1584) which suggests (on the basis of a not-unreasonable claim made by a Benedictine monk at Westminster Abbey) that Edward's mother had appointed Edward as Ælfwynn's guardian but that Ælfwynn had not told Edward she had promised herself to Rægnald: 'wherevpon, king Edward, to preuent his enimie, entred the land of Mercia, and seazed the same [Ælfwynn] to his owne hands, and caried also the said Ladie with him into Westsex.'[5] It might sound like a creative imagination trying to make sense of the holes in the evidence. But it does, however, provide reasons for the gap between two key Mercian events of 918: Ælfwynn's succession, and her dramatic removal by Edward months later. It has to be said, that an unmarried heiress to an ancient and resurgent kingdom would undoubtedly have attracted suitors and there does seem to be a hint of fear in Edward's government about the potency of Ælfwynn.

Judging by Edward's actions his vision for the future of Mercia seems to have differed from that of his sister. But during that six months, had Ælfwynn really reached out with a marriage proposal not to Edward's liking, or had she somehow failed to impress? Had she fallen short in her role as *subregulus* in some way? Her deposition would not come as a result of an internal Mercian revolt, however. Instead, it was a forced move by the Anglo-Saxon king, which was greeted with disapproval by the author of the *Mercian Register*. This suggests the Mercians were not entirely unhappy with Ælfwynn. It is perhaps worth noting a record in the fourteenth-century *Book of Hyde*, which may or may not preserve a genuine West Saxon (and abridged) interpretation of events: 'Elfleda's [*sic*] only daughter, named Elfwyna [*sic*], was carried by King Edward the elder into west Saxony, when the government of the Mercians was taken from him.'[6]

There has to be a good reason for Edward to have risked the ire of the Mercians by removing Ælfwynn. And if he had always planned to do it, there needs to be a reason why it took him so long. No matter what concessions were made, there will always have been a faction, however big or small, who were opposed to the move and were very resentful of it. The notion that Ælfwynn's faction may have encouraged a revolt against Edward, who had presumably taken control of Mercia in the summer after all, is not supported elsewhere, but is intriguing nonetheless. In this extraordinary school of thought, the coup d'état is the other way around.

Edward, in order to mitigate Mercian distress at the removal of Ælfwynn, *may* have offered the Mercian witan an obvious and almost irresistible candidate in Mercia, his first son Æthelstan. Æthelstan may have been earmarked for the succession not immediately, but upon Edward's death, with Edward holding all power in the interim. Ælfweard, his other son by his second marriage, would perhaps by the same agreement inherit Wessex at his father's death. It may have been Edward's intention that Ælfweard would rule as king of the Anglo-Saxons as he himself had done, and that Æthelstan would rule Mercia as Lord of the Mercians, just as his uncle Æthelred had. To what extent such an arrangement would be accepted by the Mercians is unclear. But then again, if Æthelstan had instead been intended to rise to the dormant Mercian throne itself (as a long-awaited king), would this not inevitably lead to the resurrection of an independent Mercia and the end of the successful overarching concept of the kingdom of the Anglo-Saxons? It all rather depends on the way that the Mercians looked at it. We might also ask that if this was Edward's policy all along, why he did not install Æthelstan immediately in June 918 in Mercia to begin with. The presence of a gap in time must surely mean there was a period of acceptance or tolerance of Ælfwynn by Edward, before somehow by political intrigue or a more prosaic unfolding of events, things went wrong. It is also important to remember that we know next to nothing of the relationship between Edward and his son Æthelstan.

This leaves us to ponder what happened to Ælfwynn, the second Lady of the Mercians. Are we really to imagine the darkest of outcomes? One theory, although perhaps stretching the imagination, is that Ælfwynn did in fact later go on to marry after all, a man named Æthelstan 'Half-King' sometime after 932. This man, the son of Ealdorman Æthelfrith, would go on to gain considerable power in East Anglia in the next generation, and he married a woman named 'Ælfwynn'. But her connections seem to have been in the East Midlands and it is thought she is unlikely to be the daughter of Æthelflæd. The most likely fate of Ælfwynn is that she was taken into a West Saxon religious house, and was not (as some contend), simply done away with. Although not uncommon, it was still a big step for Edward to take. By removing his niece to such an institution, Edward would ensure that Ælfwynn would have lived comfortably, but also may have been removed from the attentions of any suitor (depending on her status there) and would have been permanently removed from the Mercian political arena. The question is, to what institution could she have been taken? Shaftesbury, where Edward's sister Æthelgifu had become an abbess, is one candidate. But there were other religious institutions associated with Edward's family. Two daughters from Edward's second marriage entered the religious life. These were Eadflæd and Æthelhild, who went to Wilton Abbey (the latter as a lay sister). Another name is associated with Wilton: that of their mother, Ælfflæd. The woman who had given Edward many children, including the Æthelings Ælfweard and Edwin, seems to have been cast aside in favour of a new wife at around this time. Ælfflæd, according to William of Malmesbury, ended her days at Wilton and was buried there. Could Ælfwynn have been carried into Wessex and also ended up at Wilton?

Nobody is quite sure why Edward abandoned Ælfflæd. Perhaps she could no longer bear children and perhaps Edward, having seen the crisis of the Mercian succession at first hand, wanted more of a long-term assurance for his dynastic intentions than merely Æthelstan, Ælfweard and Edwin. Edward's third wife was another redoubtable Anglo-Saxon woman who held considerable influence over the royal court for years to come. Her name was Eadgifu. She was the daughter of Sigehelm, ealdorman of Kent, the man who we recall was killed in the bloodbath at Holme in 902 (see pages 34–7). The choice of Eadgifu was a wise one, if Anglo-Saxon unity was the goal. Kent had proved itself to be a powerful and necessary military resource in the wars against the Danes and Kentish blood ran through Edward's family right back to his great-grandfather Ecgberht and beyond, or at least that is the way it was portrayed. Moreover, Edward possibly had some political repair work to do with the Kentish aristocracy in the years after Holme. Eadgifu would bear a number of children for the king, two of whom, Edmund and Eadred, would play no small part in the creation of the Kingdom of England. And there was a young girl too, by the name of Eadburh. She may have been a little older than the two boys. Her story, although a later twelfth-century recollection, provides a distant glimpse into King Edward's life as a family man, although it is imbued with the sort of symbolism and elaboration we might expect. Osbert of Clare wrote that Edward was keen to know if his three-year-old daughter Eadburh was destined for the secular world or the church. On one side of her he placed jewels and toys and on the other he placed a gospel book, chalice and paten, a small plate used to hold Eucharistic bread. The girl went for the religious items, upon which Edward had her placed in her grandmother Ealhswith's foundation at Nunnaminster in Winchester. Eadburh thrived at the foundation. At one stage King Edward went to visit his daughter and he asked her to sing for him. She hesitated. Then the king promised her a just reward. Eadburh then sang to the king and then in what is perhaps the most suspicious part of the story, reminded him not only of his duty to continue his mother's

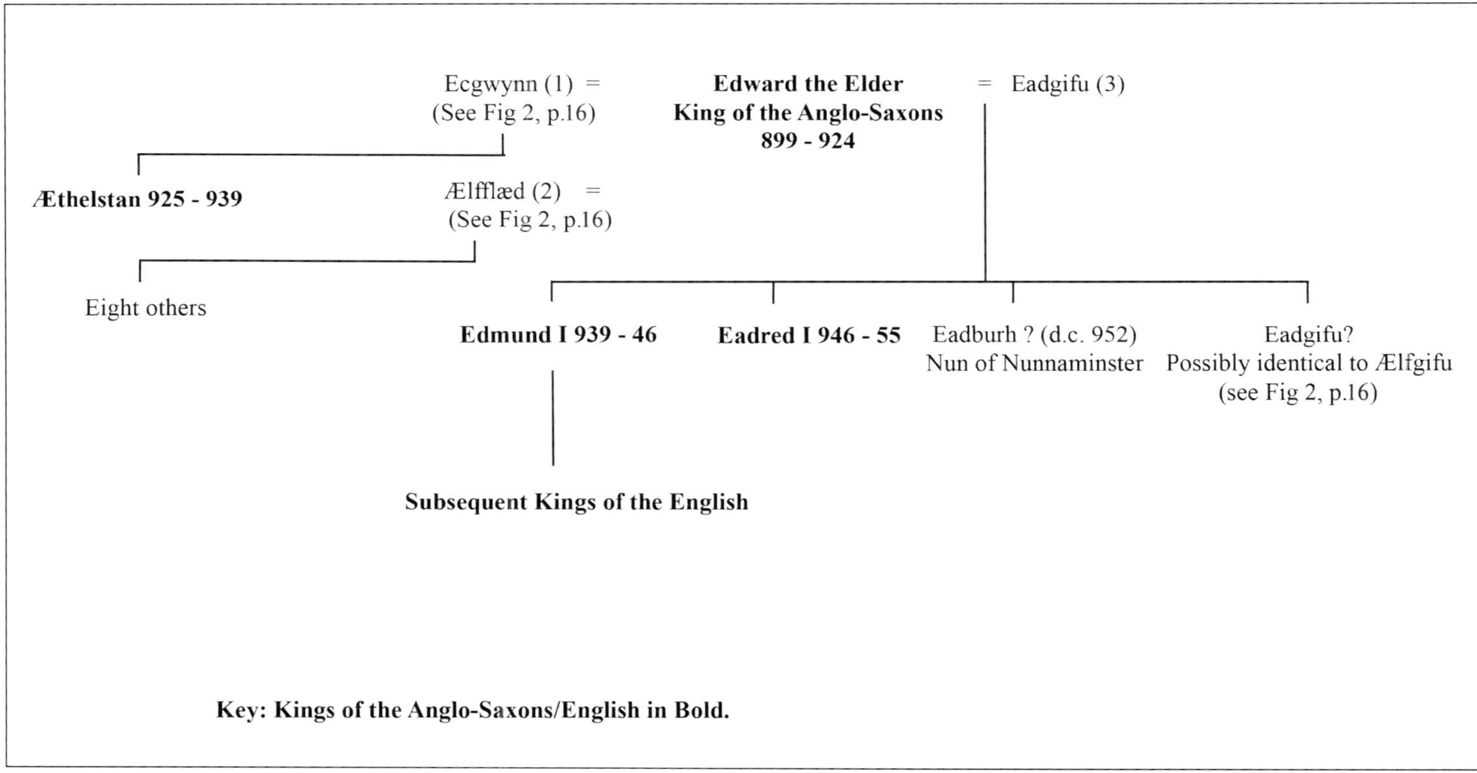

Fig. 11: *The family of Edward the Elder with Eadgifu.*

patronage of the convent, but also demanded the estate of All Cannings in Wiltshire which she knew had recently been forfeited to the king. The estate, incidentally, was still in the hands of Nunnaminster by the time of the Norman Conquest.[7]

We know little about how long Eadgifu had known Edward. However, thanks to a land dispute which rumbled on through the tenth century, there is something to help. Before the battle at the Holme, in 902, her father Sigehelm had endeavoured to pay off a debt, as if he was in some way getting his house in order before going on military campaign. He had owed thirty pounds to a man named Goda. Sigehelm had previously entrusted an estate at Cooling to Goda as security. Sigehelm, believing the debt to have been repaid, then entrusted the estate to his daughter, Eadgifu and even gave her the landbook which went with it. Goda did not see it this way at all. He denied the debt had been repaid, and he held on to Cooling for a full six years after Sigehelm's death, which brings the story of the dispute up to the year 908 or early 909. The witan, the country's powerful assembly of important magnates and clerics, ordered that Eadgifu should swear an oath concerning her father's repayment. This she did, but she was only able to recover the estate when her allies came to her side, and one of these was King Edward himself. But we do not know exactly what relations the two shared at that particular time, although it would seem likely that these events predated their marriage. It might even have been this legal case which brought the young Eadgifu to the king's attention. Alternatively, it could be that Edward, with wide knowledge of the families of Kent, had known Eadgifu for much of her life. The king, displeased with Goda for reasons unclear, granted all his property to Eadgifu 'to dispose of as she wished'. But the wise Eadgifu, though keeping the land books in her back pocket, gave back much of the land to Goda, save for some land at Osterland, which she kept along with the estate of Cooling. It was an interesting tactic. Goda, long after the death of King Edward, continued to lobby for the return of the land books. Eventually, Eadgifu gave him the books for the land, except for that at Osterland. But the dispute had a long shelf-life. The sons of Goda, later in the tenth century, seized Eadgifu's lands which were not restored until the reign of King Edgar (959–75), her grandson. Eadgifu then gave both Cooling and Osterland to Christ Church, Canterbury (S 1211).[8] As Anglo-Saxon land disputes go, this one is a good example (alongside the famous Fonthill letter, for which see below, pages 184–6) of how they could be very protracted and easily stretch from one generation to the next.

But we must return to the mystery of Ælfwynn, the second Lady of the Mercians, and her final destination on her lonely journey into Wessex in the winter of 918. It seems Wilton is a strong candidate for it. One historian has drawn attention to a much later charter of 948 (S 535), which has as its beneficiary one 'Ælfwynne', described as 'a religious woman' living in a nunnery, most probably as a lay sister.[9] It is a grant of six hides at Wickhambreux in Kent, in exchange for two pounds of purest gold. It seems the grant was given by the English king at the time and was done so at the request of the mother of that king, none other than Eadgifu, who was closely associated with Wilton. It is therefore argued that the beneficiary of this grant may in fact have been Ælfwynn, the erstwhile second Lady of the Mercians. If so, she would have been around 60 years old – a woman with a tale to tell, if only there had been someone to write it down.

The Laws of Edward the Elder

Neither of King Edward's two surviving law codes are dated. One of them, the second (promulgated at Exeter), refers to the other, so must post-date the first. Unlike the law codes of his father King Alfred, Edward does not declare that he had consulted anyone in their making, and his laws are more authoritarian and direct in their language.

The first code concentrates on trade, land disputes and perjury. It begins with a strict warning to the king's reeves to not fail to interpret the public law and to be sure to set a date for case hearings. He also refers to the adherence of the written laws, probably referring to those of his father. Whilst Alfred's laws opened with an understandable appeal to all men to keep to their oaths and pledge (Alfred had often been on the wrong end of the oathbreaker), Edward seems also to have been concerned with economics: 'And my will is that every man shall have his warrantor and that no-one shall buy except in a market town; but he shall have the witness of the port-reeve or of other men of credit [who could vouch that the goods were not stolen], who can be trusted.'

Also notable is Edward's lack of inclusion of religious matters, although it is possible he felt that his father's laws covered all this adequately enough. Edward, for the first time since the days of Ine, refers to the trial of ordeal for those whose oaths have proved worthless, having perjured themselves. As such, his laws mark the beginning of a continuous legal apparatus which lasted for centuries.

In his second (Exeter) code, Edward expresses dissatisfaction with the way in which his previous orders had been executed. His concern was with keeping the public peace better that it had been. His language is more direct and mainly in the first person, including terms such as '*ic wille þæt*' ('I will that . . .'). Here, he is beseeching his councillors to cooperate with him. He asks which of his councillors would join him by 'favouring what he favoured and discountenancing what he discountenanced, both by land and sea'. That there was a general oath of allegiance to the king in existence is also highlighted by a phrase in the second code stating 'If anyone neglects this and breaks his oath and pledge which the whole nation has given, he shall pay such compensation as the written laws declare.'

Edward's second code required his reeves to hold meetings every four weeks and to assign a hearing date to every lawsuit. It is generally taken to mark a regularization of procedures perhaps already in existence and which also marked the transition from the Old English folcmots of yesteryear towards the hundred courts of the middle tenth century. But the second code is interesting for the language it uses when describing Edward's wider realm. Concerning the punishment due to those who harbour a fugitive, it states 'if the offence is committed in the eastern or northern kingdoms, compensation shall be paid in accordance with the provisions of the treaties'. It is possibly an indicator that the second code dates from after 917 or even later, after the East Anglian Danes had sworn union with Edward, but the meaning of the phrases 'eastern' and 'northern' is not made explicit, and the 'northern' kingdom cannot have been Northumbria at this time, but may refer to other areas beyond Watling Street. The haunting phrase '. . . in accordance with the provisions of the treaties', is a reminder of how much legal documentation from Edward's reign is missing.

Chapter 23

Father and Lord

That Edward assumed mastery of Mercia is not in doubt. From 919 he is to be found shoring up the northern and north-western frontiers of the ancient kingdom where it met with Gwynedd and western Northumbria respectively. Late into harvest time in 919, Edward took an army to Thelwall where he ordered a stronghold to be made and manned. Thelwall's position, just nine miles east of Runcorn on the Mersey, would suggest that Edward shared the same concerns in the region as his late sister and was seeking to continue her policy of guarding the Mercian border, particularly against seaborne incursion from the west. Thelwall is another of our 'lost' fortifications. It is suggested that its name means 'deep pool at a plank' or perhaps 'pool with a plank bridge'.[1] Candidates range from structures near to Chaigeley School, to nearby Grappenhall, under the present village, or a site near Warrington situated inside a curve in the Mersey on its north bank near to where the old Roman road crossed the river.[2] A combination of the construction of the Manchester Ship Canal and other engineering works have made identifying Thelwall's fort a difficult task indeed.

It had been a Mercian army which Edward had taken to Thelwall, and it would also be another Mercian army (its geographic origins are not recorded) which Edward ordered to go to Manchester 'in Northumbria' to 'improve' and man it. John of Worcester, with his mention of 'valiant soldiers' stationed at Manchester, seems to imply that this force was an elite Mercian group. Manchester is immediately north of the traditional Mercian border with Northumbria. The fortification which Edward had ordered to be 'improved' is thought to have been the third-century fort at Mancunium. The rivers Irwell and Medlock protected this place on three sides where the routeway crossed the latter. Manchester was vital to Edward because it commanded the Roman road from Chester to York. Edward's strategic policy was still to prevent a physical link between Dublin and York by placing troops between the two, so as to dominate strategic routeways across western Northumbria. The burhs at Thelwall and Manchester would combine with the one already built by Æthelflæd at Runcorn to ensure that communication and transport between the two great Scandinavian power centres of the northern world would at the very least, be severely hampered.

Where Edward stayed and what he did between harvest 919 and midsummer 920 is not recorded, but it is of note that John of Worcester (writing two centuries later) places the abduction of Ælfwynn at this point, after the 'repair' of Manchester, and not, as the *Mercian Register* would apparently have it, in December 918. This may be to do with the fact that he was following the *Mercian Register*'s entry for 919 which describes the event by commencing with 'here also. . ' probably referring to the continuation of the previous year's entry.

Probably as part of the same grand strategy emphasized by the building of Thelwall and the repair of Manchester, in the summer of 920 Edward marched with an army back to

Nottingham and ordered a burh to be built on the south side of the Trent opposite the one he had manned with an Anglo-Danish force earlier. The intention might seem obvious. As in other doubly fortified places, the denial of enemy river movement was part of the goal. To reinforce this notion, Edward built a bridge between the burhs to ensure no vessels from the north-east could penetrate into the heart of the Trent Valley.[3]

The furious engineering activity did not stop. From Nottingham an army was sent to Bakewell in the Peak District. Bakewell was already a settlement on the River Wye at this time and it was situated roughly halfway between Nottingham and Manchester in a south-east to north-west line. It may have represented a frontier position at the edge of Edward's now-expanded kingdom. Bakewell was only a few miles from the Roman road from Manchester to Æthelflæd's recently-captured Derby. John of Worcester implies that the burh was not built at Bakewell itself, but 'not far off', which may be of significance. Some structures on the east bank of the Wye south of Bakewell Bridge and a site west of the river close to Castle Street have been offered as candidates, but again, this burh remains elusive. An area to the north and west of All Saints Church has also been given as a potential and promising site but no evidence (save for the existence of two ninth-century stone crosses) has been found to support the proposition.[4]

Not long after Bakewell's completion in 920, an event occurred which the (A) version of the *Anglo-Saxon Chronicle* rejoices in telling us about. The event, a 'submission' to Edward of the major regional leaders of northern Britain, has engendered much debate, which centres around the exact meaning of the 'submission' and the true extent of the power Edward was now able to wield in the British Isles. It has also been coloured by notions of Scottish and English nationalism over the centuries. Here is how the chronicle puts it, as it describes Edward heading out from Nottingham:

> . . . and from there [King Edward] went to Bakewell in the Peak District, and ordered a stronghold to be made in the neighbourhood and manned. And then the king of Scots and all the nation of Scots chose him as father and lord; and [so also did] Rægnald and Eadwulf's sons and all those who live in Northumbria, both English and Danish and Norwegians and others; and also the king of the Strathclyde Britons and all the Strathclyde Britons.

Perhaps the first observation to make about this entry is that it does not explicitly state that the meeting of kings – if indeed, it was a meeting – took place at Bakewell. We assume there was a meeting at Bakewell because of the chronicler's wording.

Another observation is the meaning of the term 'Father and Lord'. We have seen that during the height of the Danish wars in the southern Mercian theatre, a defeated jarl would come to Edward and 'seek him as Lord'. But the phrase used to describe the royal 'submissions' here is different and its meaning unclear. Some have interpreted this to be the first example of English dominance over Scotland. But it is unlikely that the submission included any territorial gains from the Scots. It is perhaps unwise to see the event in stark terms. What really seems to have happened here is a gathering of regional rulers, brought together in the wake of a huge political and military upheaval in the region. Edward (with the notable help of his sister) had extended southern Anglo-Saxon dominance to the borders of Northumbria. Arguably, since his sister's death he may even have extended it to the line of the Ribble. Constantín had fought his way south and had protected Scottish interests in a fight with Rægnald. Rægnald had taken York and begun to set himself up as king there. He would soon mint coins in his name, with the name of York on their reverse. In fact, his first penny type has a head on the obverse based on a rare portrait type of Edward's. His second type incorporated a hand on the reverse, probably also influenced by Edward's issues in Western Mercia under his sister's immediate authority (see pages 127–9). His third type, however, displaying a hammer and a bow and arrow (apparently), may have drawn inspiration from Frankish types. As for Eadwulf's sons at Bamburgh and the king of Strathclyde at Govan, neither of these were in any way minor players in the politics of the north.

Although the kings may have seen each other as 'equals', this meeting between them signified a recognition of recent conquests and in particular, an endorsement of Edward's gains. Rægnald too may have had claims which he wished to be recognized over and above his position in York itself. It is argued that the meeting was held in the context of both Edward and Rægnald's recent conquests.[5] Rægnald may have argued for the recognition of York's hegemony over Lincoln and its dependencies, a region seemingly just beyond the grasp of Edward at this time. But to even up the status of each of the attendees at the 'meeting' of 920, as seems to be the current trend, is to stretch credulity too far: for all we have said regarding the notional 'equality' of the kings at the meeting of 920, it is unlikely that any one of them walked away from the place not knowing who the first among them was. Admittedly, they may have been paying lip-service to their nominal overlord. For now, they had chosen Edward as 'Father and Lord'. It all depends of course whether we choose to believe the only account of it we have, written down in a triumphant pro-Edward chronicle. But then, if the events at or near to Bakewell unfolded in the way the scribe recorded them, can he not be forgiven for his choice of words? Nothing like this had been seen since the days of Edward's grandfather Ecgberht who had marched a West Saxon army all the way up to Dore at the edge of Mercia nearly a hundred years earlier and obtained a form of submission from Northumbria. But the events of 920 were seemingly greater even than that. And the chronicler knew it.

The Fonthill Letter

Put simply, the document known as the Fonthill Letter is a letter written by, or dictated by, Ealdorman Ordlaf of Wiltshire to his king, Edward the Elder. However, what fascinates people is what the letter reveals about Anglo-Saxon land tenure, theft, the question of secular literacy, the concept of oath-taking, the intricacies of cattle rustling, local 'policing' and detective work, corruption (that is, as we would understand it) and the contemporary concept of bad character.[6]

Although there is a case for a later date based on what seems to be a fading memory, it appears Ealdorman Ordlaf wrote the letter in the early part of King Edward's reign. It relates, however, to events which went back to the time of King Alfred. Because of a claim to the land being made by a man named Æthelhelm Higa, Ordlaf essentially summarizes the history of the Fonthill estate, formerly in his possession, whilst providing background on his unfortunate godson Helmstan, who had twice got himself into trouble with the law. Ordlaf's main concern was to show that the five hides at Fonthill had rightly been his when he handed it over to New Minster Winchester, in exchange for land elsewhere.

The Letter

The letter explains that Fonthill had been in the hands of Helmstan during the later years of King Alfred's reign. However, Helmstan had stolen a belt belonging to a man named Æthelred. After this, Æthelhelm Higa sought to win the land by litigation along with others by bringing a charge against Helmstan. Helmstan had then gone to Ordlaf for intervention (because Ordlaf had stood sponsor at his confirmation before the crime was committed), and Ordlaf spoke with King Alfred. The king allowed Helmstan the right to prove his case and appointed Ordlaf and others (of whom Ordlaf could name six) to bring Helmstan and Æthelhelm Higa to agreement. After these men had deliberated, they agreed Helmstan should come forward with the charters to prove his right to the land. A lady called Æthelthryth had apparently sold it to Oswulf. She told him she had title to the land because it was her morning gift when she had married a man named Æthelwulf. The charter was produced at Wardour when the reconciliation was being undertaken. It had been signed by King Alfred and had the names of Edward, Æthelnoth and Deormod as witnesses as well as others. Ordlaf and the others felt that Helmstan's case was strong: he was 'nearer to the oath', says Ordlaf.

But Æthelhelm Higa, who was present at the time, did not see it that way at all. He demanded they all explain their decision to the king himself, who was washing his hands in his chamber next door. So, in they all went. Alfred asked Æthelhelm Higa why he felt their decision to proceed in this way was unjust. Alfred could not think of anything more just than that Helmstan should be allowed to give the oath if he could. Ordlaf asked the king to appoint a day for the oath to be taken and the king did so.

When the day came, Helmstan performed the oath fully. But there was a twist. Ordlaf writes that Helmstan wished to give Fonthill to Ordlaf. Ordlaf would help him obtain justice provided he got the land. And so the pledge was made. As soon as the oath was over, Helmstan gave Ordlaf the charter and Ordlaf allowed Helmstan to have Fonthill on loan for life 'if he would keep himself out of disgrace'. But, recalls Ordlaf, Helmstan did not.

Some time up to two years later Helmstan stole 'untended' or 'wretched' cattle at Fonthill and took them to an adjoining estate at Chicklade. He was 'discovered' or 'apprehended' there – the man who traced his route had recovered the tracks. But when Helmstan fled, he had scratched his face on a bramble and when he tried to deny the crime, this was brought in evidence against him. At this point the reeve Eanwulf Penearding intervened. He confiscated all Helmstan's property which he owned at Tisbury. Ordlaf enquired of Eanwulf why this had happened and Eanwulf had told him that the property was forfeit to the king because Helmstan was a thief and had been the king's man (perhaps a king's thegn). Helmstan could not forfeit Fonthill, because it was loaned from Ordlaf, who once again succeeded to the land. Ordlaf is curiously mentioned in the third person here, perhaps indicating that he had dictated the letter after all. Helmstan was, however, then pronounced an outlaw by the king.

When Ordlaf was with the king at Chippenham, Helmstan had sought out King Alfred's body (i.e. his tomb) and 'brought a seal' to Ordlaf. Ordlaf gave the seal to the king and the king removed Helmstan's outlawry 'and gave him the estate to which he still has withdrawn'. Ordlaf then succeeded to his land and in the witness of the king and his councillors, he gave it to the bishop of Winchester, 'five hides in exchange for the land of five hides at Lydiard', four of which were to be Ordlaf's and one subject to tithe.

This land exchange of Fonthill to the bishop seems to have been what irked Æthelhelm Higa. Helmstan's earlier gift of Fonthill to Ordlaf was arguably invalidated, so the later exchange was invalid too. The document ends with a plea by Ordlaf for things to be kept as they are. It also has a separate endorsement summarising the result of the case – Æthelhelm Higa eventually withdrew from the suit when the king was at Warminster. The fascinating issues arising from the letter are numerous, not least of which is the nature of and authorship of the language used. Also, Æthelhelm Higa's constant fight to win the land sounds like a disputed inheritance.[7] The belt at the beginning of the story is not described, but must have been one of remarkable finery, perhaps even a bejewelled sword belt. Its owner Æthelred may or may not have been a relative of Æthelhelm Higa's. Helmstan's oath-worthiness had become an issue after the belt incident and Ordlaf's efforts on his behalf have been interpreted as sitting anywhere between the reasonable expectations of friendship and downright bribery or corruption.

Quite what Helmstan was trying to do with the cattle is not clear. He may have been moving them from one estate (the one he occupied) to another. The oxen may or may not have been the inhabitants of the estate and might even have been misled on to it, in which case, moving them on would have been a mitigating factor, depending on why he was doing it and exactly where he took them.[8] It was certainly enough to land him in trouble though. And he did try to escape, after all.

It is the passion of the protagonists which is the most beguiling part of the story, especially in view of the fact that the land in question was 'only' five hides. The desperate flight of Helmstan to the tomb of Alfred, and the dogged persistence of Æthelhelm Higa's party are such examples. As for Ordlaf himself, who may seem to us a little cagey in his recollection of matters, his own sense of frustration comes out in the letter. In a direct plea to the king he says 'when will any suit be closed if one can end it neither with money nor with oath? And if one wishes to change every judgment which King Alfred gave, when shall we have finished disputing?'

Chapter 24

The 'Mercian' Revolt

The *Anglo-Saxon Chronicle* falls strangely silent for a few years after relating the northern submission. This curious absence of information makes the dating of events between c. 920 and 924 difficult to reconstruct and may even hint at some problems for Edward in holding his kingdom together during these years. It may also be indicative of the death in 920 of the king's brother Æthelweard, one of the speculative candidates for the authorship of the (A) version of the *Anglo-Saxon Chronicle* in those recent years. Æthelweard left two young sons, Æthelwine and Ælfwine, who would both go on to fight for the kingdom in the next generation. But something seems to have happened in 920 which may have undermined the foundations of the northern submission to Edward. Sihtric of Dublin, Rægnald's kinsman, launched a raid into northern Mercia. He attacked an estate near Davenport in Cheshire. The 920 date comes from a record in the *Historia Regum Anglorum*, which is thought to be accurate. But some argue for Sihtric's raid to have occurred in 919 and to have consequently been the trigger for Edward's building activity in the region. Others still argue for 921 and see the raid as the first thing Sihtric will have done in England when he began a new and aggressive career at none other than York. Rægnald, whose reign at York had begun promisingly, died in 921. His successor was Sihtric, who abandoned Ireland and was succeeded at some stage back in Dublin by another kinsman, Guthfrith.

The question of the raid on Davenport is a vexed one. If Sihtric had conducted the raid with a fleet from the Irish Sea, he may have chosen not to sail down the heavily defended Mersey, but instead taken his vessels south from the Mersey Estuary up the River Weaver and then along the River Dane, which meets with the Weaver at Northwich. The River Dane leads up to Congleton, near Davenport. It is probably no coincidence that Northwich and Middlewich both lie on this route and it is conceivable that these salt-producing areas were the target of an audacious economic attack on Edward's kingdom. If this is the case, Æthelflæd's short-lived burh at Eddisbury may have been abandoned by this time, since we might expect its garrison to have pounced on the invaders.

The circumstances of Sihtric's assumption of power in York are not known. Nor is it known how or why Rægnald died. But if these events represented an opportunity for King Edward to complete a master-stroke at York he did not, or perhaps could not, take it. Sihtric quickly became powerful at York. Numismatic evidence points to coins being minted in his name at Lincoln, too. The coinage of Sihtric presents an interesting possibility. Although the St Peter coinage continued in his reign, one later type of Sihtric's coinage showed a sword with a cross on the reverse. On one of these cross type coins is the inscription LVDO SITRIC. This may be an abbreviation of *Ludovicus*, which could have been Sihtric's baptismal name. A man perhaps with Frankish connections. What is clear, however, is that something had changed at York since the visit of the York-folk to

Æthelflæd and their offer to be at her disposal in the summer of 918. Sihtric had not been at the meeting of kings in 920 and his activity shows him very unlikely to have agreed to any submission to Edward, nor indeed, to anyone at all.

> Her Eadweard cing getimbrede þa burh æt Cledemuþan.
>
> 'Here, King Edward built the stronghold at the mouth of the Clwyd.'
>
> The *Mercian Register*, or 'Annals of Æthelflæd'. Entry for 921 (C)

Were it not for the *Mercian Register*, we would not know that Edward had another burh-building project on his hands in 921. Strangely, the (B) version of the *Mercian Register* does not include this particular record. The mouth of the Clwyd is situated west of modern Rhyl in North Wales. The most favoured place for Edward's 'final' burh is Rhuddlan, situated at the last crossing point on the Clwyd before it reached the Irish Sea, where no doubt, the maritime traffic from Ireland was closely observed. The motive for building an English burh in this area so far into North Wales at the long-disputed western edge of the Welsh region of Tegeingl was obviously strategic. It has been suggested that Edward may have been concerned that traders were bringing their goods into Gwynedd via the Clwyd and thereby bypassing the English tax collectors of Chester. This much notwithstanding, the construction of the burh at the mouth of the Clwyd may have jarred with Idwal, king of Gwynedd, who is supposed to have submitted to Edward. It may be

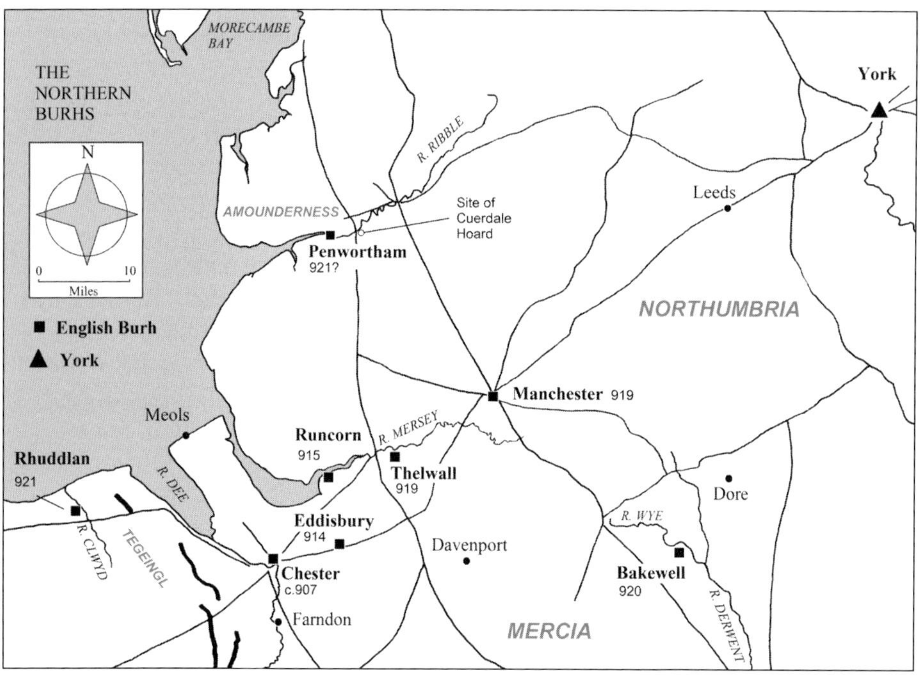

Map 23: *The northern burhs.*

that the burh's construction led to a Welsh retaliatory strike, since the *Annales Cambriae* records a mysterious 'battle of the New Fortress' in 921.[1]

Edward's activities between 921 and 924 are almost completely missing from the record. We can only generalize about what may have occurred in these two years, based on what happened before and what came to pass after this period. Some have postulated that there was another (unrecorded) burh built in around 921 by Edward, this time on the banks of the Ribble at Penwortham, near Preston where the Roman road crosses the river.[2] If so, this would have extended Anglo-Saxon royal influence up to the boundary of Amounderness, arguably a long term goal of English Mercia under Edward's forbears.

> Her Eadweard cing gefor on Myrcum æt Fearndune, ⁊ Ælfwerd his sunu swiðe hraðe þæs gefor æt Oxnaforda, ⁊ hira lic lið æt Wintanceastre. ⁊ Æþelstan wæs of Myrcum gecoren to cinge ⁊ æt Cingestune gehalgod, ⁊ he geaf his sweostor . . . [Ofsæ Ealdseaxna cynges suna].
>
> 'Here King Edward died at Farndon in Mercia, and very soon after that his son Ælfweard died at Oxford; and their bodies lie at Winchester. And Æthelstan was chosen as king by the Mercians, and consecrated at Kingston; and he gave his sister . . . [across the sea to the son of the king of the Old Saxons].'
>
> The *Mercian Register*, or 'Annals of Æthelflæd'. Entry for 924 (C)
> With section in brackets [ ] restored from the (D) version
> of the *Anglo-Saxon Chronicle*.

Edward was by now approaching 50 years old, roughly the same age as his father and sister had been when they died. During these short years, Edward must have been preoccupied with thoughts and preparations for the succession. The *Mercian Register* tells us that Edward was at Farndon (on-Dee, a royal estate) seven miles south of Chester, in 924. What it does not say is why. For this, we turn to William of Malmesbury, the only source of a curious revelation. Edward had been supressing a revolt in Chester, an uprising against him which had seemingly carried the support of the Welsh. The direct trigger for this uprising is lost to us. Some speculate that the administrative arrangements Edward had made in Mercia for the 'shiring' of the kingdom had been too much of an alien imposition on local tribal identities and had fostered resentment across Mercia. This argument depends on whether it was Edward who had initiated Mercia's 'shiring' in the first place,[3] and it does not explain a specific Chester-based resentment. However, it is certainly the case that the tenth-century boundary between Staffordshire and Warwickshire run directly through the historic Mercian capital of Tamworth, an insensitive administrative development likely to cause Mercian consternation no matter when exactly it had happened.

But it is also possible that the merchants of Chester were targeted for taxation in disproportionate ways, leading to local dissatisfaction with the king. It may also be that there was wider indignation felt by the Mercians who had supported Ælfwynn and whose bitterness had turned perhaps to anger. The Welsh assistance given to the rebels at Chester is perhaps explainable by the building of the fortress in the mouth of the Clwyd and the battle which may have taken place there the year after its completion. Unfortunately, William of Malmesbury does not expand on the matter. What he does say, however, is that Edward had successfully put the rebellion down and had even installed a garrison in Chester. He also says that Edward died just days later, at Farndon, from a sickness. The chronicler Æthelweard somewhat abruptly simply stated 'here ended his name and his perseverance', although he does pointedly accord Edward with title of *rex Anglorum*, king of the English. The date of this event is usually assigned to 17 July 924 (as mentioned in the New Minster *Liber vitae*). Edward was taken to Winchester for burial in the New Minster alongside his parents.

It had been an extraordinarily successful reign, during which the constant theme was warfare. Whilst the community at Old Minster in Winchester might have seen the king in a different light, it is difficult not to feel that most contemporaries within the kingdom, particularly secular leaders, would have been in awe of Edward the Elder. He had taken on his father's 'kingdom of the Anglo-Saxons' and expanded it, adding land and lordship ties to the growing power base of his family. It is clear that Edward was a consummate military commander, capable of overseeing a vast and sustained series of strategic campaigns, the focus of which was territorial domination from central strongholds. Season after season of success characterized the middle and later years of his reign. And yet, only rarely are we given notice of pitched battles in the old-fashioned sense of the term. Edward was no battle-seeker. His military apparatus was far more sophisticated than that. Warfare in England under Edward the Elder and his redoubtable sister Æthelflæd had become a very serious game of domination and subjection made possible by the central fortified place. Enemy lords were left with the stark choice of submission or ejection. Another feature of the campaigning was the punitive nature of some of the expeditions. A king had to be seen to act firmly with those who had broken peace agreements, and here Edward was not unwilling to devastate territories in an effort to punish oath-breakers. His use of combined regional forces is also important. Both Mercian and West Saxon forces fought under him during his reign, and so too did those Danes who had submitted to the king and who now formed part of an Anglo-Danish loyalty base beyond Watling Street. The Danes of Bedford and the combined garrison at Nottingham serve as good examples of this.

The overwhelming impression given by the twelfth-century historians (obviously writing in hindsight about an age dominated by warfare) is one of overwhelming military power. William of Malmesbury described King Edward as 'much inferior to his father in the cultivation of letters' but 'incomparably more glorious in the power of his rule'. John of Worcester saw the march back to Stamford as having been conducted by 'the most invincible King Eadward [*sic*] the elder'. John, who was sometimes given over to the glorification of kings also says, in his entry for 924 that 'After accomplishing many signal achievements, Eadweard the Elder, that most invincible king of the English, who had ruled with the greatest glory over all the inhabitants of Britain, whether English, Scots, Cumbrians, Danes, or Welsh, departed this life at a king's vill named Fearndun . . .'.

The difficulties which seem to have arisen at the end of Edward's reign should not necessarily cloud his achievements, although there is a hint of single-mindedness bordering on heavy-handedness about Edward's administrative affairs. At the beginning, he was insecure in his seat as his cousin Æthelwold gathered powerful forces against him, but Edward rose to the challenge and was able to see off the threat to his throne. Then slowly, with a mixture of treaties and military campaigns, he extended his family's power into lands long lost by Englishmen to Danish lords, with no shortage of help from his sister.

Edward's reputation has waxed and waned over the centuries. In the *Liber Monasterii de Hyda* he was recalled as *rex gloriosus*, which no doubt reflected his generous support of New Minster. But he was also remembered at Old Minster as *rex avidus*, or 'greedy' (S 814) probably for much the same reason.[4] Perhaps, on the secular side, some of the negativity may be due to the memory of the affairs in Mercia from around 918 to his death. Edward has always found himself sandwiched between the memory of his father and that of his firstborn son, whose exploits we will soon recall. But he also found himself in places eclipsed by his own sister, a strong personality, whose personal achievements were no small matter in a male-dominated world. When and where Edward is mentioned in the medieval and later histories, his power and military prowess, of course, reverberate. And yet as we have seen, there were fewer pitched battles than there were strategic manoeuvres and fortress building. The exceptions perhaps are the battles at Holme (902) and Tettenhall (910) and possibly a battle in the campaign which involved the arrival of the Scandinavian forces in the Severn Estuary in 914 (see pages 103–05) and the confrontation in the region of Maldon in 917 which had after all, involved a combined garrison and field force responding to a siege. We might add the assault against Tempsford and the sorties of the men of Luton and Bedford as well, but this is to miss the point about how warfare had considerably changed in Edward's era.

From what we can observe, Edward and Æthelflæd were consummate strategists during their wars against Danish lords. Bringing your enemy to a point where he has no choice but to negotiate, submit or leave, has a ring of classical training behind it and begs the obvious question of whether any of the roughly contemporary Byzantine military manuals and other classical military texts such as Vegetius's *De re militari* were being poured over in early tenth-century England. Vegetius, known to the Venerable Bede, was a hugely popular text in medieval times. It was also known in later tenth-century England. Pleading for army reform in the later Roman period, Vegetius wrote in the late fourth or early fifth century. For him, there had been an earlier age of Roman military dominance. The fortification of camps, the training of troops, the instillation of discipline, and how to fight, how to march and how to carry out tactical and strategic measures, were all topics covered in the four books of the work. Book I concentrated on the recruitment, organization and training of soldiers, whilst Book II presents as an infantry manual. Book III contained useful military maxims. Here, the emphasis was on battle-evasion, arguably a conspicuous aspect of King Edward's approach to warfare. There were other ways to defeat your enemy. Keeping your forces provisioned and denying the enemy their access to provisions was one of the maxims. The starvation of the Danes in 914 in the Severn Estuary was perhaps an example. Defeating through manoeuvres other than open battle in the field was another. The combined campaigns of brother and sister in Mercia during 917 are perhaps an example. Book IV contained a feast of material for the historian of siege and naval warfare, which is perhaps where the comparison with King Edward the Elder becomes a little weaker, but one of the key maxims encouraging those who desire peace to prepare for war might just be pertinent

Above left and above right: 51 and 52. *Two statues of Edward the Elder. On the outside of the Town Hall at Colchester (above). On the outside of Nos. 15 and 16 Market Place, Kingston, formerly Boots the Chemists.*

to the earlier years of the king's reign during which he can be seen to exchange land in order to acquire strategically-significant land, a period during which his thegnhood were encouraged to purchase lands from the Danes.

Edward's campaign of 912 to 913 had seen him split his army into two units at Hertford and take one part of it across hostile territory to Maldon and with its own engineering detachment, it built the burh at Witham, which of course had to be garrisoned. Meanwhile the force left behind at Hertford had commenced work on another burh on the southern side of the Lea. This all smacks of the requisite command, control and communication capabilities required of the traditional 'Vegetian' audience. None of this was possible without logistical planning, engineering equipment (however rudimentary) and a huge baggage train of supplies, weapons, armour and other materiel. And yet it was all for one purpose: to extend lordship into areas where it had either been lost or needed to be established. Edward's wars were not those of annihilation, but are characterized by the language of submission and of political cooperation. This all sounds very 'Vegetian' indeed.

The demonstrable threat of military force was frequently enough to get the king good results. His armies were capable of building and holding fortified places and of rapid movement in a landscape mapped out for warfare. But importantly, as the attacks on Tempsford and Colchester in 917 demonstrate, Edward's armies (like his sister's at Derby in the same year) were capable of successfully storming fortifications. It is striking how different Edward and Æthelflæd's campaigns were when compared to the attritional and repeated pitched battles which characterized the early part of their father's Danish wars. But whether Edward, Æthelflæd or any of their sub-commanders ever had a copy of Vegetius in their hand must remain a mystery.

Although his military prowess is undeniable, we know nothing at all of Edward's personal character and how this may have affected the way he had approached things during his reign. There are no recorded speeches attributed to the king, for example, except for the proclamations in his law codes. There are no personal references to the king's feelings or sentiments (compared to some revealing words as to how his sister had viewed her relations with her loyal thegns). But it is clear the king of the Anglo-Saxons was an astute organizer and a highly energetic figure. A mixed reputation may simply reflect the diversity inherent in the vast amount of people from various cultural and political backgrounds, each with their own views, who were touched by the events and policies of his reign. Clearly feared by his enemies and perhaps by some of his own subjects towards the end of his reign, King Edward had become the most powerful man in Britain in the years leading up to his death.

All the talk amongst the ealdormen, thegns and churchmen both at Farndon and on the long journey back to Winchester, will have been about the succession. Sixteen days after the cortege had left Farndon in Mercia, an event occurred in Oxford which would change the course of English history. Ælfweard, Edward's son and heir, mysteriously passed away. William of Malmesbury said of Ælfweard that he had been 'deeply versed in literature, much resembling his grandfather Alfred in features and disposition'. We have no idea what kind of a king Ælfweard would have been, but if William of Malmesbury was right, he would surely have ruled intelligently. But now he was dead. His brother Edwin was still alive, but so too, was someone else.

PART FIVE

ÆTHELSTAN

Chapter 25

A Protracted Succession

> In stature, from what I have heard, [Æthelstan was] not above the average in height, slim in build, with fair hair, as I have seen for myself in his remains, beautifully intertwined with gold threads.
>
> William of Malmesbury, *Gesta Regum Anglorum* 134.5

The scenes at Oxford on or around 2 August 924 are quite imaginable. The most powerful man in the British Isles had just died and now Ælfweard, his apparent 'heir', lay dead. There are many unanswered questions which surround the rise to power of England's most remarkable pre-Conquest king, the man who eventually followed on from his father's rule. Was Æthelstan present at Oxford when his half-brother Ælfweard perished? Had he been at Farndon with his father when he had died, as seems likely? Had the cortege only come as far as Oxford by 2 August and were the two half-brothers part of it, or had Ælfweard travelled up from Winchester to meet with it? Was Edwin with him? It is generally believed that Ælfweard was in Wessex and Æthelstan had been with his father in Mercia. The sequence of events, although tersely reported in the *Mercian Register*, might tend to support this. But the most obvious of all the questions one could ask at this juncture, is of course, how did Ælfweard die? He was almost certainly only in his twenties.

Firstly, it is quite possible that the cortege had only made it down to Oxford by 2 August. The distance from Farndon to Oxford as the crow flies is 115 miles. Even if we assume that the cortege left Farndon on the same day Edward died and arrived in Oxford on the same day Ælfweard expired, this would give a rate of travel at a sedentary seven miles a day. However, allowing for a day or two of observances at Farndon and a day or two of heated debates at Oxford before Ælfweard's unexpected 'departure', we would realistically be looking at a rate of travel of around nine or 10 miles a day, just about right for the era, if we include the necessary stops en route. Rates of march for armies could be much higher than this under certain circumstances (up to half as much again), but it is hardly likely that Edward was brought south at the same speed as an army might move on campaign.

But there is a fly in the ointment. A West Saxon regnal list in the twelfth-century *Textus Roffensis* gives Ælfweard a reign of four weeks. Depending on where that reign started, it could mean he did not die until around 14 August, unless he had been elected as Edward's successor a few weeks before his father had died. This makes it possible for him to have at the very least begun the process of preparing for the kingship. And this may be why a passage of text preserved in the *Liber vitae* of New Minster, Winchester (originally written in the 980s) mentions the burials at Winchester of Æthelweard *Clito* (who was clearly *Alfred's* and not Edward's son) and Ælfweard who had been 'crowned with kingly badges'. Nor is this the only reference to Ælfweard actually making it as far as a consecration of some sort. The *Liber Monasterii de Hyda* mentions a son of Edward named *Elfredus* (probably Ælfweard) who was crowned during his father's lifetime, but died not long after. One interpretation of all this could be that by the time Edward's sons by Ælfflæd were given the bad news of their father's death Ælfweard was already de facto king.[1] It is also possible that on hearing the news, both Ælfweard and Edwin moved swiftly to make the ideal a reality. This might mean that the Oxford event played no part at all in the journey of Edward's cortege. It could even be that after Edward's burial at Winchester, Ælfweard was formally crowned king and then sometime soon afterwards a meeting was arranged between Æthelstan and Ælfweard at Oxford to establish arrangements in Mercia.[2]

So, what happened at Oxford? Again, we might be tempted to draw the darkest of conclusions. Grim endings are not exactly rare in this era. We cannot be certain what Edward's exact intentions for the succession were at this particular stage in his long reign. It is quite possible those plans changed more than once. Was Ælfweard really destined to succeed to the whole of his father's kingdom as king of the Anglo-Saxons? Where did Æthelstan (always a favourite of his grandfather's) feature in the arrangements? If Æthelstan was to succeed in Mercia only, then why did Ælfwynn initially do so instead? At the time of Edward's annexing of Mercia and removal of Ælfwynn, had Edward elevated Æthelstan to the Mercian succession?

The plan to split the kingdom between Ælfweard and Æthelstan may still have been in existence on the eve of Ælfweard's death. The next day, however, would see the whole thing turned upside down. It would be satisfying to be able to answer the question of the circumstances of Ælfweard's death, but it remains elusive and may forever stay that way. It may have been as a consequence of the geographic separation of Æthelstan and Ælfweard's parties at the time of Edward's death that Mercia and Wessex made separate electoral decisions, or it may be that the split was intended. Æthelstan, says the *Mercian Register* in its last entry before it tails off in mid-sentence, 'was chosen as king by the Mercians, and consecrated at Kingston, and he gave his sister . . .', according to a standard modern translation. The Mercians are interpreted here as being the electors of Æthelstan. The words, in Old English are

> . . . Æþestan wæs of Myrcum gecoren to cinge (B)

or

> . . . Æþelstan wæs of Myrcum gecoren to cinge (C)

But crucially, it is not easy to establish if this election by the Mercians is to all of his father's domains or to Mercia alone. The words, again in Old English, in the Worcester (D) version of the *Anglo-Saxon Chronicle*, which at this point still weaves-in material from the *Mercian Register*, are:

> . . . Æþelstan wæs gecoren to cynge of Myrcum . . .

It is possible that the price of Edward's takeover of Mercia was being paid. Could it really be that Mercia at last had a king again? It is a complex issue dependant for its interpretation on syntax, and not everyone is entirely in agreement on its meaning. 'Of Myrcum' even in this context could still mean 'by the Mercians'.[3] But what is not in question is the ability and power of the Mercians to express their wishes at the time, and convert those desires into political action. Æthelstan, however, when he was finally crowned on 4 September 925, was not crowned simply as king of the Mercians. Archbishop Æthelhelm of Canterbury consecrated the king at Kingston at the border of Wessex and Mercia, as *rex Saxonum et Anglorum* (see below, page 201). We should not forget that William of Malmesbury, although biased, stated that Æthelstan was also elected at Winchester 'with the overwhelming support of the nobles'. William also says, in a section of his work derived from an 'ancient volume' on Æthelstan written originally in a bombastic style, that after the death of Edward, '. . . on his father's instructions, and by the terms of his will, Æthelstan was chosen king by acclamation, recommended as he was by his age – he was now thirty – and his mature wisdom'.

William of Malmesbury clearly knew of Æthelstan's close associations with Malmesbury, and it is not clear if he is compressing events or exaggerating his source. It could be that in 924, politics moved quicker than we think. The surviving candidates for Edward's crown had been Ælfweard's brother Edwin, a throne-worthy man in his early twenties, and two infant boys, Edmund and Eadred. Something therefore, must have happened sometime between Ælfweard's premature death and the accession of Æthelstan to all of his father's kingdom, at the expense of the only realistic West Saxon candidate, Edwin. This something, arguably, was Æthelstan himself. And just perhaps, that is why the page which records Edward's dealings at Bakewell in the (A) version of the *Anglo-Saxon Chronicle* remains blank and a new page starts with the record of the accession of King Æthelstan.

Not everyone was happy in Winchester. William of Malmesbury provides a lengthy story of a Winchester-based rebellion against Æthelstan at the beginning of his reign. He says it was led by a certain Alfred and his co-conspirators. The story has some imaginative facets and seems to be linked to Malmesbury Abbey's ongoing claims to land given to the community by Æthelstan in the wake of Alfred's forfeiture. But with that in mind, the story captures the essence of a succession crisis well enough, and makes a good tale. It may even be the reason for Æthelstan's delayed coronation.

Alfred, we are told, objected to Æthelstan's rule because Æthelstan was the son of a mere concubine. The allegation is probably highly unfair on Æthelstan's mother Ecgwynn, who seems to have merely fallen prey to the vicissitudes of dynastic politics, but this propaganda would have made Æthelstan seem in the eyes of the supporters of Ælfweard (and by association, Edwin) an inappropriate candidate for his father's throne. Edwin, for example, was the surviving son of a 'legitimate' marriage between Edward and Ælfflæd. Æthelstan, who in his youth had frequented the West Saxon court even after his apparent departure to Mercia and the court of his aunt and uncle, must have heard it all before. But it does appear that Æthelstan regarded Winchester with some caution for a while. A charter of 925 (S 395), witnessed only by Mercian clergy, although regarded by some as a forgery, was issued from Burton-on-Trent in Mercia. Here, Æthelstan is accorded the title *rex Anglorum*, amid a tortured and far from certain wording which also describes him as '. . . supervisor of the Christian household . . . well-nigh in the whirlpools of cataclysms'. The beneficiary was one Eadric, a thegn, who was given an estate at *Hwituntune* (probably Whittington, near Chesterfield in Derbyshire). The king may therefore have been moving around Mercia for some time before he came to Winchester. As if to reinforce the notion of an unstraightforward rise to power, this charter contains an odd reference to the king 'investigating the matter of discussed obedience brought to notice by the careful sagacity of my faithful men'. It was a year full of uncertainty.

Æthelstan did, however, enter Winchester at some stage after his father's death. According to William's account, which he describes in the words of Æthelstan himself from a charter, Alfred ('who was always jealous of my prosperity and of my life') was 'party to the wickedness of my enemies' when they tried to blind him when he entered Winchester after his father's death. The motive is not entirely clear, but the attempt was unsuccessful. A blinded Æthelstan would be automatically incapable of wielding power and would be removed from office, and the conspirators could at least assure themselves that they were not murderers, whilst they would then presumably have supported Edwin in a bid for the throne. But because the plot failed, Alfred went into exile and to Rome to defend himself in the presence of Pope John X (914–28). Later, goes the tale, Alfred, having sworn an oath at the altar of St Peter, collapsed and was taken to the Schola Anglorum, where he died two nights later. Æthelstan agreed to Alfred's burial as a Christian, and his possessions were given over to the king who then gave them to God and St Peter. Bath Abbey and Malmesbury Abbey allegedly acquired Alfred's lands and recorded their acquisitions by retelling the tale of the plot in various charters. But the whole story of Alfred in this section of William's work reads as almost a hagiographical tale. The evasion of a blinding elevates Æthelstan to a saint-like status, as does the grudging allowance of Alfred's Christian burial. But, according to what William had heard in popular songs, not only did Alfred, a man of 'overweening insolence' decline 'to submit to a lord not of his own choosing', he was also put to death after resisting in secret for 'as long as he could'. More alarmingly, it was suggested to the king by some that Edwin was implicated in the plot, with what would eventually be far-reaching consequences for him in years to come. This memory of Edwin's involvement, however spurious, does not seem to have escaped the public imagination

For a few years, however, Edwin seems to have maintained close relations with Winchester and with Bishop Frithestan in particular. Frithestan, appointed during the great reforms of 909, had been close to Edwin's mother Ælfflæd, who had given gifts to him in the form of a stole and maniple now preserved at Durham cathedral. These items found their way in c. 934 to St Cuthbert's shrine at Durham, donated by King Æthelstan. Edwin also appears as Eadwine [*sic*] *Clinton* (a Latin term equating to Ætheling) in a charter of uncertain date, drawn up between 924 and 933 (S 1417). The document is a lease from the New Minster community at Winchester to a thegn of Æthelstan's (who happens to be called Alfred) of land at Chisledon, Wiltshire. Whether Edwin's position in the witness list here (second behind Æthelstan) points to a reconciliation and an implication that the Winchester community expected Edwin to succeed Æthelstan, is unclear. What is clear, is that Edwin's popularity at Winchester was certainly a factor during the early years of Æthelstan's reign and it is not out of the question that Edwin for a while represented a similar 'threat' to Æthelstan as Æthelwold had to Edward at the beginning of his reign.

William of Malmesbury goes on to tell the rest of the tale concerning the ultimate fate of Edwin, which ended in tragedy in a controversial drowning in 933, which we will explore.[4] But at the end of the account, he expresses words of caution. William was convinced that Æthelstan had shown 'remarkable affection' towards his other brothers, the two infants Edmund and Eadred. He 'brought them up lovingly in childhood'. Crucially, in one version of William's work, the phrase '. . . never, out of respect for them, turning his thoughts towards marriage' is included. Perhaps Æthelstan may have become king on the promise to hold the kingdom open not for any of his own heirs, but for the children of Edward by Eadgifu, his father's redoubtable third wife. This opens the possibility that Eadgifu, who survived long into the tenth century, may have run Æthelstan's court as a dowager queen, looking after the interest of her sons but not attesting the king's charters. If this agreement had been reached in 924, it might well have clinched the coronation for Æthelstan and left his half-brother disgruntled. But we do not know exactly when the agreement was reached, if it was reached at all.

Chapter 26

Coronation

> Concerning this king there is a vigorous tradition in England that he was the most law-abiding and best-educated ruler they have ever had.
>
> William of Malmesbury, *Gesta Regum Anglorum* 132.

Æthelstan, either through hard negotiation, or on the strength of a binding promise, or even by sheer force of personality, managed to make it through to his coronation day on 4 September 925. If there is any uncertainty about his father's place of consecration, the same cannot be said for the coronation of Æthelstan. The *Mercian Register*, for example, gives Kingston as the place and John of Worcester adds that 'Æthelstan was proclaimed king at Kingston, which signifies the king's town'. William of Malmesbury of course, follows suit. The reasons for the choosing of Kingston have been noted above (pages 17–18), along with the possible arguments for the place also having been the 'coronation' place for Edward the Elder. For Æthelstan, perhaps more so than for his father, the necessity to bring together Wessex and Mercia at Kingston was important in the light of recent events. This of course, has led to the suggestion, which has some weight to it, that it was Æthelstan himself who started the practice of royal consecrations at Kingston.

One document (S 394), more of a memorandum of a gift, is dated to the day of the consecration. It styles the king *rex Saxonum et Anglorum* and was probably drawn up by a continental scholar resident in England, who spells the king's name as *Adalstan*. In the memorandum, the king restores fourteen sulungs (a land assessment in Kent similar to a hide) at Thanet to St Augustine's, Canterbury. Present were *Athelm* (Æthelhelm) the archbishop of Canterbury and seven other bishops. A notable absentee was Bishop Frithestan, who was most likely back in Winchester ruminating over recent developments.

This brings us to the question of the Second English Coronation *Ordo* used at Æthelstan's coronation. It survives in documents no earlier than the late tenth century. One argument in favour of it having first been used at Edward the Elder's ceremony in 900 (see page 18), is that the new ceremonial ritual contained a procedure for anointing a queen as well as a king. At the turn of the century, arguably Ælfflæd had been that queen and the provision was made for her. Moving forward to 925 we find Æthelstan, on the other hand, remaining unmarried. However, it has been argued that there need not necessarily be a queen in existence but simply that the ceremonial apparatus for one needed to be there.[1]

The ceremony involved the bestowal and blessing of the regalia, which included a ring (a mark of the king's duty to support the True Faith), a sword (to help widows and orphans and to 'restore things left desolated'), a sceptre (to defend the Holy Church and Christian people under him) and a rod (to 'teach the right way to those who stray', among other things). But there was now a crown too – for the very first time – replacing the use of a helmet. Æthelstan would go on to make the most of this symbolism, being depicted wearing a crown on his coinage and also in some portraits in contemporary manuscripts.

There were several new prayers (developed from Carolingian examples) which were brought into the service to be included at various moments, one in particular when the bishop was about to anoint the king. This was *Omnipotens sempiterne Deus*, drawing from a ninth-century Carolingian source, which encouraged God to bestow on the king various characteristics of biblical kings. Especially significant is the implication in the consecration prayer that the king was to be supported by the subjection of both the 'Angles' and the 'Saxons', surely a reference to the people of Mercia and Wessex combined (as it then stood). The theme of the unity of both peoples ran through the whole of the proceedings.

Another prayer, said at the end of the ceremony by the archbishop after the enthronement of the king, contained the phrase '. . . hold fast the state which you have held by paternal suggestion . . . ; remember to show honour to the clergy in due places, so that the mediator between God and men may strengthen you as mediator between clergy and people in the throne of this kingdom'.

One of King Æthelstan's earliest acts, perhaps even played out in front of the crowds at Kingston, was to symbolically free a slave. This act, a manumission, concerned a man called Ealdhelm. It is recorded as a contemporary passage in one of the king's much older gospel books and the record is witnessed by two of the king's Mass priests and other household men. One of the Mass priests, Alfheah, also witnessed the memorandum granted to St Augustine's, Canterbury on the day of the coronation. The symbolism is clear. Here, the man at the very top of society was showing his compassion for a man at the very bottom. William of Malmesbury, perhaps unsurprisingly, would later say of Æthelstan that 'to lesser folk . . . he laid aside the haughty heir of royalty and was mild and affable'. Here at his coronation, not only did Æthelstan bestow freedom on the slave, but also did so on his children. The gospel book, an early sign that the king was an avid collector, may even have been the very one on which Æthelstan had just sworn his coronation oath.

At some stage in 926 King Æthelstan issued two important confirmation charters for two separate thegns. They both bore something in common in that they both confirmed land formerly purchased from Danes. One concerned the five hides of land at Chalgrave and Tebworth in Bedfordshire (to Ealdred), the purchase of which King Edward and Lord Æthelred had encouraged (see page 52) and the other concerned sixty hides at Hope and Ashford in Derbyshire, to an Uhtred (S 397). Interestingly, the witness lists, which include the Archbishop of Canterbury and eight other bishops, do not include Frithestan, Bishop of Winchester, an omission perhaps indicating simmering tension in the old West Saxon capital. But Æthelstan was able to concentrate on other important matters during the first full year of his reign, courtesy of his rather large extended family.

Æthelstan, although apparently childless,[2] was blessed with a sister and numerous half-sisters from his father's marriages or unions. Some, as we have seen, would enter the religious life, but others became very powerful secular women in royal courts overseas and Æthelstan made widespread use of the political tool of the marriage alliance. His father Edward had begun the policy by marrying one of his daughters Eadgifu (not to be confused with Edward's third wife of that name) between 917 and 919 to the Frankish king Charles 'the Simple'. Charles was deposed in 922 and imprisoned the following year, but he and Eadgifu had already had a boy, a mere infant named Louis. The boy, for his own safety, was sent to England by his concerned mother, lest any one of Charles's enemies should find him and kill him, according to one French source.[3] Here, he found protection under Æthelstan. Louis, who became known by the French as Louis d'Outremer ('of Overseas'), would be nurtured in England and the time would come in his teenage years when he would launch a bid for power in France.

Within months of his coronation, Æthelstan himself was playing the marriage alliance card much closer to home. William of Malmesbury tells us the impetus had come not from the English king, but from none other than Sihtric at York. His initial overtures to Æthelstan were followed up by a trip to the king in person. The Worcester manuscript (D) of the *Anglo-Saxon Chronicle* says that Sihtric had come all the way to Tamworth to meet with Æthelstan on 30 January 926. Here, Æthelstan 'gave him [Sihtric] his sister'. Quite what was said in Tamworth is unknown. But the prospect of an alliance through marriage with York will undoubtedly have appealed to Æthelstan. In his mind, perhaps it would lead to a familiar link to a key part of the northern English political scene which had eluded his father. Sihtric's angle on the agreement is less easy to discern, although an alliance with the most powerful man south of the Humber will have done him no harm. There are arguably echoes of the overtures made to Æthelflæd by the men of York in 918 in all this, but we can't be entirely sure that a marriage alliance was truly in the offing back then. It is of note that the chronicler gives Sihtric the title of 'king', however. The identity of the sister is also not certain. It is likely to have been Æthelstan's only full sister (at least according to William of Malmesbury), with whom he may have grown up in Mercia when he himself was fostered at the court of his aunt and uncle. William was at pains to point out that he could find no details about the sister in any of his sources, but he does contend that she was the daughter of Edward and his first 'wife' Ecgwynn. She is not named however, until much later the thirteenth century, when Roger of Wendover names her as Eadgyth.[4] This thirteenth-century account (based on a twelfth-century Bury tradition), also recorded by Matthew Paris, claimed that Sihtric broke his side of the 'agreement' with Æthelstan by renouncing Christianity and also claimed that the marriage was never consummated. Sihtric then died, and Eadgyth returned to Mercia and founded a nunnery at Polesworth near Tamworth where she spent her life in virginity.

However, this story of St Eadgyth of Polesworth may be inaccurate. A different variant of the Bury tradition claims that Eadgyth was buried at Tamworth and was the daughter of the king's second marriage to Ælfflæd. Later sources simply serve to confuse the issue further. John of Wallingford said that Sihtric's wife was named *Orgiue*, for example. Also, in Holinshed's sixteenth-century *Scottish Chronicle*, a reference is made to a daughter of Edward named Beatrice, who was wed to *Sithrike, king of Northumberland*. It is possible that Roger of Wendover has confused the woman with Æthelstan's half-sister of the same name, but although the Edith of Polesworth story has become interlinked with the fate of Æthelstan's full sister, the fact that the union between this woman and Sihtric took place need not be doubted.

Whatever her identity, it was a desperately short-lived union. But there was another sister who had been the focus of an approach from Francia. This particular marriage is mentioned in Flodoard of Reims' entry for 926. 'Hugh, son of Robert', married a daughter of Edward the Elder who was 'the sister of the wife of Charles'. Hugh, the Count of Paris, had recently attained the title of 'Duke of the Franks', although William of Malmesbury called him 'king'. His father Robert had risen to the western Frankish throne in the wake of the ousting of Charles the Simple. But Robert was killed in 923, leaving Hugh's brother-in-law Rudolph to obtain the throne. Charles had sought help from Herbert of Vermandois, but it had been Herbert who had imprisoned Charles. It has been suggested that Hugh's attentions towards Æthelstan's half-sister may have been brokered by Eadgifu, the motive here would presumably have been to drive a wedge between Hugh and Herbert.[5]

The target of Hugh's desire, through envoys, was Eadhild. If William of Malmesbury, drawing once again from that 'ancient volume', is correct, it is surprising Eadhild had not found a suitor earlier: in her, he says, 'the whole mass of beauty, of which other women have only a share, had flowed into one by nature'. The envoy was Æthelstan's own cousin, a man named Adulf (Adelolf), son of Baldwin, Count of Flanders, who had married Æthelstan's aunt Ælfthryth sometime before 899. The party which came to England in search of Eadhild's hand on behalf of Hugh gets a remarkable write-up by William of Malmesbury, or perhaps more accurately, his source. They came to the English king at Abingdon. Here, Adulf revealed the gifts he had brought over the sea. They included 'fragrant spices, never before seen in England' and fine emeralds. But far more importantly than that, the impressive list of gifts as recited by William included 'many swift horses with their trappings "champing at their teeth" as Virgil says . . .'. These horses were no idle or casual gift. It is quite likely that they were of Arab or Barb stock, probably stallions, and were quickly employed in the Wessex royal studs. If so, it was a gift with a long-term benefit for the king, given that mobility in the landscape had become an important part of early tenth-century warfare.

The other gifts sound almost magical in their description, but were hugely important to Æthelstan. They included 'the tawny gold', a reflective classical onyx vessel depicting lifelike pastoral scenes; the sword of Constantine the Great with its owner's name in gold letters and a nail from the Passion embedded in its scabbard; Charlemagne's lance (said to have been driven into Christ's side by a centurion); the banner of St Maurice; a precious and dazzling crown of solid gold; a small piece of the 'holy and wonderful Cross' encased in crystal and a small portion, similarly mounted, of the crown of thorns. For a devout and avid relic collector such as Æthelstan, these gifts were hugely welcome, and were an endorsement of his notion of a 'Carolingian'-style rulership. The king, it is said, responded in kind with similar gifts, and of course, handed over his sister.

That the year 926 was one of marriage alliances, gift-giving and of international recognition for Æthelstan, is hardly in dispute. There would be another very important marriage alliance in 929 – that of Athelstan's other half-sister Eadgyth to Otto, the son of the East Frankish King Henry the Fowler. Another half-sister (called either Ælfgifu or Eadgifu) would go on to marry 'a certain king near the Alps', according to the chronicler Æthelweard, who does not name her as such. However, of the earlier marriages, one in particular was about to mysteriously collapse. Whether Sihtric had indeed repudiated his wife and abandoned Christianity is uncertain, but what is more certain is that in 927, he died. William of Malmesbury says Sihtric's end was 'violent'. Whatever had happened to him and whatever became of his wife, Sihtric had left a vacuum in York no smaller than the one Rægnald had stepped into a few years earlier. But who now, would be the quicker to fill it?

Chapter 27

Perfecta Saxonia – An 'England' Made Whole?

> His [Æthelstan's] subjects, who admired his courage and modesty, loved him dearly; on rebels, invincible and unsleeping, he descended like a flash of lightning.
>
> William of Malmesbury, *Gesta Regum Anglorum* 134.5

It was Guthfrith, veteran of Corbridge and kinsman of Sihtric, who came over from Dublin, bringing forces from there and from the *Longphort* at *Linn Duachaill* (Anagassan, Co. Louth) to England. Once again, the record is so sparse as to deceive us into another time compression. We do have the *Annals of Ulster*, William of Malmesbury and John of Worcester to assist, though.

It would appear that Æthelstan allowed Guthfrith no time at all to even make a mark on Northumbrian government at York. The *Annals of Ulster* have the Dane back in Dublin inside just six months. The *Anglo-Saxon Chronicle* gives up very little, however. The Worcester manuscript, after telling us that this was a year in which 'fiery rays appeared in the northern part of the sky' simply states '. . . Sihtric perished and King Æthelstan succeeded to the kingdom of Northumbria', with the Canterbury and Peterborough versions simply stating in their entry for 927 'here [King] Æthelstan drove out King Guthfrith'. For the drama and the thunder, we turn to William of Malmesbury and his much-cited 'ancient volume'. Æthelstan, it is said, had already brought the whole of England under his rule 'by the mere terror of his name', with the single exception of the Northumbrians. William even claims, through the source, that Sihtric's death had given Æthelstan the opportunity to add Northumbria to his own 'share' in that Northumbria was Æthelstan's through 'ancient right', although such an extraordinary claim is not mentioned elsewhere.

William of Malmesbury provides two separate narratives of events in the north at the time of Æthelstan's takeover. The first mention of the aftermath of Sihtric's death and Æthelstan's response is in a section not attributable to the 'ancient volume' but is instead a simple, although sometimes garbled, narrative of the reign of Æthelstan. Here, William says that Æthelstan 'subdued the whole province, after driving out a certain Ealdwulf [*sic*] who was in revolt'. He goes on to say that the king compelled Idwal, king of all the Welsh, and Constantín, king of the Scots, to abdicate. Æthelstan then restored the kings to reign under him, 'declaring it more glorious to make kings than to be one'. The reference to 'Ealdwulf' is thought to be an error. William may have meant Ealdred, son of Eadwulf of Bamburgh, unless 'Ealdwulf' refers to an otherwise unknown family member 'who was in revolt'.

William's account from the 'ancient volume', however, provides many peculiar twists and some new names. Sihtric's son, Anlaf (that is, Olaf Sihtricson, whose career in the north would prove to be long and eventful) apparently fled to Ireland and his 'brother'

Guthfrith to Scotland. English envoys then followed them and went to Constantín and Owain 'king of the Cumbrians' (Strathclyders) to get the fugitive (Guthfrith) back. 'The barbarians', says William, 'had no spirit to utter a word of protest' and subsequently gathered willingly 'at a place called Dacre', placing themselves and their kingdoms in the hands of the English king. At this meeting, Æthelstan stood godfather to Constantín's son, who was baptised. Guthfrith, however, had slipped away 'with a certain Turfrith' and commenced an unsuccessful siege of York. They were both then besieged themselves in 'a certain fortress' and subsequently escaped, after which Turfrith was shipwrecked and drowned. Guthfrith, also troubled by the seas, eventually 'came at length to the king's court to surrender'. He was entertained by Æthelstan for four days and then sent off to his ships once more. In the meantime, Æthelstan levelled to the ground the fortress the Danes had built 'long ago' at York 'in order to leave disloyalty no place of refuge'. During the course of the levelling, the English discovered many riches in the fortress, which Æthelstan distributed amongst 'individuals'. Æthelstan, we are told, made it a principle not to accumulate his own wealth, but to spend it on monasteries, or on his own loyal followers, a reflection perhaps of the idealised role of the warrior king as gift-giver.

The Worcester (D) version of the *Anglo-Saxon Chronicle* follows up its brief notice of Æthelstan's acquisition of Northumbria with what appears to be a summary of the king's success over other kings to date:

> . . . and he governed [*gewylde*, more accurately, 'subjected'] all the kings who were in this island: first Hywel, king of the West Welsh, and Constantín, king of the Scots, and Owain, king of Gwent, and Ealdred, Ealdwulf's offspring, from Bamburgh [John of Worcester says Ealdred was expelled from his citadel]. And they confirmed peace with pledges and with oaths in a place which is called River's Meeting on 12 July [iiii Udus Iulii]; and they forbade all devil-worship and then parted in concord.

The River Eamont flows out of Ullswater to join with the Eden further east. It passes through the south side of Penrith where a little further to the east, it is joined by the Lowther. There was also a junction of Roman roads here, with one in particular leading all the way south to the restored fort of Manchester. Another road led east through Stainmore, and branched north-east into the heart of St Cuthbert's lands situated to the south of Chester-le-Street. Another branch led directly south towards York.

The order of the list of kings is probably chronological to begin with, in terms of who submitted first. Hywel, for example, had already submitted to the English earlier (see above, page 175). Then come the others in apparent order of seniority. The inclusion of Hywel and Owain has led some to conclude that although the list includes those who submitted to Æthelstan, it does not necessarily imply that they all travelled up to Eamont in the far north for the meeting. However, it is not at all impossible either. That there was a meeting, is not in dispute, and it is most likely to have been convened to confirm Æthelstan's position as ruler of Northumbria and to establish a subsequent peace.

We cannot be sure of events leading up to this tumultuous meeting of kings at Eamont. It is very unlikely that Æthelstan's descent on York and his driving-out of Guthfrith was entirely bloodless. In fact, it is likely to have involved an overt demonstration of military

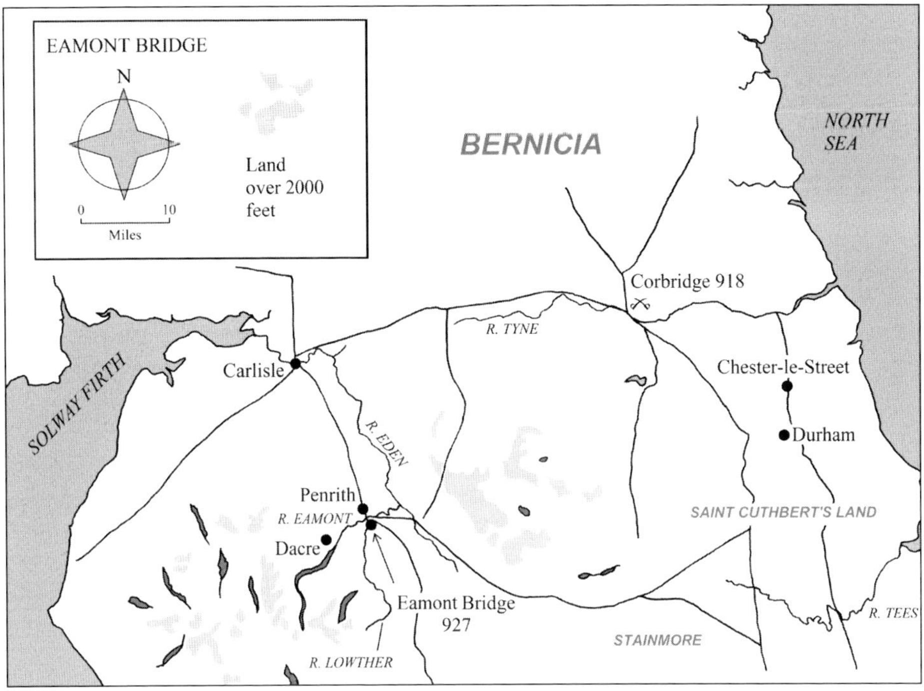

Map 24: *Eamont Bridge.*

power. It may even be that the Welsh kings listed by the chronicler (Hywel and Owain) had fulfilled their lordship obligations to the king and had accompanied him on the York campaign to expel Guthfrith. There may also be a king missing from the list. Eamont Bridge (William of Malmesbury says Dacre) by the Eamont, is situated at the southern border of the Kingdom of Strathclyde and as William says, the Owain at the meeting was *Eugenium regum Cumbrorum*, Owain, king of the Cumbrians. Hence, the confusion over which 'Welsh' kings actually attended. They may both have done, one in the king's army and the other coming down from Govan.

The curious mention at the end of the chronicle's passage that they 'forbade all devil-worship' is perhaps explained by the fact that now all of Britain south of the Orkneys had once again returned to Christian rule. Despite their political differences, it is probably the case that each of the Christian leaders at Eamont Bridge was confirming a pact to no longer make alliances with the pagans. The exact site of the meeting is not identified. Candidates range from Westmorland Holme (formed by the junction of the Eamont and the Lowther), to two prehistoric henge monuments near Eamont Bridge, or the old Roman fort at Brougham where a later castle was built, or even an earlier monastery at Dacre, although this last relies solely on William of Malmesbury. Most of these sites might have been suitable for a denouncement of paganism. But Mayburgh Henge, just to the north of the modern M6 motorway, offers a dramatic setting, with its ancient cobblestone banks still rising to form an amphitheatre-like arena which once enclosed numerous standing stones, of which only one now remains. Alternatively, just a short walk away to the east, was a smaller and more open henge monument now called King Arthur's Round

Table. This may also have offered a suitable venue for the meeting, and what better places than at these henges could there be to forbid 'devil-worship'?

Æthelstan had pushed the boundaries of the kingdom of the Anglo-Saxons to previously unheard-of geographical limits. With the acquisition of Northumbria and the agreement at Eamont, it must have seemed to contemporaries that the vision of Alfred the Great of a single united kingdom of all the English, given to him by St Cuthbert, had been realized through the industry of his son and daughter, and the sheer power of his grandson Æthelstan. The Worcester version of the *Anglo-Saxon Chronicle* does not exaggerate when it describes the position in 927. Æthelstan's power was enormous, and everyone knew it. Æthelstan himself, from this time forwards, believed himself to be the overlord not just of the English people but of all of Britain. It was a belief that would reflect itself in his use of a title in both royal documents and on his coinage. In his charters, he would begin to style himself *rex Anglorum* 'king of the English', and on his coinage came an even grander title, *Rex Totius Britanniae*, 'king of all Britain'. The aspiration would continue to grow as the opening years of Æthelstan's reign went by. Perhaps the visit from the envoys of Hugh, the Duke of the Franks, had bolstered the image which Æthelstan had of himself. More illustrious titles would be claimed, and they would be everywhere supported by the legitimacy of heavenly approval. The kingdom of the Anglo-Saxons, an idea which had lasted from around 880 to 927, was being eclipsed by something even grander. At Eamont Bridge, the kingdom of the English had been born. But, in the colourful world of the north, things could – and indeed did – change again, though not for another six years or so. For now, the achievements of the king, so early in his reign, were enough to inspire one particular clerk in Æthelstan's household (possibly from New Minster),[1] called Petrus to burst into poetry in the wake of the Eamont Bridge gathering, a meeting which he quite possibly attended in person.

The poem *Carta dirige gressus* ('Letter direct your steps') was addressed to the royal court. Petrus, almost certainly a man of Continental origin, knew what it had all meant to those present and despite the difficulties experienced by Æthelstan at Winchester, Petrus was keen to let people know the extent of what had taken place and the character of the king. It is triumphant in its tone and probably is based on an earlier poem written about Charlemagne which also uses the device of directing itself towards the imperial palace.

Carta dirige gressus per maria nauigans tellurisque spacium ad regis palacium	Letter, direct your steps sailing across the seas and an expanse of land to the king's burh.
Rege primum salutem ad reginam, clitonem claros quoque comites armigeros milites	Direct first of all your best wishes to the queen, the prince, the distinguished ealdormen as well, the arm-bearing thegns.
Quos iam regit cum ista perfecta Saxonia: uiuit rex Æþelstanus per facta gloriosus!	Whom he now rules with this England [now] made whole: King Æthelstan lives Glorious through his deeds!

Ille, Sictric defuncto
armat tum in prelio
Saxonum exercitum
per totum Bryttanium

He, with Sitric having died,
in such circumstances arms for battle
the army of the English
throughout all Britain.

Constantinus rex Scottorum
aduolat Bryttanium:
Saxonum regum saluando,
fidelis seruitio.

Constantine, king of the Scots,
hastens to Britain:
by supporting the king of the English
[he is] loyal in his service.

Dixit rex Æþelstanus
per Petri preconia:
sint sani, sint longeui
saluatoris gratia!

King Æthelstan said [these things]
through the announcements of Peter:
may they be well, live long,
Through the saviour's grace!

The 'letter' had seemingly endured a combined land and sea journey from Eamont Bridge, unless this is merely a literary device. The 'queen' and the 'prince' to which greetings are extended, could be both Ælfflæd and her son Edwin (the word for the prince is *clitonem*, in English, Ætheling), or more likely perhaps Eadgifu and her son Edmund, or indeed Eadgifu and Edwin. Although Edwin was still very much at large in Winchester at this time, Ælfflæd had almost certainly been removed to a religious house (see above, page 178). It is, however, just possible that none of these combinations are being referred to here, and that the poet's 'queen' is referring to our other Eadgifu (Æthelstan's half-sister who married Charles the Simple). She had given birth to the young Louis who had been packed off to England for his own safety (see above, page 203). Although it is generally believed that this Eadgifu sent her son to the English court and remained abroad, it is possible she might have come to England at some stage. If so, Eadgifu and Louis might be outside candidates for the couple in question. The likely combination however is Edward's third wife and widow Eadgifu and the older surviving Ætheling of Edward's second marriage, Edwin.[2]

The suggestion is that Æthelstan had summoned an army from all the English parts of his realm, perhaps implying a joint Mercian and West Saxon force like those his father had commanded in the wake of his aunt's death. The result of the campaign and the submission had been an 'England [*Saxonia*] made whole'. Interestingly, the poet does not describe any fighting. The mere threat of warfare seems to have been enough for Æthelstan's opponents to submit to his lordship. Arguably, this is what his father and aunt had tried to do as well, mixing war and the meaningful threat of war, to establish and extend their lordship.

An example of this threat of violence to enforce overlordship may be present in William of Malmesbury's account of what happened next in the aftermath of Eamont Bridge. Again drawing from the 'ancient volume', William tells of 'the princes of the Northwalians [the Welsh]' whom Æthelstan 'compelled to meet him at the city of Hereford'. After a 'spell of reluctance' from the Welsh, Æthelstan forced them to change their minds and surrender. No king before him had even contemplated what followed, says William. The Welsh were to pay Æthelstan by way of annual tribute 20 pounds of gold and 300 pounds of silver '. . . and to hand over by the count 25,000 oxen, besides as many as he might wish of hounds that with their keen scent could track down the lairs and lurking-places of wild beasts, and birds of prey skilled in pursuing other birds through empty air'. That the Welsh only submitted due to the threat of warfare is perhaps indicated by a Welsh prophesy poem *Armes Prydein*, written in around 930. This poem, which called Æthelstan a 'great king', also bemoaned the loss of Welsh land to the English over many hundreds of years and prophesied that one day revenge would come.

According to William of Malmesbury, Æthelstan went straight from his meeting with the Welsh at Hereford (where he fixed the boundary at the River Wye), to Cornwall. He forced the Cornish to leave Exeter where they had lived until now on an equal footing with the English. He then fixed the boundary at the River Tamar, and rebuilt Exeter with towers and a wall of squared stone. Although this part of William's account is usually treated with scepticism due to the fact that Exeter's walls were already extant, and that there are doubts as to the 'cleansing' of the Cornish at this time from the place, William's mention that Æthelstan was still remembered in these parts in the twelfth century, may have had some truth in it.

By 927, Æthelstan was showing himself to be the ultimate embodiment of the early medieval warrior king. Whilst it is true that Alfred, Æthelflæd and Edward's campaigns had both laid the foundations for and then built up the kingdom of the Anglo-Saxons, Æthelstan, in just his first three years of rule, established the family's power further north than ever before and built a new political entity out of it, a kingdom of the English. The idea that 'England' as a country was an inevitable consequence of all this, is perhaps an exaggeration, but not by much. What we are observing here is the foundation work in the building of that country. It is probably not a coincidence that the Edwardian version of the *Anglo-Saxon Chronicle*, if that is what we can call version (A) and the Mercian or Æthelflædan version as captured in the *Mercian Register* of (B), (C) and woven into (D) both end with submissions of insular rulers across Britain to the main subjects of their texts: Edward in the case of (A), and Æthelstan in the case of the *Mercian Register*, who follows on as a subject in the annals from his aunt, and his cousin, up to the submission at Eamont Bridge.[3] A new era had begun. Those who compiled the chronicles clearly knew it. But it would be a while before they and their successors could put a narrative together again. The stage was being set for one of the greatest military showdowns ever seen in the British Isles.

For the rule of any early medieval dynasty to be effective, a family needed a recurrence of strong leaders from generation to generation, and here, throughout the lifetime of Alfred, Edward and Æthelflæd, they had had just that. Then of course, came Æthelstan. And yet, embodying perhaps every quality needed to succeed as an early medieval leader in a brutal world, there had been one woman. A daughter to a visionary king, a sister to a powerful brother and a mother to a woman who under other circumstances may have gone on to a brighter future, Æthelflæd was also for a long time the wife of another successful man, Æthelred, Lord of the Mercians, who does not always get the plaudits he deserves for his part in the family project. He had married into that family and his daughter and foster son Æthelstan were in some way its heirs, although one of these had been cruelly spirited away. But Æthelflæd was also a military commander with a special talent for strategy, a devout patroness of the church, a collector of royal and distinctly Mercian saintly relics, a founder therefore of churches and fortresses, a shrewd negotiator, and much loved by those who must have seen her as the symbol of a resurgent Mercia. In many ways, she was almost too good at leadership, leaving a palpable sorrow at her premature death, and a memory which strongly persists in the English Midlands even to this day. It is to this woman, who profoundly excelled in warfare and diplomacy against male opponents, that England owes its childhood years.

And so, in 927, King Æthelstan, *rex Anglorum* and self-styled king of all Britain, packed Wulfhelm, his new Archbishop of Canterbury, off to Rome where for the first recorded time, an English archbishop made the journey to collect his ecclesiastical vestment, a pallium, from the pope. If the new English king already had the power, he was now looking for continuing legitimacy and Rome was where his family had always looked for it. Like his grandfather and his aunt, he was fiercely intellectual and highly devoted to God.

For King Æthelstan, the work was just beginning. Despite the flattering poetry, the visits from foreign dignitaries with offers of marriage proposals and hugely symbolic gifts, and the enormous wealth now being accrued by the king, not everyone was content in Æthelstan's England. Nor was there any acceptance of things amongst the Scandinavian dynasties in the northern world. Their long held dream of ruling across the Dublin-to-York axis had been shattered by Æthelstan. In the *Longphorts* of the east coast of Ireland, and in the valleys of Wales and the mountains of Scotland and on the banks of the Clyde, plots would be hatched once more. Alliances would be born. Danes living beyond Watling Street, who had no choice but to submit to the king of the English, might well be persuaded to switch allegiance in the years to come. What had newly become a kingdom of the English, could easily become something else in no space of time at all. As we have frequently seen, in Anglo-Saxon England, as in many other places across the early medieval world, memories died hard. And the memory of what would happen next in this, the reign of England's first king, would resonate well beyond all the other milestones and turning points of England's colourful and bloody history.

Notes

Introduction

1. See Keynes, S. (2015), 'Alfred the Great and the Kingdom of the Anglo-Saxons', in Discenza, N.G. and Szarmach, P.E. (eds), *A Companion to Alfred the Great*. Leiden/Boston: Brill, pp. 13–47 for a background and discussion of the concept of the 'kingdom of the Anglo-Saxons'.
2. See Keynes, S. (2001), 'Edward, King of the Anglo-Saxons', in Higham, N.J. and Hill, D.H. (eds), *Edward the Elder 899 - 924*. Abingdon: Routledge, pp. 40–66, for an influential paper on the concept of the Alfredian 'kingdom of the Anglo-Saxons'.

Part One: The Lady Emerges

Chapter 1: The Thwarted King

1. For the terms of King Alfred's will, see Keynes, S. and Lapidge, M. (eds and trans) (1983), *Alfred the Great. Asser's Life of King Alfred and other contemporary sources*. Penguin Classics. London: Penguin, pp. 173–8.
2. Herbert, K. (1997), *Peace Weavers and Shield Maidens: Women in Early English Society*. Milton Keynes: Anglo-Saxon Books, pp. 23–5, for the suggestion that Æthelflæd may have been denying her husband a male heir. See also Crick, J. (1999), 'Men, Women and Widows: Widowhood in Pre-conquest England', in Cavallo, S. and Warner, L. (eds), *Widowhood in Medieval and Early Modern Europe*. London: Routledge, pp. 26–36.
3. Bailey, M. (2001), 'Ælfwynn, Second Lady of the Mercians', in Higham, N.J. and Hill, D.H. (eds), *Edward the Elder 899 – 924*. Abingdon: Routledge, pp. 112–27, particularly pp. 113–15 for birth, early years and upbringing.
4. Lapidge, M. (1981), 'Some Latin poems as evidence for the reign of Athelstan', *Anglo-Saxon England. Vol. 9*. Cambridge: Cambridge University Press, pp. 61–98 discusses the poetic links to Æthelstan's 'investiture'. See also Nelson, J. (1997), 'The Franks and the English in the Ninth Century Reconsidered', in Rosenthal, J.T. and Szarmach, P.E. (eds), *The Preservation and Transmission of Anglo-Saxon Culture*. Kalamazoo: Western Michigan University, pp. 141–58, for a discussion, among other things, of the meaning of Æthelstan's 'investiture'.
5. Foot, S. (2011), *Æthelstan: the First King of England*. London: Yale University Press. See pp. 30–3 for a discussion of Ecgwynn, Æthelstan's mother. Also, more generally see Sharp, S. (2001), 'The West Saxon Tradition of Dynastic Marriage', in Higham, N.J. and Hill, D.H. (eds), *Edward the Elder 899 – 924*. Abingdon: Routledge, pp. 78–88.

6. Heighway, C. and Bryant, R. (1999), 'The Golden Minster. The Anglo-Saxon Minster and Later Medieval Priory of St Oswald at Gloucester', *CBA Research Reports No 117*. York: Council for British Archaeology, p. 43 for the translation of the 'lost' charter of Æthelstan in respect of the 1304 dispute over St Oswald's at Gloucester.
7. Yorke, B. (2001), 'Edward as Ætheling', in Higham, N.J. and Hill, D.H. (eds), *Edward the Elder 899 – 924*. Abingdon: Routledge, pp. 33–4 for an outline of the arguments for the identity of Æthelhelm, father of Ælfflæd.
8. For an analysis of this issue, see Nelson, J.L. (1986), 'The Second English Ordo', in Nelson J.L. (ed.), *Politics and Ritual in Early Medieval Europe*. London: Hambleton Press, pp. 361–74. See also a later paper by the same author – Nelson, J.L. (2008), 'The First Use of the Second Anglo-Saxon Ordo', in Barrow, J. and Wareham, A., *Myth, Rulership, Church and Charters: Essays in Honour of Nicholas Brooks*. Aldershot: Ashgate, pp. 117–26. But see also Pratt, D. (2017), 'The Making of the Second English Coronation Ordo', *Anglo-Saxon England 46*. Cambridge: Cambridge University Press, pp. 147–258.
9. See Baker, J. and Brookes, S. (2013), *Beyond the Burghal Hidage: Anglo-Saxon Civil Defence in the Viking Age*. Leiden: Brill, for an integrated and comprehensive discussion of Anglo-Saxon fortifications in the landscape for the whole period. For an argument for an early date for the Burghal Hidage, see also Haslam, J. (2005), 'King Alfred and the Vikings: Strategies and Tactics 876–886', *Anglo-Saxon Studies in Archaeology and History 13*. Oxford: Oxford University School of Archaeology, pp. 121–53.
10. For an analysis of this whole episode, see Lavelle, R. (2009), 'The Politics of Rebellion: The Ætheling Æthelwold and West Saxon Royal Succession, 899–902', in Skinner, P. (ed.), *Challenging the Boundaries of Medieval History: The Legacy of Timothy Reuter*. Turnhout: Brepols, pp. 51–80.
11. See Atherton, M. (2021), *The Battle of Maldon. War and Peace in Tenth-Century England*. London: Bloomsbury Academic, in particular Chapter 8, pp. 118–27.
12. Ross, M.C. (1985), 'Concubinage in Anglo-Saxon England', *Past and Present 108*. Oxford: Oxford University Press, pp. 3–34. Page 32 for the suggestion that Æthelwold's abducted nun may have been taken as a concubine.
13. Kershaw, J. (2015), 'Viking-Age Silver in North-West England: Hoards and Single Finds', in Harding, S., Griffiths, D. and Royles, E. (eds), *In Search of Vikings. Interdisciplinary Approaches to the Scandinavian Heritage of North-West England*. London and New York: CRC Press. Taylor and Francis Group, pp. 149–64. Includes a discussion of bullion and display economies. See pp. 155–7 for Silverdale.
14. Biddle, M. (2018), *The Search for Winchester's Anglo-Saxon Minsters*. Oxford: Winchester Excavations Committee (Archaeopress Archaeology), pp. 22 and 66–7.
15. See Sawyer (S 359) and also Rumble, A.R. (2001), 'The Churches of Winchester and Wessex', in Higham, N.J. and Hill, D.H. (eds), *Edward the Elder 899 – 924*. Abingdon: Routledge, pp. 230–45. Also, see Yorke, B. (1984), 'The Bishops of Winchester, the Kings of Wessex and the Development of Winchester in the Ninth and Early Tenth Centuries', *Proceedings of the Hampshire Field Club Archaeological Society 40*. Gloucester: Alan Sutton, pp. 61–70. For the comparison between Edward's New Minster policy and earlier Northumbrian and Mercian models, see

Thacker, A. (2001), 'Dynastic Monasteries and Family Cults', in Higham, N.J. and Hill, D.H. (eds), *Edward the Elder 899 – 924*. Abingdon: Routledge, pp. 253–4.

16. Campbell, J. (2001), 'What is not known about the Reign of Edward the Elder', in Higham, N.J. and Hill, D.H. (eds), *Edward the Elder 899 – 924*. Abingdon: Routledge, pp. 12–24. Especially for observations on John of Salisbury's comments on the men of Kent being in the forefront of Anglo-Saxon armies and therefore possibly forming the vanguard.
17. For a discussion of the location of and consequences of the Battle of the Holme, see Key, M.J. (2019), *Edward the Elder. King of the Anglo-Saxons. Forgotten Son of Alfred*. Stroud: Amberley, pp. 107–09. For a literary comparison to the famous Battle of Maldon poem, see Atherton, M. (2021), *The Battle of Maldon. War and Peace in Tenth-Century England*. London: Bloomsbury Academic, in particular Chapter 8, pp. 118–27. See also Hart, C. (1992), *The Danelaw*. London: Hambledon Press, pp 511–15. For the suggestion of Biggleswade, drawing from earlier work by W.J. Corbett, see Angus, W.S., 'The Chronology of the Reign of Edward the Elder', *English Historical Review* Vol. 53, No. 210. Oxford: Oxford University Press, p. 194.
18. Szarmach, P.E. (1998), 'Æthelflæd of Mercia: Mise en Page', in Baker, P.S. and Howe, N. (eds), *Words and Works: Studies in Medieval English Language and Literature in Honour of Fred C. Robinson*. Toronto: University of Toronto Press, pp. 105–26, especially for an analysis of the *Mercian Register*. See also Wainwright, F.T. (1945), 'The Chronology of the Mercian Register', *English Historical Review* Vol. 60, No. 238. Oxford: Oxford University Press, pp. 385–92. Also, see Stafford, P. (2008), '"The Annals of Æthelflæd": Annals, History and Politics in early tenth-century England', in Barrow, J. and Wareham, A. (eds), *Myth, Rulership, Church and Charters: Essays in honour of Nicholas Brooks*. Aldershot: Ashgate Publishing Ltd, pp. 101–16.
19. It is suggested that the *Mercian Register* or 'Annals of Æthelflæd' once formed the end of a larger text in Old English which was already in vernacular form and which began with the Alfredian Chronicle. It might therefore be a distinctly Æthelflædian continuation of the *Anglo-Saxon Chronicle* in much the same way as version (A) can be interpreted as an Edwardian one. But see also Szamarch (1998) above, for the case for a Latin *Gesta* being behind the annals. The topic is covered extensively in a formidable book, Stafford, P. (2020), *After Alfred: Anglo-Saxon Chronicles and Chroniclers, 900 – 1150*. Oxford: Oxford University Press, pp 52–78.

Chapter 2: Ingimund

1. For a thorough analysis of the place names of Wirral and the Viking enclave, see Harding, S. (2016), *Ingimund's Saga. Viking Wirral*. Chester: University of Chester Press. See also Matthews, S. (2003), 'Viking Settlement in the Wirral', *Journal of the Chester Archaeological Society 78*. Chester: Chester Archaeological Society, pp. 107–17. Also, for an earlier scholarly analysis of the Ingimund tale, see Wainwright, F.T. (1948), 'Ingimund's Invasion', *English Historical Review* Vol. 63, No. 247. Oxford: Oxford University Press, pp. 145–69.

2. Translations taken from that published in Harding, S. (2016), *Ingimund's Saga. Viking Wirral*. Chester: University of Chester Press, pp. 5–7. Translated by the late Professor I.L. Foster of Jesus College, Oxford.
3. See Henry Bradshaw's *Life of St. Werburge*, Stanza 90, line 625 for the transfer of the dedication of St Peter to the centre of Chester. Available at http://www.medievalchester.ac.uk/texts/scholarly/bradshaw-page=0.html [Accessed 20/10/2021]. For a general analysis and comparison of Chester and Gloucester and Æthelred and Æthelflæd's roles in ecclesiastical organization, see Thacker, A. (1982), 'Chester and Gloucester: Early Ecclesiastical Organization in Two Mercian Burhs', *Northern History. Vol. 18. Issue 1*. Taylor Francis Online, pp 199–211. Available at https://www.tandfonline.com/doi/pdf/10.1179/007817282790176555 [Accessed 20/10/2021].
4. For a summary of archaeological evidence for Anglo-Saxon Chester, see Ward, S. (2001), 'Edward the Elder and the re-establishment of Chester', in Higham, N.J. and Hill, D.H. (eds), *Edward the Elder 899 – 924*. Abingdon: Routledge, pp. 160–6.
5. Thacker, A. (2020), 'St Wærburh: The Multiple Identities of a Regional Saint', in Langlands, A. and Lavelle, R. (eds), *The Land of the English Kin. Studies in Wessex and Anglo-Saxon England in Honour of Professor Barbara Yorke*. Leiden/Boston: Brill, pp. 443–66.

Chapter 3: Peace

1. A summary of the reorganization of the West Saxon dioceses is to be found in Rumble, A.R. (2001), 'Edward the Elder and the Churches of Winchester and Wessex', in Higham, N.J. and Hill, D.H. (eds), *Edward the Elder 899 – 924*. Abingdon: Routledge, especially pp. 238–45.
2. Campbell, J. (2001), 'What is Not Known about the reign of Edward the Elder', in Higham, N.J. and Hill, D.H. (eds), *Edward the Elder 899 – 924*. Abingdon: Routledge, pp. 12–24, especially pp. 12–14 for a discussion of the amount of material probably lost from the reign of Edward. See also Wormald, P. (2001), 'On þa wæpnedhealfe: kingship and royal property from Æthelwulf to Edward the Elder' (in the same volume), p. 275 for a discussion of the silence surrounding land transactions in the later part Edward's reign.
3. Campbell, A. (ed. and trans) (1962), *The Chronicle of Æthelweard*. London, Edinburgh, New York: Oxford University Press. Nelson's Medieval texts. See also Keynes, S. and Lapidge, M. (eds and trans) (1983), *Alfred the Great. Asser's Life of King Alfred and other contemporary sources*. Penguin Classics. London: Penguin, pp. 189–91 for a slightly different translation of the final years of King Alfred's reign.
4. Keynes, S. (2001), 'Edward, King of the Anglo-Saxons', in Higham, N.J. and Hill, D.H. (eds), *Edward the Elder 899 – 924*. Abingdon: Routledge, pp. 52–5 for discussion of these charters.
5. The location and meaning of the treaty at Tiddingford is discussed by Key, M.J. (2019), *Edward the Elder. King of the Anglo-Saxons. Forgotten Son of Alfred*. Stroud: Amberley, pp. 134–9.

6. For a discussion of the hoards in this area see Kershaw, J. (2015), 'Viking-Age Silver in North-West England: Hoards and Single Finds', in Harding, S., Griffiths, D. and Royles, E. (eds), *In Search of Vikings. Interdisciplinary Approaches to the Scandinavian Heritage of North-West England* London and New York: CRC Press. Taylor and Francis Group, pp. 149–64. See also Campbell, J. (2001), 'The Northern Hoards', in Higham, N.J. and Hill, D.H. (eds), *Edward the Elder 899 – 924*. Abingdon: Routledge, pp. 212–29, though based on evidence known up to 2001.
7. Quanrud, J. (2015), 'Taking Sides: North-West England Vikings at the Battle of Tettenhall', in Harding, S., Griffiths, D. and Royles, E. (eds), *In Search of Vikings. Interdisciplinary Approaches to the Scandinavian Heritage of North-West England.* London and New York: Taylor and Francis Group, pp. 71–94 for an argument in support of the importance of the Scandinavians of north-west England in the regional politics of the early tenth century after their expulsion from Ireland in 902 and in their being involved in the subsequent battle at Tettenhall.
8. Heighway, C. and Bryant, R. (1999), *The Golden Minster. The Anglo-Saxon Minster and Later Medieval Priory of St Oswald at Gloucester. CBA Research Reports No 117.* York: Council for British Archaeology. The exact date of the dedication remains elusive. See pp. 34–5.
9. Little, G.R. (2007), *Dynastic Strategies and Regional Loyalties: Wessex, Mercia and Kent, c.802 – 939.* Unpublished PhD thesis. Dept. of History, University of Sheffield. Pages 238–41 for the argument that the retrieval of the relics of St Oswald by Æthelflæd and Æthelred was in some way linked to Æthelred's illness and the search for a cure.

Chapter 4: The Battle of Tettenhall, 5 August 910

1. Quanrud, J. (2015), 'Taking Sides: North-West England Vikings at the Battle of Tettenhall', in Harding, S., Griffiths, D. and Royles, E. (eds), *In Search of Vikings. Interdisciplinary Approaches to the Scandinavian Heritage of North-West England.* London and New York: Taylor and Francis Group, pp. 71–9.
2. Horovitz, D. (2017), *Æthelflæd, Lady of the Mercians; the Battle of Tettenhall 910AD; and other West Mercian Studies*. Stafford: Horovitz. For the Battle of Tettenhall, Camp Feld and Wednesfield, and for extensive discussions of the philological, place-name and other evidence, see pp. 446–9, 516–19, 577–81 and 585–9.
3. Belford, P. (2008), 'Archaeological Evaluation at St Mary's Road Wednesbury', *Coalbrookdale: Ironbridge Archaeology, Report: 300.* Ironbridge: Ironbridge Archaeology.

Chapter 5: *Bremesbyrig*

1. A point made by Blake, M. and Sargent, A. (2018), 'For the Protection of All the People': Æthelflæd and her Burhs in Northwest Mercia', *Midland History* Vol. 43 Issue 2. Routledge (Taylor and Francis), pp 120–54. (at p. 17 of the separately-downloadable paper). Available at https://www.tandfonline.com/doi/full/10.1080/0047729X.2018.1519141. [Accessed 06/07/2021].

2. The case for Bromborough is briefly summarized by Wolfe, J. (2001), *Æthelflæd. Royal Lady, War Lady*. Chester: Fenris Press, p. 26, who also promotes Beeston. For Beeston Castle excavations, see Ellis, P. (ed.) (1993), *Beeston Castle, Cheshire. A report on the Excavations 1968-85 by Laurence Keen and Peter Hough*. Archaeological report No 23. London: HBMC (English Heritage). See also Clarkson, T. (2018), *Æthelflæd. The Lady of the Mercians.* Edinburgh: John Donald (an imprint of Berlin Ltd), pp. 101–02 for a general discussion.
3. For a discussion of the early history of Bromsgrove see Dyer, C. (2000), 'Bromsgrove: A Small town in Worcestershire in the Middle Ages', *Worcestershire Historical Society. Occasional Publications: No. 9*. Worcester: Worcestershire Historical Society.
4. See Clarkson, at Note 2 above.
5. See Dalwood, H., Robson-Glyde, S. and Rogers, T. (2013), *The Historic Environment of Bromsgrove Town Centre, Worcestershire: a Baseline Survey*. Worcester: Worcestershire County Council, p. 7 for a discussion of Bromsgrove's early medieval evidence.
6. For a discussion of the position of Leintwardine in the West Mercian landscape, and its nearby 'tot' sites, see Stone, D.J.F. (2017), *Mutually Assured Construction. Æthelflæd's burhs, Landscapes of Defence and the Physical Legacy of the Unification of England, 899-1016*. PhD thesis. Exeter University, pp. 96, 183 and 222. The implication of the pottery is that the site was militarily connected, perhaps with a garrison. For an analysis of integrated communications, see Baker, J. and Brookes, S. (2015), 'Signalling Intent: Beacons, Lookouts and Military Communications', in Hyer, M.C. and Owen-Crocker, G.R. (eds), *The Material Culture of the Built Environment of Anglo-Saxon England*. Liverpool: Liverpool University Press, pp. 216–34.
7. Except perhaps for the comment made in the *Mercian Register* at the entry for 918, for which see page 172.
8. Heighway, C. and Bryant, R. (1999), *The Golden Minster. The Anglo-Saxon Minster and Later Medieval Priory of St Oswald at Gloucester. CBA Research Reports No 117*. York: Council for British Archaeology. See p. 8 for discussions about the location of the church.

Part Two: The Fortresses of the Conquest

Chapter 6: How did a Fortress Work?

1. For an analysis of Anglo-Saxon burhs in this era, see Hill, D. and Rumble, A.R. (eds) (1996), *The Defence of Wessex: The Burghal Hidage and Anglo-Saxon Fortifications*. Manchester: Manchester University Press. Also Lavelle, R. (2003), *Fortifications in Wessex c. 800-1066*. Oxford: Osprey. For a discussion of the fortress-building heritage in Æthelflæd's region, see Bassett, S. (2013), 'Anglo-Saxon Fortifications in Western Mercia', *Midland History* Vol. 36 Issue 1. Routledge (Taylor and Francis). Available at https://www.tandfonline.com/doi/abs/10.1179/004772911X12956221816169 pp. 1–23. [Accessed 25/10/2021]. See also Bassett, S. (2008), 'The Middle and Late Anglo-Saxon Defences of Western Mercian Towns', in Crawford, S. and Hamerow, H. (eds), *Anglo-Saxon Studies in Archaeology and History 15*. Oxford: Oxbow Books, pp. 180–239. Available at https://doi.org/10.2307/j.ctvh1dw9r.7. [Accessed 27/10/2021]. See also Williams, G. (2013), 'Military and Non-Military Functions of

the Anglo-Saxon burh, c.878-978', in Baker, J., Brookes, S. and Reynolds, A. (eds), *Landscapes of Defence in Early Medieval Europe*. Turnhout: Brepols, pp. 129–64.

2. For a discussion of the word 'burh' as a place name in its variant forms during the Anglo-Saxon era, see Draper, S. (2008), 'The Significance of Old English Burh in Anglo-Saxon England', in Crawford, S. and Hamerow, H. (eds), *Anglo-Saxon Studies in Archaeology and History 15*. Oxford: Oxbow Books. Available at https://doi.org/10.2307/j.ctvh1dw9r.8. pp. 240–53. [Accessed 27/10/2021]. See also Baker, J. (2013), 'The Language of Anglo-Saxon Defence', in Baker, J., Brookes, S. and Reynolds, A. (eds), *Landscapes of Defence in Early Medieval Europe*. Turnhout: Brepols, pp. 65–90.
3. In a sumptuous and detailed book, John Blair re-appraises the archaeology of the Anglo-Saxon built environment era by era. Blair, J. (2018), *Building Anglo-Saxon England*. Princeton and Oxford. Princeton University Press. For the period considered here, see Part II: Consolidation, circa 700-920, Chapters 6 to 8, pp. 179–305, dealing with Mercian origins, the Burghal Hidage and rural settlement.
4. For an extensive discussion of the terminology surrounding burhs, see Stone, D.J.F. (2017), *Mutually Assured Construction. Æthelflæd's burhs, Landscapes of Defence and the Physical Legacy of the Unification of England, 899-1016*. PhD thesis. Exeter University, pp 17–20. See also Baker, J. and Brookes, S. (2013), *Beyond the Burghal Hidage: Anglo-Saxon Civil Defence in the Viking Age*. Leiden: Brill, for a ground-breaking and interdisciplinary approach to the subject. For how burghal territories may have worked in this era, see Haslam, J. (2019), 'Burhs, burghal territories and 'proto-hundreds' in the English central Midlands in the early tenth century'. Available at https://www.academia.edu/38697054/Burhs_burghal_territories_and_proto-hundreds_in_the_English_central_Midlands_in_the_early_tenth_century. [Accessed 25/10/2021].

Chapter 7: *Scergeate* 912 (Æthelflæd)

1. This general location for Scergeate is suggested by Sharp, T. (2013), *Chronicles, Treaties and Burhs; the Burghal Hidage and the Mercian Register. Part 2: The Mercian Reconquest*. Available at: https://www.academia.edu/5565935/Chronicles_Treaties_and_Burhs_the_Burghal_Hidage_and_the_Mercian_Register_Part_2_The_Mercian_Reconquest_910_919. p.19. [Accessed 31/10/2021].
2. Horovitz, D. (2017), *Æthelflæd, Lady of the Mercians; the Battle of Tettenhall 910AD; and other West Mercian Studies*. Stafford: Horovitz. See pp. 134–53 for an extensive discussion of *Scergeate* in respect of an identification with Shrawardine and its near neighbour.

Chapter 8: *Bricge* 912 (Æthelflæd)

1. See Horovitz, D. (2017), *Æthelflæd, Lady of the Mercians; the Battle of Tettenhall 910AD; and other West Mercian Studies*. Stafford: Horovitz, pp. 116–33 for an extensive discussion of 'Æthelflæd's *burh* at *Cwatbrycge*' summarized here.
2. Blake, M. and Sargent, A. (2018), '"For the Protection of All the People": Æthelflæd and her Burhs in Northwest Mercia', *Midland History* Vol. 43 Issue 2. Routledge (Taylor and Francis), pp. 120–54. Available at https://www.tandfonline.com/

doi/full/10.1080/0047729X.2018.1519141. [Accessed 06/07/2021]. Contains a useful discussion on the siting similarities in Æthelflæd's known burhs, including the topographic details and the foundation of churches within.

Chapter 9: Hertford 912/13 and Witham 913 (Edward)

1. Hertford's Anglo-Saxon heritage and its burghal evidence is neatly summarized by Clive Partridge. See Partridge, C. (2008), 'Hertford and Ware: archaeological perspectives from birth to middle age', in Slater, T. and Goose, N. (eds), *A County of Small Towns. The Development of Hertfordshire's Urban Landscape to 1800.* Hatfield: University of Hertfordshire Press, pp. 127–58. See especially pp. 142–6 for Edward's burhs.
2. The chronology of Edward's reign is notoriously fraught with difficulty, due to uncertainties in establishing the commencement of each year (the entry for 912, for example, seems to have started from the autumn Roman indictional New Year in September, hence Martinmas falling before summertime). Also, the manuscript of version (A) at this point is littered with later chronological corrections in numerous hands. A good starting point is Angus, W.S. (1938), 'The Chronology of the Reign of Edward the Elder', *English Historical Review* Vol. 53, No. 210. Oxford: Oxford University Press, pp. 194–210. See also Vaughan, R. (1954), 'The Chronology of the Parker Chronicle 890 – 970', *English Historical Review* Vol. 69, No. 270. Oxford: Oxford University Press, pp. 59–66. More recently, see Sparks, N. (2011), 'The 'Parker Chronicle': Chronology Gone Awry', *The Medieval Chronicle VII.* Brill, pp. 63–84. Available at https://brill.com/view/book/edcoll/9789401200417/B9789401200417-s005.xml. [Accessed 05/11/2021].

Chapter 10: Tamworth and Stafford 913 (Æthelflæd)

1. For a good general history of Tamworth through the Anglo-Saxon period, see Pollington, S. (2011), *Tamworth. The Ancient Capital of Mercia.* Tamworth: Tamworth Borough Council. See pp. 47–55 for Æthelflæd's activities in the famous burh.
2. For an analysis of Stafford's Anglo-Saxon archaeology, see Carver, M. and Cane J. (2010), *The Birth of a Borough: An Archaeological Study of Anglo-Saxon Stafford.* Woodbridge: Boydell Press. Also Carver, M. (2010), *Anglo-Saxon Stafford. Archaeological Investigations 1954-2004.* Field Reports On-line. York: Archaeology Data Service. Available at https://doi.org/10.5284/1000117. [Accessed 26/10/2021].
3. The same type of pottery has also been known as Chester Ware, Chester-type Ware, Stafford-type Ware, and West Midlands Early Medieval Ware. See Ford, D.A. (1999), 'A Late Saxon Pottery Industry in Staffordshire: A Review', *Medieval Ceramics 22-23*, pp. 11–36. Available at https://medievalpottery.org.uk/medieval-ceramics-online/volume-22-3-1998-99/. [Accessed 26/10/2021]. See Stone, D.J.F. (2017), *Mutually Assured Construction. Æthelflæd's burhs, Landscapes of Defence and the Physical Legacy of the Unification of England, 899-1016.* PhD thesis. Exeter University, pp. 179–87 for a more detailed and recent breakdown of the distribution of Stafford Ware.

4. Dodd, A. (ed) (2014), *Excavations at Tipping Street, Stafford, 2009–10*. Walsall: Stafford Archaeological and Historical Society. See also a collaborative article based on the latest landscape and bioarchaeological research: Bogaard, A., Charles, M., Forster, E., Hamerow, H., Holmes, M., McKerracher, M., Neil, S., Ramsey, C.B., Stroud, E. and Thomas, R. (2020), 'An Integrated Bioarchaeological Approach to the Medieval "Agricultural Revolution": A Case Study from Stafford, England, c. AD 800–1200', *European Journal of Archaeology 23 (4)*. Cambridge: Cambridge University Press, pp. 585–609. doi:10.1017/eaa.2020.6. Also available at https://www.cambridge.org/core/journals/european-journal-of-archaeology/article/an-integrated-bioarchaeological-approach-to-the-medieval-agricultural-revolution-a-case-study-from-stafford-england-cad-8001200/7CC93DF3D9E1ECB0E18F8B8816683F2A. [Accessed 05/11/2021].
5. See Note 2 above. See also Carver, M. (2011), 'What were they thinking?: Intellectual Territories in Anglo-Saxon England', in Hinton, D.A., Crawford, S. and Hamerow, H. (eds), *The Oxford Handbook of Anglo-Saxon Archaeology*. Oxford: Oxford University Press, pp. 914–47.

Chapter 11: Eddisbury and Warwick 914 (Æthelflæd)

1. See Varley, W.J. (1950), 'Excavations at the Castle Ditch, Eddisbury, 1935-1938', *Transactions of the Historic Society of Lancashire and Cheshire 102*. Liverpool: Historic Society of Lancashire and Cheshire, pp. 1–68. Available at https://www.hslc.org.uk/wp-content/uploads/2017/06/102-2-Varley.pdf. [Accessed 26/10/2021]. For more recent work, see Cocroft W.D., Everson, P., Jecock M. and Wilson-North, W.R. (1989) 'Castle Ditch hill fort, Eddisbury, Cheshire, reconsidered: the excavations of 1935-8 in the light of recent field survey', in Bowden, M., Mackay, D.A. and Topping, P. (eds), *From Cornwall to Caithness: Some Aspects of British Field Archaeology. Papers presented to Norman V. Quinnell*. Oxford: British Archaeological Reports British Series 209, pp. 129–73. See also Webster, T. (2006), *Archaeological Recording at Eddisbury Hillfort, Delamere, Cheshire*. Chester: Gifford & Partners; and Shaw, M. and Clark, J. (2003), *Cheshire Historic Towns Survey: Eddisbury Archaeological Assessment*. Chester: Cheshire County Council and English Heritage.
2. For the oven, see Garner, D. (2012), *Hillforts of the Cheshire Sandstone Ridge*. Chester: Cheshire West and Cheshire Council, p. 66. See also Stone, D.J.F. (2017), *Mutually Assured Construction. Æthelflæd's burhs, Landscapes of Defence and the Physical Legacy of the Unification of England, 899-1016*. PhD thesis. Exeter University. See p. 54 for discussion of the oven and the 2010–11 excavations.
3. See Sharp, T. (2013), *Chronicles, Treaties and Burhs; the Burghal Hidage and the Mercian Register. Part 2: The Mercian Reconquest*. Available at: https://www.academia.edu/5565935/Chronicles_Treaties_and_Burhs_the_Burghal_Hidage_and_the_Mercian_Register_Part_2_The_Mercian_Reconquest_910_919, p. 24. [Accessed 31/10/2021].
4. For an introduction to the early history of Warwick, see Allison, K.J., Dunning, R.W. and Jones, S.R. (1969), 'The Borough of Warwick: Introduction', in Stephens,

W. B. (ed.), *A History of the County of Warwick: Volume 8: The City of Coventry and Borough of Warwick. Victoria County History*, pp. 417–51, and also pp. 476–80 for political and administrative history to 1545. For an analysis of Anglo-Saxon Warwick, see Bassett, S. (1989), 'Anglo-Saxon Warwick', *Midland History* Vol. 34 Issue 2. Routledge (Taylor and Francis). Available at https://www.tandfonline.com/doi/abs/10.1179/175638109X417332, pp. 123–55. [Accessed 06/11/2021]. For a summary of excavations see Hill, D. and Rumble, R. (eds) (1996), *The Defence of Wessex: The Burghal Hidage and Anglo-Saxon Fortifications*. Manchester: Manchester University Press, pp. 222–23.

Chapter 12: Buckingham 914 (Edward)

1. See Haslam, J. (2018), 'The two burhs of Buckingham', *Southern History 39*. Available at https://www.academia.edu/37404273/The_two_burhs_of_Buckingham, pp. 1–35. [Accessed 07/11/2021]. The arguments for a burh at Newport and for the events of 914 being seen by the chronicler through the lens of later developments, are explored.

Chapter 13: Chirbury and *Weardbyrig* 915 (Æthelflæd)

1. For a discussion of the limited investigations undertaken at Chirbury, see Stone, D.J.F. (2017), *Mutually Assured Construction. Æthelflæd's burhs, Landscapes of Defence and the Physical Legacy of the Unification of England, 899-1016*. PhD thesis. Exeter University, pp. 69–76.
2. Blunt, C.E. and Elmore Jones, F. (1958), 'The Tenth Century Mint æt Weardbyrig', *British Numismatic Journal Vol. 28* pp. 494 – 8. Available online at https://web.archive.org/web/20190802121023/http://www.britnumsoc.org/publications/Digital%20BNJ/pdfs/1955_BNJ_28_37.pdf. [Accessed 19/09/2021].
3. This identification of Ælfwynn is powerfully argued by Bailey, M. (2001), 'Ælfwynn, Second Lady of the Mercians', in Higham, N.J. and Hill, D.H. (eds), *Edward the Elder 899 – 924*. Abingdon: Routledge, p. 119.
4. Hislop, M., Kinsey, M. and Williams, G. (2011), *Tutbury: 'A Castle Firmly Built'. Archaeological and Historical Investigations at Tutbury Castle, Staffordshire.* Oxford: Archaeopress, pp. 50–6.
5. Discussed by Blunt and Elmore Jones. See Note 2 above.
6. Pointed out by Professor Michael Wood in a British Library (and HistFest) online lecture. See Wood, M. (2021), *Æthelflæd: Lady of the Mercians* [online video]. Available at https://www.youtube.com/watch?v=YJ78whSSo7E. [Accessed 07/11/2021].
7. Warburton's case is discussed in Clarkson, T. (2018), *Æthelflæd. The Lady of the Mercians.* Edinburgh: John Donald (an imprint of Berlin Ltd), p. 127.
8. Coates R. (1998), 'Æthelflæd's fortification of "Weardburh"', *Notes and Queries 45. Issue 1*. Oxford: Oxford University Press, pp. 8–12 for the north Welsh argument in favour of Gwespyr.

Chapter 14: Bedford (Edward) and Runcorn 915 (Æthelflæd)

1. The archaeology of the King's Ditch is discussed in Edgeworth, M. (2011), 'The Weir and the Flowing Earthworks of Bedford', *British Archaeology No 121*. York: Council for British Archaeology, pp. 22–7.
2. The drawing reproduced here comes from Beaumont, W. (1873), *A History of the Castle at Halton and the Priory or Abbey of Norton*. Warrington: P. Pearse, p. 4 and purportedly shows the rampart reported earlier in the century by J.H. Hanshall in 1823 in *History of the County Palatine of Chester. 2nd edition*. Chester: J.H. Hanshall, p. 418.
3. Clarkson, T. (2018), *Æthelflæd. The Lady of the Mercians*. Edinburgh: John Donald (an imprint of Berlin Ltd), p. 131. See also Baggs, P., Kettle, A., Lander, S., Thacker, A. and Wardle, D. (1980), 'House of Augustinian canons: The abbey of Norton', in Elrington C.R. and Harris B.E. (eds), *The Victoria County History of the County of Chester, Vol. 3*. Oxford: Oxford University Press, pp. 165–71.
4. The plateau theory and alternative location for the burh at Runcorn is examined in Blake, M. and Sargent, A. (2018), '"For the Protection of All the People": Æthelflæd and her Burhs in Northwest Mercia', *Midland History* Vol. 43 Issue 2. Routledge (Taylor and Francis), pp. 120–54. Available at https://www.tandfonline.com/doi/full/10.1080/0047729X.2018.1519141. [Accessed 06/07/2021].

Chapter 15: Maldon 916 (Edward)

1. A point raised and discussed by Key, M.J. (2019), *Edward the Elder. King of the Anglo-Saxons. Forgotten Son of Alfred*. Stroud: Amberley, p. 198.
2. See Karkov, C. (1995), 'Æðelflæd's Exceptional Coinage?', *Old English Newsletter 29.1: 41*. Available online at http://www.oenewsletter.org/OEN/archives.php?volume=29&issue=1. [Accessed 18/09/2021]. See also Lyon, S. (2001), 'The Coinage of Edward the Elder', in Higham, N.J. and Hill, D.H. (eds), *Edward the Elder 899 – 924*. Abingdon: Routledge, pp. 67–78, for an analysis of the coinage of the reign including (p. 73) the decorative issues from Western Mercia.

Part Three: The Offensive of 917–918

Chapter 16: Æthelflæd and the Welsh

1. The complexity of the changes in political subjection in Wales from King Alfred's time to King Edward's time is summarized by Charles-Edwards, T.M. (2013), *Wales and the Britons 350 -1064*. Oxford: Oxford University Press, pp. 504–07. Brycheiniog in particular is discussed at p. 506.
2. Campbell, E. and Lane, A. (1989), 'Llangorse: a 10th-century royal crannog in Wales', *Antiquity, 63(241)*. Cambridge: Cambridge University Press, pp. 675–81. doi: 10.1017/S0003598X0007681X. See also Lane, A. and Redknap, M. (2020), *Llangorse Crannog: the Excavation of an Early Medieval Royal Site in the Kingdom of Brycheiniog*. Oxford: Oxbow Books, especially pp. 413–14.
3. Welton, M. (2018), 'Domina et Fidelibus Eius: Elite Households in Tenth Century Francia and Anglo-Saxon England', in Earenfight, T. (ed), *Royal and Elite Households*

in Medieval and Early Modern Europe: More than Just a Castle. Explorations in Medieval Culture 6. Leiden: Brill, pp. 15–41. Examines the household dynamics of Æthelflæd and of Gerberga of Francia. See particularly, pp. 33–4 for Æthelflæd's retaliation against Brycheiniog as an example of household targeting.

Chapter 17: Spring and Summer 917

1. For an earlier opinion on the location of Wigingamere (since revised), see Haslam, J. (1988), 'The Anglo-Saxon Burh at Wigingamere', *Landscape History 10*. Taylor Francis online. Available at https://www.tandfonline.com/doi/abs/10.1080/01433768.1988.10594413. [Accessed 19/09/2021]. For the reappraisal, see Haslam, J. (1997), 'The Location of the Burh of Wigingamere – a reappraisal', in Rumble, A.R. and Mills D. (eds), *Names, Places and People: An Onomastic Miscellany in Memory of John McNeal Dodgson*. Stamford: Paul Watkins Publishing, pp. 111–37. See also Dodgson, M. (1997), 'Wigingamere', in Rumble, A.R. and Mills D. (eds), *Names, Places and People: An Onomastic Miscellany in Memory of John McNeal Dodgson*. Stamford: Paul Watkins Publishing, pp. 383–9.
2. For a discussion of the methodology behind finding Viking fortifications and the effects of antiquarian research, see Raffield, B. (2013), 'Antiquarians, Archaeologists and Viking Fortifications', *Journal of the North Atlantic. No 20*. Steuben: Eagle Hill Institute, pp. 1–29. Raffield also discusses Tempsford in an unpublished MPhil thesis – Raffield, B. (2010), *'Inside that fortress sat a few peasant men, and it was half-made'. A Study of 'Viking' Fortifications in the British Isles AD793-1066*. Available at https://etheses.bham.ac.uk/id/eprint/1102/1/Raffield10MPhil.pdf, pp. 38–62. [Accessed 27/11/2021].
3. Key accepts the existence of Guthrum II and his death at Tempsford. See Key, M.J. (2019), *Edward the Elder. King of the Anglo-Saxons. Forgotten Son of Alfred*. Stroud: Amberley, pp. 135, 168, 214 and 217.

Chapter 18: Derby, Late July 917

1. Derby's development at this time is outlined in Hall, R.A. (1974), 'The Pre-Conquest Burh of Derby', *Derbyshire Archaeological Journal 94*. Derbyshire Archaeological Society. Available online at https://archaeologydataservice.ac.uk/archives/view/daj/contents.cfm?vol_id=1083. [Accessed 18/09/2021].
2. Thompson, V. (2002), *Dying and Death in Anglo-Saxon England*. Woodbridge: Boydell Press, in particular, pp. 11–12 for Æthelflæd and a discussion of the taking of Derby and the meaning of the word '*besorge*' and the relationship between Æthelflæd and her retainers.

Chapter 19: The Autumn Onslaught

1. See Pelteret, D.A.E. (2009), 'An Anonymous Historian of Edward the Elder's Reign', in Baxter, S., Karkov, C.E., Nelson, J. and Pelteret, D.A.E. (eds), *Early Medieval Studies in Memory of Patrick Wormald*. Farnham: Ashgate, pp. 319–36 for an analysis

of the question of the authorship of the section of the *Anglo-Saxon Chronicle* dealing with the campaigns of Edward between 912 and 920.

2. This line of argument is put forward by Wood, H.H. (2018), *Edward the Elder and the Making of England*. Available at http://www.amazon.co.uk/kindlestore [downloaded 16 March 2021], p. 197 of the Kindle edition. The story is translated by Fairweather, J. (2005), *Liber Eliensis. A History of the Isle of Ely From The Seventh Century to the Twelfth*. Woodbridge: Boydell and Brewer, pp. 121–2. For the wider legal issue of how such disputes were settled, and for the role of compurgation, see Roffe, D. (2000), *Domesday. The Inquest and the Book*. Oxford: Oxford University Press, p. 66.

Chapter 20: Leicester and Stamford 918

1. For a thorough analysis of the archaeology and development of post-Roman Leicester, see Courtney, P. (1998), 'Saxon and medieval Leicester: the making of an urban landscape', *Transactions of the Leicestershire Archaeological and Historical Society 72*, pp. 110–45. Available at https://www.le.ac.uk/lahs/downloads/1998/1998%20(72)%20110-145%20Courtney.pdf. [Accessed 11/11/2021].
2. For Stamford Ware pottery, see Kilmurry, K. (1980), *The Pottery Industry of Stamford, Lincolnshire, c.A.D. 850-1250: Its Manufacture, Trade and Relationship with Continental Wares, with a Classification and Chronology*. Oxford: BAR Publishing. For the archaeological work undertaken, see Mahany, C. and Roffe, D. (1983), 'Stamford: the Development of an Anglo-Scandinavian Borough', *Anglo-Norman Studies 5*. Woodbridge: Boydell and Brewer, pp. 198–219. Not everyone is in agreement with how things developed at Stamford: see Haslam, J. (2017), 'The territorial and strategic context of Stamford, Lincolnshire, in the early tenth century', *Journal of Historical Geography 58*, pp. 23–38. Available at https://doi.org/10.1016/j.jhg.2017.09.003. (https://www.sciencedirect.com/science/article/pii/S0305748817302049). [Accessed 11/11/2021]. Haslam sees Edward building two burhs either side of the river on the West Saxon model, thus creating two burghal territories in the landscape.

Part Four: Securing the North

Chapter 21: The Battle of Corbridge

1. Identifying the date for the Battle of Corbridge, and establishing exactly how many times a battle was fought there, have been problematic. For the English source and a discussion of the two entries, which on the face of it seem to present two different battles, see South, T.J. (2002), *Historia de Sancto Cuthberto: A History of Saint Cuthbert and a Record of His Patrimony. Anglo-Saxon Texts No 3*. Cambridge: D.S. Brewer, pp. 105–09. The battle(s) were discussed by Wainwright in an influential 1950 paper reprinted in 1975: Wainwright, F.T. (1975), 'The Battles at Corbridge', in Finberg, H.P.R. (ed.), *Scandinavian England. Collected Papers by F.T. Wainwright*. Chichester: Phillimore, pp. 163–80. For a recent analysis, see Woolf, A. (2007), *From Pictland to Alba 789 – 1070*. Edinburgh: Edinburgh University Press, pp. 142–4. This is a view accepted in Clarkson, T. (2014), *Strathclyde and the Anglo-Saxons*

in the Viking Age. Edinburgh: John Donald (an imprint of Berlin Ltd), pp. 69–70. South's explanation is also accepted by Downham, C. (2008), *Viking Kings of Britain and Ireland. The Dynasty of Ívarr to A.D. 1014*. Edinburgh: Dunedin Academic Press Ltd, pp. 92–3. Although far from resolved, the weight of opinion may now be moving towards just one, and not two, battles of Corbridge.

2. William of Malmesbury's account of Matilda and its similarities with the memory of Æthelflæd is explored by Arman, J. (2017), *The Warrior Queen. The Life and Legend of Æthelflæd, Daughter of Alfred the Great*. Stroud: Amberley, pp. 221–2.
3. See Bovey, A. (2005), *The Chaworth Roll: a Fourteenth-Century Genealogy of the Kings of England*. London: Sam Fogg Rare Books, p. 41 for the translated passage on Æthelflæd.
4. Nichols, P.W. (2005), 'Excavations at St Andrew's Church, Churchdown, Gloucestershire, 2000', *Transactions of the Bristol and Gloucestershire Archaeological Society 123*. Bristol: Bristol and Gloucestershire Archaeological Society, pp. 87–93.
5. For a detailed analysis of the history of the Edith Gittins bequest to Leicester, including background on the life and work of Gittins herself, see Orlandi, M. and Smurra, R. (2021), 'The role of women in the shaping of civic identity in Edwardian Leicester: Edith Gittins and the Anglo-Saxon past of Æthelflæd's fountain. Historical reconstruction and 3D visualization', in *Urban History*. Cambridge: Cambridge University Press, pp. 1–29. doi:10.1017/S0963926821000158. [Accessed 28/11/2021].
6. Dunn, C. (2015), *God's Chosen: The Cults of Virgin Martyrs in Anglo-Saxon England*. https://digitalrepository.unm.edu/engl_etds/4. [Accessed 20/07/2021]. The University of New Mexico, pp. 50–69, for an in-depth discussion about the importance of St Margaret of Antioch and St Juliana to Anglo-Saxon women, in particular to Æthelflæd herself.

Chapter 22: A New Lady

1. Thompson, V. (2002), *Dying and Death in Anglo-Saxon England*. Woodbridge: Boydell Press, in particular pp. 8–24 for Æthelflæd and a discussion of her death and the cult centre at Gloucester.
2. For an expert analysis and discussion of the life and fate of Ælfwynn, see Bailey, M. (2001), 'Ælfwynn, Second Lady of the Mercians', in Higham, N.J. and Hill, D.H. (eds), *Edward the Elder 899 – 924*. Abingdon: Routledge, pp. 112–27.
3. Charles-Edwards, T.M. (2013), *Wales and the Britons 350-1064*. Oxford. Oxford University Press, pp. 498–9 for a discussion about the meaning and application of the verb '*cirran*'.
4. Woolf, A. (2001), 'View from the West: an Irish perspective on West Saxon dynastic practice', in Higham, N.J. and Hill, D.H. (eds), *Edward the Elder 899 – 924*. Abingdon: Routledge, pp. 89–101, especially pp. 99–100 for the suggestion that Ælfwynn may have once been betrothed to the young Æthelstan. The paper draws comparisons with the contemporary Irish experience.
5. *Caradoc, of Llancarvan: The historie of Cambria, now called Wales: a part of the most famous yland of Brytaine, written in the Brytish language aboue two hundreth yeares past: translated into English by H. Lhoyd Gentleman: corrected, augmented, and continued out of records and best approoued authors, by Dauid Powel Doctor in diuinitie*. London:

1584. Imprinted at London by Rafe Newberie and Henrie Denham, p. 50. Available at http://name.umdl.umich.edu/A17946.0001.001. [Accessed 12/11/2021].
6. Stevenson, J. (ed.) (1854), *The Church Historians of England. Vol II. Part II. Containing The Chronicle of Fabius Ethelwerd, Asser's Annals of King Alfred, The Book of Hyde, The Chronicles of John Wallingford, The History of Ingulf, Gaimar*. London: Seeleys, p. 514.
7. See Ridyard, S.J. (1988), *The Royal Saints of Anglo-Saxon England. A Study of West Saxon and East Anglian Cults*. Cambridge: Cambridge University Press, pp. 96–139.
8. S 1211, the grant by Eadgifu to Christ Church, Canterbury contains an extensive history of the dispute.
9. Bailey, M. (2001), p. 125. See Note 2 above.

Chapter 23: Father and Lord

1. Dodgson, J. McN. (1970), *The Place-Names of Cheshire: Part ll. The Place-Names of Bucklow Hundred and Northwich Hundred*. Cambridge: Cambridge University Press, p. 138.
2. Carter, G.A. (1989), *A History of Latchford From the Bronze Age to the Twentieth Century*. Latchford: Keith Thompson, p. 14.
3. See Wildgoose, R.H. (1961), 'The Defences of the Pre-Conquest Borough of Nottingham', *Transactions of the Thoroton Society of Nottinghamshire. 65*. Nottingham: Thoroton Society of Nottinghamshire, pp. 19–26. See also Haslam, J. (1987), 'The Second Burh of Nottingham' *Landscape History 9*. Taylor Francis online. Available at https://www.tandfonline.com/doi/abs/10.1080/01433768.1987.10594405. [Accessed 19/09/2021].
4. See Stetka, J. (1997), *King Edward the Elder's Burh: The Lost Village of Burton by Bakewell*. Bakewell: Bakewell and District Historical Society.
5. The extent of Edward's power at this time is discussed in Davidson, M.R. (2001), 'The (non) Submission of the Northern Kings in 920', in Higham, N.J. and Hill, D.H. (eds), *Edward the Elder 899 – 924*. Abingdon: Routledge, pp. 200–11. See also Wainwright, F.T. (1975), 'The Submission to Edward the Elder', in Finberg, H.P.R. (ed.), *Scandinavian England. Collected Papers by F.T. Wainwright*. Chichester: Phillimore, pp. 325–44.
6. The Fonthill Letter has obviously been much discussed. In particular, see Keynes, S. (1992), 'The Fonthill Letter', in Korhammer, M. (ed.), *Words, Texts and Manuscripts: Studies in Anglo-Saxon Culture Presented to Helmut Gneuss on the Occasion of His Sixty-fifth Birthday*. Cambridge: D.S. Brewer, pp. 53–97. Because there are so many aspects of Anglo-Saxon life touched upon by the document, see also Gretsch, M. (1994), 'The Language of the Fonthill Letter', *Anglo-Saxon England 23*. Cambridge: Cambridge University Press, pp. 57–102; and Hough, C. (2000), 'Cattle Tracking in the Fonthill Letter', *English Historical Review*, Vol. 115, No. 463. Oxford: Oxford University Press, pp. 864–92; and Boynton, M and Reynolds, S. (1996), 'The Author of the Fonthill Letter', *Anglo-Saxon England 25*. Cambridge: Cambridge University Press, pp. 91–5; and Smith, S.T. (2007), 'Of Kings and Cattle Thieves: The Rhetorical Work of the Fonthill Letter', *Journal of English and Germanic Philology 106*. Champaign: University of Illinois Press, pp. 447–67; Brooks, N.P. (2009), 'The

Fonthill Letter. Ealdorman Ordlaf and the Anglo-Saxon Law in Practice', in Baxter, S., Karkov, C.E., Nelson, J. and Pelteret, D.A.E. (eds), *Early Medieval Studies in Memory of Patrick Wormald*. Farnham: Ashgate, pp. 301–17; and Niles, J.D. (2012), 'The Fonthill Ghost Word, the Fonthill Thief, and Early West Saxon Scribal Culture', in Hussey, M. and Niles, J.D. (eds), *The Genesis of Books: Studies in the Scribal Culture of Medieval England in Honor of A.N. Doane*. Turnhout: Brepols, pp. 69–95.

7. Keynes, S. (1992), 'The Fonthill Letter', in Korhammer, M. (ed.), *Words, Texts and Manuscripts: Studies in Anglo-Saxon Culture Presented to Helmut Gneuss on the Occasion of His Sixty-fifth Birthday*. Cambridge: D.S. Brewer, pp 71–2.
8. See Niles, J.D. (2012), 'The Fonthill Ghost Word, the Fonthill Thief, and Early West Saxon Scribal Culture', in Hussey, M. and Niles, J.D. (eds), *The Genesis of Books: Studies in the Scribal Culture of Medieval England in Honor of A.N. Doane*. Turnhout: Brepols, pp. 83–4.

Chapter 24: The 'Mercian' Revolt

1. The identification was made by Wainwright, F.T. (1950), 'Cledemutha', *English Historical Review* Vol. 65, No. 255. Oxford: Oxford University Press, pp. 203–12. For a history of the excavations, see Griffiths, D. (2001), 'The North-West Frontier', in Higham, N.J. and Hill, D.H. (eds), *Edward the Elder 899 – 924*. Abingdon: Routledge, pp. 171–4. See also Manley, J. (et al) (1987), 'Cledemutha: A Late Saxon Burh in North Wales', *Medieval Archaeology 31*. Available online at https://archaeologydataservice.ac.uk/archiveDS/archiveDownload?t=arch-769-1/dissemination/pdf/vol31/31_013_046.pdf. [Accessed 19/09/2021].
2. Higham, N.J. (1988), 'The Cheshire Burhs and the Mercian Frontier to AD 924', *Transactions of the Antiquarian Society of Lancashire and Cheshire 85*. Liverpool: Historic Society of Lancashire and Cheshire, pp. 193–222. See also Griffiths, D. (2015), 'A Brief History and Archaeology of Viking Activity in North-West England', in Harding, S., Griffiths, D. and Royles, E. (eds), *In Search of Vikings. Interdisciplinary Approaches to the Scandinavian Heritage of North-West England*. London and New York: Taylor and Francis Group, pp. 33–50.
3. For discussion of the topic, see Hill, D. (2001), 'The Shiring of Mercia – again', in Higham, N.J. and Hill, D.H. (eds), *Edward the Elder 899 – 924*. Abingdon: Routledge, pp. 144–59.
4. For a breakdown of Edward's subsequent reputation, see Higham, N.J. (2001), 'Edward the Elder's Reputation. An Introduction', in Higham, N.J. and Hill, D.H. (eds), *Edward the Elder 899 – 924*. Abingdon: Routledge, pp. 1–11.

Part Five: Æthelstan

Chapter 25: A Protracted Succession

1. McDermott, D. (2021), 'Winchester, Æthelings and *Clitones*: the Political Significance of the City for Anglo-Saxon Aristocracy and Norman nobility', in Lavelle, R., Roffey, S. and Weikert, K. (eds), *Early Medieval Winchester: Communities, Authority*

and Power in an Urban Space, c.800 – c. 1200. Oxford: Oxbow Books, pp. 103–24, particularly p. 114 for Ælfweard. For the *Liber Monasterii de Hyda*'s mention of Elfredus, see Edwards, E. (ed) (1866), *Liber Monasterii de Hyda*. London: Longmans, Green, Reader and Dyer, p. 113.
2. Foot, S. (2011), *Æthelstan: the First King of England.* London: Yale University Press, p. 17.
3. A point covered in Stafford, P. (2020), *After Alfred: Anglo-Saxon Chronicles and Chroniclers, 900 – 1150.* Oxford: Oxford University Press, p. 68.
4. Edwin's fate will be considered in the next volume of this series. But see also Foot, S. (2011), *Æthelstan: the First King of England.* London: Yale University Press, pp. 40–2.

Chapter 26: Coronation

1. See Note 8, page 213 above.
2. There is a reference in the *Liber Eliensis* (III. 50) to a possible daughter of Æthelstan named there as 'Æðitha filia regis Æðelstani'. However, this is thought to be an error for Eadgyth, his sister. Blake E.O. (ed) (1962), *Liber Eliensis.* London: Camden Society, p. 292.
3. Holder-Egger, O. (ed.) (1881), *Folcuin. Gesta Abbatum Sithiensium.* Hanover: Hahn. Ch 101, p. 626. See also Bachrach, B.S. and Fanning, S. (eds and trans) (2004), *The Annals of Flodoard of Reims. 919 – 966.* Peterborough, Ontario: Broadview Press, entry for 923 (para 5EF). See also MacLean, S. (2008), 'Making a Difference in Tenth-Century Politics: King Athelstan's Sisters and Frankish Queenship', in Fouracre, P. and Ganz, D. (eds), *Frankland: the Franks and the World of the Early Middle Ages.* Manchester: Manchester University Press, pp. 167–90.
4. See Thacker, A. (2001), 'Dynastic Monasteries and Family Cults', in Higham, N.J. and Hill, D.H. (eds), *Edward the Elder 899 – 924.* Abingdon: Routledge, pp. 257–8 for a discussion of the cult of Edith of Polesworth. See also Foot, S. (2011), *Æthelstan: the First King of England.* London: Yale University Press, p. 48. For a more recent study of the identity and history of Edith of Polesworth, see Tringham, N. (2020), 'St Edith of Polesworth and her Cult', *The Journal of Ecclesiastical History. Volume 71. Issue 1.* Cambridge: Cambridge University Press, pp. 1–19. She is likely to have been a seventh-century Mercian princess and was buried at Polesworth with possible relics in the nearby collegiate church at Tamworth.
5. See Foot, S. (2011), *Æthelstan: the First King of England.* London: Yale University Press, p. 47, Note 63.

Chapter 27: *Perfecta Saxonia* – An England Made Whole?

1. Lapidge, M. (1981), 'Some Latin poems as evidence for the reign of Athelstan', *Anglo-Saxon England. Vol. 9.* Cambridge: Cambridge University Press, pp. 92–3.
2. Foot, S. (2011), *Æthelstan: the First King of England.* London: Yale University Press, p. 112.
3. An observation brought to light by Stafford, P. (2020), *After Alfred: Anglo-Saxon Chronicles and Chroniclers, 900 – 1150.* Oxford: Oxford University Press, pp. 52–78.

Bibliography

In the summer of 2018 a conference was held at Tamworth to mark the 1,100th anniversary of Æthelflæd's death. Not all the papers are published at the time this present book went to press. However, the conference contributors are listed at http://www.visittamworth.co.uk/sites/default/files/documents/conference.pdf. [Accessed 15/11/2021].

Also, an unrelated volume of papers on Æthelflæd and the role of women in the tenth century is planned for publication in 2023. Hardie, R. (ed.) (forthcoming), *Æthelflæd, Lady of the Mercians, and Women in Tenth-Century England*. Part of the series of Publications of the Richard Rawlinson Center. Berlin: De Gruyter. Available for pre-order at https://www.amazon.co.uk/AEthelflaed-Mercians-Tenth-Century-Rawlinson-Anglo-Saxon/dp/1501517619. [Accessed 15/11/2021]. Also listed elsewhere as published by Michigan Institute Press.

Primary Sources

Included below are some useful translations of some of the key works written during the Anglo-Saxon era covering the period represented by this book, plus some later medieval sources, many of which draw from Anglo-Saxon sources themselves.

Firstly, there is an invaluable online resource based on Peter Sawyer's *Anglo-Saxon Charters: an Annotated List and Bibliography, published by the Royal Historical Society in 1968.* This is to be found at https://esawyer.lib.cam.ac.uk/about/index.html [Accessed 19/12/2020].

Secondly, there is the *Prosopography of Anglo-Saxon England*, an online database featuring details and facts about all the recorded inhabitants of England from the late sixth to the late eleventh century. This is to be found at http://www.pase.ac.uk/ [Accessed 10/01/2021].

Bachrach, B.S. and Fanning, S. (eds and trans) (2004), *The Annals of Flodoard of Reims. 919 – 966.* Peterborough, Ontario: Broadview Press.

Blake, E.O. (ed.) (1962), *Liber Eliensis.* London: Camden Society.

Campbell, A. (ed. and trans) (1962), *The Chronicle of Æthelweard.* London, Edinburgh, New York: Oxford University Press: Nelson's Medieval texts.

Dumville, D. and Keynes, S. (gen. eds) (1983 onwards), *The Anglo-Saxon Chronicle: A Collaborative Edition.* Cambridge: D.S. Brewer. A series of volumes of the *Anglo-Saxon Chronicle* in all its forms including material from other works which draw on the chronicles.

Edwards, E. (ed.) (1866), *Liber Monasterii de Hyda.* London: Longmans, Green, Reader and Dyer.

Giles, J. (trans) (1849), *Roger of Wendover's Flowers of History. 2 Vols.* London. Also, a facsimile was published in 1996 by Llanerch Enterprises, Lampeter.

Greenway, D. (1996), *Henry Archdeacon of Huntington. Historia Anglorum. The History of the English People. Oxford Medieval Texts.* Oxford: Clarendon Press.

Hennessy, W.M. and MacCarthy, B. (1887–1901), *Annala Uladh: Annals of Ulster otherwise Annala Senait, Annals of Senat: a chronicle of Irish affairs from A.D. 431 to A.D. 1540.* Dublin: Printed for H.M. Stationery Office by A. Thom and Co Ltd.

Holder-Egger, O. (ed.) (1881), *Folcuin. Gesta Abbatum Sithiensium.* Hanover: Hahn.

Keynes, S. and Lapidge, M. (eds and trans) (1983), *Alfred the Great. Asser's Life of King Alfred and other contemporary sources.* Penguin Classics. London: Penguin.

Mynors, R.A.B., Thomson, R.M. and Winterbottom, M. (eds) (1998), *Oxford Medieval Texts: William of Malmesbury: Gesta Regum Anglorum, Vol. 1.* Oxford: Oxford University Press.

Nelson, J.L. (ed. and trans) (1991), *The Annals of St-Bertin.* Manchester: Manchester University Press.

Radner, J. (ed. and trans) (1978), *The Fragmentary Annals of Ireland.* Dublin: Dublin Institute for Advanced Studies.

South, T.J. (2002), *Historia de Sancto Cuthberto: A History of Saint Cuthbert and a Record of His Patrimony. Anglo-Saxon Texts No 3.* Cambridge: D.S. Brewer.

Stevenson, J. (ed. and trans) (1853), *Florence of Worcester. A History of the Kings of England.* First published by Seeley's in the series *The Church Historians of England.* Florence's history was written in part by John of Worcester in the twelfth century. A modern and accessible facsimile was published in 1996 by Llanerch Enterprises, Lampeter.

Stevenson, J. (ed. and trans) (1858), *Simeon of Durham. A History of the Kings of England.* London. Another accessible facsimile is published by Llanerch Enterprises, Lampeter.

Stevenson, W.H. (ed. and trans) (1904), *Asser's Life of King Alfred: together with the Annals of Saint Neots erroneously ascribed to Asser.* Oxford: Oxford University Press.

Swanton, M.J. (ed. and trans) (2000), *The Anglo-Saxon Chronicles.* London: Phoenix.

Whitelock, D. (ed.) (1996), *English Historical Documents 500 – 1042.* Second Edition. London: Routledge.

Some Useful Books and Collections of Research Papers

Available as either traditional published books or eBooks.

Abels, R. (1992), *Lordship and Military Obligation in Anglo-Saxon England.* Berkeley: University of California Press. In-depth explanation of how the Anglo-Saxon lordship ties worked in respect of military recruitment.

Adams, M. (2017), *Ælfred's Britain. War and Peace in the Viking Age.* Available at http://www.amazon.co.uk/kindlestore. [Downloaded 20 September 2020].

Arman, J. (2017), *The Warrior Queen. The Life and Legend of Æthelflæd, Daughter of Alfred the Great.* Stroud: Amberley.

Atherton, M. (2021), *The Battle of Maldon. War and Peace in Tenth-Century England.* London: Bloomsbury Academic.

Baker, J. and Brookes, S. (2013), *Beyond the Burghal Hidage: Anglo-Saxon Civil Defence in the Viking Age*. Leiden: Brill.

Barrow, J. and Wareham, A. (2008), *Myth, Rulership, Church and Charters: Essays in Honour of Nicholas Brooks*. Aldershot: Ashgate.

Baxter, S., Karkov, C.E., Nelson, J. and Pelteret, D.A.E. (eds) (2009), *Early Medieval Studies in Memory of Patrick Wormald*. Farnham: Ashgate.

Belford, P. (2008), 'Archaeological Evaluation at St Mary's Road Wednesbury', *Coalbrookdale: Ironbridge Archaeology, Report: 300*. Ironbridge: Ironbridge Archaeology.

Biddle, M. (2018), *The Search for Winchester's Anglo-Saxon Minsters*. Oxford: Winchester Excavations Committee (Archaeopress Archaeology). Sumptuously illustrated, with all you need to know about the history of excavations at Winchester in respect of both the Old and New Minsters.

Blair, J. (2018), *Building Anglo-Saxon England*. Princeton and Oxford: Princeton University Press.

Blair, J., Keynes, S., Lapidge, M. and Scragg, D. (2014), *The Wiley Blackwell Encyclopedia of Anglo-Saxon England (Second Edition)*. Blackwell Publishing Ltd. Essential handbook for students of Anglo-Saxon England.

Blunt, C.E., Stewart, B.H.I.H. and Lloyn, C.S.S. (1989), *Coinage in Tenth Century England: From Edward the Elder to Edgar's Reform*. Oxford: Oxford University Press.

Bovey, A. (2005), *The Chaworth Roll: a Fourteenth-Century Genealogy of the Kings of England*. London: Sam Fogg Rare Books.

Brownworth, L. (2014), *The Sea Wolves. A History of the Vikings*. Available at http://www.amazon.co.uk/kindlestore. [Downloaded 20 May 2020].

Caroll, J., Harrison, S. and Williams, G. (2014), *The Vikings in Britain and Ireland*. London: British Museum Press. Good general background for the 'Viking' phenomenon.

Carver, M. (2010), *Anglo-Saxon Stafford. Archaeological Investigations 1954-2004*. Field Reports On-line. York: Archaeology Data Service. Available at https://doi.org/10.5284/1000117. [Accessed 26/10/2021].

Carver, M. and Cane J. (2010), *The Birth of a Borough: An Archaeological Study of Anglo-Saxon Stafford*. Woodbridge: Boydell Press.

Charles-Edwards, T.M. (2013), *Wales and the Britons 350-1064*. Oxford. Oxford University Press. A monumental history from the end of the Roman Empire to the last Anglo-Saxon campaigns in Wales prior to the Norman Conquest.

Clarkson, T. (2014), *Strathclyde and the Anglo-Saxons in the Viking Age*. Edinburgh: John Donald (an imprint of Berlin Ltd).

Clarkson, T. (2018), *Æthelflæd. The Lady of the Mercians*. Edinburgh: John Donald (an imprint of Berlin Ltd).

Discenza, N.G. and Szarmach, P.E. (eds) (2014), *A Companion to Alfred the Great*. Leiden/Boston: Brill.

Dockray-Miller, M. (2000), *Motherhood and Mothering in Anglo-Saxon England*. New York: St Martin's Press. Especially pp. 43–76 for Æthelflæd.

Dodd, A., Goodwin, J., Griffiths, S., Norton, A., Poole, C. and Teague, S. (2014), *Excavations at Tipping Street, Stafford, 2009–10. Transactions of Staffordshire Archaeological and Historical Society, 47*. Stafford: Stafford Archaeological and Historical Society.

Downham, C. (2008), *Viking Kings of Britain and Ireland. The Dynasty of Ívarr to A.D. 1014*. Edinburgh: Dunedin Academic Press Ltd.

Dumville, D.N. (ed.) (1992), *Wessex and England from Alfred to Edgar: Six Essays on Political, Cultural and Ecclesiastical Revival. Studies in Anglo-Saxon History*. Woodbridge: Boydell Press.

Dunn, C. (2015), *God's Chosen: The Cults of Virgin Martyrs in Anglo-Saxon England*. https://digitalrepository.unm.edu/engl_etds/4. [Accessed 20/07/2021].

Dyer, C. (2000), 'Bromsgrove: A Small Town in Worcestershire in the Middle Ages', *Worcestershire Historical Society. Occasional Publications: No. 9*. Worcester: Worcestershire Historical Society.

Farmer, D.H. (2011), *The Oxford Dictionary of Saints. Fifth Edition. Revised*. Oxford: Oxford University Press.

Finberg, H.P.R. (ed.) (1975), *Scandinavian England. Collected Papers by F.T. Wainwright*. Chichester: Phillimore. Essential reading, containing the famous paper on Æthelflæd which more or less rescued her from obscurity.

Foot, S. (2011), *Æthelstan: the First King of England*. London: Yale University Press.

Garner, D. (2012), *Hillforts of the Cheshire Sandstone Ridge*. Chester: Cheshire West and Cheshire Council.

Grossi, J. (2021), *Angles on a Kingdom. East Anglian Identities from Bede to Ælfric*. Toronto: Toronto University Press.

Hadley, D. (2006), *The Vikings in England. Settlement, Society and Culture*. Manchester: Manchester University Press.

Harding, S. (2016), *Ingimund's Saga. Viking Wirral*. Chester: University of Chester Press.

Harding, S., Griffiths, D., and Royles, E. (eds) (2015), *In Search of Vikings. Interdisciplinary Approaches to the Scandinavian Heritage of North-West England*. London and New York: Taylor and Francis Group.

Hart, C. (1992), *The Danelaw*. London: Hambledon Press.

Haslam, J. (ed.) (1984), *Anglo-Saxon Towns in Southern England*. Chichester: Phillimore.

Heighway, C. and Bryant, R. (1999), *The Golden Minster. The Anglo-Saxon Minster and Later Medieval Priory of St Oswald at Gloucester. CBA Research Reports No 117*. York: Council for British Archaeology.

Herbert, K. (1997), *Peace Weavers and Shield Maidens: Women in Early English Society*. Milton Keynes: Anglo-Saxon Books.

Higham, N.J. and Hill, D.H. (2001), *Edward the Elder 899–924*. Abingdon: Routledge. Essential collection papers on the reign of Edward the Elder with perspectives on the Celtic west and also on Æthelflæd.

Higham, N.J. and Ryan, M.J. (2013), *The Anglo-Saxon World*. London: Yale University Press.

Hill, D. (1984), *An Atlas of Anglo-Saxon England*. Oxford: Wiley-Blackwell. Essential atlas covering the whole era.

Hill, P. (2004), *The Age of Athelstan*. Stroud: Tempus.

Hill, P. (2012), *The Anglo-Saxons at War*. Barnsley: Pen and Sword Books Ltd.

Hislop, M., Kinsey, M. and Williams, G. (2011), *Tutbury: 'A Castle Firmly Built'. Archaeological and Historical Investigations at Tutbury Castle, Staffordshire*. Oxford: Archaeopress, pp. 50–6.

Holland, T. (2019), *Æthelflæd. England's Forgotten Founder*. London: Ladybird Expert Series/Michael Joseph.

Horovitz, D. (2017), *Æthelflæd, Lady of the Mercians; the Battle of Tettenhall 910AD; and other West Mercian Studies*. Stafford: Horovitz. Exhaustive analysis and multidisciplinary approach to early tenth century West Mercian studies concentrating on the Lady of the Mercians.

Hunt, J. (2016), *Warriors, Warlords and Saints: the Anglo-Saxon Kingdom of Mercia*. Alcester: West Midlands History Ltd.

Huscroft, R. (2019), *Making England, 796 – 1042*. Abingdon: Routledge.

Jones, M.C. (2018), *Founder, Fighter, Saxon Queen. Æthelflæd. Lady of the Mercians*. Barnsley: Pen and Sword.

Key, M.J. (2019), *Edward the Elder. King of the Anglo-Saxons. Forgotten Son of Alfred*. Stroud: Amberley.

Kilmurry, K. (1980), *The Pottery Industry of Stamford, Lincolnshire, c.A.D. 850-1250: Its Manufacture, Trade and Relationship with Continental Wares, with a Classification and Chronology*. Oxford: BAR Publishing.

Korhammer, M. (ed.) (1992), *Words, Texts and Manuscripts: Studies in Anglo-Saxon Culture Presented to Helmut Gneuss on the Occasion of His Sixty-fifth Birthday*. Cambridge: D.S. Brewer.

Lane, A. and Redknap, M. (2020), *Llangorse Crannog: the Excavation of an Early Medieval Royal Site in the Kingdom of Brycheiniog*. Oxford: Oxbow Books.

Lavelle, R. (ed.) (2010), *Alfred's Wars: Sources and Interpretations of Anglo-Saxon Warfare in the Viking Age*. Woodbridge: The Boydell Press. Covers more than just Alfred's wars and includes those of the tenth and eleventh centuries.

Lavelle, R. and Roffey, S. (eds) (2015), *Danes in Wessex: The Scandinavian Impact on Southern England, c. 800 – c.1100*. Oxford and Philadelphia: Oxbow Books.

Lavelle, R., Roffey, S. and Weikert, K. (eds) (2021), *Early Medieval Winchester: Communities, Authority and Power in an Urban Space, c.800 – c.1200*. Oxford: Oxbow Books.

Little, G.R. (2007), *Dynastic Strategies and Regional Loyalties: Wessex, Mercia and Kent, c.802 – 939*. Unpublished PhD thesis. Dept. of History, University of Sheffield.

Marafioti, N. (2014), *The King's Body: Burial and Succession in Late Anglo-Saxon England*. Toronto: University of Toronto Press.

Molyneaux, G. (2015), *The Formation of the English Kingdom in the Tenth Century*. Oxford: Oxford University Press.

North, J.J. (1994), *English Hammered Coinage. Vol I. Early Anglo-Saxon to Henry III. AD 600-1272. 3rd revised edition*. London: Spink and Sons. Invaluable reference book.

Owen-Croker, G. and Schneider, B.W. (eds) (2013), *Kingship, Legislation and Power in Anglo-Saxon England*. Woodbridge: Boydell.

Parker, E. (2018), *Dragon Lords. The History and Legends of Viking England*. Available at http://www.amazon.co.uk/kindlestore. [Downloaded 02 June 2019].

Pollington, S. (2011), *Tamworth. The Ancient Capital of Mercia*. Tamworth: Tamworth Borough Council.

Raffield, B. (2010), *"Inside that fortress sat a few peasant men, and it was half-made". A Study of 'Viking' Fortifications in the British Isles AD793-1066*. Available at https://etheses.bham.ac.uk/id/eprint/1102/1/Raffield10MPhil.pdf.

Ridyard, S.J. (1988), *The Royal Saints of Anglo-Saxon England. A Study of West Saxon and East Anglian Cults*. Cambridge: Cambridge University Press.

Rollason, D., Leyser, C. and Williams, H. (eds) (2010), *England and the continent in the tenth century: studies in honour of Wilhelm Levison (1876-1947)*. Turnhout: Brepols.

Rumble, A.R. and Mills D. (eds) (1997), *Names, Places and People: An Onomastic Miscellany in Memory of John McNeal Dodgson*. Stamford: Paul Watkins Publishing.

Sawyer, P.H. (1982), *Kings and Vikings: Scandinavia and Europe AD 700–1100*. New York: Methuen.

Sawyer, P.H. (1997), *The Oxford Illustrated History of the Vikings*. Oxford: Oxford University Press.

Shaw, M. and Clark, J. (2003), *Cheshire Historic Towns Survey: Eddisbury Archaeological Assessment*. Chester: Cheshire County Council and English Heritage.

Staden, A. (2018), *King Edward the Elder and Æthelflæd, Lady of the Mercians*. Available at http://www.amazon.co.uk/kindlestore [Downloaded 9 February 2020].

Stafford, P. (1998), *Queens, Concubines, and Dowagers: The King's Wife in the Early Middle Ages*. Leicester: Leicester University Press.

Stafford, P. (2002), *Unification and Conquest. A Political and Social History of England in the Tenth and Eleventh Centuries*. Oxford: Oxford University Press.

Stafford, P. (2020), *After Alfred: Anglo-Saxon Chronicles and Chroniclers, 900 – 1150*. Oxford: Oxford University Press.

Stansbury, D. (1993), *The Lady Who Fought the Vikings*. South Brent: Imogen Books.

Stenton, Sir F. (1971), *Anglo-Saxon England*. Oxford: Oxford University Press. With numerous reprints and editions, this is still a classic.

Stetka, J. (1997), *King Edward the Elder's Burh: The Lost Village of Burton by Bakewell*. Bakewell: Bakewell and District Historical Society.

Stone, D.J.F. (2017), *Mutually Assured Construction. Æthelflæd's burhs, Landscapes of Defence and the Physical Legacy of the Unification of England, 899-1016*. PhD thesis. Exeter University.

Thompson, V. (2002), *Dying and Death in Anglo-Saxon England*. Woodbridge: Boydell Press.

Townend, M. (2014), *Viking Age Yorkshire*. Available at http://www.amazon.co.uk/kindlestore [Downloaded 26 February 2020].

Walker, I.W. (2000), *Mercia and the Making of England*. Stroud: Sutton.

Webster, T. (2006), *Archaeological Recording at Eddisbury Hillfort, Delamere, Cheshire*. Chester: Gifford & Partners.

Whitehead, A. (2018), *Mercia. The Rise and Fall of a Kingdom*. Available at http://www.amazon.co.uk/kindlestore [Downloaded 05/04/2019].

Whitehead, A. (2020), *Women of Power in Anglo-Saxon England*. Barnsley: Pen and Sword. Containing a useful appendix on female saintly cults featuring many linked to the activities of Æthelflæd.

Williams, T. (2017), *Viking Britain: A History*. London: William Collins.

Wolfe, J. (2001), *Æthelflæd. Royal Lady, War Lady*. Chester: Fenris Press.

Wood, H.H. (2018), *Edward the Elder and the Making of England*. Available at http://www.amazon.co.uk/kindlestore [Downloaded 16 March 2021].

Woolf, A. (2007), *From Pictland to Alba 789 – 1070*. Edinburgh: Edinburgh University Press.

Individual Papers Covering the Period c. 899–927

Abrams, L. (2001), 'Edward the Elder's Danelaw', in Higham, N.J. and Hill, D.H., *Edward the Elder 899 – 924*. Abingdon: Routledge, pp. 128–43.

Allison, K.J., Dunning, R.W. and Jones, S.R. (1969), 'The Borough of Warwick: Introduction', in Stephens, W. B. (ed.), *A History of the County of Warwick: Volume 8: The City of Coventry and Borough of Warwick. Victoria County History*, pp. 417–51.

Angus, W.S. (1938), 'The Chronology of the Reign of Edward the Elder', *English Historical Review* Vol. 53, No. 210. Oxford: Oxford University Press, pp. 194–210.

Baker, J. (2013), 'The Language of Anglo-Saxon Defence', in Baker, J., Brookes, S. and Reynolds, A. (eds), *Landscapes of Defence in Early Medieval Europe*. Turnhout: Brepols, pp. 65–90.

Baker, J. and Brookes, S. (2015), 'Signalling Intent: Beacons, Lookouts and Military Communications', in Hyer, M.C. and Owen-Crocker, G.R. (eds), *The Material Culture of the Built Environment of Anglo-Saxon England.* Liverpool: Liverpool University Press. pp. 216–34.

Bailey, M. (2001), 'Ælfwynn, second Lady of the Mercians', in Higham, N.J. and Hill, D.H., *Edward the Elder 899 – 924*. Abingdon: Routledge, pp. 112–27.

Bassett, S. (1989), 'Anglo-Saxon Warwick', *Midland History* Vol. 34 Issue 2. Routledge (Taylor and Francis). Available at https://www.tandfonline.com/doi/abs/10.1179/175638109X417332, pp. 123–55. [Accessed 06/11/2021].

Bassett, S. (2008), 'The Middle and Late Anglo-Saxon Defences of Western Mercian Towns', in Crawford, S. and Hamerow, H. (eds), *Anglo-Saxon Studies in Archaeology and History 15.* Oxford: Oxbow Books, pp. 180–239.

Bassett, S. (2013), 'Anglo-Saxon Fortifications in Western Mercia', *Midland History* Vol. 36 Issue 1. Routledge (Taylor and Francis). Available at https://www.tandfonline.com/doi/abs/10.1179/004772911X12956221816169, pp. 1–23. [Accessed 25/10/2021].

Blackburn, M.A.S. (2001), 'Expansion and Control: Aspects of Anglo-Scandinavian Minting South of the Humber', in Graham-Campbell, J., Hall, R., Jesch, J. and Parsons, D., *Vikings and the Danelaw. Select Papers from the Proceedings of the Thirteenth Viking Congress, Nottingham and York, 21-30 August 1997*. Oxford: Oxbow Books, pp. 125–42.

Blake, M. and Sargent, A. (2018), '"For the Protection of All the People": Æthelflæd and her Burhs in Northwest Mercia', *Midland History* Vol. 43 Issue 2. Routledge (Taylor and Francis), pp. 120–54. Available at https://www.tandfonline.com/doi/full/10.1080/0047729X.2018.1519141. [Accessed 06/07/2021].

Blunt, C.E. and Elmore Jones, F. (1958), 'The Tenth Century Mint æt Weardbyrig', *British Numismatic Journal Vol. 28*, pp. 494–8. Available online at https://web.archive.org/web/20190802121023/http://www.britnumsoc.org/publications/Digital%20BNJ/pdfs/1955_BNJ_28_37.pdf. [Accessed 19/09/2021].

Bogaard, A., Charles, M., Forster, E., Hamerow, H., Holmes, M., McKerracher, M., Neil, S., Ramsey, C. B., Stroud, E. and Thomas, R. (2020), 'An Integrated Bioarchaeological Approach to the Medieval 'Agricultural Revolution': A Case Study from Stafford, England, c. AD 800–1200', *European Journal of Archaeology 23 (4)*. Cambridge: Cambridge University Press, pp. 585–609. doi:10.1017/eaa.2020.6. Also available at https://www.cambridge.org/core/journals/european-journal-of-archaeology/article/an-integrated-bioarchaeological-approach-to-the-medieval-agricultural-revolution-a-case-study-from-stafford-england-cad-8001200/7CC93DF3D9E1ECB0E18F8B8816683F2A. [Accessed 05/11/2021].

Boynton, M. and Reynolds, S. (1996), 'The Author of the Fonthill Letter', *Anglo-Saxon England 2*. Cambridge: Cambridge University Press. pp. 91–5.

Brooks, N.P. (2009), 'The Fonthill Letter. Ealdorman Ordlaf and the Anglo-Saxon Law in Practice', in Baxter, S., Karkov, C.E., Nelson, J. and Pelteret, D.A.E. (eds), *Early Medieval Studies in Memory of Patrick Wormald*. Farnham: Ashgate, pp. 301–17.

Campbell, E. and Lane, A. (1989), 'Llangorse: a 10th-century royal crannog in Wales', *Antiquity 63(241)*. Cambridge: Cambridge University Press, pp. 675–81.

Campbell, J. (2001), 'What is not known about the Reign of Edward the Elder', in Higham, N.J. and Hill, D.H. (eds), *Edward the Elder 899 – 924*. Abingdon: Routledge, pp. 12–24.

Carver, M. (2011), 'What were they thinking?: Intellectual Territories in Anglo-Saxon England', in Hinton, D.A., Crawford, S. and Hamerow, H. (eds), *The Oxford Handbook of Anglo-Saxon Archaeology*. Oxford: Oxford University Press, pp. 914–47.

Charles-Edwards, T.M. (2001), 'Wales and Mercia 613-918', in Brown, Michelle P. and Farr, Carol A. (eds), *Mercia: An Anglo-Saxon Kingdom in Europe*. London: Continuum, pp. 89–105.

Coates R. (1998), 'Æthelflæd's fortification of "Weardburh"', *Notes and Queries 45. Issue 1*. Oxford: Oxford University Press, pp. 8–12.

Cocroft, W.D., Everson, P., Jecock, M. and Wilson-North, W.R. (1989), 'Castle ditch hill fort, Eddisbury, Cheshire, reconsidered: the excavations of 1935-8 in the light of recent field survey', in *From Cornwall to Caithness: Some Aspects of British Field Archaeology. Papers presented to Norman V. Quinnell.* Oxford: British Archaeological Reports British Series 209, pp. 129–73.

Courtney, P. (1998), 'Saxon and medieval Leicester: the making of an urban landscape', *Transactions of the Leicestershire Archaeological and Historical Society. 72*, pp. 110–45. Available at https://www.le.ac.uk/lahs/downloads/1998/1998%20(72)%20 110-145%20Courtney.pdf. [Accessed 11/11/2021].

Crick, J. (1999), 'Men, Women and Widows: Widowhood in Pre-conquest England', in Cavallo S. and Warner, L. (eds), *Widowhood in Medieval and Early Modern Europe*. London: Routledge, pp. 26–36.

Davidson, M.R. (2001), 'The (non) Submission of the Northern Kings in 920', in Higham, N.J. and Hill, D.H. (eds), *Edward the Elder 899 – 924*. Abingdon: Routledge, pp. 200–11.

Dodgson, M. (1997), 'Wigingamere', in Rumble, A.R. and Mills, D. (eds), *Names, Places and People: An Onomastic Miscellany in Memory of John McNeal Dodgson*. Stamford: Paul Watkins Publishing, pp. 383–9.

Dolley, R.H.M. (1958), 'The post-Brunanburh Viking coinage of York', *Nordisk Numismatisk Arsskrift 1957-8*. Stockholm: Almqvist & Wiksell, pp. 13–88.

Draper, S. (2008), 'The Significance of Old English Burh in Anglo-Saxon England', in Crawford, S. and Hamerow, H. (eds) *Anglo-Saxon Studies in Archaeology and History 15*. Oxbow Books. Available at https://doi.org/10.2307/j.ctvh1dw9r.8. pp. 240 – 53. [Accessed 27/10/2021].

Edgeworth, M. (2011), 'The Weir and the Flowing Earthworks of Bedford', *British Archaeology No 121*. York: Council for British Archaeology, pp. 22–7.

Ford, D.A. (1999), 'A Late Saxon Pottery Industry in Staffordshire: A Review', *Medieval Ceramics 22-23*, pp. 11–36. Available at https://medievalpottery.org.uk/medieval-ceramics-online/volume-22-3-1998-99/. [Accessed 26/10/2021].

Gretsch, M. (1994), 'The Language of the Fonthill Letter', *Anglo-Saxon England 23*. Cambridge: Cambridge University Press, pp. 57–102.

Griffiths, D. (2001), 'The North-West Frontier', in Higham, N.J. and Hill, D.H. (eds), *Edward the Elder 899 – 924*. Abingdon: Routledge, pp. 171–4.

Griffiths, D. (2015), 'A Brief History and Archaeology of Viking Activity in North-West England', in Harding, S., Griffiths, D. and Royles, E. (eds), *In Search of Vikings. Interdisciplinary Approaches to the Scandinavian Heritage of North-West England*. London and New York: Taylor and Francis Group, pp. 33–50.

Hall, R. (2001), 'A kingdom too far: York in the early tenth century', in Higham, N.J. and Hill, D.H. (eds), *Edward the Elder 899 – 924*. Abingdon: Routledge, pp. 188–99.

Hall, R.A. (1974), 'The Pre-Conquest Burh of Derby', *Derbyshire Archaeological Journal 94*. Derbyshire Archaeological Society. Available online at https://archaeologydataservice.ac.uk/archives/view/daj/contents.cfm?vol_id=1083. [Accessed 18/09/2021].

Haslam, J. (1987), 'The Second Burh of Nottingham', *Landscape History 9*. Taylor Francis online. Available at https://www.tandfonline.com/doi/abs/10.1080/01433768.1987.10594405. [Accessed 19/09/2021].

Haslam, J. (1988), 'The Anglo-Saxon Burh at Wigingamere', *Landscape History 10*. Taylor Francis online. Available at https://www.tandfonline.com/doi/abs/10.1080/01433768.1988.10594413. [Accessed 19/09/2021].

Haslam, J. (1997), 'The Location of the Burh of Wigingamere – a reappraisal', in Rumble, A.R. and Mills D. (eds), *Names, Places and People: An Onomastic Miscellany in Memory of John McNeal Dodgson*. Stamford: Paul Watkins Publishing, pp. 111–37.

Haslam, J. (2017), 'The territorial and strategic context of Stamford, Lincolnshire, in the early tenth century', *Journal of Historical Geography 58*, pp. 23–38. Available at https://doi.org/10.1016/j.jhg.2017.09.003. (https://www.sciencedirect.com/science/article/pii/S0305748817302049). [Accessed 11/11/2021].

Haslam, J. (2018), 'The two burhs of Buckingham', *Southern History 39*. Available at https://www.academia.edu/37404273/The_two_burhs_of_Buckingham, pp. 1–35. [Accessed 07/11/2021].

Haslam, J. (2019), 'Burhs, burghal territories and "proto-hundreds" in the English central Midlands in the early tenth century'. Available at https://www.academia.edu/38697054/Burhs_burghal_territories_and_proto-hundreds_in_the_English_central_Midlands_in_the_early_tenth_century. [Accessed 25/10/2021].

Heighway, C. (2001), 'Gloucester and the New Minster of St Oswald', in Higham, N.J. and Hill, D.H., *Edward the Elder 899 – 924*. Abingdon: Routledge, pp. 102–11.

Higham, N.J. (1988), 'The Cheshire Burhs and the Mercian Frontier to AD 924' *Transactions of the Antiquarian Society of Lancashire and Cheshire 85*, pp. 193–222.

Higham, N.J. (2001), 'Edward the Elder's Reputation. An Introduction', in Higham, N.J. and Hill, D.H. (eds), *Edward the Elder 899 – 924*. Abingdon: Routledge, pp. 1–11.

Hill, D. (2001), 'The Shiring of Mercia – again', in Higham, N.J. and Hill, D.H. (eds), *Edward the Elder 899 – 924*. Abingdon: Routledge, pp. 144–59.

Hough, C. (2000), 'Cattle Tracking in the Fonthill Letter', *English Historical Review* Vol. 115, No. 463. Oxford: Oxford University Press, pp. 864–92.

Insley, C. (2016), 'Collapse, Reconfiguration or Renegotiation? The Strange End of the Mercian Kingdom, 850-924', *Reti Medievali Revista, Vol. 17, No. 2*. Florence: Firenze University Press, pp. 231–49.

Karkov, C. (1995), 'Æðelflæd's Exceptional Coinage?', *Old English Newsletter 29.1:* 41. Available online at http://www.oenewsletter.org/OEN/archives.php?volume=29&issue=1. [Accessed 18/09/2021].

Kershaw, J. (2015), 'Viking-Age Silver in North-West England: Hoards and Single Finds', in Harding, S., Griffiths, D. and Royles, E. (eds), *In Search of Vikings. Interdisciplinary Approaches to the Scandinavian Heritage of North-West England*. London and New York: CRC Press. Taylor and Francis Group, pp. 149–64.

Keynes, S. (1992), 'The Fonthill Letter', in Korhammer, M. (ed.), *Words, Texts and Manuscripts: Studies in Anglo-Saxon Culture Presented to Helmut Gneuss on the Occasion of His Sixty-fifth Birthday*. Cambridge: D.S. Brewer, pp. 53–97.

Keynes, S. (1998), 'King Alfred and the Mercians', in Blackburn, M.A.S. and Dumville, D.N. (eds), *Kings, Currency and Alliances: History and Coinage of Southern England in the Ninth Century*. Woodbridge: Boydell, pp. 1–45.

Keynes, S. (2001), 'Edward, King of the Anglo-Saxons', in Higham, N.J. and Hill, D.H., *Edward the Elder 899 – 924*. Abingdon: Routledge, pp. 40–66.

Keynes, S. (2015), 'Alfred the Great and the Kingdom of the Anglo-Saxons', in Discenza, N.G. and Szarmach, P.E. (eds), *A Companion to Alfred the Great*. Leiden/Boston: Brill, pp.13–47.

Klimek, K. (2013), 'Æthelflæd: History and Legend', *Quidditas: The Journal of the Rocky Mountain Medieval and Renaissance Association, 34*, pp. 11–28. Available online at https://rmmra.byu.edu/files/2018/12/34.pdf. [Accessed 18/09/2021].

Lapidge, M. (1981), 'Some Latin poems as evidence for the reign of Athelstan', *Anglo-Saxon England. Vol. 9*. Cambridge: Cambridge University Press, pp. 61–98.

Lavelle, R. (2009), 'The Politics of Rebellion: The Ætheling Æthelwold and West Saxon Royal Succession, 899 – 902', in Skinner, P. (ed.), *Challenging the Boundaries of Medieval History: The Legacy of Timothy Reuter*. Turnhout: Brepols, pp. 51–80.

Lyon, S. (2001), 'The Coinage of Edward the Elder', in Higham, N.J. and Hill, D.H. (eds), *Edward the Elder 899 – 924*. Abingdon: Routledge, pp. 67–78.

MacLean, S. (2008), 'Making a Difference in Tenth-Century Politics: King Athelstan's Sisters and Frankish Queenship', in Fouracre, P. and Ganz, D. (eds), *Frankland: the Franks and the World of the Early Middle Ages*. Manchester: Manchester University Press, pp. 167–90.

Maddox, M.C. (2015), 'Queen or Puppet Lady?: Æthelflaed's role in the Politics, Economics and Identity of Mercia', *Quaestiones Medii Aevi Novae, 19 (2014)*. Warsaw: Historical Institute of the University of Warsaw, pp. 111–26.

Mahany, C. and Roffe D. (1983), 'Stamford: the Development of an Anglo-Scandinavian Borough', *Anglo-Norman Studies 5*, Woodbridge: Boydell and Brewer, pp. 198–219.

Manley, J. (et al) (1987), 'Cledemutha: A Late Saxon Burh in North Wales', *Medieval Archaeology 31*. Available online at https://archaeologydataservice.ac.uk/archiveDS/

archiveDownload?t=arch-769-1/dissemination/pdf/vol31/31_013_046.pdf. [Accessed 19/09/2021].

Matthews, S. (2003), 'Viking Settlement in the Wirral', *Journal of the Chester Archaeological Society 78*. Chester: Chester Archaeological Society. pp. 107–17.

McDermott, D. (2021), 'Winchester, Æthelings and *Clitones*: the Political Significance of the City for Anglo-Saxon Aristocracy and Norman Nobility', in Lavelle, R., Roffey, S. and Weikert, K. (eds), *Early Medieval Winchester: Communities, Authority and Power in an Urban Space, c.800 – c. 1200*. Oxford: Oxbow Books, pp. 103–24.

Meijns, B. (2011), 'The Policy on Relic Translations of Baldwin II of Flanders (879–918), Edward of Wessex (899–924) and Æthelflaed of Mercia (d. 924): A Key to Anglo-Flemish Relations?', in Rollason, D., Leyser, C. and Williams, H. (eds), *England and the continent in the tenth century: studies in honour of Wilhelm Levison (1876-1947)*. Turnhout: Brepols, pp. 473–92.

Nichols, P.W. (2005), 'Excavations at St Andrew's Church, Churchdown, Gloucestershire, 2000', *Transactions of the Bristol and Gloucestershire Archaeological Society 123*. Bristol: Bristol and Gloucestershire Archaeological Society, pp. 87–93.

Ní Ghrádaigh, J. (2015), 'The occluded role of royal women and lost works of pre-Norman English and Irish art (tenth to twelfth centuries)', *Journal of Medieval History 42:1*, pp. 51–75. https://www.tandfonline.com/doi/full/10.1080/03044181.2015.1107750. [Accessed 18/09/2021].

Niles, J.D. (2012), 'The Fonthill Ghost Word, the Fonthill Thief, and Early West Saxon Scribal Culture', in Hussey, M. and Niles, J.D. (eds), *The Genesis of Books: Studies in the Scribal Culture of Medieval England in Honor of A.N. Doane*. Turnhout: Brepols, pp. 69–95.

Pelteret, D.A.E. (2009), 'An Anonymous Historian of Edward the Elder's Reign', in Baxter, S., Karkov, C.E., Nelson, J. and Pelteret, D.A.E. (eds), *Early Medieval Studies in Memory of Patrick Wormald*. Farnham: Ashgate, pp. 319–36.

Quanrud, J. (2015), 'Taking Sides: North-West England Vikings at the Battle of Tettenhall', in Harding, S., Griffiths, D. and Royles, E. (eds), *In Search of Vikings. Interdisciplinary Approaches to the Scandinavian Heritage of North-West England*. London and New York: CRC Press, Taylor and Francis Group, pp. 71–94.

Raffield, B. (2013), 'Antiquarians, Archaeologists and Viking Fortifications', *Journal of the North Atlantic. No 20*. Steuben: Eagle Hill Institute, pp. 1–29.

Rumble, A.R. (2001), 'The Churches of Winchester and Wessex', in Higham, N.J. and Hill, D.H. (eds), *Edward the Elder 899 – 924*. Abingdon: Routledge, pp. 230–45.

Sharp, S. (2001), 'The West Saxon Tradition of Dynastic Marriage', in Higham, N.J. and Hill, D.H. (eds) *Edward the Elder 899 – 924*. Abingdon: Routledge, pp. 78–88.

Sharp, T. (2013), *Chronicles, Treaties and Burhs; the Burghal Hidage and the Mercian Register. Part 2: The Mercian Reconquest*. Available at: https://www.academia.edu/5565935/Chronicles_Treaties_and_Burhs_the_Burghal_Hidage_and_the_Mercian_Register_Part_2_The_Mercian_Reconquest_910_919. [Accessed 31/10/2021].

Smith, S.T. (2007), 'Of Kings and Cattle Thieves: The Rhetorical Work of the Fonthill Letter', *Journal of English and Germanic Philology 106*. Champaign: University of Illinois Press, pp. 447–67.

Smurra, R., and Orlandi, M. (2021), 'The role of women in the shaping of civic identity in Edwardian Leicester: Edith Gittins and the Anglo-Saxon past of Æthelflæd's fountain. Historical reconstruction and 3D visualization', *Urban History*, pp. 1–29. doi:10.1017/S0963926821000158. [Accessed 19/01/2022].

Sparks, N. (2011), 'The "Parker Chronicle": Chronology Gone Awry', *The Medieval Chronicle VII*. Leiden: Brill. pp. 63–84. Available at https://brill.com/view/book/edcoll/9789401200417/B9789401200417-s005.xml. [Accessed 05/11/2021].

Spiegel, F. (2005), 'The heroic biography of Æthelflæd of Mercia and the Old English Judith: A re-examination', *Quaestio Insularis, 5* (2004). Cambridge: Quaestio Insularis, pp. 111–44.

Stafford, P. (2001), 'Political Women in Mercia: Eighth to Early Tenth Centuries', in Brown, M.P. and Farr C., (eds), *Mercia: An Anglo-Saxon Kingdom in Europe*. London: Continuum, pp. 35–49.

Stafford, P. (2008), '"The Annals of Æthelflæd": Annals, History and Politics in early tenth-century England', in Barrow, J. and Wareham, A. (eds), *Myth, Rulership, Church and Charters: Essays in honour of Nicholas Brooks*. Aldershot: Ashgate Publishing Ltd, pp. 101–16.

Szarmach, P.E. (1998), 'Æthelflæd of Mercia: Mise en Page', in Baker, P.S. and Howe, N. (eds), *Words and Works: Studies in Medieval English Language and Literature in Honour of Fred C. Robinson*. Toronto: University of Toronto Press, pp. 105–26.

Thacker, A. (1982), 'Chester and Gloucester: Early Ecclesiastical Organization in Two Mercian Burhs', *Northern History. Vol. 18. Issue 1.* Taylor Francis Online, pp. 199–211. Available at https://www.tandfonline.com/doi/pdf/10.1179/007817282790176555 [Accessed 20/10/2021].

Thacker, A. (1985), 'Kings, Saints, and Monasteries in Pre-Viking Mercia', *Midland History* Vol. 10 Issue 1. Routledge (Taylor and Francis). Available at https://www.tandfonline.com/doi/abs/10.1179/mdh.1985.10.1.1 pp. 1–25. [Accessed 07/07/2021].

Thacker, A. (2001), 'Dynastic Monasteries and Family Cults: Edward the Elder's Sainted Kindred', in Higham, N.J. and Hill, D.H. (eds), *Edward the Elder 899 – 924*. Abingdon: Routledge, pp. 248–63.

Thacker, A. (2020), 'St Wærburh: The Multiple Identities of a Regional Saint', in Langlands, A. and Lavelle, R. (eds), *The Land of the English Kin. Studies in Wessex and Anglo-Saxon England in Honour of Professor Barbara Yorke*. Leiden/Boston: Brill, pp. 443–66.

Tringham, N. (2020), 'St Edith of Polesworth and her Cult', *The Journal of Ecclesiastical History. Volume 71. Issue 1.* Cambridge: Cambridge University Press, pp. 1–19.

Varley, W.J. (1950), 'Excavations at the Castle Ditch, Eddisbury, 1935-1938', *Transactions of the Historic Society of Lancashire and Cheshire 102*, pp. 1–68. Available at https://www.hslc.org.uk/wp-content/uploads/2017/06/102-2-Varley.pdf. [Accessed 26/10/2021].

Vaughan, R. (1954), 'The Chronology of the Parker Chronicle 890 – 970', *English Historical Review* Vol. 69, No. 270, pp. 59–66.

Wainwright, F.T. (1948), 'Ingimund's Invasion', *English Historical Review* Vol. 63, No. 247. Oxford: Oxford University Press, pp. 145–69.

Wainwright, F.T. (1950), 'Cledemutha', *English Historical Review* Vol. 65, No. 255. Oxford: Oxford University Press, pp. 203–12.

Wainwright, F.T. (1975), 'Æthelflæd, Lady of the Mercians', in Finberg, H.P.R. (ed.), *Scandinavian England. Collected Papers by F.T. Wainwright*. Chichester: Phillimore, pp. 305–24.

Wainwright, F.T. (1975), 'The Battles at Corbridge', in Finberg, H.P.R. (ed.), *Scandinavian England. Collected Papers by F.T. Wainwright*. Chichester: Phillimore, pp. 163–80.

Ward, S. (2001), 'Edward the Elder and the re-establishment of Chester', in Higham, N.J. and Hill, D.H. (eds), *Edward the Elder 899 – 924*. Abingdon: Routledge, pp. 160–6.

Welton, M. (2018), 'Domina et Fidelibus Eius: Elite Households in Tenth Century Francia and Anglo-Saxon England', in Earenfight, T. (ed.), *Royal and Elite Households in Medieval and Early Modern Europe: More than Just a Castle. Explorations in Medieval Culture 6*. Leiden: Brill, pp. 15–41.

Wildgoose, R.H. (1961), 'The Defences of the Pre-Conquest Borough of Nottingham', *Transactions of the Thoroton Society of Nottinghamshire 65*. Nottingham: Thoroton Society of Nottinghamshire, pp. 19–26.

Williams, G. (2013), 'Military and Non-Military Functions of the Anglo-Saxon burh, c.878-978', in Baker, J., Brookes, S. and Reynolds, A. (eds), *Landscapes of Defence in Early Medieval Europe*. Turnhout: Brepols, pp. 129–64.

Woolf, A. (2001), 'View from the West: an Irish perspective on West Saxon dynastic practice', in Higham, N.J. and Hill, D.H. (eds), *Edward the Elder 899 – 924*. Abingdon: Routledge, pp. 89–101.

Yorke, B. (1984), 'The Bishops of Winchester, the Kings of Wessex and the Development of Winchester in the Ninth and Early Tenth Centuries', *Proceedings of the Hampshire Field Club Archaeological Society 40*. Gloucester: Alan Sutton, pp. 61–70.

Yorke, N. (2001), 'Edward as Ætheling', in Higham, N.J. and Hill, D.H. (eds), *Edward the Elder 899 – 924*. Abingdon: Routledge, pp. 25–39.

Index

Written entries in *italics* indicate references to written works.